PURE PRAGMATICS

and

POSSIBLE WORLDS

The Early Essays of

WILFRID SELLARS

Edited and Introduced by J. Sicha

Ridgeview Publishing Company

Paper Text: ISBN 0-917930-06-1
Cloth Text: ISBN 0-917930-26-6

Library of Congress Catalog Card No.: 78-65271

Published in the United States of America
by Ridgeview Publishing Company
P.O.Box 686
Atascadero, CA 93423

Printed in the United States of America
by Ridgeview Letterpress & Offset Inc.
Independence, OH 44131

CONTENTS

Other Books by Wilfrid Sellars

Science, Perception and Reality
    Routledge and Kegan Paul

Science and Metaphysics
    Routledge and Kegan Paul

Essays in Philosophy and Its History
    D. Reidel Publishing Co.

Philosophical Perspectives: History of Philosophy
    Ridgeview Publishing Co.

Philosophical Perspectives: Metaphysics and Epistemology
    Ridgeview Publishing Co.

Naturalism and Ontology
    Ridgeview Publishing Co.

ACKNOWLEDGEMENTS

"Pure Pragmatics and Epistemology", *Philosophy of Science*, vol. 14, no. 3, July, 1947, The Williams & Wilkins Co. Reproduced by permission.

"Epistemology and the New Way of Words", *The Journal of Philosophy*, vol. 44, no. 24, November, 1947.

"Realism and the New Way of Words", *Philosophy and Phenomenological Research*, vol. 8, no. 4, June, 1948. Reprinted by permission of the editor.

"Concepts as Involving Laws and Inconceivable without Them", *Philosophy of Science*, vol. 15, no. 4, October, 1948, The Williams & Wilkins Co. Reproduced by permission.

"Language, Rules and Behavior", in Sidney Hook. (ed.), *John Dewey: Philosopher of Science and Freedom* (Dial Press, Inc., 1950). Reprinted by permission of Sidney Hook.

"On the Logic of Complex Particulars", *Mind*, vol. 58, no. 231, 1949. Reprinted by permission of the Mind Association.

"Quotation Marks, Sentences and Propositions", *Philosophy and Phenomenological Research*, vol. 10, no. 4, June, 1950. Reprinted by permission of the editor.

"A Semantical Solution of the Mind-Body Problem", *Methodos*, vol. V, no. 17, 1953.

"Inference and Meaning", *Mind*, vol. 62, no. 247, 1953. Reprinted by permission of the Mind Association.

CONTENTS OF INTRODUCTION

I. OPENING REMARKS

A. THE ORGANIZATION AND PLAN OF THE BOOK

This book is a collection of Wilfrid Sellars' "early" essays, i.e., essays written in the period (roughly) from 1946 to 1953. Though Sellars wrote other essays during that period, the ones collected in this book are (along with ITSA and SRLG in SPR) the most important and constitute, in pages, the overwhelming portion of his work in that period.

With one notable exception, very little has been done to the essays themselves. Obvious typographical and other errors have been corrected (when possible); new pagination has been added to the old; but the old pagination has been preserved so that references in footnotes or in the text to other pages in the essays did not have to be changed. No attempt has been made to achieve consistency among the essays in grammatical style or, more importantly, in technical notation. The latter lack is particularly noticeable with regard to quotation: Quotation marks have been left in the styles dictated by the manuals of the editors and typesetters of the different publishers of the essays.

The notable exception mentioned in the previous paragraph is "Realism and the New Way of Words" (RNWW). This essay was revised by Sellars for inclusion in *Readings in Philosophical Analysis* which was edited by Feigl and him. It is the revised "Realism and the New Way of Words" (RNWWR) which has been reproduced in this volume.

There are no footnotes in this introduction. All references to philosophical works are in the text. The references are made by the use of abbreviations of the titles of the works. The abbreviations for works not by Sellars are in the general "Bibliography" at the end of this introduction; those for works by Sellars, in "The Philosophical Works of Wilfrid Sellars" at the end of the book. This latter bibliography is complete.

Though most readers will not lament the loss of footnotes, many may
not be happy to hear that there is no index. I did not think that an index
would be much help. But I hope that I have provided something that is
better: Each essay is preceded by an outline. The entries in the outline are either summaries of what is said in a paragraph or paragraphs or
a phrase or two indicating the topic(s) of the paragraph or paragraphs if
I deemed the topic(s) unsuitable for short restatement. It was not
possible to establish a uniform way of doing the outlines; each essay has
been outlined in the manner I judged most suitable for the content and
organization of the essay. Finally, it goes without saying that, in
general, I have allotted larger entries to the points and the topics that
are most germane to my introduction; thus the outlines have to some
degree a built-in emphasis and interpretation.

B. THE PURPOSES OF THIS INTRODUCTION

My overriding aim in writing this introduction is, to use a colloquial
phrase, "to give you an idea of what's going on" in Sellars' philosophy.
There are several noteworthy consequences of having this aim.

First, I do not think of the introduction as being, to any large extent,
an attempt at an accurate "history" of "late 40s-early 50s" Sellars'
philosophy. There are, however, "historical" elements to my remarks.
I do attempt to provide a partial guide to those early essays. Given the
combination of the introduction and the summary at the beginning of
each essay, the interested reader will, I hope, be able to work, if not
effortlessly, than at least without Herculean labour, through what are,
after all, difficult, philosophically wideranging and, even today, novel
essays. Moreover, I allow considerable space for saying what Sellars
does *not* mean in order to dispel some of the misapprehensions and
misunderstandings that an unguided reading of these essays might
produce. There are, for example, numerous pieces of terminology that
are, in one way, familiar enough to philosophers, but are used by
Sellars to his own ends. In addition, some of the essays have a
decidedly different "atmosphere" from others. Three, PPE, ENWW and
RNWW, have a distinctly Carnapian air; the tone and general impression
created by these essays is different from that of most of the others in
this volume.

Second, I try to present a reasonably unified treatment of the topics
mentioned in the title of this book: Pure Pragmatics and Possible

Worlds. Sellars' view on these matters, I think it is safe to say, were not all that well understood when he wrote these essays in the late 1940s; and I think that it is also correct to say that they have not received much attention in recent years though they are very germane to many discussions that are being carried on at the present time.

The desire to combine a reasonable systematic approach to "pure pragmatics" and "possible worlds" with the mildly historical goals mentioned above led to a variety of difficulties. Many of the essays in this volume are long and develop topics over many pages. To what extent could I enter into the details of any one essay without losing the general thrust of the discussion? Added to this problem is the fact that there are many formulations that Sellars would no longer employ since they suggest things that are not part of his view at the present time. How much of the details of these earlier formulations should be discussed as opposed to emphasizing the general "spirit" of the discussions in these essays?

I am not entirely satisfied with the compromise course by means of which I have steered through my problems. I have, when it seemed to me important and not overly distracting, commented on the terminology, the formulations, the specific steps of Sellars' discussion. It would be a mistake to pass too lightly over the differences between the earlier work of Sellars and the later. Such a procedure would have made it very difficult for the reader to understand many, many passages in the early writings. For the most part, however, I have tried to present a unified view, one that is in keeping with Sellars' more recent work. All in all, then, I have tried to lay more stress on the basic themes of Sellars' work than on the specific formulations he gives in these early essays.

An apparently inevitable result of sticking to "the basic themes" is that more than a cursory glance be paid to *specific* pronouncements in four essays not in this volume. In one way, reliance on these essays is reasonable enough. The essay "Is There a Synthetic A Priori" (ITSA) was published in 1953, the same year that two of the essays in this volume were published (SSMB and IM); "Some Reflections on Language Games" (SRLG), in 1954. A somethat later essay, "Empiricism and the Philosophy of Mind" (EPM), contains passages that are direct outgrowths of the material in PPE, ENWW and RNWW. Finally, "Empiricism and Abstract Entities" (EAE), though published in 1965, was written in the early 50s and deals with topics from Carnap's work that are, at times, of great concern for the interpretation of the early essays. It is true that interpreting Sellars' early writings by appeal to these essays has a tendency to obscure, more than would be otherwise, the development of Sellars' philosophy. All I can do is plead guilty to this charge and repeat my previously stated intention to relegate "historical" issues to the (near) background. Doubtless Sellars' views changed and developed during the period from 1946 to the publication of EPM in 1956. While an attempt to trace these developments is, I think, a philosophically profitable task, it is not possible to accomplish it along with my previously stated aims. (Moreover, anyone who has read Sellars' "Autobiographical Reflections" (AR) in *Action, Knowledge, and Reality* will realize that what I am here calling "the early essays" is at least the "middle" period of Sellars' work and that it would be difficult, indeed, given the long period of philosophical work before these essays, to be greatly confident about any scheme which attempted to catalog the stages of growth in Sellars' views).

As a final word of warning, let me say that I have not attempted to organize my comments in any of a variety of recognizably rigorous fashions. I would not wish, in many cases, to defend the exact formulations I produce. I have written this introduction in a fashion consistent with the primary aim mentioned earlier: to present the material so that even a reader who had never looked into it before would be able to come away with "a good idea of what is going on" in Sellars' philosophy.

II. SOME FUNDAMENTAL THEMES

A. NATURALISM

Both PPE and ENWW open with remarks on the nature of philosophy and its relation to other disciplines. The aim of these remarks is to indicate the sort of distinction Sellars wishes to draw between philosophy and "the empirical sciences", particularly psychology. But though most of Sellars' readers would agree that some such distinction should be drawn, many of them would be surprised to read that philosophy "is properly conceived as the *pure theory of empirically meaningful languages*" (ENWW 645.2). However, careful reading of these introductory remarks and other passages which accompany remarks about the "pure theory of empirically meaningful languages" (e.g., PPE 182.2; ENWW 647.1; RNWWR 431.3; 433.2 & 440.1) might convince one that Sellars is thinking *primarily* of "epistemology" and not of philosophy in general. So, it might seem proper to suppose that the pure theory of empirically meaningful languages would be directed, as many places in the text indicate, toward problems concerning knowledge, truth, "experience" and "meaning" (to the degree that this last subject is involved in epistemological discussions). On this understanding, Sellars' use of the term 'philosophy' was, though perhaps misleading, in keeping with a long tradition which saw the "distinctively philosophical" parts of philosophy as those dealing with human knowledge.

I do not intend to discuss directly the question of whether any such conception of epistemology, or philosophy as a whole, would be illuminating. However, I will offer the observation that the magnitude of what Sellars has in mind by "the pure theory of empirically meaningful languages" would not occur to most readers for, perhaps, a variety of reasons. One of the by-products of this introduction, I would hope, is the raising in readers' minds of the possibility that such a conception of epistemology, or philosophy, might be defensible and thus that all genuinely epistemological (philosophical) issues could be organized in one unified approach to philosophy. Be that as it may, my immediate concern in beginning with these remarks is to ask a different question: viz., Why does Sellars think it important to mention such a view of epistemology (philosophy)? What, to speak colloquially, is "behind" such a view? Two suggestions arise naturally from a reading of PPE, ENWW and RNWW.

To a post–30s reader, the phrase 'empirically meaningful language' suggests virulent empiricism. Add to that Sellars' other Carnapian terminology (e.g., 'syntax', 'semantics' and 'pragmatics') and most readers would doubtless be inclined to conclude that subsequent material would fit happily into the positivism of the '30s and early 40s (Indeed, Sellars insistence on a "Pure" Pragmatics to accompany a "Pure" Syntax and a "Pure" Semantics is reasonably interpreted as a response to Carnap's treatment of "pragmatics" as a "descriptive" discipline (see, e.g., ISFL 8-15).) On this interpretation, the suggestion that epistemology (philosophy) is the pure theory of empirically meaningful languages is of a piece with similar-sounding Carnapian pronouncements.

There is *something* to be said for the above suggestion. That Sellars
finds important insights in Carnap's work is well attested by Sellars'
references to Carnap (see, in particular, EAE, section VIII). But not only
does this suggestion not really explain what is "behind" Sellars' remark,
it would also, as a general assumption to guide one in interpreting Sellars
lead to error. *If* we understand "empiricism" as that view which in
"history of philosophy" writings is contrasted with "rationalism",
then Sellars' "empiricism is *mostly* (but *not all*) in the terminology.
Sellars may have seen himself as "a rationalistic realist who has deserted
to the camp of logical empiricism" but even then he was quite clear that
such a "desertion" was *not* primarily a matter of having "rejected one set
of philosophical propositions in favor of another" (ENWW 645.1). (AR
shows just how many traditionally "non-empiricist" views and inclin-
ations existed in the "prior to the late 1940s" Sellars.)

An other suggestion occurs to the reader of the 70s for whom the
terminology of 'syntax', 'semantics' and 'pragmatics' is bound up with the
machinery of much of modern logic. Moreover, sprinkled throughout the
PPE, ENWW and RNWW are such terms as 'formal', 'formally decideable',
'formation rule', 'transformation rule', 'predicate' and 'individual
constant' which reinforce the impression that Sellars is among those who
think the fruits of modern logic will bring succor to philosophy. There
is also *something* to this. But it too is misleading as a guide to Sellars'
philosophy, for his account of language is not, as will be seen, in the
contemporary tradition spawned by the study of formal languages though
he does wish to utilize these studies in his own way.

What, then, is really "behind" Sellars' remark about epistemology
(philosophy)? Sellars' position is that a distinction between "factual"
propositions on the one hand and philosophical propositions and
propositions containing troublesome philosophical terms such as 'means',
'true', 'about' and logical terms on the other hand is essential to a
viable *naturalistic* philosophy. While it is not possible in this introduction to deal with naturalism in detail, I shall make two points that
are central to the upcoming discussion.

First, the main foe of a naturalistic philosophy is what Sellars usually
refers to as "psychologism" (e.g., RNWWR section IV). Psychologism
takes a variety of forms and appears both within the classical rationalist
and classical empiricist traditions. In the rationalist tradition, it
appears in the account of meaning and truth and leads to doctrines involving the "direct awareness", "intuition", "givenness", "apprehension" of abstract entities (RNWWR section IV; ENWW 648.2, 649
note 6; LRB 289.1, 290.1, 308.1,. 2 & .3; ITSA sections 5 & 6). It is
these doctrines, ones that include such *psychological* relations between

"minds" and abstract entities, that are truly "Platonistic" (ENWW 649
note 6; RNWWR 430 note 3; LRB 395 note 7). In the empiricist tradition,
it leads to doctrines that hold that all "genuine" concepts are "factual".
A satisfactory naturalistic philosophy abjures platonism *in the sense
described* (and thus accepts "psychological nominalism" (EAE section
III, particularly 445.1)) and yet is unwilling to forget the insights of the
rationalist tradition. Thus such a philosophy must steer a course
between these two products of "psychologism" and, of course,
assiduously avoid psychologism itself with respect to meaning, truth,
indeed *all philosophical* concepts (RNWWR section IV; LRB 289.1,
290.1):

> (ENWW 646.1 & .2) The present paper amounts to the contention
> that classical rationalism, insofar as it was concerned with
> genuinely philosophical issues, made explicit the grammar of
> epistemological and metaphysical predicates, but—owing to
> certain confusions, particularly with respect to *meaning* and
> *existence*—came to the mistaken conclusion that philosophical
> statements were factual statements, albeit of a peculiar kind.
> Classical empiricism, on the other hand, argued that these
> statements were common or garden variety factual statements,
> and usually put them in the psychological species. Rationalism
> gave the grammar, but contaminated it with platonizing factualism.
> Classical empiricism threw out the platonizing, but continued to
> factualize, and confused the grammar of philosophical predicates
> by attempting to identify them with psychological predicates. In
> many cases the grammar was so seriously confused that certain
> of the more consequent empiricists can hardly be called
> philosophers.
>   It is now time to realize that classical rationalism was
> essentially sound as a naive syntax of philosophical predicates,
> and not only can but must be absorbed into the empiricist camp
> if the latter is to be a philosophy. As a matter of fact, such a
> process of absorption has been going on for sometime, and is
> proceeding, according to all indications, at an accelerated
> rate.   The essential task is to rob rationalism of the illusion
> that it is making factual statements. But in order to do this,
> empiricism must first recognize that a certain group of concepts
> which, when they are recognized at all to fall within the province
> of the philosopher, are hurled into the psychologistic dump
> known as pragmatics, are as genuinely philosophical and non-
> factual as those of pure syntax. Empiricism, too, has its

Introduction

factualistic illusions to lose. Thus the conflict between rationalism and empiricism is a conflict of illusions and must cease when these factualistic illusions are dispelled.

My second point concerns the naturalistic strategy of giving a "non-psychologistic" account of philosophical propositions and philosophical concepts. A slogan that more than any other directs this strategy is one derived from a remark of Wittgenstein:

My fundamental thought is that the "logical constants" do not represent
(Tractatus 4.0312)

Let me state very crudely what Sellars takes this remark to say. It sums up the crucial point in a doctrine of the functioning of logical constants, a doctrine which is free from an assumption that can easily lead to platonism. This assumption is that, in order for logical constants to function in language, there must be items "in the world" which logical constants "stand for" ("mean"). Since logical constants do what they do only in partnership with other linguistic expressions, the existence "in the world" of items "stood for " by logical constants would seem to require other items to join them ("propositions", "properties", "functions", etc.) Then to account for our knowledge of all these "abstract objects", which are not usually held to partake of the familiar causal processes involving our senses, special psychological relations between us and the abstract objects are invoked (e.g., Church, NAE 104). To avoid such platonism, the slogan that Sellars derives from Wittgenstein directs a "non-representational" account, not only of logical constants, but also of terms which are "akin" to them (e.g., 'means', 'true', etc.). The word, which, for Sellars, encompasses all these terms is 'formal' and his Tractarian slogan is "formal terms do not represent."

Thus Sellars plans to pilot his philosophical naturalism between classical rationalism and strong empiricism by developing an account which holds that "formal" concepts, such as meaning and truth, function in a "non-representational" way as fundamental concepts in the pure theory of empirically meaningful languages. One intended effect of this move is, as we have seen, to preserve the insights of classical rationalism and yet to avoid the "factualistic" tendencies which led it to platonism and to other epistemological excesses.

B. "KNOWLEDGE ABOUT"

Before pursuing the details of Sellars' strategy, I wish to comment, in general terms, on Sellars' view of language. There is utility in presenting an overview of Sellars' "formal" theory of language at this point. First, the reader will have some idea where the more detailed remarks of the following sections fit into the total view. Second, though the Carnapian terminology of "syntax", "semantics", and "pragmatics" is useful (and I intend to stick with it), it is difficult to counteract the impression it creates (mentioned above) that Sellars' view of language is of a piece with the now familiar contemporary accounts of "formal languages". I hope that my brief remarks in this section will begin to dispel that impression. (Remember: I have given myself a license—well, not to kill, but at very least to maim polished formulations all in the good cause of promoting understanding.)

Borrowing a traditional philosophical term, I shall say that a "representation" is anything which can properly be said to be "of" or "about" something or to "mean" something. Thus, utterings, writings, typings, and so on can be representations; to utter, to write, and so on can be to represent something.

For Sellars, a language is a system (or, structure) of representation one of the main elements of which are those representations called "rules". There is one very general classification of representations that is most important for Sellars' account. I shall say that "blue" representations are representations of items that are *not* linguistic in the sense of 'language' that I am presently characterizing. (Roughly speaking, blue representations are all those that are not of either of the two remaining sorts—though this way of putting it depends on the correctness of several parts of Sellars' philosophy.) "Green" representations are the rules which "regulate" (or "govern") linguistic items, i.e., representations, and are thus representations of representations. "Red" representations are the remaining representations of representations including representations of the rules of language and the items that the rules govern. (The reader will no doubt be delighted to discover that there is a reason for my unfamiliar terminology). Anything which is a language must provide for these three sorts of representations. Other things may, for good reason, be called language because of some similarity or other they bear to a language in the proper sense, but no system of items which lacks the provisions for even one of these kinds of representations is a language in the full-fledged sense that it is the aim of Sellars' pure theory of empirically meaningful languages to elucidate.

Why have I refrained, the reader may well ask, from employing the familiar terminology of "objectlanguage", "metalanguage", "meta-metalanguage" and so on? (Sellars avails himself of these terms as even a casual glance through his essays will show.) I am happy to admit that there are important points to be made in the Sellarsian scheme by employing these familiar terms. But the structure I have so briefly sketched is *not* the one that is usually discussed in the "object-meta" terminology. First of all, in standard logical works, the "metalanguage" is usually described as "the language one is using to talk about another (perhaps the same) language." Such a distinction, while no doubt useful and important, is clearly not the same as the distinction indicated by my terminology of "red", "blue" and "green". Second, as we shall discover, the "blue-green-red" classification is not a "hierarchy" in the sense in which the "object-meta-metameta-etc." division is. Indeed, the "red-blue-green" division does, in certain ways, cut across the usual hierarchy. The importance of these points will emerge, I hope, as this introduction develops.

What needs to be emphasized (and will become clear as my exposition progresses) is that the "green-red-blue" classification is the important one because of the aims Sellars has for his theory of language. First, the theory must supply an account of the notion that appears in my characterization of representation: i.e., "aboutness". Sellars says of the aim of much of his argument in PPE that it is

> (PPE 187.3) *the attempt to give a formal reconstruction of the common sense notion that an empirically meaningful language is one that is about the world in which it is used.*

Second, the theory must set out what is required in order that a language can formulate sentences "worthy of the term 'knowledge'" (RNWWR 433.2). As we shall see, the requirements here deal principally with what is necessary in order that a being might properly be said to be a "knower of its own world" (EPH 45.5 & 59.1; see also CIL 305.1). Though I shall not, because of space limitations, be able to deal in any *complete* way with these two aims of the pure theory of empirically meaningful languages, it is nevertheless crucial to realize that much of what Sellars says about language is guided by his concern (if I may wrap up both goals in one phrase) to give an account of a being that has *"knowledge about* its own world".

III. The Pure Theory of Empirically Meaningful Languages: PURE
SYNTAX, PURE SEMANTICS, and PURE PRAGMATICS.

A. PURE SYNTAX

(1) FIRST STEPS

In ENWW and RNWW, Sellars never gives a *tidy* classification of
"what goes where." In part, he does not worry about "syntax" and
"semantics" because he seems to suppose that everyone has a
working grasp of the distinction between them. His main aim is to
explain what additional resources go to make up "pragmatics." He
employs this term even though, in the writings of others, it is a term
for a psychological and sociological subject. Such a terminological
choice pushes Sellars to emphasize strongly his condemnation of
"psychologism" which, being present in pragmatics, is in danger
of "infecting" semantics by promoting a treatment of "meaning" as
a psychological relation (ENWW 645.3; PPE 182.1 & .2). Such
concerns do not produce a scheme of exposition into which a cut-
and-dried classification of the parts of the pure theory of
empirically meaningful language fits nicely.

A cursory look at PPE, ENWW and RNWW would suggest that
syntax (or, syntactics) treats of the "grammar" of languages,
semantics of meaning (or, designation) and truth, and pragmatics
of (roughly) verification, confirmation and meaningfulness (PPE
section I, particularly 182.2; ENWW 647.1; RNWWR section V).
This suggestion, while there is some point to it, can be grossly misleading. For one thing, a mere list of terms such as the one above
leaves unclear why the term 'semantics' would not be sufficient for
what is covered under both "semantics" and "pragmatics" in the
above scheme (indeed, Sellars, in a sense, makes this point himself
and admits that it might be satisfactory to extend the subject of
semantics (PPE 183.3)). A more important drawback from Sellars'
point of view is that the "list of terms" approach to distinguishing
these subjects makes syntax and semantics appear to be independent
subjects on a par with pragmatics, on a par in the sense that their
subject matter is independent of the subject matter of pragmatics.
But this is not Sellars' view (RNWWR 440.1; PPE 186.1 & 187.1).

The key to an understanding of "pure pragmatics" and its relation
to "pure syntax" and "pure semantics" is not to be found in

attempts to parcel out terminological territory like so many parts of
Poland. As a beginning to an understanding of these subjects and
their relations, we must come to grips with a remark in RNWWR 431.2
that contrasts two senses of the term 'language', the "descriptive"
and the "normative." The first step in appreciating the significance
of this remark is to note that pure pragmatics, indeed, even syntax
and semantics, as we shall see, are crucially involved with *rules*.

  Though this point is made conspicuously by Sellars (e.g., PPE
182.2; ENWW 651.1; RNWWR 431.1, 435.1 & 445.3), its importance may
easily pass unnoticed because the term 'rule' appears regularly in
logic books and in works on logic in connection with principles that
are *not*, in Sellars' sense, rules. Thus Carnap uses the term 'rule'
in discussions of "syntax" and "semantics" in such a way that no
prescriptive (normative) expressions are present in "rules" (IFSL
10-12 & sections 7 & 8; MN 4 & 5). Sellars does not do this; indeed
he devotes the greater share of section IV in IM to criticizing Carnap
for losing sight of the "normative flavour" (IM 328.2) that must be
present in a rule by means of such words as 'ought', 'may', and so on.

  In fact, the attentive reader of Sellars would find that the
"normative", the "prescriptive", is on Sellars' mind whenever he discusses rules. Thus in LRB, as well as IM, a long passage (LRB
296.3-299.2) is devoted to insisting, in a general fashion, on the
importance of rules and "rule-regulated (governed) activity" and on
the fact that a rule requires normative expressions such as 'correct',
'proper', and 'right' (LRB 299.1). In a paragraph in that passage (and
a footnote to it) (LRB 299.2), Sellars talks of the similarity of
his discussion of rule-regulated activity to Kant's discussion of
"Practical Reason." (In this period as well are OM and OMR in which
Sellars attempts to specify what is characteristic of statements with
'ought'.) And, of course, SRLG is a whole article devoted to issues
concerning rules and rule-regulated behavior. Suffice it to say that
there is overwhelming evidence that even in the earliest of his
writings, Sellars understood the word 'rule' in epistemological contexts in much the way it is understood in ethical contexts and that he
thought of himself as pursuing a view strikingly similar to Kant's
views on "Practical Reason."

  Let us adopt some convenient terminology. Let us call sentences
with 'ought' such as

  (1) everyone ought to feel sympathy for victims of crimes

"rules" or "prescriptive" (or, "normative") sentences and 'ought' a "prescriptive" (or, "normative") term. It may be true that we can find good reasons for thinking that there are other sentences and other terms which also have such features that would qualify them as "rulish" or "prescriptive." But for the purposes of this introduction, I shall stick to sentences like (1) for my illustrations of rules. And I shall rewrite them, without wishing to commit myself on a host of issues that may occur to the reader (and did occur to Sellars (see, e.g., OMR; IILOR; SM, ch. VII; FCET)) as

(2) ought (everyone feels sympathy for the victims of crimes).

The arrangement illustrated by (2) is sufficient for our purposes.

So, (2) is a prescriptive (normative) sentence and 'ought' a prescriptive (normative) term. But can the term 'language' (in one sense) be a normative term in this sense? Clearly that would not be what Sellars wants. Thus we must recognize that when Sellars says that there is a sense of the term 'language' in which it is a "normative" term, he has in mind a relatively wide sense for the term 'normative'. This wider sense can be indicated by saying that it is a sense of 'normative' in which not only is a rule a normative expression, but the *term* 'rule' is also a normative expression. In the wider sense of 'normative,' the sentence

that (e.g., what Smith just said) is a rule

is a normative sentence even though it does not contain the word 'ought' and is not itself a rule. Moreover, in this sense of 'normative', terms defined with the help of the term 'rule' and other such terms as are necessary to the discussion of rules are normative terms and the subjects which use these terms are normative subjects.

But the word 'normative' is too closely connected with the term 'norm' and the word 'prescriptive' with 'prescribe' to be stretched in the fashion which I have just indicated without courting confusion. So, I shall, following Sellars, substitute the term 'practical' for the term 'normative' in its wider sense. (This arrangement will serve to remind us of the Kantian parallels which Sellars himself has come to emphasize more and more.) When I need a convenient noun, as well as the adjective 'practical', I shall use 'practical discourse' or 'practical reasoning' (without making any commitments about the word 'reason') as the context demands. So, 'language', in one sense, is a term of practical discourse.

The misleading aspect of much of Sellars' terminology in PPE, ENWW
and RNWW can now be, at least in general, explained: The term
'Formal' and other terms from the logician's vocabulary appear regularly in these three essays, but all these terms, for Sellars, are terms
of practical discourse. Indeed, the term 'formal' itself does no more
in some cases than indicate that the item so described is part of
practical discourse. (Unfortunately, there are other uses of the word
'formal' which mark other distinctions. Sellars himself repents his
over-liberal employment of this term (QMSP 520 note 3).) The word
'formal' in this wide sense I generally avoid in favor of the term
'practical'.

(2) SYNTACTICAL RULES AND "PURITY" IN PURE SYNTAX

Thus, though it is true that Sellars holds that syntax is concerned
with what are, in one way, the most general features of language, viz.,
those concerning the "grammar" and the "logical structure" of
language (PPE 181.1 & .2; ITSA 312.1,.2 & .3), Sellars also
hold that syntax deals with these aspects of language through its
treatment of "formation" and "transformation" *rules*. It is here that
care must be taken.

I shall set out a formation rule and a transformation rule as examples of the *sort* that would appear in Sellars' early accounts.
(Nothing really prevents Sellars from incorporating, for example, much
more complicated rules of formation, i.e., of grammar.) Using the
standardized form of the previous subsection, I offer the following
as an example of a formation rule

(3) ought (anything which is a sentence joined to a sentence by
a conjunction is a sentence)

and the following as an example of a transformation rule

(5) ought (from a sentence which is sentence joined to a sentence
by a conjunction is inferred the sentences so joined).

The exact import of (3) and (4) is not, of course, completely clear. I
shall have more to say about them a bit later once another important
theme of Sellars' philosophy has been introduced. But, for now, (3)
and (4) are sufficient for the following observations.

Both (3) and (4) are rules in the proper sense. They are, in an explicable way, general. They do not claim the existence of any linguisitc items. Moreover, the only kinds of linguistic items mentioned in (3) and (4) are sentences and conjunction. A similar point is true of other such rules, some of which speak of predicates and individual constants as well as sentences and some of which speak of disjunction, negation and quantifiers as well as conjunction. No *specific* example of any of these kinds of linguistic items is presented or mentioned by any of these rules. I shall call such rules "logical rules" or "rules of logic".

Is it then the task of "pure syntax" to set out and study *specific systems* of logical rules? I do not think that it matters much whether we answer this question "yes" or "no". If we decide to call the study of systems of logical rules "logic", then a "yes" answer to the above question would have the acceptable, though perhaps unexpected, consequence that logic is part of pure syntax. For terminological convenience, I shall answer this question "no". I shall say that logic is the subject which sets out systems of such rules as (3) and (4) and studies them (in ways that can be delimited). Logic is a subject distinct from pure syntax but, as we shall see, one closely related and, in a sense, subordinate to pure syntax.

What I have called "logical rules" do not exhaust what I shall call "syntactical rules". (Another sort of syntactical rule is introduced in subsection IIIB(1).) So, in what follows I shall, in many cases, speak of "syntactical rules" and not of the narrower group of syntactical rules that are logical rules. In keeping with the decision of the previous paragraph, the study of *specific systems* of syntactical rules, whether they be logical or not, is *not* part of pure syntax.

It may seem that leaving the study of specific systems of syntactical rules out of pure syntax leaves nothing "syntactical", pure or not. But, on Sellars view, this is not so.

First, there are things which might reasonable enough be called "syntactical" but are not "pure" (and thus are not studies by pure syntax). I shall discuss these in a few pages.

Second, there are syntactical studies which are pure but are not studies of specific systems of syntactical rules. These studies are *similar* to (but *not* the same as) what is sometimes discussed under the heading of "theoretical syntax" or the "general theory of the syntax of formal systems". So, pure syntax does, in a sense

"study" rules, but in a different sense from that in which logic studies
specific systems of rules. For example, pure syntax says what sort of
rules syntactical rules are and what kinds of syntactical rules there are. In
short, it attempts a general account of syntactical rules and what
appears in such rules: e.g., the notions of inference, of joining, of
sentence (or, of statement—the exact terminology need not concern us
here), of predicate, of individual constant and of logical constant.

Of course, I do not have the space here to do pure syntax, but I can
make several important points about it.

The generality of the account that pure syntax gives must be
emphasized. Pure syntax sets down, according to Sellars, what is true
of *any* language with regard to having syntactical rules, sentences, predicates and so on. Of course, pure syntax does not tell us everything about
language; after all, it is just one part of the pure theory of empirically
meaningful languages. Moreover, pure syntax is limited in certain ways
with respect to what it does discuss. For example, though pure syntax
characterizes the notion of a logical constant, it does not characterize
conjunction since this latter characterization can be accomplished only
for a specific system of syntactical rules (or, a group of specific
systems). (Thus, in LFST, it is not primarily pure syntax that I am doing,
but, rather, this latter task.) Pure syntax is, however, not entirely silent
on the matter of conjunction since its account of syntactical rules applies
to ones like (4) which are central to characterizing conjunction; in
addition, the account of logical constants includes an account of
sentence connectives that sets down the pattern for giving characterizations of such logical constants as conjunction in terms of appropriate
rules (for part of this work, see Sicha, LFST sections CII & CIII(b)).

The Sellarsian pure syntactical characterization of any basic
syntactical term is part of Sellars' general account of language. Such an
account, in its intended generality, cannot be inductive. Inductive
definitions, the required definitions of basic syntactical terms for formal
systems, depend, in the end, on the base clauses that simply list items
that are to count as items of the syntactical kind being defined. In some
cases, the syntactical kind is (roughly speaking) defined merely by the
list. As a consequence, there is *no one single* definition of a basic
syntactical term in the theory of formal languages (though there are uniform instructions for constructing the needed inductive definitions for
different formal systems). In this respect, Sellars' account of basic
syntactical terms is of different ilk altogether: There in *one single*
characterization of basic syntactical terms (such as 'sentence',
'predicate', 'logical constant') provided as part of the general account
of language; this characterization does not change from language to
language.

It is a consequence of the above observations that Sellars' account of basic syntactical terms is strikingly different from that to be found in works on formal systems and, in particular, in Carnap's work. (I should like to emphasize that this consequence is one that rests on views that can be found in PPE, ENWW and RNWW. That Sellars is aware of this consequence clearly emerges in IM (328ff, especially 330.2), is a direct subject of discussion in EAE (Sections V, VI & VII), and is the background assumption against which SRLG is written.)

Another illustration of the difference between Sellars' account of basic syntactical terms and the familiar accounts found in most logic books is provided by considering an aspect of Carnap's treatment of these matters in FLM and ISFL. In order to draw this contrast, I must return to pick up a point made earlier.

There is activity that might properly be called "syntactical" but is not "pure". Suppose that, in accordance with the precepts of pure syntax, one sets out a system of syntactical rules for a language L1 and proceeds to characterize conjunction with respect to these rules. One might then say,

(5) let asterisks (in L1) be conjunctions.

Sentence (5) picks out natural linguistic objects of a certain kind, i.e., asterisks, and proclaims, that they are to be taken as fitting the rules for logical constants and, in particular, conjunctions. Such acts of fiat, or "positing", of classes (or, kinds) of natural linguistic objects with regard to the concepts of pure syntax and of logic is familiar enough from the way in which examples of formal systems are given in logic books; but insofar as such "positing" mentions natural objects of specific kinds, it is, for Sellars, not part of pure syntax.

Moreover, the investigation of natural languages to determine whether certain natural objects are logical constants, and, say conjunctions, is not part of pure syntax either, though such an investigation does proceed with the help of pure syntax. The sentences which result from such an investigation, for example,

(6) "and"s (in English) are conjunctions

are not pure syntactical sentences.

In the early essays, Sellars' usual way of talking about kinds of natural linguistic objects that are "posited" to conform to linguistic rules or are discovered by investigation so to conform is talking about "token-classes" (ENWW 653.1; RNWWR 445.2). In addition, he contrasts "tokens" and "token-classes" with "types". For the moment, let the following illustrate the desired contrast: Suppose it is true in L1 that there is only one item which is conjunction ("type"); yet because of (5),

there may well be, in L1, many conjunctions ("tokens"). Tokens of a
given type and non-empty classes with these tokens as members exist
only if natural objects of a specific kind (a kind of sign design, for
example) exist.

With these points in mind, let us consider several of the features of
Carnap's treatment of syntax. In FLM (16.2), Carnap defines the "formal"
as that which has a definition which involves reference only

> to the expressions of the object-language (or, more exactly, to the
> kinds of signs and the order in which they occur in the expressions)
> but not to any extra-linguistic objects and especially not to the
> designata of the descriptive signs of the object language

(see also ISFL 10.2). (As an aside, notice that this definition of 'formal'
would not work for Sellars since he insists that semantical and pragmatic
as well as syntactical terms are "formal" terms. But Carnap wishes to
contrast "formal" terms with "semantical" ones (FLM 16.3; ISFL 9.1)
since all definitions of semantical terms, for Carnap, "refer directly or
indirectly to designata".) The sorts of definitions of "formal" terms
that Carnap has in mind are ones that *at some stage* involve giving a list
(FLM section 5). The lists contain expressions that refer to kinds of
sign designs and are understood to contain, in addition to terms referring
to sign designs, only syntactical terms and logical terms. The following
are characteristic examples (though not actually form Carnap):

> (7) x is an individual constant of L2 =df x = 'a' or x = 'b'
> or ..... or x = 'n'

and

> (8) (i) 'P' is a variable of L2
>   (ii) If A is a variable of L2, then A followed by a stroke is a
>   variable of L2.
>   (iii) Something is a variable of L2 if and only if it is obtained by
>   repeated applications of (i) and (ii).

Such definitions, even when, as in (8), they have a base clause and an inductive clause, make syntactical terms defined predicates built up, in the
end, from logical constants and descriptive terms (in this case, descriptive
terms for kinds of sign designs and their relations).

That Sellars does not utilize such definitions we have already seen.
Indeed, Sellars attacks such definitions as failing to provide adequate

explanations of syntactical terms (and, for that matter, semantical terms like truth) (see, in particular EAE sections VI and VII). Part of the reasons for this attack have been discussed. The preceding paragraphs highlight one more reason why Sellars rejects Carnap's definitions of syntactical terms: Reference to "kinds of sign designs" is, I have said, not a part of pure syntax as Sellars conceives of it. Of course, instances of kinds of sign designs (or, kinds of acoustical events, etc.) must exist in order for there to exist, in a given language, non-empty classes of tokens. But sentences which formulate the picking out or discovering of kinds of natural objects, as in (5) or (6), are, though part of practical discourse, *not* part of the *pure* theory of empirically meaningful languages.

Before I make additional observations, let me remind you of a crucial point made a few pages back: It is a consequence of Sellars' approach that pure syntax has a single syntactical term, say, 'individual constant', not a family of terms which are defined in a uniform way for different languages. Pure syntax gives a characterization of individual constants that does not vary with the *vocabulary* (the lexicon) of different languages. (Compare (7) above.) It does, of course, allow for a family of restricted syntactical terms that reflect the exact *syntactical rules* of such languages which have different syntactical rules (see my attempts in this regard in LFST section IV).

This view of syntactical predicates has consequences for the examples we have looked at. In (5) and (6), the term 'conjunction' can be univocal even though (5) is uttered in constructing an artificial language and (6) is uttered as a result of an investigation of English. Contrary to familiar accounts, (5) does not have the predicate 'conjunction-in-L1' where L1 is the language being constructed and (6) does not have the predicate 'conjunction-in-English' where English is the language under study. Of course, there are such "relativized" predicates and they can be defined as follows:

> x is a conjunction-in-L1 = df in L1, x is a conjunction and x is an asterisk or x is an . . . . . or . . . . . .

where the last conjunct of the definiens list all those kinds of natural linguistic objects that are, in L1, conjunctions and

> x is a conjunction-in-English = df in English, x is a conjunction and x is an "and" or x is an . . . . . or . . . . . .

where the last conjunct of the defininens lists all those kinds of natural

linguistic objects that are, in English, conjunctions. (Of course,
in English, not all "and"'s are conjunction. For that matter, in L1,
all asterisks need not be conjunctions. In such cases, the "where"
clauses above would have to be more precisely formulated.)

For ease of reference in later sections, I shall say that the major
points of this subsection delineate (though not completely) the
"purity" of pure syntax.

(3) TOKEN, TYPE AND THE LANGUAGE USER IN PURE SYNTAX

The rather provisional remarks of subsection IIIA(2) on types and
tokens are sufficient for the purposes of sketching another important
concept in the pure theory of empirically meaningful languages.

I said, in subsection IIIA(2), that the existence of tokens depends on
the existence of sign designs of one sort or another. According to
(5), there are no conjunctions (tokens of conjunction) in L1 unless there
are asterisks (assuming that asterisks are the sole natural objects
selected to be conjunctions). But though the existence of tokens and
membership in token-classes depends on the existence of sign designs
of various specific kinds, it in no way follows that the concept of a
token cannot be employed without commitment to the existence of
tokens. The term 'token' is a predicate and like other predicates it
can appear in many sentences that are meaningful (and some that are
true as well) even though there are no objects of the sort that the
predicate is true of.

Of even more importance for pure syntax is that it does not follow
from the fact that something is a token that it has any one specific
natural property. A token, to put it in crudest terms, is a natural
object of *some sort* that conforms to linguistic rules. Of course,
natural objects must have determinate natural properties, but such
properties are not referred to merely by talking about tokens. The
importance of this will emerge as I introduce the new concept
alluded to above.

One of the sources of the difficulty in understanding the exact
import of rules (3) and (4) is that we are inclined to think that,
strictly speaking, what rules regulate or govern are not such things
as sentence, logical constants, and so on. What would help is having
a different "subject" for the rules, a subject about which it can be
plausibly said that the rules regulate it. Let us think of this subject

as being the sort of thing that can have dispositional properties.
The term I shall use for this subject is 'language user'. With this
term, it is possible to reformulate the syntactical rules (3) and
(4). Rule (4), for example, becomes:

> (4') ought(a language user is disposed to infer, from a sentence
> which is a sentence joined to a sentence by a conjunction,
> the sentences so joined).

What I said at the beginning of this subsection about the concept
of a token holds also for the concept of a language user. The
existence of language users is, of course, dependent on the
existence of natural objects (indeed, natural objects which have
dispositional properties). Yet the generalities of pure syntax and
even rules like (4') do not require the existence of language users.
Moreover, the concept of a language user in no way brings with it
determinate natural properties. A language user is something of
some sort or other that is governed by such rules as (4'). Rule
(4'), for example, tells us, roughly speaking, that it ought to be
that a language user would token in a certain way *if* the language
user were to token in another way. But neither the concept of a
language user nor the concept of tokening in a certain way need
involve determinate *natural* properties.

I do not wish to mislead the reader: no instant clarification is
gained by rewriting (4) as (4'). But the concept of a language user,
as we shall see, is central to a full formulation of many of Sellars'
doctrines. For the moment, though, I shall do no more than recast
the central themes of section II with the aid of the notion of a
language user.

First, the matter of naturalism was broached in II A. We can now
begin to see a little about how pure syntax and logic might be fit
into a naturalistic framework without losing their "purity".
Syntactical discourse and syntactical rules like (4') must, for Sellars,
fit into a total view of language that avoids two pitfalls. On the
one hand, we must avoid thinking of syntactical rules and syntactical
structure as being intelligible only in light of the attribution of
special psychological powers to language users, powers which bring
language users into relation to abstract entities. That way lies
platonism. On the other hand, we must avoid construing syntactical
discourse and syntactical rules as speaking of natural objects
merely as natural objects. This way leads to a view which, Sellars
holds, would be unable to preserve the insights of classical

rationalism (see the quote from ENWW in IIA). Sellars' course
between these two options should now be a little clearer: Put in
blunt terms, Sellars wishes to treat syntactical discourse as practical
discourse about natural objects, i.e., as discourse about natural
objects *as* involved in a structure of rules. Most fundamentally, these
natural objects are language users. Secondarily, of course, there are
the natural objects which are the tokenings, i.e., the activities of the
language users with respect to which the syntactical rules govern the
language users.

Now let us remember the second theme of section II: language as
the structure of blue, red and green representations. (Notice that the
term 'representation' is conveniently, and sometimes unfortunately,
ambiguous between types and tokens.) In IIB, I said that, for Sellars,
a language is a system of representations—blue, green and red
representations. Let me now restate succinctly and generally a
fundamental tenent of pure syntax: Among the rules of language
(green representations) are syntactical rules, some of which are
what I have called "logical rules"; syntactical rules govern the
language user in the "formation" and "transformation" of
representations. So, part of the structure of language is that contributed by syntactical rules and their governance of the language
user in the activities of "forming" and "transforming" items of
language.

Notice that the way I have recast the themes of section II makes
it clear that some part of the pure theory of empirically meaningful
languages must show *in detail* how syntactical rules and, in general,
practical discourse, are to be accommodated within Sellars' naturalistic
framework. Attention to this point must be deferred till later since our
next step, dictated by the division of the pure theory of meaningful
languages into syntax, semantics and pragmatics, is to obtain further
insight into the structure of language.

B. PURE SEMANTICS

(1) MEANING AND RULES

Not unexpectedly, the central question in this subsection is the
question of what pure semantics adds to our understanding of the
structure of language. However, traditional and contemporary treatments of the issues I am discussing force a number of digressions.

A complete exposition of Sellarsian pure semantics would discuss both meaning and truth. Such an undertaking is not possible in this introduction, for with respect to these two concepts Sellars has elaborated his views tremendously since the '40s. To truth and issues connected with truth, Sellars has devoted many pages, sometimes whole essays (see, e.g., TC; sections of EAE and AE; SM chs. IV & V). I shall confine my illustrations of pure semantics largely to the topic of meaning. And even my treatment of meaning is, for the most part, restricted to the early formulations of Sellars' views on meaning. Even with such a restricted compass, it will be clear that as much as Sellars' account of syntax differs from accounts of syntax presented within the framework of the theory of formal languages, that much does Sellars' account of semantics differ from such accounts of semantics.

Sellars' account of meaning weaves together several strands. We already know, though, the general pattern into which these strands must fit. Talk about meaning is "formal," i.e., part of practical discourse. Thus sentences which say something about meaning must, for Sellars, say something that brings them within the scope of practical discourse. Moreover, such sentences must say something that involves in some way rules since rules are the heart of practical discourse. The wherewithal to make the *details* of all these (and yet other) strands clear is not present in Sellars' work until AE; but the salient points are there from beginning and can easily be set out.

Since the terms of pure semantics are part of practical discourse, it is a natural question whether there are any rules that belong distinctively to pure semantics. The answer unfortunately is not very illuminating: One can arrange for such rules but the terminological divisions I find most convenient do not allow it. Nevertheless, a discussion of two possible candidates for the title "semantical rules" illuminates important aspects of Sellars' view.

Sellars is committed to the claim that there are rules that are rules of inference but are not such as (4') illustrates. That is, he is committed to the idea that there are what he variously calls "conformation rules" (PPE 188.3; ENWW 651.1; RNWW 438.3), "material transformation rules" (IM section II) or "material(or, extra-logical) rules of inference" (IM, *passim;* ITSA section 9; SRLG paragraphs 28 & 29). In structure, these rules are like the "formal" (i.e., "logical") rules of inference we have looked at; they say what ought to be the case about inference. But rather then being generally about sentences, predicates and

individual constants and about specific logical constants as the
logical rules are, the material rules are about specific predicates.
(Note that this contrast between "material" and "formal" is a contrast between two kinds of rules; it should also be kept in mind
that the predicates talked about by material rules of inference are
undefined predicates that appear in blue representations. Whether
there are any other predicates which require material rules of inference is a matter that shall remain uncommented upon in this
introduction.) Thus the sort of thing the *simplest* of these material
rules of inference might say is that it ought to be that for any individual constant, a language user is disposed to infer a sentence with
that individual constant combined with a given predicate from a
sentence with that individual constant combined with another
predicate.

Such rules as these might be construed as semantical rules (and
certainly in his later work Sellars is content to say that all these
rules are "semantical;" see SM ch. IV, 61). However, since material
rules of inference are directly connected with inference and do in a
sense the same thing that formal (i.e., logical) rules of inference do
and since I have already classified the logical ones as syntactical,
it seems reasonable to classify the material ones as syntactical
too. Such a policy follows Sellars' own in the early essays and has
advantages that will become apparent in time.

The other sorts of rules that might qualify as semantical rules
are those that purport to connect "words with the world" (what
Sellars calls in LRB 301ff, "sense meaning rules"). A small
complication sets in here. Sellars always, in his earlier works
(LRB 301ff; IM 335.3; ITSA section 8; SRLG paragraphs 30-38),
argues against the claim that there are any such rules. But most
of these arguments depend on a specific conception of such rules
as rules of action(in the sense in which hiccoughing and sneezing
are not actions). Given this conception of these rules, Sellars is,
I think, correct in arguing that the recognition of such rules would
lead to just the sort of platonistic view he is struggling to avoid.
However, in SM, Sellars makes a distinction between rules of action
and rules of criticism (SM ch. III, section VI). And among the rules
of criticism which guide the language teacher in the instruction of
the language, there can be rules such as the following (crudely-
formulated) one:

(9) ought (a user of our language is disposed to token (utter,
write, etc.) "red" when confronted by a red object in standard conditions).

Such rules might be classified as semantical, but given the arrangements of my exposition, it is more convenient to think of these as
pragmatic rules.

So the distinction, as I have drawn it, between semantics and
the other parts of the theory of empirically meaningful languages
leaves no room for rules which are distinctively semantical rules.
Yet pure semantics does offer us concepts that do reflect something
about rules. To show this, I now turn to the pure semantical
account of meaning.

What is it to say that an item, E, has meaning? Crudely put,
it is to say that E has a specific place in a language. An
important element in having such a specific place is being governed
by rules (more accurately, of course, being tokened by a language
user who is governed by rules; for some of the refinements that
must go with this account of meaning, see Sicha MEM sections
2A & 2B). In certain cases it can be argued that only some rules
are relevant to the item in question. Thus consider a logical
constant like conjunction. The rules that are primarily relevant
to its meaning are the logical transformation rules. In the case of
the sort of undefined predicates discussed above, the rules that
are primarily relevant to their meaning are the material transformation rules.

Let us consider how this works out in the case of "sameness
of meaning." In "Meaning and Syntax," section VII of RNWWR,
Sellars asks when a predicate, A, should be accounted the same
as the predicate, B. And the answer he gives is that:

> the predicates of a language are differentiated from one another
> in terms of the formal roles they play in the language. Using
> the term 'syntax' in a broader sense than is current we would
> say "different syntax,different predicate; same syntax; same
> predicate." We shall prefer to say that predicates are
> differentiated only by the conformation rules which specify
> their combining properties.

Sellars' view of what he has claimed is quite clearly brought out

xxxiv   Introduction

by the remark, in the same subsection, that *"we have here a coherence theory of meaning characterized in purely syntactical terms."*

Let me extend these remarks on meaning by borrowing a little from the later work of Sellars (particularly AE). Pure semantics' study of meaning is a study of that practical discourse about language in which terms are *classified with respect to the structure of language and the rules which govern them.* Talk about the meaning of a term is really talk about what sort of term it is with respect to a specific linguistic structure involving rules. So, from the point of view of pure semantics, where there is no difference in classification there are not two terms but only one. (Of course, we have discussed neither all the sorts of linguistic rules nor all the structure of language.)

(2) "E MEANS---"

It may well come as a surprise to some that Sellars thinks that such classification is exactly what is going on in (some of) the familiar sentences that are examples of

(10) E means ---.

A complete defense of this claim cannot be set forth without the resources of AE. But a selection of important points is available even though Sellars' later view of 'means' cannot be set out here and even though his earlier view is not trivially different from the later one.

A warning must be given before I begin. It is *not* part of *pure* semantics to discuss *directly* the English sentences which are instances of (10) and the English term 'means' (a similar point holds for 'true'). The following example of (10) is not a sentence of pure semantics though it is, in a sense, a "semantical" sentence of English:

(11) "rot" (in German) means *red.*

Sentence (11) is a "semantical" sentence in a sense of 'semantical' which is analogous to the sense of 'syntactical' in which sentences (5) and (6) are "syntactical." It is the business of *pure* semantics to discuss meaning and semantical terms in the manner in which pure syntax discusses syntactical terms, items which are of basic syntactical kinds, and syntactical rules. Thus pure semantics is about classifications with respect to rules and the features of any sentences that state such classifications. But, were I to approach pure semantics

in its "pure" form, I should need much more machinery than I
presently have developed (and much of it would be a restatement
of AE or of ch. 2 of my MEM). Moreover, I would be unable, in any
convenient way, to explain several features of Sellars' remarks in
PPE, ENWW and RNWW. So, the ensuing discussion contains
"purity" but embedded in "impure" example.

In PPE, ENWW and RNWW, Sellars is primarily concerned with
such sentences as (11) in connection with their relation to the
distinction between "types" and "tokens". This distinction
(which briefly appears in subsection IIIA(2)) is most important
to pure pragmatics, but it does figure into semantics insofar as
semantics attempts to discuss (11). Let me quote a remark that
appears almost word for word in all three of the essays mentioned
above (PPE 186.1; ENWW 554.1; RNWWR 440.2). (I quote from
RNWWR 440.2.)

> .....Thus, 'token' is a metalinguistic predicate and is used
> properly when it is said that the state of affairs designated
> by one expression in a language is a token of another
> (perhaps the same) expression in the language. The formal
> significance of the concept of token is brought out by the
> following: If 'p' designates p, and p is token of
> 'q', then all the metalinguistic predicates which apple to
> 'q' apply also to p. In other words, we have here a grammar
> in accordance with which metalinguistic predicates can be
> associated with certain expressions belonging on the
> "right-hand side of designation sentences."

The occurrence of the variable 'p' in

(12) 'p' designates p

and

(13) p is a token of 'q'

may well be a source of puzzlement.

The puzzlement is not removed by noting that exactly the
same thing is in Carnap. Consider the following simple example
(ISFL 12.2):

(14) 'igloo' means (designates) house.

In (14), the term 'means' is followed by an unquoted expression. An
"open sentence" which was exactly like (14) except in having a
variable in place of 'house' would have the same appearance as (12).
Since Carnap is convinced that designation is a relation between
"words" and "objects," it is understandable that he has the terms
on the right-hand side of designation sentences appear without quotes:
they simply stand for their objects. But Sellars wants no part of
this: of that much we can be assured by the general strategy of
Sellars' naturalism (see IA). In any case, that meaning (designation)
is *not a relation* follows from many remarks Sellars makes in the early
essays (IM 335.1; PPE 198.2; RNWWR 433.2); for example,

> (RNWWR 433.2) To say that 'means' is a formal term in such a
> language is to say that 'means' or 'designates' is one of the bones
> of the skeleton of the language, enabling it to contain a logic of
> meaning and truth, just as logical words enable any language to
> contain a logic of implication. *Meaning* in this sense is no more
> to be found in the world than is a referent for 'or'.

(See also SSMB sections V & VI; sections IV through VII of EAE,
especially 466; ITSA 314.1ff; SRLG paragraphs 31, 32 & 80; EPM
section VII.) Why then does Sellars wish to preserve what appears
to be a feature of Carnap's account which depends on a doctrine that
Sellars rejects?
   The answer to this question is that Sellars is not preserving a
feature of Carnap's account as such but is trying to preserve a
feature of such statements as (11) which seems to be essential to
their function. What is it that statement (11) must do? Surely (for
a speaker of English) it should *give* the meaning of 'rot'. Sentences
such as

(15) 'rot' (in German) has the same meaning as 'red' (in English),

as these have usually been understood, do not, it has been repeatedly
argued, do this. Sentence (15) can be understood, accepted as true
and tokened meaningfully by those who do not understand the meaning
of 'red'. Once this point has been taken to heart there seems no
alternative but to accept the claim that (11) has some *restriction*
on it such that it cannot function as does (15) for those who do not

understand the meaning of 'red'. This restriction can be no other than one that insures that anyone tokening (11) meaningfully understands the meaning of 'red'.

Well, what sentences containing 'red' are such that anyone tokening them meaningfully understands the predicate 'red'? I answer using a terminology popularized by Quine: Those sentences in which 'red' is *used,* not *mentioned.* This point seems to dictate understanding (11) as having a *use* of *some sort* of 'red'. Of course, it cannot be its ''ordinary use'' since in that use 'red' is a predicate and the 'red' in (11) is not functioning as a predicate (nothing, after all, is said to be red) (SSMB 63.1; EPM 163.1).

At the time Sellars wrote PPE, ENWW and RNWW, standard logical notation provided only the obvious choice: mention with quotes (or some such device) or don't. Once one adopts the latter alternative and formulates sentences like (11) with the occurrence of 'red' *unquoted,* one is forced, in order that complex sentences containing sentences with 'means' should be well formed, to continue as one began; thus we have

   (16) if 'p' designated p and p is a token of 'q', than all the metalin-
        guistic predicates which apply to 'q' apply also to p

instead of

   if 'p' designates p and 'p' is a token of 'q', than all the metalinguistic predicates which apply to 'q' apply to 'p'.

The latter does not say what Sellars wants it to say.

One more reason that Sellars formulates his sentences as illustrated by (12) and (13) is that, as the quote from RNWWR 440.2 indicates, a great concern in his earliest essays is not with insuring that expressions as types are classifiable with respect to rules and linguistic structure in general but that expressions as *tokens* are so classifiable. Thus (16) (from RNWWR 440.2) is a principle concerning the classification of tokens.

In one sense, as I pointed out before, there is at most one conjunction (or, anyway, at most one with respect to every system of logical rules). *Actual* conjunctions make their appearance only with the aid of sentences which mention specific kinds of sign designs as sentences (5) and (6) do. But, as I also insisted in subsection IIIA(3), the concept of a token is a perfectly useful concept even if one has not either set out by fiat or discovered some sign designs that are to be produced or are produced in the tokenings of types. Thus Sellars must have a place in his formal

apparatus for using the term 'token' and for talking *in general* about tokens
and "token-classes" even if he is not entertaining any sentences about
specific kinds of sign designs. Moreover, tokens, being as they are tokens of
types, have the same "formal" properties as their type. Suppose we say,
"Assume that there is a token of conjunction. What can we say about it?"
The answer is that at very least we must say that this assumed token is a
conjunction and that it is a logical constant and so on for whatever else is
true of conjunction. In somewhat different terms, that is what (16) tells us
about tokens.

Let me summarize the considerations that I have claimed helped to shape
Sellars' account of (10) 'E means----'. First, (at least some) such sentences,
e.g., (11) and (14), must actually *give* the meaning of the expression E. As a
consequence of this function of these sentences, the truth of such a sentence
insures that the expression E has a meaning. Second, a crucial feature of
such sentences appears to be the fact that a *token* of the speaker's language
has *some sort* of "use" in the sentence. Or, anyway, at very least the expressions on the "right-hand" side of a sentence like (11) is *not*
"mentioned" in the sense of 'mentioned' that made its appearance in the
now classical discussions of "use" and "mention". Third, (at least some)
such sentences as are of the form of (10) appear to be eminently suited,
given the features just mentioned, to be intimately involved in reasoning
concerning the classification of *both tokens and types* (see PPE 186.2 & .3;
RNWWR 445.2).

In a sense, Sellars has wound up too many things into one package. By
SRLG, Sellars has come to see that while the resources of an adequate account
of meaning allow for the sort of talk about tokens and types that he wishes to
have, he does not have as yet the resources he needs. (Once again the reader
must look to AE (and SM) for the details.) Though the complete sorting out
of all this is a large project, several points are enough for present purposes.

It is easily shown that Sellars has, in the early essays, a way of getting
much of what he needs concerning "semantic classification" through his
view of the relationship of such sentences as (11) and (15). Part of Sellars'
view of 'means', expressed in a great many articles after RNWW (IM 335.1;
EAE 460ff; SSMB section VI, 78.2; ITSA 314.3, 315.1 & .2; SRLG paragraphs
31 & 80; EPM 163.1), is that sentences like (11) do "give us the information"
stated by sentences like (15). What Sellars has in mind here would take a
while to explain. But suffice it to say that (15) is not, Sellars claims, a
logical consequence of (11) alone. (The exact relationship of the two requires material from AE to explain.) However, be that as it may, you will

notice that part of what sentences like (11) do, given the relationship between (11) and (15) just suggested, is enable us to classify tems with respect to the determinate structure and the rules of the language. In fact, the general remarks on meaning made at the end of the previous subsection show that sentences like (15) tell us something that can be stated in pure semantical terms: namely, that *the semantical classifications of the tokens of two different token-classes are exactly the same.* In short, (15), on Sellars' view, does tell us that from the vantage of pure semantics, only one item, a predicate, is involved in (15) even though there are two determinate kinds of sign designs produced in tokenings of that predicate (RNWWR 445.2; QMSP sections III, IV & VI). The job of clarifying the relation of (11) to (15) is a significant part of providing a pure semantical account of sentences like (11), an account which makes clear their connection with pure semantical classification with respect to linguistic structure.

An example of how Sellars' view of the relationship of (11) and (15) gives him part of what he wants is obtained by considering, instead of (11), the sentence from Carnap:

(14) 'igloo' means house.

The sentence (14) ''conveys the information'' that

(17) 'igloo' (in Eskimo) has the same meaning as 'house' (in English).

But (17) says *(in crudest terms),*

semantically speaking, 'igloo' (in Eskimo) is of the exact same kind as 'house' (in English): i.e., the ''formal'' properties of the one are also the ''formal'' properties of the other.

Thus, for example, if 'house' is a predicate, then 'igloo' is a predicate—and so on for any other formal properties.

Of course, Sellars' doctrine, in AE, is the *stronger* one, mentioned at the start of this subsection, that a sentence like (11) *is* a special sort of classificatory sentence. Nonetheless, AE does hold to a relationship between (11) and (15) and between (14) and (17) that is *much* the same as that described above. But, in AE, the difference between the sentences in these pairs is like the difference between, respectively,

A is of kind K

and

A is of the same kind as B.

(Note that the first of these sentences does not, of course, *alone* logically imply the second.) The claim that (11) *really is* a special sort of classificatory sentence is a development that helps Sellars to clarify all of what is involved in classifying tokens and to nail down the point that meaning is not a relation because 'means' turns out to be a specialized version of 'is'.

I hope that this discussion has not only shed light on some unusual passages in PPE, ENWW and RNWW, but that, more importantly, it has shown that there is a great deal for pure semantics in Sellars sense to say (and I have not even touched on truth) and has illustrated what pure semantical discourse about language tells us about the structure of language. In the next short subsection, I summarize my remarks about language thus far and take up briefly one point that greatly concerned Sellars in his early essays.

(3) SEMANTICS AND MATERIAL RULES OF INFERENCE

I am very anxious to emphasize the unusual character of what Sellars is suggesting as the task of pure semantics. Let me remind the reader of one of the major points of IIIA(2): That the typical definitions of syntactical terms which are found in accounts of formal languages are not, for several reasons, a part of Sellars' account of pure syntax. While it is not possible to discuss the point at length, the reader will find in many treatments of formal languages definitions of semantical terms (in particular, 'designates' and 'true') which are of a piece with definitions of syntactical terms. Clearly Sellars is unwilling to accept such definitions of semantical terms if what I have said about pure semantics is correct. (Moreover, in at least the case of Carnap, Sellars quite explicitly disavows the sort of definitions of semantical terms that Carnap offers (EAE section VII.) According to pure semantics, sentences which say that an item has meaning say no more than (crudely put) that the item has a determinate place in a language. For an item A, and an item, B, to have the same place in this structure is for A and B not to be different but to be one and the same *semantically speaking*.

This extremely sketchy and crudely formulated summary of the points of the previous two subsections emphasizes what is crucial: Pure semantics, like pure syntax, aims at saying something about language in general, at setting out semantical distinctions that apply to language in general and at explaining semantical notions. None of this requires exhibiting the items of any language; one does not even have to begin by assuming that there are languages. The principles of pure syntax and pure semantics explain (in part) what something is *if* it is a language.

What pure semantics has added to our conception of a language is the claim that each language must have ("red") representations which classify items of the language with respect to their place in the linguistic structure and, in particular, with respect to the rules of the language. Certain sentences of English with the word 'means' were offered *(not* as a matter of pure semantics of course) as examples of sentences which, when tokened by speakers of English, actually do such classifying.

With all this in mind, let us look again at one sort of rule that was briefly mentioned in the previous sections. These rules were called "conformation rules," "material rules of inference," and "material transformation rules." Not enough was said at the time such rules were first mentioned about why such rules are necessary to the scheme Sellars is proposing. But at least one reason for admitting such rules is now clear in retrospect: Such rules, *in prescribing the inferential relations of undefined predicates* (in blue representations), are primary in determining the classification of such predicates; without them, there could be no semantical differentiation of these predicates and thus no semantical classifications of them. Nothing else thus far mentioned could accomplish this differentiation. (Views that accept psychological relations between minds and abstract entities have, at least, something to say about such differentiation though Sellars does not find such doctrines satisfactory for obvious reasons; in addition he thinks that, in many cases, the invoking of such psychologistic machinery does not really provide the slightest enlightenment (ITSA sections 7 & 8).)

However, the need for conformation rules brings up an important side issue: *viz.*, the possibility that Sellars' readers might construe him as maintaining a doctrine of "synthetic a priori" truth. The

magnitude of his concern about this construal is reflected in the
occurrence of passages related to this matter (PPE 185.2; ENWW
650.2 & 651.1; RNWWR 443.3; IM 337.1; SRLG paragraphs 81-83)
and a whole article on the topic (ITSA). In one respect, Sellars was
perhaps right to be concerned about the interpretation of his remarks
on conformation rules. These remarks tend to emphasize his Kantian
connections (e.g., RNWWR 446.1). Anyone who read Sellars from the
viewpoint of classical (Humean) empiricism would be very tempted to
conclude that Sellars did agree with Kant. Conformation rules are
"synthetic" by most standards that would appeal to a classical
empiricist (they are not rules of logic or justifiable merely by appeal
to logic; their contradictories appear to be "possible"). They are not
"known a posteriori" if that phrase is taken to mean, as it often does
for classical empiricists, "known by direct observation or inductive
generalization from direct observation." On Sellars' view, the material
rules of inference are essential to having undefined predicates of blue
representations and thus are essential to having observational knowledge (as we shall see). So, it might seem very reasonable to conclude
that material rules of inference are at once "synthetic" and also
"a priori". (Furthermore, there is even a sense of 'necessary' in
which they are "necessary".)

   However, such problems are largely terminological. Sellars argues
that any judgment about whether a doctrine involves commitment to
synthetic a priori truth is a matter that calls first for terminological
"decisions" (ITSA 319.2). With sufficient terminological adjustments,
it would be correct to say all of the following about material rules of
inference: They are synthetic and a priori (and necessary), synthetic
and a posteriori (and necessary), analytic and a priori (and not
necessary). Nothing much is gained by such observations and Sellars
was no doubt correct in wishing to argue that it is more to the point
to forget such terms in setting out the logical and epistemological
status of material rules of inference. (The controversies about synthetic
a priori truth are, however, so enduring that I have written parts of
section VI with these questions in mind.)

   However, the crucial point is that, for Sellars, "experience" is
central to our adopting one system of material rules of inference rather
than another; as Sellars puts it (ITSA 319.2), each such system must
"compete for adoption in the market-place of experience." *The pure
theory of empirically meaningful languages says that each language must
have material rules of inference; it does not say that we should use one
language rather than another* (see RNWWR 443.3).

C. PURE PRAGMATICS

(1) INDEXICALS

Pure pragmatics has a variety of different components and I shall approach them one by one. The first is a theory of indexicals or "token-reflexive" expressions. The idea that a study of such expressions might belong to a subject akin to semantics and called "pragmatics" has been made, in recent times, familiar by the work of Montague and others. In the late 1940s, however, such an idea was unusual and contrary, as Sellars emphasized, to the then empiricist understanding of pragmatics (Carnap, FLM sections 2 & 3 and ISFL sections 4 & 5; PPE 183.3; ENWW 645.3; RNWWR 432.1 & 440.1). Since the general attitude towards there being a "theory" that treats indexicals is now favorable and since my main aim is to explain the general outlines of Sellars' theory of language, I do not intend to spend much space expounding the details of Sellars' view of indexicals. But I hope to illustrate by an example of Sellars' treatment of indexicals that Sellars' subject of pure pragmatics is, like his subjects of syntax and semantics, part of his doctrine of practical reason and thus is different from the now familiar pragmatics. Moreover, I hope it will be clear from the example that the theory of indexicals is illuminatingly assigned to pragmatics rather than semantics for reasons having to do with the way in which the concept of tokening is utilized in the theory.

As a small historical note, it is true that Sellars does not lean too much weight on separating pragmatics from semantics. He is willing to consider the possibility that the term 'semantics' should be extended to cover the matters discussed in this section. Moreover, at a point in the early 50s, he gives up using the word 'pragmatics' (see 453 note 29 in EAE, an essay which was written in the early 50s), presumably because its use had not caught on and to continue employing it was not to bring any clarity to his readers. However, there is at least one, if not more than one, important distinction that can be marked by distinguishing between semantics and pragmatics.

My example is taken from section VIII, "The Pragmatics of 'Now'", of RNWWR. Section VIII does more than offer an account of 'now' and, indeed, does "more" right in the process of presenting an account of the workings of 'now'. So, the remarks I make here about section VIII are a considerable filtering of what is there.

The essential point in understanding the workings of 'now' concerns
the concepts of tokening and time (for other indexicals, space, rather
than time, would be crucial). Put crudely (and ignoring that in some cases
much more than a point in time is at issue), "now" is the time at which the
tokening of the sentence containing 'now' takes place. If we let this crude,
but apparently accurate, remark guide us, any rules for 'now' must involve
in a very special way the notion of tokening: in a way that it is not involved in syntactical rules. Of course, all syntactical rules can be recast
as general rules about *all* tokenings of a given type. But such general
rules are indifferent to time and place; nothing about specific place or
time (or, for that matter, the specific tokener) forms an integral part of
the instructions given by the rule. Clearly the same is not so for any rule
that is constructed for 'now' on the basis of the crude principle set down
above. (Thus we have one reason for distinguishing pragmatics from the
other parts of the pure theory of empirically meaningful languages.)

Any rule for 'now' must, on Sellars' view, connect 'now' with whatever
"skeletal" relation(s) is(are) present in the language (RNWWR sections
VI & VII; ENWW 655.1; see also SM ch. IV, section VIII). These
skeletal relations provide a fundamental sort of ordering; our ordinary
spatial and temporal relations are examples of skeletal relations. Let us
suppose that 'before' is one of the skeletal relations. Then what ought
to be inferred from

> Smith's joke occurred before Jones' laugh,
> Jones is laughing now, and
> The token of 'Jones is laughing now' that just occurred did so at tl

is

> Smith's joke occurred before tl.

Rules that would be devised on the model of such examples can, with the
help of machinery not developed in this essay, be connected intelligibly with
a principle for the truth of such sentences as 'Jones is laughing now'.
This principle would have as a consequence that (roughly)

> 'Jones is laughing now' is true

if and only if the time, tl, at which the tokening of 'Jones is laughing now'
takes place is the time (i.e., tl) at which Jones is laughing. (It must be

noted that in a principle such as this, the present tenses, including that of
'is true', must be taken seriously. The sentence 'Jones is laughing now'
is true but not necessarily was true or will be true. We need not conclude
from this that we must recognize a predicate 'true at t' rather than simply
'true'; the most that follows is that sentences containing 'true' are as temporal as 'Jones is laughing now'.)

The example of the preceding paragraph is not an example of *pure*
pragmatics. Pure pragmatics, like pure syntax and pure semantics, states
rules and definitions that are entirely general and do not refer directly to
sign designs of specific languages. Our inability to state such rules and
definitions is due, in part, to a lack of syntactical resources. For
example, I do not have at hand a pure syntactical account of sentences
like 'Smith's joke occurred before tl' (not to mention the premises of the
illustrated inference). The formulation of pure pragmatic rules also depends
on having appropriate pragmatic terms. The term 'indexical' is one of these
pragmatic terms; it would also be necessary to have terms for kinds of
indexicals. Only with all this machinery is a pure pragmatic account of
indexicals actually formulable.

A point that surely strikes anyone who reads the above remarks on
'now' is that the rules governing 'now' (and presumably the rules for any
other indexical) do not in any interesting sense eliminate the indexical.
And this is so. But I do not think that anyone should have expected it to
be otherwise. Compare the rules for logical constants and the principles
of truth for sentences containing logical constants. These rules and
principles do not eliminate logical constants entirely, for logical constants
appear in the rules and principles themselves and in connection with the
reasoning necessary for the use of these rules and principles. Similarly,
in the case of 'now' and other indexicals, these are eliminable from sentences
only in the weak sense that from a given sentence with an indexical -
we may correctly infer, with the aid of sentences with indexicals, a sentence
without *that* indexical. Let me put this in the slogan "language is
irreducibly indexical".

This slogan is one that Sellars subscribes to for additional reasons over
and above the ones already given. Tokening is temporally and spatially and,
in a sense, by tokener locatable. One of the basic differences between
pragmatics on the one hand and syntax and syntax and semantics on the
other is that part of pragmatics is a general account of tokening and its
relationship to space and time; in fact, the account of indexicals is one

part of this larger account. Let me develop this point: Among other things, a token is an item with spatial and temporal location, but not in virtue of its being of a given type. It is up to pure pragmatics to formulate, with the sort of generality and "purity" found in syntax and semantics, the truths of practical discourse about the relationships of tokens, types and space and time and to characterize the sentences by which language talks of *its own* spatio-temporal involvement. The irreducibly indexical character of language thus arises, for Sellars, also from the fact that the pure pragmatic resources of a language outfit the language to talk about itself *as tokened in space and time*, as, in a sense, "here" and "there", "now" and "then". According to the pure theory of empirically meaningful languages, any language must have the resources to talk about itself not simply in the time and place in-different terms of syntax and semantics, but in pure gragmatic terms which allow it to deal with its occurrence in space and time. It is a distinctive feature of pure pragmatics that it has responsibility for formulating the "formal" rules and "formal" truths about the occurrence, the tokening, of language in space and time and for characterizing the linguistic resources that enable the language itself to represent that occurrence.

The following two subsections are, in part, an elaboration of the points of the previous paragraph.

(2) OBSERVATION REPORTS

Two introductory remarks: First, the materials for this subsection and the next are, for reasons I shall comment on later,mixed together in various sections of PPE, ENWW and RNWWR (PPE section II; ENWW sections II & IV; RNWWR sections V, VI & VII). I shall follow the lead of later Sellars' writings and sort the various strands out. Second, the strand picked out for this subsection I have labeled with the phrase 'observation reports'. This is *not* the terminology of Sellars' early essays. The usual terminology with which he discusses the topics of this subsection and the next is 'confronting sentence' or 'verified sentence'. I prefer to use his later terminology because it makes a more intelligible connection for the reader between the earlier and later work and because it is a step to providing myself sufficient terminology for all the distinctions I draw.

Sellars is anxious to insist that, besides meaning in the sense in which pure semantics discusses it, there is something else that is relevant to our usual talk of meaning. After all, there is nothing in the pure semantical sense of 'meaning' which requires that a language be tokened in order to have meaning. It is a part of the purity of pure semantics and pure syntax

that the meanings of sentences, predicates, logical constants and so on
can be discussed perfectly well (with respect to a given system of rules)
without producing examples of these items and even without supposing
that there are anywhere tokens of these items. Yet traditionally philosophers have wished to claim that the "meaning" (in some sense) of at
least some terms in the language is importantly connected with
"experience". With this claim, Sellars is in *qualified* agreement:

> (RNWWR 431.3) . . . .if epistemology has anything to say about the
> relation of *meaning* to *experience*, then the term 'experience' as used
> by the epistemologist must belong to the same frame as 'meaning' and
> 'implication'. 'Experience' in this use must be contrasted with
> 'experience' as a term of empirical psychology, just as we have already
> contrasted 'language' as an epistemological term with 'language' as
> an expression in socio-psychologico-historical linguistics.

> (RNWWR 433.2) This leads to the conclusion that whether or not a
> language is *used*, there corresponds to it a meta-language which contains
> (formally) true meaning-statements about the expression of the language.
> In this sense, then, the expressions of any constructible language
> designate or mean. Consequently, the difference between an applied and
> a non-applied language has nothing to do with the *meanings* of its ex-
> pressions. (4) On the other hand, it is obvious that a language that is
> not applied is, in a sense to be clarified, *empty*. At the present stage
> in our argument we are considering the possibility that the opposite of
> empty is *meaningful*, and that a language is meaningful (as opposed to
> *has meaning*—in the semantic sense) by virtue of being *applied*.

So, we need to explain a pure pragmatic sense of 'experience' in order to
explain in what sense a language might be "applied".

What is usually at issue when the philosophical tradition speaks of
"experience" (at least in empiricist circles) is our response to the
physical world, i.e., one form or another of "observation" (seeing, hearing,
etc.). Observing is frequently construed as a matter of coming to represent
the world as a result of some sort of causal "contact" or "commerce"
with objects. (I shall, for convenience, henceforth talk of "stimulation".)
I have already pointed out in subsection IIIB(1) that something of this
sort is involved in Sellars' view. He is willing to contemplate that there

are rules which govern a language user's responses to objects; my crudely
formulated example was:

(9) ought (a user of our language is disposed to token "red" when con-
    fronted by a red object in standard conditions).

(Such a rule, I said at the time I first gave it, would most conveniently be
classed as a rule of pragmatics; I am about to discuss something which indicates why this should be so.)

So much, then, by way of background. What sort of "application" is involved
in "meaningfulness"?   In order for a language to be applied, certain sentences
(and certain predicates) and objects must appear in the regularities it is the
purpose of such rules as (9) to bring about. Rule (9), however, has a drawback
from the viewpoint of our present task. It is a perfectly good rule of English
(or, in any case, would be with some patching up). But if we are to gain a
glimpse of pure pragmatics, we must avoid beginning our investigation by considering a rule that has a *use* of the predicate 'red' which is an English word.
To appreciate what can be done in pragmatics, the first step is to note that the
regularity at which (9) aims is not just any regularity: It is that one without
which the linguistic item which is the response to the visual stimulation could
not be true. Crudely put, in the case of 'red', the regularity, to be present as
a disposition in the language user, is that of tokening, in standard conditions,
'red' when visually stimulated by a red object (for a detailed discussion of
standard conditions of perception, see Aune, KMN chs. V & VII). How shall
this be put in pragmatic terms?

Let us look at a simpler case. Suppose that there is, in standard conditions
C, a token of 'this is red' in the presence of a red object as a result of the
visual stimulation of the language user by the red object. How shall we
formulate this correspondence, this "presence", in pragmatic terms? For
Sellars, it will not due to invoke "awareness" of facts (or states of affairs,
qualities, relations or whatever). This is the sort of move that Sellars'
naturalism leads him to avoid (ENWW 648.2 & 649.1; see also LRB 304ff).
The correspondence that is formulable in pragmatic terms is a quite straight-
forward one: It involves the sentence with the predicate 'red', a token of which
occurred in C, and (close enough for present purposes) a sentence about the
former sentence saying that a token of the former sentence occurred in C. At
this stage, it is important to incorporate into the account that the correspondence is the one in which, as I said above, the token of the sentence
"reflects" the "presence" of what it is about (in this case, a red object).

This matter is handled by noting that this correspondence is assured by the condition that

> (18) in C, if a token of 'this is red' (which contains a token of the predicate 'red') is produced by a user of our language, than 'this is red' is true.

What is embedded in the example (18) is *(roughly)* the main condition that Sellars sets down in the definition of 'verified sentence' (though he does so in different terminology)(PPE 187.4 & 190.1; ENWW 656.1 & 658.1; RNWWR 435.1 & 440.3).

Given this example, it is easy enough to formulate the main condition for being an observation sentence in terms of the regularity of which we have considered one instance:

> (19) in standard conditions C, whenever a token of the sentence S (which contains a token of the predicate P) is produced by a user of our language, then S is true.

So, the regularity formulated by (19) is the regularity to be present as a disposition in the language user. For reasons I will comment on in a moment, the best way to state this in pure pragmatics is to treat an observation sentence S (and an observation predicate P) as a sentence for which there is a rule that

> (20) it ought to be that from the sentence

>> this token of S (containing a token of P) is produced in standard conditions by a user of our language

> is inferred the sentence

>> S is true.

With such a rule, if what ought to be "comes to pass", then a generalization like (19) is true. (Actually it would do no great harm, given the less than adequate treatment I am producing, if we thought of the pure pragmatic rule as one that simply said that a generalization of which (19) is an example, ought to be (see LRB 299.1).)

Of course, pure pragmatics does not specify which sentences are observation sentences and which predicates are observation predicates; it does specify that such sentences and such predicates are the sentences and predicates mentioned in such rules as fit the pattern illustrated by (20). Moreover, pure pragmatics does not worry about the specific ways in which regularities like (19) come about. But it does say that it is part of being an empirically meaningful language that there be natural laws which connect the language, though the tokening of the language user, to natural objects. Such a natural law is, for Sellars, a "material transformation rule". (Thus we have one reason for my above formulation in terms of a rule of inference.)

Pure pragmatics thus aims to provide a "formal" account of the "application" of a language as it does a "formal" account of the occurrence of language in space and time. Notice that, like all the "pure" accounts we have looked at, it is possible to discuss the application of language without it being a logical consequence that there are any tokens of any language, any actual applications or any examples of the relevant regularities. Adequately formulated, these remarks would appear as the conditions for the "meaningfulness" of a language: Crudely put, an empirically meaningful language has observation sentences and observation predicates as these are briefly characterized above. These remarks would also provide the materials for characterizing *one* pure **pragmatic** concept of "experience". (Additionally, other material transformation rules of a language may tell us things about the natural features of language users which contribute to an appreciation that observation sentence regularities involve "experiences" in another sense; but, though pure pragmatics allows for this, it does not *itself* distinguish "sensory" experience as a kind of "experience"—a machine might have "experiences" in the pure pragmatic sense I have sketched.)

Though observation reports are the tokenings of observation sentences, the above remarks barely scratch the surface of Sellars' account of observation reports, for there is another traditional claim about observation that Sellars finds a prominent place for in his view. This claim concerns observation as a "mode" of knowledge. To have observed (e.g., seen) that it is raining is (in the best conditions) to know that it is raining. Pure pragmatics must tell us about this matter as well. (Sellars has written no small amount on observation and knowledge; the reader completely unversed in Sellars can do no better than read EPM. A more elaborate treatment is found in SM and a well-stated exposition of similar views is to be found in Aune's KMN.) Thus I finally approach the theme first introduced in IIB: knowledge and the claims of the pure theory of empirically meaningful languages to be epistemology. On this enormous topic, I shall make one central point.

For Sellars, knowledge is the result of a "critically responsive" language. A language user does not have knowledge simply by responding to stimulation, not even with reliably true responses to stimulation. There is a sense in which a thermometer gives us "reliable" responses to stimulation. The conception of a language user as participating in lawful relations to natural objects through tokening is essentially the notion of a thermometer, a device that responds in a "reliable" manner to changes in the world. In order for the language user to have *observational knowledge*, the language user must be, as we would usually say, "conscious" of "what is going on" in a way that a thermometer is not. By this time it will come as no surprise to the reader that pure pragmatics has a "formal" concept of "consciousness" (and thus another concept of "experience").

What is it, according to Sellars, that the language user must be conscious of in order to have observational knowledge? Well, *one* thing that is necessary in order to rise above the status of a thermometer is that one must be conscious that, in observation reporting, what is happening is a manifestation of a causal regularity that is prescribed by one of the rules of one's language. To put it in terms of the language, it is as if the language had to be "conscious" that *its very rules* had insured (with the help, of course, of changes in the world) that the observation sentence is tokened in the specified circumstances. How would the language or the language user do this? Among other things, by being able to represent a token which is an observation sentence by a metalinguistic sentence with the *pure pragmatic predicate* 'observation sentence'. The only way in which the language user can do so is if there are regularities connecting tokens of sentences which *are not metalinguistic* with tokens of sentences which *are metalinguistic*, that is, which are in *practical discourse* about language. In short, the language user must participate in a process *like* observation reporting with respect to the pragmatic part of his language.

Let us return to the example of the language user tokening, in C, the sentence 'this is red'. The language user's "consciousness" of what it is doing is (in part) manifested in the language user's inferring (in C), *in accordance with (20)*, that 'this is red' is true. But (20) is, according to the pure pragmatic account of observation sentences, a rule for an observation

sentence. Thus this appeal to (20) requires that the language user realize
(in C) that

> This token of 'this is red' is a token of an observation sentence (i.e., it
> is one part of a regularity prescribed by a material transformation rule of
> my language (*viz.,(20)*)).

These moves have put the language user in the position to consider his
observation report from a sufficiently ''critical'' point of view'', i.e., from
the point of view of a being who can token sentences about itself and its
tokening which sentences require being governed by rules that·prescribe
regularities involving itself and its tokening. Such a being understands the
place and nature of observation reporting and thus can evaluate observation
reports properly.

The ''transition'' that the language user makes into the pragmatic meta-
language is, I said, *like* that involved in observation reporting. However, it
is, for reasons too complicated to explain here, *not* an observation report.
It is true, though, that there must be something like what, in SRLG, Sellars
calls ''language entry transitions'' into practical discourse about language
(i.e., into the metalanguage). This point brings us to an immensely important
matter in Sellars' philosophy. Though Sellars is adamant that practical discourse is not reducible to any other form of discourse and stands on its own
feet, he also holds that practical discourse has causal relations to natural
objects. In the case of practical discourse, Sellars is not at all inclined to
abandon his naturalism for a doctrine of ''noumenal intervention'' in the
world (LRB 299 note). A great deal of Sellars' energy in his writings on
practical reasoning and ethics has been directed toward filling in his view
of the place of practical discourse in the spatio-temporal order. What I
have briefly discussed above is one aspect of this topic: namely, entry
into that part of the language which contains rules and that part that
contains talk about rules.

Before turning to the last topic of this treatment of pure pragmatics, I
should like to take a paragraph to comment on the way in which observation
reports are treated in PPE, ENWW and RNWW. Though most of the elements
I have mentioned appear in one form or another in these essays, Sellars'
discussion of these matters is complicated by a variety of things. First,
as I pointed out before, Sellars is supposing that the basic individuals are
events. Among these events are the sensory events of the language user
(RNWWR 432.2). In addition, tokens of the language user's language appear
in the language user's sensory experience. Thus there is truly a

"confrontation" of "sensory events" and tokens. Indeed, they are "co-experienced". The "formal" counterpart of being "co-experienced" is what is packed into the term 'coex'. There are many things about this presentation that Sellars would no longer accept. At best it presents a special case of what I have discussed in connection with observation reports. On the account I have given, the causal regularities involving observation reports are of *whatever* sort that material transformation rules of the language say they are. Second, the formulations of Sellars' remarks involving 'coex' are affected by the need to make the variables conform to the formulation of sentences with 'means'. Thus one finds 'p coex q' to match 'E means p'. Such problems are avoided in my discussion which follows the strategies of Sellars' later work. Third, the most difficult aspect of Sellars' treatment of 'coex' in these three essays is that while discussing "experience" and "observation", he is also discussing the topic of the next subsection. And while, as we shall seem these two topics can be discussed simultaneously and do, in a sense, "coincide" in a certain special case, they are different and do need separate treatment (which they do get in Sellars' later writings).

(3) PICTURING

Again I use as the heading of a subsection a term from Sellars' later writings (though the word 'picture' occurs in some of the early essays, it is not a well-established term). What appears of the doctrine of picturing in the early essays is only a part of what the doctrine becomes. My discussion is, till near its end, restricted to the contents of the early essays (for those who wish more there is BBK, TC and SM ch. V). This restriction has two consequences. First, my view of picturing is through the lens of pure pragmatics and, as will be apparent, from the vantage of an as yet submerged issue, viz., the status of proper names. Sellars' approach to picturing is usually through the topic of truth (SM ch. V) aided by comment on Hume or Wittgenstein (TC section II & III) or through a contrast between meaning ("signification") and picturing (BBK). Second, I shall not attempt to lay out what Sellars takes to be some of his "later" reasons for holding a doctring of picturing (see, in particular, SM ch. V, paragraphs 56, 57 & 75).

A theme that has surfaced obsurely before must now be brought clearly into
the light: What the pure theory of empirically meaningful languages sets out
as a characterization of language is an "ideal" (one might say, a "regulative
ideal" in a Kantian sense). Thus a language, according to the theory, is
considerably more "tidied-up" and complete than what each of us individually
speaks. In particular, the pure theory of empirically meaningful languages
attributes to a language a complete (though not, of course, necessarily
adequate) group of formation and transformation rules. Now then, the segment
of a language that is not about language, i.e., the segment comprised solely
of what I called "blue" representations, includes sentences that are individual
constants combined with predicates as well as sentences that are complex
because of the appearance in them of logical constants or defined terms. Within
a structure of formation and transformation rules, it can be made clear which
kinds of entities are "made up" of other kinds of entities. Thus the idea of a
non-complex individual is part and parcel of the pure pragmatic framework. In
fact, this idea, within the context of pure pragmatics, is the idea of an undefined
individual constant. In general, the defined versus the undefined is clearly
demarcated within a language as language is characterized by the pure theory
of empirically meaningful languages. So, the segment of language that is not
about language has atomic sentences: i.e., sentences containing only undefined
individual constants and undefined predicates (one-place or more).

With respect to the formation and transformation rules, all undefined individual constants of a language, as contrasted with predicates, have the same
features and are thus formally indistinguishable. What differentiates undefined
individual constants from each other is not, then, their place in the syntactical
structure of the language. But, pure pragmatics tells us, each language has
"distinguished" atomic sentences, the "world-story" of the language. The
undefined individual constants that have "determinate meaning" must appear
in atomic sentences of the world-story of the language. Indeed, such an individual constant must appear in at least one sentence with a one-place
predicate and at least one sentence with a relational predicate of a special
sort. (I shall comment further on these restrictions in a moment.) The effect
of having a world-story is that each undefined individual constant in this
world-story is differentiated from every other. Of course, we must think of a
complete world-story, for, to speak in an ordinary way, the world-story is the
"true history" of the basic individuals of that language and one basic
individual is not necessarily differentiated from all the rest by anything less
than the whole history. (This "completeness" is compatible with Sellars'
point in paragraph 76, ch. V of SM.)

In any language, there are other histories than the world-story. The
world-story is simply one history out of many that can be constructed with
the undefined individual constants and undefined predicates of the language.
But, as I indicated above, what "distinguishes" the world-story is its
connection with truth: It is the "true history". Every sentence of a world-
story is a true sentence while other histories contain at least one false
sentence. (I have deviated slightly from Sellars' terminology, but I do
not think that I have mis-stated any point in doing so.)

Rather than try to discuss the many restrictions on histories and world-
stories, I shall comment only on the two I have mentioned. While, for
convenience, I have a tendency to treat all syntactical rules as "transformation" rules or "formation" rules, there are other syntactical rules
that might not fit handily into either group though they are clearly
"like" rules of the two kinds in certain respects. For example, such a
rule might tell us that we ought not to be disposed to token any sentence
which (roughly speaking) has a conjunctive predicate containing two
predicates of a specific kind (e.g., 'red and blue' is a crude example).
These rules provide a structure for the undefined predicates (of the blue
representations) which is important in separating them into "families"
(color predicates, shape predicates, etc.) which are related in specific
ways. The sentences of a history must not break such rules. Moreover,
any undefined individual constant in a history in a given language might
well be required to appear in at least one sentence with a predicate of
each family of predicates.

The relational sentences in which the undefined individual constants
appear in a history are the sentences that reflect spatio-temporal
structure. This structure varies from language to language; the transformation rules of the language determine the features of that structure.
Thus a history, in conforming to all the rules of its language, may have
the undefined individual constants of that language appearing with more
than one ("skeletal") relational predicate and in more than one sentence
with each such relational predicate. The general pragmatic restriction
that must not be broken is that from any undefined individual constant
in any (atomic) relational sentence in a history one must be able, by
the transformation rules and other sentences in the history, to reach another
(atomic) relational sentence in the history that has the original undefined
individual constant and any other undefined individual constant in the
history.

What we have so far is that, according to pure pragmatics, a language must have atomic sentences. Out of all the histories formulable from these atomic sentences, there is one true history, the world-story. That an atomic sentence is true if and only if it is in the world-story of its language is a claim that is true by the definition of 'world-story'. (Sellars sometimes puts this point, in the three earliest essays, by saying that the truth of atomic sentences is "formally decidable".) Of course, pure pragmatics tells us, for a given language, neither *which* atomic sentences are in the world-story of that language nor *which* history is the world-story.

In Sellars' early writings, perhaps the foremost importance of the concept of a world-story of a language is in the matter, already mentioned, of the meaning of undefined individual constants. Let us now call such individual constants "proper names". Proper names, as I pointed out above, cannot be semantically differentiated by looking to formation or transformation rules of the language. To put it crudely, all those rules say the same things about every proper name. So, a proper name, A, is different from a proper name, B, just in case the "place" of one in the world-story is different from the "place" of the other. That is, A and B are different if and only if there is something true of A with respect to the world-story that is not true of B with respect to the world-story.

But the importance of the world-story is not solely semantical. It is clear that a (non-omniscient) spatio-temporally located language user does not have the ideally complete world-story at any given time and place (an *ex hypothesi* omniscient language user is not quite in our position; see Sellars' remarks on "omniscient Jones" (ENWW section II; RNWWR 426.2ff & section VI)). What can the language user do to enlarge the part of the world-story that it has? Among other things, the language user can "move" itself, change its spatio-temporal position. (In general, of course, pure pragmatics would offer an account of language users as not only subjects of change but "initiators" of it; but this part of pure pragmatics is, except for the occasional comment, well beyond the scope of this introduction.) Part of the language user's language contains principles relevant to the language user's bringing about changes in its spatio-temporal location. In at least some cases, the language user needs sentences about the spatio-temporal location, properties and relations of other objects at the present and in the future. *In general,* such sentences cannot be inferred with the aid of anything but fundamental natural laws, i.e., material rules of inference of the language. But this utilization of fundamental natural laws requires premises which are sentences of the world-story. After all, the fundamental natural laws (as

opposed to those concerning ''complex'' objects) pertain to the predicates
of the basic individuals of the world. And, even if, in one's movements,
one deals primarily with sentences concerning the spatio-temporal location,
properties and relations of ''complex'' entities (this would be true of some
language users), the language user cannot in general predict things about
these complex objects without the help of the fundamental natural laws,
for, in at least some cases, a complex object is so-and-so because it is
composed in a certain way of basic individuals which are such-and-such.
So, sentences from the world-story must be utilized as premises to derive
conclusions needed by a language user in the process of extending its
knowledge.

However, not even with the above reflections have I exhausted the
importance of the world-story—what Sellars now calls a "picture". To
close this subsection I shall entertain largely ''later Sellars'' reflections
on world-stories.

When pure pragmatics speaks of a world-story, it is not, of course,
speaking of spatio-temporally located items since a world-story is composed of sentences as types. But the world-story as tokened is spatio-
temporally located and, in one way or another, the sentences of the world-
story can be spatio-temporally indexed. For the present, let us suppose
that with the world-story goes a commentary about the places and times
at which the sentences of the world-story are tokened. Remember
that, as I noted earlier, from the point of view of a (non-omniscient)
language user the (history which is a candidate for the) world-story
''develops''. (Even in the case of an omniscient (as understood by
Sellars) language user, it develops.) Let us think of what happens as
(roughly) this: The anguage user tokens a sentence S at a time tl and
place pl. If S is atomic and is to be part of the world-story, then at tl
and pl (so indicated in the commentary) the language user tokens (in the
commentary) that S is true.

But this way of putting things raises a problem: How does the language
user know which sentence to stick in the world-story and which to leave
out? Well, in general, language users cannot be protected from making
mistakes of one sort or another about this. Sellars holds *no* view that
would require that knowledge must be set on some ''foundation'' with
respect to which no mistakes are possible. Thus, it in no way bothers
him that what a language user puts in a developing history might be wrong:

All that follows, if such a situation occurs, is that the history in question is
not the world-story.

But there are ways in which the world-story of a language is "generated",
in a sense, by the language itself and causal action. Remember that the
language user is understood to have that tremendous battery of dispositions
that the rules of the language enjoin. So, let us look at a simple case which
involves the "aplication" of the language: i.e., a case of observation reporting. This example will also be an illustration of *one* way in which indexicals
can be connected with world-stories (see SM ch. V, section IV).

Let us suppose that in standard conditions and as a result of visual
stimulation by a red object, one of the language user's dispositions is
actualized and that results in a tokening:

(20) this is red.

In accordance with the arrangements set down in the section on observation
reports, the language user can conclude, from a premise stating the
occurrence of (20) in standard conditions, that the sentence of which (20)
is a token is true. For simplicity (otherwise I would open yet another can
of worms), let us suppose that the language user, by indexing with whatever
expressions it uses for place and time, constructs an individual constant,
thus: 'this(p,t)'. So, 'this(p,t)' is an individual constant for the object that
confronts the language user at the place p and the time t of the tokening
of (20). Now 'this(p,t)' and the predicate of (20) form the sentence

(21) this(p,t) is red.

But (21) need not be an atomic sentence. It is entirely possible that the
original response was to a complex object and that the proper place of
'this(p,t)' is as a defined term. If (21) is atomic, then (simplifying matters)
sentence (21) goes into the world-story (with appropriate commentary).
If (21) is not atomic, then (once again oversimplifying considerably) a
great deal of inference must occur as a result of the transformation rules
of the language (including rules that state definitions) to obtain whatever
atomic sentences follow from the observation sentence (given additional
premises about place, time, conditions, other objects, etc.). These atomic
sentences (the ones that are in effect necessary conditions of the truth
of the observation report) go into the world-story. In short, the world-story
is developed by the dispositions of the language user being actualized by

causal activity of objects (including the language user as such an object). That is, the world-story is "generated" by a complicated *method of* *"projection"*—which is no more that the totality of "observational" and "transformational" dispositions which the language user has in light of the *prescriptions of the rules of its language* (SM ch. V, paragraph 56; TC 215ff; BBK paragraph 37ff).

Now, let us think for a moment of the *(ideal) complete* histories, including the world-story, of a language. The following is true of each such history: No sentence containing a proper name already in the history and no sentence with a proper name not already in the history can be added without producing inconsistency *(given* the rules of the language, the sentences of the history and the non-atomic sentences connected with the history). Thus an (ideal) complete history is "maximal". As tokened through the actualization of the observational and transformational dispositions of the language user (a "projection"), each token of an (ideal) maximal history is in complicated relations to the other tokens of the history. That is, each token, *as a spatio-temporal item,* has natural relations to other tokens in the history through a projection; speaking a little freely, an (ideal) maximal history *as tokened through a projection* is a vast spatially and temporally extended complex entity, a *picture* of the entire world.

The condition for the *adequacy* of such a picture with respect to a projection is that the natural relationships within the picture "match up" with the natural relationships of the basic individuals. A world-story, as tokened by a method of projection, is literally, if adequate with respect to that method of projection, "isomorphic" to the non-linguistic spatio-temporal items of the world (BBK paragraphs 24, 52, 53 & 58; SM ch. V, sections VIII & IX). (That a language also has *something like* a mirroring of the world-story as natural object and how this is related to judgments of the world-story's adequacy are points that I can do no more than offer a few limited remarks on in the next subsection.)

At rock bottom, then, the function of proper names is to be *elements in an adequate picture, a world-story that is generated by language and causal activity.* What differentiates proper names is their place in this picture, a picture which is at one and the same time a spatio-temporal item as tokened and a system of atomic sentences in a language. (The last two paragraphs have brought us as close as I can come in this introduction to Sellars' discussion of picturing in SM ch. V.)

(4) A FEW SUMMARY COMMENTS

From our present position, it might occur to anyone that a more orderly
system of exposition would begin with pure pragmatics and then discuss syntax
and semantics along the way. The need to *introduce* my readers to Sellars'
early essays made it seem reasonable to conduct the exposition in the order that
appears here. But it is possible and helpful to recover briefly part of the ground
already trod and, at the same time, to add here and there a bit more flesh to the
skeleton which I have been exposing.

The point of this introduction is not the detailed exposition of Sellars' views
on this topic or that in epistemology or philosophy of language, but rather an indication of the scope and content of the pure theory of empirically meaningful
languages. So, my partial summary will proceed without regard to what might be
basic and what derivative in the pure theory of empirically meaningful languages.
I shall not even explain what, out of all that I say, would be enough for a
Sellarsian definition of 'language'. My summary is a statement of truths (or
what would be truths given cleaning-up and reformulation) of the pure theory
without regard to the systematization of that theory.

For Sellars, language is a system of representation, a system of elaborate
structure without which no occurrence can count as a tokening and no occurrence
can be an item of knowledge. The structure provides what is necessary for
a "critical" appraisal of claims to knowledge.

Let me review, at this point, the formal concept of a language user. The
notion of a language user in the pure theory is that of the language, so to speak,
localized in a spatio-temporal framework. As such, the (ideal) language user
participates in the structure of language through its vast array of dispositions
to token. These dispositions, these "iffy" properties about what the language
user would token if. . . . are prescribed by the rules of the language. Of course,
tokenings are *not* specified with respect to natural properties (e.g., according
to sign design) but only with regard to the structural connections enjoined by
the rules.

Consider the dispositions of the language user with respect to what I called
in IIB "blue" representations. Actualizations of such dispositions of the
language user are tokenings containing individual constants and predicates and
logically complex tokenings involving these. Some of these tokenings are
causally evoked by sensory stimulation (observation reporting) and others, by

other tokenings (inferring). (In addition, there are those tokenings I have not discussed which are causally efficacious in changing the language user as a natural object.) The important structure at this level is the world-story of atomic sentences which is, as tokened, being generated by this causal activity.

In addition to these dispositions, the language user has dispositions concerning what I called "green" representations, the "rules" of the language. The language user appeals to these rules in criticizing reasoning, in developing by inference the world-story and in planning by practical reasoning its own "moves" in the future. (Thus rules are involved in the production of "actions" and this is a matter, in some cases, of the tokening of rules in reasoning. This complicated topic is part of pure pragmatics and its significance cannot be brought out in syntax even though syntactical rules are involved in practical reasoning.)

Finally, we come to what I called "red" representations. According to pure pragmatics, a language user must be disposed, in appropriate circumstances, to respond to tokenings with tokenings in a pragmatic metalanguage. Thus, for example, a language user must be able to represent tokenings by such other tokenings as:

    that's a rule,
    that's an atomic sentence,
    that tokening was brought about by visual stimulation,
    that tokening contains the predicate 'red',

and on and on for syntactical, semantical and pragmatic predicates of all sorts. A language user, on Sellars' view, does not simply respond in regular fashion as enjoined by the rules of the language; the language user (*qua* natural object (of whatever sort) which is a realization of the language in space and time) has all the dispositions necessary to token sentences which *say that the various features and regularities of linguistic tokenings* are *because of* the rules. In short, a language user is disposed to token pragmatic sentences which are part of practical discourse about the language user as a being which is governed by rules.

I wish to be clear about why pure pragmatics requires metalinguistic responses of an (ideal) language user. This requirement is part of what insures that the metalinguistic *tokenings,* the ones by which, to put it ordinarily, we talk about rules and about other tokens and types as having syntactical, semantical and pragmatic properties and relations, are "lawfully related" to the tokenings they are "about". The relationship between these *metalinguistic sentences and,* speaking ordinarily, *the items they are "about" is just as much part of the causal order and structure of language as those tokenings which are not metalinguistic.*

It is crucial at this point to note that among the tokenings of these metalinguistic sentences are those that *say* what is in the world-story (in a sense, "mirror" it) and are the needed "commentary" on the world-story. Moreover, with subsidiary premises supplied by the commentary, premises about the occurrence of tokens in space and time, a pragmatic metalanguage is capable of formulating sentences about the causal impact of rules and the causal connections between practical discourse and other discourse in the language itself. So, a language has means for representing *rules as items in a causally organized spatio-temporal world* the basic objects of which are pictured by the language and thus has means for dealing with the function of rules in the causal economy.

Such then is an example of the complexity of the linguistic dispositions that a language user must have in order to be sufficiently "critical". Of course, I have barely scratched the surface of what goes into all this. For example, the language user's conception of itself as a rule user must reflect the various kinds of rules and the kinds of the dispositions it has so that it is able to criticize sentences which place other tokens within the structure of language. It is only by seeing itself in this (ideally) articulated "self-conscious" fashion (to borrow an Hegelian turn of phrase) that the language user comes to know the truth about its own world.

I will not, however, persevere in discussion of the theme of a "being that has knowledge about its own world" (section IIB), for it would lead into some central issues in epistemology and in the end to a detailed treatment of truth and knowledge. What I shall do is turn to a topic related to the topic of the complexity of the structure of language. Among other things, I shall consider that part of language use which is a reflection of the language user's "critical" attitude toward the rules it uses. This directly depends on what I have been discussing, for if a language user does not see itself as subject to rules, it cannot contemplate being subject to *other* rules (i.e., *changing* its rules) and if it does not conceive the place of rules in the structure of language, it cannot appreciate *the point and the impact of changing its rules,* i.e., it cannot appreciate that changing rules is one of the keys to coming to have *better* pictures and patterns of reasoning.

IV. POSSIBLE WORLDS

A. THE SELLARSIAN STRATEGY

In its main outlines, the Sellarsian strategy on possible worlds and modality is largely determined by the considerations that have shaped the pure theory of empirically meaningful languages. These considerations stand out most clearly against the background of what Sellars thinks of as the *main* alternative to the sort of view he espouses: It is what he calls "naive realism", In its *most advanced* (and, of course, not "naive") *form,* naive realism is a philosophical view that pushes our ordinary talk about properties, relations, numbers and such like to its limits. It takes seriously the existence of abstract entities: (some selection of) states of affairs, universals, propositions, facts and possibilities of all sorts including possible worlds and possible "particulars" (i.e., possible spatio-temporal individuals). Out of the various reasons that might be given for Sellars' rejection of naive realism, two are especially relevant to the discussion of this introduction.

The first point is easily made by restatement of my remarks in section IIA on Sellars' Tractarian slogan "formal terms do not represent". The defenders of naive realism attribute to abstract entities a variety of properties and relations to other abstract entities. Among such properties and relations are logical ones (being disjunctive, being general, being entailed by other abstract entities) and others such as truth, possibility, necessity, and so on. Conspicuously absent are such things as spatio-temporal location, causal dispositions and any properties or relations that would require such location and such dispositions. Clearly, abstract entities are intimately connected with those concepts that Sellars wishes to interpret as "formal" concepts. It would, of course, be difficult to incorporate these concepts into the pure theory of empirically meaningful languages and, as it were, leave the abstract entities behind.

The second point is closely connected with the first. Abstract entities are not characterized in such a way that it is easy to see how they would participate in the causal order. Yet, as the last section tries to make clear, knowledge is obtained through the structure of language which is, for Sellars, thoroughly causal. In order for Sellars to accept naive realism, he would have to find a place in this causal order for abstract entities as naive realism characterizes them. Attempts to do exactly this, I pointed out in IIA, are made. But these attempts accept special psychological relations between minds and abstract entities: thus such views hold to what Sellars calls "psychological platonism". As I emphasized in IIA, the rejection of psychological platonism is a central element in Sellars' naturalism.

These two points also make it relatively clear what Sellars' strategy with respect to possibility (and modality in general) and abstract entities must be. On Sellars' view, discourse involving modal terms and terms for abstract entities must be a part of practical discourse about the structure of language (though the exact details of this strategy are, as we shall have some small indication, not simple). Thus, on Sellars' view (but not naive realism), that modality and abstract entities *are* involved in causal processes is defensible: *But that involvement is a special case of the involvement of practical discourse in causal processes.*

At this point, my exposition strikes the same reefs that have been there throughout this introduction. I cannot, with the space I have, embark on the details of Sellars' primary account of modal sentences and sentences with abstract singular terms. That would take a book (most of my MEM is, in fact, devoted to just that). (The best introduction to Sellars' views on these matters is AE and CAE.) What I shall do is briefly explain a bit more about the general features of Sellars' account of possibility in the pure theory of empirically meaningful languages before turning to several related matters.

The following is the bluntest way of putting what I take to be the fundamental point in Sellars' treatment of possibility. The framework of talk about possibility is just the framework in terms of which a language user represents to itself *alternative (other)* linguistic tokening than it is presently disposed to. This is not to say that every sense of the word 'possible' is to be explicated directly by means of this remark; that is not so. What is true is that the notions that explicate possibility and the other modalities are linguistic in that they reflect the (pragmatic) framework in which a language user can be properly critical toward its present and past linguistic tokening. A particularly important, but not the only, case is the language user's critical attitude toward the rules of its language which are so essential to that linguistic tokening. A language user, given its abilities with regard to a (pragmatic) metalanguage, is in a position to modify its language, particularly the rules of the language, to satisfy its epistemic desires for better pictures and better reasoning. To put the point at the beginning of this paragraph once again: A linguistic activity that is essential to such modification is discourse about what is possible; such discourse expresses the language user's understanding of the epistemic alternatives (the ''others'') that are open to it and that demarcate its choices for improving its epistemic position.

Before attempting to sketch the range of such alternatives that are provided by Sellars' account and thus with it some of what Sellars' has to say about the ''possibilities'', I wish to discuss one point Sellars made in early (and ''near early'') essays about the word 'necessarily'. This discussion I wish to serve as a warning: It would be a great mistake to think of Sellars' explication of specific modal constructions in some language as being nailed down to one simple pattern. The remarks I have made about the general framework of possibility insure that in *some* way Sellars' account of modal terms will be ''linguistic''. However, the following example, with the subsequent discussion, will, I hope, impress on the reader that no quick conclusions about the details of Sellars' view can be drawn from the observation that Sellars account of modality is ''linguistic''.

B. 'NECESSARILY'

Besides serving as a warning, the example of this section gives me the opportunity to remind the reader not to forget about the "purity" of the pure theory of empirically meaningful languages. One of the jobs of the pure theory is to investigate languages with regard to the differences between the systems of rules and world-stories found in them. This investigation, if carried through, would lead to a very general characterization of the differences among languages. As an adjunct to this investigation, the pure theory also characterizes modal terms since, as I indicated in the previous section, these terms are part of the framework that enables a language user to contemplate trading in its language for another. Of course, the characterization of modal terms is entirely "pure"; that there are tokens in specific languages such as English which are this modal term or that is to be decided only by an investigation of the language.

Sellars does, in a way, lend comfort (if not exactly aid) to losing sight of this last point, for he presents, just as I generally do in this introduction, "pure" characterizations only by way of "impure" example. The reason for this is one I have alluded to before: Pure characterizations are an elaborate undertaking which interfere with frying other important fish. So, he commonly puts his points by saying something about specific tokens (tokens of English since that is the language he is writing in) such as those which are tokens of 'necessary', 'necessarily', and 'necessitates' (LRB 296.1 & 309.1 & .2; IM section V; SRLG paragraph 88). Doubtless Sellars *qua* sophisticated tokener and lay investigator of English does have views about these English tokens. But these views should not be confused with the pure pragmatic account of modal terms.

Let us look for a moment about what Sellars has to say about 'necessarily'. He is convinced that, in many cases, an instance of the sign design 'necessarily', produced in an English sentence tokening, has the function of indicating, if its appearance is correct, that the tokening of the sentence to which the instance of the sign design is attached is a "reflection" of a rule of inference (material or formal) of our language in that tokenings of this sentence are sanctioned by the rule of inference. Let me compare this view to one concerning tokens of 'therefore' in English. It is not implausible to suggest that English tokenings that involve the production of an instance of the sign design 'therefore' are "indicators" of an inference sanctioned by a rule of inference of our language. To hold this view of 'therefore', one does *not* need to suppose that the English word 'therefore' is to be rewritten as something like 'the following sentence is correctly inferred from the preceding ones' or 'there is a rule by which the inference of the following sentence from the preceding ones is justified'. All one need hold is that *properly* occurring tokens of the word 'therefore' are such that (roughly) it ought to be that any speaker of English, from

> an English tokening of 'therefore' is preceded by some sentences and followed by another sentence,

infers

> the former sentences are premises and the latter is a conclusion and there is a rule of our language according to which this conclusion is correctly inferred from these premises.

The above principle, though it concerns a word of English, is the basis for a pure characterization of —let me call it—an "inference indicator" term. (Of course, convictions about the tenability of such a pure characterization are different from convictions about the truth of the claim that the English word 'therefore' is an "inference indicator" term.)

Similarly, Sellars' remarks on the English term 'necessarily' point to a pure characterization of what I shall call "rule indicator" terms. The pure characterization of such terms and the claim that in English some tokens of 'necessarily' are such terms are quite different. As important is the fact that this claim about 'necessarily' *does not imply* that there are no other sorts of modal terms in English and *does not even imply* that *all* tokenings of 'necessarily' in English are "rule indicator" terms.

Sellars has a special reason for remarking on what I have called "rule indicator" terms: He wishes to suggest, in some essays not primarily directed toward the issues of modality (LRB 309.1 & .2; IM 333.1, .2 & .3; SRLG paragraphs 27 & 88), that modal terms can find a place in the naturalistic account of language as   rule-governed. So, he chooses a relatively simple example to illustrate one such place.   But this example is no guide to the much more elaborate treatments in Sellars' later writing (AE; CAE; SPB; NAO). That Sellars' general therapy for discourse containing modal terms or abstract singular terms is linguistic (in his sense of this term) does not imply that he has but one treatment to prescribe for such items as are claimed to be part of that discourse.

C. POSSIBLE INDIVIDUALS AND POSSIBLE WORLDS

In CIL, "Concepts as Involving Laws and Inconceivable Without Them" (and in P, "Particulars"), Sellars directly discusses possible worlds from the viewpoint of "naive realism" (see IVA). Sellars is perfectly happy to reflect, in the spirit of naive realism, on possible worlds and possible individuals even though, as I pointed out in IVA, all such reflection must, in the end, turn out to be "about language". In CIL, Sellars has a specific reason for embarking on an elaboration of the naively realistic view of possibilities: He is anxious to tackle a problem, raised by claims of C.I. Lewis in *An Analysis of Knowledge and Valuation*, which concerns "real connections" and to do so in a way that fits well with Lewis' own approach. But, even more generally, Sellars sees merit in dealing with and solving problems, if possible, within the naively realistic assumptions that lead to them. A paragraph in P sums up these points well:

(P 296.1) .....the 'ontological' jargon of worlds and possibilities has long been used by philosophers and logicians in their attempts to understand the structure of conceptual systems..... Most of the puzzles which are the inherited stock-in-trade of contemporary philosophy either belong in this frame, or else concern the very status of the frame itself. Even should this 'ontological' frame be but the shadow of rules of language, it by no means follows that there is no point in the effort to develop it more consistently and systematically than has been done in the past. Puzzles and antinomies within the frame (though not perplexities concerning the

frame itself) *can* be resolved within the frame, even though the resulting clarification is but a shadow of an insight into linguistic usage
that *might* have been obtained directly.

Nothing, I have said before, short of a statement of major parts of
Sellars' later writings can give an accurate total rendition of Sellars'
position on modality and abstract entities. But I do intend to do something
less ambitious: to present a brief exposition of Sellars' elaboration of the
naively realistic account of possible worlds. By and large, I shall follow
the exposition of the central sections of CIL, sections III through VI
(summarized briefly in P 294ff). In addition, I shall give, as I go along,
a ''correlation'' of the concepts of naive realism and those of the pure
theory of empirically meaningful languages. I do not have the space to
spell out the force of the ''correlation'', to provide an adequate commentary
on its scope and limits, or to flesh out my discussion with ''linguistic
treatments'' of specific sentences.
  Section III of CIL opens with a review of a relatively familiar
''Leibnitzian'' account of possible worlds. More or less, the account is
this: A ''world'' is a collection of ''basic particulars'' exemplifying
simple ''universals'', both qualities and relations. The relations
establish the spatio-temporal structure of the world (or, a structure which,
while not spatio-temporal as we usually think of space and time, orders
in certain ways the basic particulars). Among the atomic ''states of
affairs'', i.e., those states of affairs which involve only the basic
particulars and simple universals of a world, are those that obtain, the
''facts'' of that world. One world in the family of worlds is the ''actual''
one; those that are not the actual world are ''merely possible'' worlds.
.(For reasons he explains (CIL 293.1), Sellars abandons the term 'world'
for the term 'history'. Since I have, for convenience, employed the latter
term in my discussion of pure pragmatics, I shall, in this section, retain
the naively realistic and familiar term 'world'. A careful reading of CIL
and this introduction would show that, in any case, I have avoided and
am avoiding the issues that lead Sellars to reject 'world' in favor of
'history'.)
  A rough-and-ready correspondence with concepts of the pure theory of

empirically meaningful languages is begun by noting that to the concept of
a world, W, corresponds that of a world-story, S, of a language, L. With
respect to W, S and L, part of the remainder of the correspondence is
conveniently set out in a table:

W	S and L
basic particular	proper name
simple universals	undefined predicates:
qualities	one-place predicates
relations	many-place predicates
atomic states of affairs	atomic sentences
facts	true atomic sentences

Continuing this correspondence depends on taking care to distinguish two
contrasts.

The one contrast is between the actual world and merely possible worlds.
In the pure theory of empirically meaningful languages, the corresponding
contrast is between the world-story of one language and the world-story of
another language. We can make this point equivalently as follows:
Consider the (material and formal) rules, R, of languages which form a
family by sharing R. With respect to R, different world-stories can be
formulated. The concept of such alternative world-stories is what
corresponds to the concept of the various worlds, actual and merely
possible.

A quite different contrast, one that Sellars is adamant in maintaining
(CIL 293.3 item VII; P 294.2,295.1), is that between a possible world, W,
and a "possible state of the world W". The facts of W specify the *actual*
(and, of course, a possible) state of W. A state of W which is "merely
possible" is specified by a collection of states of affairs some of which
do *not* obtain. I shall call the possible states of W which are *not actual*
the "counterfactual" states of W. In the pure theory, the corresponding
contrast is between a world-story of a language, L, and the *other* histories
(the "false" ones) formulable in L.

One of the reasons Sellars insists on the difference between these two
contrasts is that confusing them, he thinks, is one source of the
(unacceptable) doctrine of "bare particulars" (P 295.1). Sellars'
insistence on the difference between these two contrasts is reflected in

the fact that *no* particular of a world, W, is also a particular of another world whereas any particular of W can appear in a counterfactual state of W. The tenability of all this within naive realism I will not consider. But the corresponding point within the pure theory of empirically meaningful languages I have, in effect, argued for in IIIC(3): Strictly speaking, *no two different world-stories*, S1 and S2, in L1 and L2, respectively, *can share even one proper name* (even if L1 and L2 share the very same rules). This follows from the fact that proper names are semantically determinate only with respect to a complete world-story; what differentiates a proper name from another in a world-story is the (total) place of the proper name in that world-story. Thus, I repeat, no proper name of one world-story is a proper name of another world-story. Of course, any proper name of a world-story, S, can appear in an atomic sentence of a false history (with respect to S). (See RNWWR 441 note 10.)

Whatever may be the deficiencies of the naively realistic position just sketched, it has one overwhelming drawback for Sellars: It recognizes only one family of possible worlds. The correct development of naive realism leads, Sellars claims, to the recognition of a plurality of families of possible worlds. Sellars' strategy for supporting this claim begins with the observation that, as traditionally conceived, all possible worlds contain the same simple universals (CIL 295.3). If there were different systems of "possible" simple universals, then there would be good naively realistic grounds for thinking that there were different families of possible worlds, each family containing its own system of simple universals. That Sellars wishes to argue for the antecedent of this hypothetical is clear from the following quotation:

> (CIL 296.1) There are two closely related mistakes which are characteristic of western philosophy as a whole. They are (1) the discussion of philosophical questions in terms of a list of universals which is taken for granted, and which is a list of universals whose difference from one another is taken for granted and not clarified[11] and (2) the assumption that while it makes sense to speak of possible particulars, and to contrast actual with merely possible particulars, neither of these ways of speaking makes sense in connection with universals. Certainly some philosophers have discussed the possibility of there being universals which are not exemplified by

the actual history, but the sort of thing they have had in mind is a color
which nobody will ever happen to see. Such a universal is not conceived of as a merely possible universal as opposed to actual universals,
it is an actual universal (a phrase which is, for them, redundant) which the
world doesn't happen to have taken to its bosom. Furthermore, even this
idea has been discussed as one might discuss the possibility of there
being ghosts, as something unlikely and queer. We, on the other hand, are
soon going to assert the existence of domains of possible universals, and
not just as a queer speculation to which one should pay one's respects in
a systematic discussion, but as an integral part of our naive conceptions
concerning possibility.

(Compare **ENWW** 650.3 note 13.)
    Sellars' argument begins with an attempt to determine what a naive realist
ought to say about point (1) above: How is the difference of one simple universal from another to be understood? After trying out and rejecting as inadequate several answers to this question(CIL 297.1-299.1), he finds the most
plausible course for a naive realist to follow is to insist that (CIL 299.2)

> *the diversification of the most-determinate qualitative universals is*
> *to be understood in terms of relations which obtain between all*
> *particulars, actual or merely possible, which exemplify these universals.*

What is needed to handle the identity and difference of universals is what one
would expect: viz., properties that one universal might have and another
universal lack. The way to these properties is, the above quote tells us,
through considering the exemplifications of simple universals by "particulars,
actual or merely possible".
    The crux of Sellars' argument is at hand (remember that Sellars writes
'history' where I write 'world'):

> (CIL 299.2) *Thus, the properties of a universal as universal concern that*
> *which is involved in its being exemplified.....*For convenience of
> expression, we shall consider the set of properties which together are
> distinctive of a universal to be a single property which we shall call
> the distinctive property of the universal. Now in terms of the framework
> with which we have been working, we can say that the distinctive property
> of a universal concerns its exemplification in all possible histories in

which it is exemplified, and is identical with respect to all exemplifications in all possible histories in which it is exemplified. But in order for each universal to have such a distinctive property, the family of possible histories which exemplify the domain of universals to which the universal belongs cannot consist of the relational arrays of states of affairs which would be possible if, *per impossible*, universals were completely indifferent to the context in which they are exemplified. In other words, the family of possible histories which exemplify this domain of universals cannot consist of all "logically possible" arrays of exemplifications of the universals by sets of particulars, where by this is meant the arrays that would be possible if a domain of universals were a sheer multiplicity of *exemplifiables*, as substitutable for one another in any context as pennies. [14] The reason for this is obvious. *If the family were of this nature, then each universal would function "symmetrically" with all the others in relation to the family, and hence would have no distinctive property with respect to its exemplifications in the family. The universals would be indiscernable, and, hence, identical.*

Thus, in order to make sense out of the claim that the worlds of the family which includes the actual world share a system of simple universals, each universal of the system being *different* from others in the system, the naive realist has been led to the view that this family of worlds is *restricted* to less than the logically possible arrays of states of affairs that can be put together from the basic particulars available in the family and the simple universals of the family. There are certain, shall we say, "patterns" that *must* hold throughout the family if one is to make sense out of the family's being associated with a system of simple universals. Consider an elementary example: A universal, U1, may, in one world of a family, be exemplified by the very same particulars which exemplify U2; in another, by many more than exemplify U2; but in no world of the family, by less than exemplify U2. These "patterns", or "invariancies", as Sellars calls them, are not a matter of laws of logic:

(CIL 301.2) In exemplifying a common domain of universals, the histories of the family exhibit certain common invariancies involving the relations in which particulars stand and the qualitative universals they exemplify. Since these invariancies necessarily obtain of the family, being bound up with the fact that the universals exemplified by the family are the universals they are, and since these invariancies restrict the family to

less than what we referred to as the "logically possible arrays of
exemplifications of the universals"—and are therefore not the invariancies
which are exhibited in the formulae of logic—we may call them *material
invariancies*.

These material invariancies are the laws of nature of the possible worlds of
the family that exhibits them.

Finally, the argument approaches the conclusion stated above: There is
more than one family of possible worlds. Clearly the naive realist assents
to the claim that there are *alternative* systems of *material invariancies*, i.e.,
other systems of logically possible laws of nature. With other systems of
material invariancies come other systems of simple universals and thus other
families of possible worlds:

> (CIL 304.1) .....we began by assuming that the contrast between actual
> and possible doesn't apply to *universals*. Our argument, however, forces
> us to abandon this assumption, for the very notion that the *actual* domain
> of universals, one of the possible histories exemplifying which is the
> actual history, is characterized by a set of co-exemplification properties
> or material invariancies, leads to the conception of *alternative systems
> of universals characterized by other sets of co-exemplification properties
> or material invariancies, and exemplified in other families of possible
> histories.*

The range of possibilities, as originally envisaged by naive realism, was,
as I said earlier, too limited. The realm of possibility is "a family of
families of possible worlds". Each family is characterized by containing
a system of simple universals or, equivalently, by exhibiting a system of
material invariancies. Such, then, is Sellars' elaboration of traditional
naive realism. (Of course, if one were to consider alternative systems of
logical laws, there would be even more "possibilities" to add to the already
imposing assemblage.)

I do not wish to discuss the tenability of this elaborated naive realism
in naively realistic terms (in any case, there are many things the above
summary of Sellars' argument omits). But I am anxious to point out that
the claim that corresponds in the pure theory of empirically meaningful
languages to the one so lengthily argued for is a straightforward

consequence of my remarks on material transformation rules and undefined
predicates in IIIB(1) and IIIB(3). As a preliminary, note that the concept
corresponding to material invariancy (law of nature) is that of material
transformation rule. As I pointed out in III, material transformation rules
are required for the semantical differentiation and classification of
undefined predicates: Put bluntly, without material transformation rules,
there can be no tokens which are predicates. Different systems of material
transformation rules give different groups of undefined predicates. A
family of languages is marked off by sharing the same material rules of
inference (given that they share the same formal rules of inference);
such a family shares the same predicates. The totality of world-stories
formulable in languages sharing the same rules (material and formal),
i.e., the totality of world-stories that do not conflict with any rule of
these languages, corresponds to a family of possible worlds sharing the
same material invariancies and thus the same simple universals.

The world-stories formulable within languages sharing the same rules
include *all* of the arrays of atomic sentences that are consistent with the
material transformation rules of these languages. Since these world-
stories run through all the "materially consistent" (but *not* all the
logically consistent) arrays of atomic sentences, each undefined predicate
of the languages of these world-stories can be distinguished from every
other by the totality of its appearances in these world-stories. These
world-stories as a whole reflect *all* the differences that are *consistent with*
what is prescribed by the material transformation rules of the languages.
Thus the consideration of these world-stories provides a way equivalent
to that discussed in III for differentiating undefined predicates. (Putting
the points of this paragraph in naively realistic terms, we have: Simple
universals are differentiated from each other by the totality of exemplifications these universals have with respect to all the particulars in a family
of worlds which all exhibit the same material invariancies.)

Let me conclude my remarks on world-stories by reminding the reader
of the concept of a "false" history (which corresponds to a merely
possible (counterfactual) state of a world). In addition to the world-story
of a language, there are all the other histories that are formulable in the
language with the help of the proper names of the world-story. These
histories are, of course, "false"; they contain at least one false atomic
sentence as judged by the world-story which contains all the true atomic
sentences and fixes the semantical function of the proper names of the

language. Notice that a proper name of a world-story appears in at least one false history with respect to that world-story (in general, it will appear in many false histories with respect to that world-story). The "contrary-to-fact" sentences of a false history with respect to a given world-story may contain exactly the same proper names as the true sentences of that world-story. Put in naively realistic terms, any individual of a world appears in at least one possible but not actual state of that world. It is one and the same individual in both the actual state and this counterfactual state of the world.

Such, then, is the range of epistemic alternatives available to a language user: Differing languages with the same formal transformation rules but not the same material ones; differing world-stories of languages which share the same rules, both material and formal; differing histories with respect to a world-story of a given language. Moreover, we might, as I indicated, even wish to add the case of languages that do not share the same formal rules.

I have come as far with these matters as space allows. I shall conclude by "giving the reader an idea" of how all this machinery bears on necessity through a brief consideration of the naive realist's concept of being "true in all possible worlds". As I said near the end of IIIB(3), the treatment of such concepts calls more for decision than anything else. I shall take up two cases, both "extreme". In both cases, I confine my attention to atomic sentences and material and formal rules.

In the first case, the pure pragmatic concept corresponding to being "true in all possible worlds" is, for atomic sentences,

being true in all world-stories

and, for rules,

not being contravened by any world-story.

A transformation rule is contravened by a world-story if (roughly) the world-story contains the "premises" of the transformation but not the "conclusion".

Given such a pure pragmatic understanding of being true in all possible worlds (and a few other assumptions that will emerge), it follows that any atomic sentence, A, of any world-story is "necessary". After all, A appears in one and only one world-story, S. It is true in S. No other atomic sentence of S is in any way incompatible with A and, more surprisingly, yet just as truly, *no atimic sentence of any other world-story is incompatible with A.* The latter conjunct is true because the atomic sentences of world-stories other than S have proper names that are different from the ones in S: Every proper name belongs to one and only one world-story. So, no sentence of any world-story makes A not true and, provided that we cleave to classical logic, A is true in every world-story. Hence, A is necessary.

Similarly, every rule, T, is necessary. The world-stories of the family F, of languages which share T *ex hypothesi* do not contravene T. But the world-stories of families other than F cannot contravene T either, since the atomic sentences of those world-stories, being in languages of families other than F, contain different predicates than F: Every predicate belongs to one and only one family of languages. Hence, T is not contravened by any world-story and thus T is necessary.

Three comments are in order. First, the very same results can be obtained in a naively realistic approach to necessity (though some terminological wrinkles would have to be ironed out). After all, the pure pragmatic concepts and the naively realistic ones "correspond" uniformly (within the range I have considered). Second, the pure pragmatic concepts of necessity just sketched obviously represent one "extreme". They reflect the fact that both world-stories and rules, given Sellars' account of "meaning" (IIIB and IIIC(3)), are essential to "fixing the meaning" of at least some linguistic items (compare CIL 310.2,311.1 &.2, 312.1 & 313.1). Third, my claims about necessity are independent of the concepts of being a priori, a posteriori, analytic and synthetic. Clearly there is great scope for terminological maneuvering. For example, if I were to follow a well-established line of thought and take a sentence to be analytic if it is essential to the "meaning" of (at least some of) the terms in it, then even the atomic sentences of world-stories would be analytic. But if the condition for being analytic is the "inessential" occurrence of all but logical terms, then atomic sentences of world-stories would be synthetic—but still necessary (in the above sense of 'necessary'). (Compare the end of IIIB(3).)

Let us look at the other "extreme": Being true in all possible worlds is taken to correspond to having no epistemic alternatives. It is trivial to show that the atomic sentences of world-stories are *not* necessary in this sense. Consider an atomic sentence, A, of a world-story, S. Every proper name in any world-story appears in at least one false history (with respect to that world-story) and, in general, appears in many atomic sentences of that history which are false sentences. Thus the proper name appearing

in A also appears in false sentences in false histories (with respect to S) and
at least one of these histories does not contain A. Such a false history
(with respect to S) provides alternatives to A. Thus A is not necessary.
(Put in naively realistic terms, there are merely possible (counterfactual)
states of a possible world, W, in which a particular, P, does *not* exemplify one
of the universals P exemplifies in W but *does* exemplify some other
universal(s).)

That there are alternatives to a system of material transformation rules is
clear. And, if we wished, we can make sense out of alternatives to formal
transformation rules. Thus both sorts of rules turn out in the present sense
of 'necessary' *not* to be necessary. (It is, perhaps, amusing to note that though
in the present sense of 'necessary', atomic sentences of world-stories and
transformation rules are *not necessary*, all of them can nevertheless be
accounted *analytic* in one of the senses of 'analytic' sketched above.)

One moral to draw from this brief excursus on concepts of necessity is that,
on Sellars' view, modal discourse is important in enabling a language user to
represent many things about histories and world-stories and about relations of
world-stories to the rest of a language and of languages to families of
languages and of families of languages to each other. But necessity never
prevents the tokening of *sentences which are about "alternatives"*. Such
sentences are not inconsistent or false even though the rules or other
sentences they are about may be, in some sense, incompatible with rules or
other sentences we hold to be true. So, to say that something is necessary
may well be to say something true about your language. But that does not
prevent you from altering your language so that something else is necessary
(see IM 377.1).

(RNWWR 456.2) This paper represents a meeting of extremes. The echoes
of Leibnitz, Hume and Kant are no less obvious than those of Wittgenstein,
Carnap and Tarski. But as a matter of historical justice long due, I like
to think that we have reformulated in our own way a familiar type of
Idealistic argument. It has been said that human *experience* can only be
understood as a fragment of an ideally coherent *experience*. Our claim is
that our empirical *language* can only be understood as an incoherent and
fragmentary schema of an ideally coherent *language*. The Idealism, but

not the wisdom, disappears with the dropping of the term 'experience'. Formally, all languages and worlds are on an equal footing.

(EPM 170.3 in SPR) One seems forced to choose between the picture of an elephant which rests on a tortoise (What supports the tortoise?) and the picture of a great Hegelian serpent of knowledge with its tail in its mouth (Where does it begin?) Neither will do. For empirical knowledge, like its sophisticated extension, science, is rational, not because it has a *foundation* but because it is a self-correcting enterprise which can put *any* claim in jeopardy, though not *all* at once.

Carnap, R.

FLM   *Foundations of Logic and Mathematics*, vols. I & II of the *International
       Encyclopedia of Unified Science* (Chicago: University of Chicago Press,
       1939).

ISFL   *Introduction to Semantics and Formalization of Logic*, (Cambridge,
       Massachusetts: Harvard University Press, 1959).

MN   *Meaning and Necessity* (Chicago: The University of Chicago Press,
       1947 & 1956).

Church, A.

NAE   "The Need for Abstract Entities in Semantic Analysis", *American
       Academy of Arts and Sciences Proceedings*, vol. 80 (1951: 100-112).

Castaneda, H-N.

AKR   (ed.) *Action, Knowledge and Reality* (Indianapolis: The Bobbs-Merrill
       Company, Ind., 1975).

Sicha, J.

LFST   "Logic: The Fundamentals of a Sellarsian Theory", in J. Pitt (ed.),
       The Philosophy of Wilfrid Sellars: Queries and Extensions (Dordrecht:
       D. Reidel Publishing Co., 1978): 257-286.

MEM   *A Metaphysics of Elementary Mathematics* (Amherst, Massachusetts:
       University of Massachusetts Press, 1974).

Wittgenstin, L.

TRACTATUS   *Tractatus Logico-Philosophicus* (London: Routledge and Kegan
            Paul, Ltd., 1922).

SECTION I

(181; 182; 183.1)   The key to defending against psychologistic and, in general, factualistic accounts of philosophical concepts is the presentation of accounts of these concepts as "formal" concepts pertaining to language. Failure to give such accounts has led to a resurgence of psychologism and factualism in analytic philosophy: (182.2)

> I am now in a position to define the topic of this paper. If an analytic philosopher wishes to attack psychologism in epistemology, what fundamental concepts should he claim to be mistakenly treated as psychological or, in general, factual concepts? In other words, from the stand-point of analytic philosophy, which concepts of those traditionally classified as epistemological properly belong to philosophy? This we have interpreted to mean, *which of the concepts traditionally classified as epistemological can be interpreted as concepts of which the function and essence is to serve in rules definitive of a type of object calculus?* I shall argue that of the traditional concepts which can be so interpreted, the fundamental ones are *true, false, designates* (or *means*), *verifiable, confirmable, verified, confirmed,* and *meaningful.* I shall argue that psychologico-factualism lingers on with respect to the first three, because analytic philosophy has not yet achieved a formal treatment of the latter five. I shall argue that 'true,' 'false,' and 'designates' still receive factualistic treatment at the hands of analytic philosophers, in spite of a metalinguistic treatment of these terms obviously incompatible with a factualistic analysis, *because these terms gear in with 'verifiable,' 'confirmable,' 'verified,' 'confirmed,' and 'meaningful,' and a formal, or metalinguistic analysis of these latter terms does not yet exist.* Unrestrained factualism with respect to the latter has tarred the former with the same brush.

(183.2,.3)   The task of the present paper is "to show that 'verifiable,' 'confirmable,' 'verified,' and 'meaningful, have a status akin to that of currently recognized syntactical and semantical concepts." A major part of the treatment for these predicates as formal terms lies in "the recognition of a class of metalinguistic rules which figure in neither pure syntax, nor in pure semantics *as at present conceived;* rules which define a new dimension of calculus structure, a dimension which alone entitles them to be called *languages* in a genuinely epistemological sense of the term." It seems a reasonable suggestion to use the term 'Pure Pragmatics' for that "branch of the pure theory of language which deals with the above predicates and clarifies their relation to this new dimension of calculus structure." (These predicates are hereafter called *pragmatic predicates.*)

(184.1; 185)   An introductory investigation of discourse about "language behavior" illustrates some of the distinctions (e.g., that of "type" versus "token") that must be clarified in the course of the paper.

SECTION II

(186.1,.2,.3) An introductory discussion of 'token' and 'type' makes the point that the essential semantical relationship of 'token,' 'type,' and 'designates' is that sentences with 'designates' provide the context in which metalinguistic predicates can be applied to tokens of types.

(187.1) Both types and tokens, as well as P-lawfulness, are adequately clarified only in Pure Pragmatics rather than Pure Semantics.

(187.2,.3) The distinguishing concept of Pure Pragmatics (expressed here by the term 'coex') is the one that enables us to state the restrictions that are necessary in order that pragmatic predicates by applied to a linguistic structure. Put differently, this concept provides the means for a clarification of the claim that *"the minimum formal requirement which a formal system must fill in order to be a candidate for the position of empirically meaningful language is that it be capable of being 'about' a world in which it is used."*

(187.4; 188.1) The predicate 'coex' is crucial to the formal statement of the "empirical tie" of a sentence. Sentences that have an "empirical tie" are (provided they meet other requirements) "verifiable sentences."

(188.2) The pure pragmatic account of the concept of a "P-lawful system" has two parts.

(188.3) One part of the concept of a P-lawful system is that such a system must be governed by "conformation rules" which set down restrictions on which relational and which non-relational predicates can combine with the same individual constants to form sentences.

(189.1,.2;) The other part of the concept of a P-lawful system is that such a system be capable of formulating a highly restricted subset of sentences called a "story." It is with respect to a story that the individual constants of the system have a determinate "functioning" and thus a "determinate meaning." An adequate account of these matters would require definitions of 'text,' 'story,' 'verification base,' 'verified-in-a-story,' 'confirmable,' and 'confirmed-in-a-story', though here only tentative attempts at such definitions are provided.

(190.2) The correctness of predications of pragmatic predicates is ascertained on purely formal grounds. This fact is the fundamental point in the case for the truly philosophical status of these predicates.

(191.1; 192.1,.2) Once 'confirmed-in-S' is, through a tentative characterization of 'confirmed to degree-n-with-respect-to-S,' distinguished from this latter predicate, the distinction between 'verified-in-S' and 'confirmed-in-S' is clearly seen in the fact that, according to the tentative definitions, a sentence which is verified-in-S has "an empirical tie in S" whereas a sentence merely confirmed-in-S does not.

(192.3; 193.1,.2) An account of one sense of the term 'meaningful' allows us to appreciate the distinctions among 'predicate verified-in-S,' 'predicate (merely) confirmed-in-S,' 'primitive predicate in S' and 'predicate meaningful-in-S' and to note that pure pragmatics contains an empiricist criterion of meaningfulness by ''acquaintance'' only in the sense of requiring that a language be capable of formulating ''stories'' each of which, according to the tentative definitions given above, must have a specially restricted subset of sentences that are verified in it.

(194.1) Sketch of an account of a pure pragmatic sense of 'exists.'

SECTION III

(195.1,.2; 196.1) A discussion of the differences between ''language proper'' and ''language schemata'' and of the basis of this distinction in the utilization of variables under certain conditions. What ''definite descriptions'' do in language schemata and a comparison of them with ''logically proper names'' (in a sense defined by means of the term 'story') in languages proper.

(196.2; 197.1) How the predicates 'language schema' and 'language proper' are to be understood in relation to the philosophical criticism of our ''empirical language,''i.e.., our actual symbol behaviour.

SECTION IV

(197.2) The central issue in combating ''naive realism'' is to be found in the connection naive realism holds to exist between expressions being meaningful and their ''designating'' items of ''*the* world.''

(198.1,.2; 199.1) The notion of ''designation'' (or meaning) does *not* specify a relation between language and *the* world. Sentences with 'designates' appear in the construction of stories. Each language contains a system of expression constructed according to the definition of a story and thus ''designates'' a world. ''Thus any collection of expressions which is formulated in accordance with the requirements which define a story is ''about a world,'' for this is merely another way of saying that designation sentences are part of the mechanism of constructing a story'' (i.e., of constructing any story). Moreover, pragmatic predicates ('verified,' 'c onfirmed.' 'true') apply to every story.

(200.1,.2) The pragmatic aspect of the concept of a story is partly brought out by the observation (in the terminology just discussed) that ''the requirement that a story contains a verification base amounts to the requirement that'' (a) ''the world designated by the story include items which are tokens of sentences in the story,'' (b) these ''tokens are co-experienced with the items designated by the sentences they token'' and (c) these latter ''items'' are also designated by the tokens themselves ''as being tokens'' of the sentences which designate these latter items.

(200.3,.4) The full explication of ''aboutness'' requires the clarification of a ''world in which statements are made attributing pragmatic (hence also semantic, syntactic) predicates to empirical language expressions.'' Such a world is one that includes the tokening of ''pragmatic meta-sentences'' within itself. The story of such a world is characterized metametalinguistically in a metametalanguage which sets out the relation of metalanguage to objectlanguage.

(201.1) In a sense, there is a hierarchy of metalanguages.

(201.2; 202.1) Philosophical propositions are part of the ''pure theory of languages'' and the ''philosophical criticism'' of ordinary language (like the''mathematical criticism'' of ordinary mathematical activity) is mediated by the refined and integrated system of ''habits'' that philosophers (and mathematicians) inculcate upon their ''symbol-behavior.''

PURE PRAGMATICS AND EPISTEMOLOGY

WILFRID SELLARS

The attempt to draw a clear distinction between Philosophy and the empirical sciences can almost be taken as the defining trait of the analytic movement in contemporary philosophical thought. The empirical science that has most frequently threatened to swallow up questions of particular interest to philosophers since the time of Descartes has been psychology. Characteristic, then, of analytic philosophy has been the rejection of what it terms *psychologism*, that is to say, the mistake of identifying philosophical categories with those of psychology, whether introspective or behavioristic. It is clear that to launch an attack on psychologism, thus conceived, presupposes that one has a list of philosophical categories which one is able to identify as such; and this in turn presupposes an ability to sketch, at least in a general way, a distinctly *philosophical* account of these concepts, although a systematic account along non-psychologistic lines may be a distant and ill-defined goal. The analytic movement in philosophy has gradually moved towards the conclusion that the defining characteristic of philosophical concepts is that they are *formal* concepts relating to the formation and transformation rules of symbol structures called languages. Philosophy, in other words, tends to be conceived of as the *formal theory of languages*[1]. From this standpoint, consequently, psychologism is conceived of as the psychological treatment of concepts which are properly understood as formal devices defining a mode of linguistic structure.

Today, then, the analytic philosopher establishes his right to attack psychologism with respect to a given concept if he is able to show that it is capable of treatment as a concept the nature and function of which is constituted by its role in rules definitive of a broader or narrower set of calculi. The issue was joined first over the concepts of formal logic and pure mathematics, and it can be said with confidence that the attack on factualistic and, in particular, psychological accounts of these concepts rest on solid ground. Logic and mathematics are not empirical sciences nor do they constitute branches of any empirical science. They are not inductive studies of symbol formation and transformation behavior. (And if, at a later stage in our argument, we shall find *formal* science dealing with language *facts*, it will not be because logic is discovered by a more subtle analysis to belong to empirical science after all, but rather because of a less naive analysis of the relation of language to fact.) This first battle was won because of the development of pure syntax. The concepts of formal logic and pure mathematics were clarified through being identified with concepts which occur in the formation and transformation rules definitive of calculi. These rules constitute a logic of implication and deducibility. In this stage of the battle against psy-

---

[1] We shall draw a distinction, perhaps sharper than that usually drawn, between the formal theory of languages, and the empirical study of historical language-behavior. See below, note 10.

chologism, an apparently clear-cut distinction arose between *symbol-behavior* and *formal system*, a distinction sometimes summed up as that between *inference as fact* and *deducibility as norm*.

We have preferred to say that pure syntax is concerned with rules defining the formal structure of *calculi* rather than *languages*, for syntax, as the term has come to be used, makes no use of the concepts of designation and truth, not to say verifiability and meaningfulness. There has, however, arisen the notion of a structure of rules which define the formal features not of calculi in general, but of a special set of calculi in connection with which the term 'language' is more appropriately used. Such systems of rules are studied in pure semantics. They are richer than those formulated in pure syntax, for besides in a sense covering the same ground, they add a new dimension to the manipulation of the systems they define. Of what assistance to the analytic philosopher has been the development of this new branch of linguistic analysis? It would be encouraging if we could say that as a result of this new development, philosophers of the analytic school are agreed in attacking psychologistic and, in general, factualistic accounts of the additional concepts which make their appearance in the rules of pure semantics. Thus we should expect a clear-cut distinction between 'meaning' as a term in empirical psychology definable in terms of goal behavior, and the semantical concept of designation; and similarly, between constructed empirical relationships, however subtle, and the semantical concepts of truth and falsity. Unfortunately, not only have analytic philosophers not made proper use of the new tools made available to them, not only have they not pressed on to new victories in the battle against psychologism and factualism; ground has actually been lost! In the syntactical stage of analysis, logical syntax was used as a Procrustean bed, and if the concepts admitted to philosophy were often sorely maimed, factualism, at least, was kept at bay. Semantics, to continue with metaphor, instead of providing a gentler bed, has been functioning as a Trojan horse. As a result, factualism and psychologism are flourishing in analytic philosophy, and by no means on the fringes only. The invasion stems in part from a carry-over from the psychologism that characterized much of the controversy over sense-perception in the 'teens and twenties; but in part also, and this is indeed the decisive factor, to the incompleteness of semantics (at least as at present constituted) as a foundation from which to launch a decisive attack against these enemies of philosophy.

I am now in a position to define the topic of this paper. If an analytic philosopher wishes to attack psychologism in epistemology, what fundamental concepts should he claim to be mistakenly treated as psychological or, in general, factual concepts? In other words, from the stand-point of analytic philosophy, which concepts of those traditionally classified as epistemological properly belong to philosophy? This we have interpreted to mean, *which of the concepts traditionally classified as epistemological can be interpreted as concepts of which the function and essence is to serve in rules definitive of a type of object calculus?* I shall argue that of the traditional concepts which can be so interpreted, the fundamental ones are *true, false, designates* (or *means*), *verifiable, confirmable, verified, confirmed,* and *meaningful.* I shall argue that psychologico-factualism lingers on with respect to the first three, because analytic philosophy has not yet achieved a formal treatment of the latter five. I shall argue that 'true,' 'false,' and 'designates' still receive factualistic treatment at the hands of analytic philosophers, in spite of a metalinguistic treatment of these terms obviously incompatible with a factualistic analysis, *because these terms gear in with 'verifiable,' 'confirmable,' 'verified,' 'confirmed,' and 'meaningful,' and a formal, or metalinguistic analysis of these latter terms does not yet exist.* Unrestrained factualism with respect to the latter has tarred the former with the same brush.

But is it true that factualism and psychologism predominate in current treatments of the latter terms? Analytic philosophers take one of two courses, (1) verifiable and confirmable sentences are distinguished in terms of a psychological criterion of evidence, (2) the difference between verifiable and confirmable sentences is either held to be one of degree, or else is defined with respect to the status (defined or primitive) of the predicates of these sentences in the language in which they are formulated. Course (1) is obviously psychologism. What of (2)? Here the crucial test is to ask: "What about 'confirm*ed*' (as opposed to 'confirm*able*') and 'verif*ied*' (as opposed to 'verif*iable*')?" If the answer amounts to a denial that these are *philosophical* concepts, then it is clear than an account has not been given of verif*iable* and confirm*able* as philosophical concepts, for as such the latter make sense only as related to verif*ied* and confirm*ed*. But where we do find verified and confirmed taken into the philosophical fold, it invariably turns out that such psychological or socio-psychological notions as 'accepted' or 'belonging to a (specified) domain of opinion' are given as the core of the meaning of these terms.

I shall be asked, "Since you are making an accusation of psychologism against current treatments of these concepts, are you not, according to your opening discussion, presupposing that they are capable of formal treatment? Must you not be able to show that 'verifiable,' 'confirmable,' 'verified,' 'confirmed,' and 'meaningful' have a status akin to that of currently recognized syntactical and semantical concepts? that they belong in rules definitive of a type of object calculus? It is by justifying an affirmative answer to these questions that I hope to indicate the lines along which analytic philosophy must advance in order to regain the ground that has recently been lost. Thus, I shall explore the possibility that the assignment of the above predicates to the expressions of an object calculus can be clarified by the recognition of a class of meta-linguistic rules which figure in neither pure syntax, nor in pure semantics *as at present conceived*; rules which define a new dimension of calculus structure, a dimension which alone entitles them to be called *languages* in a genuinely epistemological sense of the term.

I have elsewhere[2] suggested that the term 'pragmatics' be rescued for philosophy through the assignment of the title 'pure pragmatics' to that branch of the

[2] "Realism and the New Way of Words," *Philosophy and Phenomenological Research,* forthcoming.

pure theory of language which deals with the above predicates, and clarifies their relation to this new dimension of calculus structure. But since, as we shall see, the concepts of pure semantics themselves can receive adequate treatment only in terms of this new dimension, it may be preferable to extend the term 'semantics' rather than propose a new one. In spite of the terminology I shall adopt in the present paper, I wish to leave this question open. The use of the 'pragmatics' in connection with verification, confirmation, and meaningfulness is now an established one, though these items are but a small part of what is now included under this heading. Shall we as philosophers extend the term 'semantics' or narrow the term 'pragmatics?' In any case, it is only if there is a pragmatics that is *not* an empirical science of sign-behavior; a pragmatics which *is* a branch of the *formal* theory of language, that the term is rescued for philosophy. And it is only if there is such a new dimension of calculus structure, whether its analysis be called 'Pure Pragmatics' or 'Pure Semantics' that the analytic philosopher can hope to give a non-psychologistic account of the key concepts of traditional epistemology.

It will be helpful to work our way into pure pragmatics by means of a problem the formulating of which will serve two purposes, that of introducing a key concept in linguistic analysis, and that of weakening the grip of naive realism in a way that will make our argument more easy to follow. Let us draw an implication of the statement that formal predicates, whether syntactical, semantical, or pragmatic, are meta-linguistic predicates. Our usual state of mind consists in being torn in two directions. On the one hand, we find it necessary to say that syntactical predicates (for example) have as their domain expressions in a calculus which is a model or norm for symbol-behavior. (The terms 'model' and 'norm' are here used to suggest a problem, rather than indicate a solution). We should point out that the decidability of syntactical predicates with respect to these expressions, and, in general, the properties to which the calculus owes its status as a norm for symbol-behavior, are due to the fact that it is *constituted* by formation and transformation rules. We should recognize that it is nonsense to say that human symbol behavior is constituted by syntactical formation and transformation rules.

On the other hand, if we are asked, "Isn't it absurd to say that syntactical properties do not apply to symbol behavior?", we should find it extremely difficult not to agree. How, indeed, can we characterize an *inference*, for example, as valid, unless it makes sense to attribute syntactical properties to symbol-behavior in the world of fact? If we say that syntactical properties belong in the first instance to expressions in a calculus or language which is a model or norm for symbol behavior, can we then go on to say that in the second instance they belong to language *as behavioral fact*? But to say this would be to put metalinguistic predicates into the object-language. Is there, then, no way out of our dilemma? Must we hold either that syntactical predicates are object-language predicates, or that syntactical predicates are not applicable to language as behavioral fact? Perhaps we can find a way out by drawing a distinction between language *as behavior* (that is, as the subject-matter of empirical psychology),

PURE PRAGMATICS AND EPISTEMOLOGY   185

and language behavior *to the extent that it conforms, and as conforming, to the criteria of language as norm*; or, in the terminology we shall adopt, between language behavior *qua* behavioral fact, and language-behavior *qua tokens* of language as *type*.

It will be part of our later purpose to clarify this distinction between *token* and *type*. Our present concern is to note that if the above distinction is to be of assistance, *language behavior as tokens* must be the subject-matter of a meta-language; for only in this way can it be eligible for syntactical characterization. But this seems to throw us back into the fire, for if it *is* the subject-matter of a *meta*-language, how can it be *factual* language behavior? Is not *fact* the subject-matter of a first-level (as opposed to a meta-) language? To recapitulate: the solution of our dilemma appears to require a three-fold distinction between (1) language as norm or type, (2) language as behavioral fact, and (3) items in the second class which token, and as tokening, items in the first class. In doing this it requires that the language-behavior of (3) belongs to both the domain of fact, and the domain of language as norm. This is only possible if the domain of *fact*, and the domain of *language as norm* turn out to be the same. But language as norm is such as being posited by metalinguistic rules. We have consequently been led from a problem to a paradox. The attempt to clarify the applicability of syntactical predicates to language behavior has led us to the curious conception of *fact* and *object-language as type* as both alike constituted by metalinguistic rules, or, to put it more loosely, by metalinguistic construction. Can such a conception be defended? The answer is to be found in the argument which follows; for it is in pure pragmatics as defined below that the lingering ghost of naive realism (as a *philosophical* perspective) is finally exorcized, and Kant's Copernican revolution receives its non-psychologistic fruition.

The historical reference at the conclusion of the preceding paragraph requires a word of explanation. There is no question of introducing a quasi-Kantian doctrine of synthetic *a priori* knowledge. The following argument belongs in the stream formed by the merging of left-wing empiricism with modern logic. The mention of Kant is intended to suggest that the linguistic tools shaped in pure pragmatics will make possible, indeed necessitate, a return to the *Aufbau* stage of Logical Empiricism, but with a conception of *Aufbau* which is as much richer than that of the learly thirties, as the psychologism of Kant is richer than that of Hume. If it be asked, "How can a world of fact be a metalinguistic construction, particularly since the constructing itself as fact belongs in the world?", I must point out that the clarification of the status of formal systems is the culminating task of a philosophy of language, *and must be treated as such*. If the question is put too soon, the answer will inevitably be empirical in a bad sense, in a word, *scientism*. If it is asked, "Are you consistent in calling your position a form of Logical Empiricism? How can philosophy, which on your interpretation is a purely formal science, give an *empirical* answer to the above or any other question?", it may suffice for the moment to point out that an *empiricist* answer need not be an *empirical* (as being *factual*) answer. Indeed, as we shall see— p.193 below—the thesis of empiricism is a *formal* rather than a *factual* truth, and by no means in the trivial sense of a definitional cut in a field of wider possibilities. The realization that philosophical truths could not be factual truths, combined with too narrow a conception of the formal has led to the Wittgensteinian contention that there are no philosophical propositions. I hope to make clear that this is a mistake, while granting that in a sense the Wittgensteinians have the last word.

II

In the above discussion of the applicability of syntactical predicates to behavioral fact, we introduced the concept of *language as token*. The first task of pure pragmatics is to clarify this concept, for it is involved in the definition of all pragmatic predicates. Yet this concept is one that is capable of at least a provisional definition in terms of the equipment available in pure semantics. 'Token' is a metalinguistic predicate, and it is used properly when it is said that the *designatum* of one expression in a language is a token of another (perhaps the same) expression in the language. The formal significance of this concept is the role it plays in the following rule: *If 'p' designates p, and p is a token of 'q,' then all the metalinguistic predicates that apply to 'q' apply also to p.*

This notion can be made concrete by the following: Suppose that psychology has classified all auditory sensations, however complex, into classes. Let one of the class-terms be 'α,' and suppose that it designates the class of complex sounds heard when people say that it is raining. Consider the sentence 'p' which says 'α(there-then),' and the sentence 'q' which says "It is raining." Consider next the semantic sentences, " 'p' designates p" and " 'q' designates q." Finally consider the sentence, " 'p' designates p, and p is a token of 'q.' " It says, roughly, that a particular auditory sensation is a token of the sentence "it is raining."

Since we are introducing a rule according to which metalinguistic predicates can be associated with expressions belonging on either side of the 'designates' in a semantic designation-sentence, we must be careful to remember that *all the expressions in a semantic sentence belong to the semantic metalanguage.* Thus, if p is a token of 'q,' and accordingly it can be said that p designates q, the latter 'p' and 'q' must not be confused with object-language expressions. It will be convenient to introduce the term 'type' as follows, if p is a token of 'q,' we shall say that 'q' is the type of which p is a token. This will enable us to distinguish between metalinguistic sentences in which metalinguistic predicates are associated with expressions ultimately belonging on the left hand side of designation sentences, from those in which they are associated with expressions ultimately belonging on the right hand side of designation sentences. We shall say that the former attribute metalinguistic predicates to language expressions as types, and the latter attribute these predicates to language expressions as tokens.

It is worth calling attention once more to the fact that the primary use of metalinguistic predicates is in connection with language as type. That is to say, the metalinguistic sentence "p designates q," presupposes the metalinguistic sentences " 'p' designates p," " 'q' designates q," and "p is a token of 'q.' " Similarly, "p is true," presupposes " 'p' designates p," "p is a token of 'q' " and " 'q' is true." This will be of importance later on when we are concerned to point out that the relation of type to token as we are using these terms is not the same as that between the class of marks *the* and a member of the class of marks *the*.

Another concept which is made available through the resources of pure semantics, but which also fails to reach its full stature within its confines, is that of P-lawfulness. The concept is not a decisive one for pure semantics, for while semantic rules can define calculi which involve P-lawfulness, a calculus defined by a set of semantic rules need not have this characteristic. Pure semantics is indifferent to the presence or the absence of P-lawfulness in object-language structures. In this respect, pure pragmatics will differ from pure semantics. We shall return shortly to this topic, and attempt to sketch the lines along which pragmatics must analyze the notion of P-lawfulness. Our present purpose has been to set the stage for the introduction of the distinguishing concept of pure pragmatics.

The concepts of linguistic token and P-lawfulness are essential to pure pragmatics, but do not suffice to distinguish it from semantics. What, then, is the concept the introduction of which makes possible the elaboration of a set of rules which define a type of object-calculus to the expressions of which pragmatic predicates ('verifiable', 'confirmable', 'verified', 'confirmed', 'meaningful', etc.) are assignable under formally specifiable conditions? The answer is that pragmatic rules require any object-calculus to contain an irreflexive, symmetrical and transitive two place predicate for which we shall use the term 'co-ex'. The model for this predicate is the common sense expression 'is-present-to-consciousness-along-with''.

It should not be necessary to point out, though it is wise to do so, that the fact that pure pragmatics lays down such a requirement on any calculus to the expressions of which pragmatic predicates can be applied, does *not* mean that in pure pragmatics we add psychology, in whole or in part, introspective or behavioristic, to pure semantics. We have not even added the psychological concept of *being present to consciousness along with*. Whatever we may have our eye on in constructing the science of pure pragmatics, (and it is not the psychology of belief, or expectation, or puzzle-solving, or persuasion, or any of the other detailed psychology that has been smuggled into philosophy under the heading 'pragmatics') the fundamental concept of pure pragmatics is that of a certain *formal* restriction on the calculi to the expressions of which pragmatic predicates are assignable. If we were putting the matter in a non-technical way, we would say that *the minimum formal requirement which a formal system must fill in order to be a candidate for the position of empirically meaningful language is that it be capable of being 'about' a world in which it is used.* This statement should be kept in mind as the key to the argument which follows, for its aim can be summarized as *the attempt to give a formal reconstruction of the common sense notion that an empirically meaningful language is one that is about the world in which it is used.*

By requiring any constructed calculus to contain such a predicate (which we shall symbolize by 'Coex,' short for 'co-experienced with'), and with the aid of the metalinguistic predicate 'token,' we can introduce the predicate 'verifiable sentence' in the following way:

'p' is a verifiable sentence in C, if C includes a sentence 'q' and a sentence 'r' such that 'q' designates *r coex p*, and *r* is a token of 'p.'

The sentences 'q' and 'r' will be called the *experiential tie* of 'p.' This concept of an experiential tie is, consequently, a purely formal one. It is the *philosophical* concept which has been sought mistakenly in the psychological object language.

As a crude aid to the understanding of the above definition, consider the following:

'Jones is seeing red' is a verifiable sentence in C, if C includes a sentence 'q' and a sentence 'r' such that 'q' designates *Jones' imaging Jonz-iz-ceeing-redd coex Jones seeing red*, and *Jones' imaging Jonz-iz-ceeing-redd* is a token of 'Jones is seeing red.'

At this stage, we should note that in addition to the requirement specifying an empirical tie, our definition has limited verifiable sentences to sentences which fulfil the formal requirements of "sentences about particular states of affairs." The predicate 'verifiable sentence' does not apply to sentences involving unrestricted general operators. We shall consider later the applicability of this predicate to sentences involving definite descriptions.

Before we introduce further fundamental concepts of pure pragmatics, we must indicate the general lines along which the pragmatic concept of a P-lawful system is to be clarified. We shall introduce this notion in terms of object-calculi the elementary expressions of which are explicitly listed sets of primitive relational and non-relational predicate-constants, and an explicitly listed set of individual-constants; and the elementary sentences of which consist of a conjoining of these predicates with the appropriate number of individual-constants. Later we shall examine the pragmatic importance of calculi in which variables play a nontrivial role. Now the pragmatic concept of a P-lawful system turns out, on examination, to have a negative and a positive phase. The former consists in a certain type of restriction on the predicates of the calculus in which such a system can be formulated; in Leibnitzian terms, *a principle of compossibility;* while the positive phase may, perhaps, be compared to his *principle of plenitude.* The following discussion is a tentative and summarizing survey of a line of thought that requires detailed and rigorous development to constitute a solid chapter in the pure theory of language. The purpose of the present paper will be amply fulfilled if it provides a general framework in terms of which specific problems of formulation and argument in epistemology can be discriminated from questions relating to matters of fact, and their status as capable of definitive solution clarified.

As a concept in the pure theory of language, the negative element in the concept of a P-lawful system might better be called a *principle of conformation,* than one of compossibility, though, as we shall see, the *designata* of a conformable set of sentences may be said to be compossible. A still more suggestive title might be "the principle of the internality of primitive relational predicates," for the conformation rules of a calculus, the expressions of which can qualify for pragmatic predicates, *specify for each non-relational predicate in the calculus, the relational predicates which can participate in sentences with one and the same individual constant which is conjoined in a sentence with the non-relational predicate in question.* A set of such rules provides what may be called the "P-restrictions" of the calculus. Note that they are metalinguistic in character, and that *the general propositions which correspond to them in the object-language are to be distinguished from "contingent" generalizations, even though they are not, in the usual syntactical sense, analytic.*

We have not yet brought out the full extent of our indebtedness to Leibnitz. The apparatus which defines a calculus to the expressions of which pragmatic predicates are applicable must include a principle of the *identity of indiscernibles.* This principle specifies that two expressions in the object-calculus which differ solely with respect to the individual-constants they contain (it will be remembered that the calculi we are discussing do not contain variables), and which are not parts of more inclusive expressions, are *synonymous.* Thus, if 'Pr$_1$(a)' and 'Pr$_1$(b)' are two expressions in such a calculus, '*a' designates not only a, but also b; and 'b' designates not only b, but also a,* that is to say, a and b are identical. Note that synonymity does not entail mutual substitutability in more inclusive expressions. This is necessary, otherwise if the inclusive expression already contained an individual constant appearing in the expression that was going to be substituted for a part of it, one might run up against a conformation rule.[3]

We are now in a position to give a tentative account of the positive phase of the pragmatic concept of a P-lawful system. A set of sentences in a calculus with a given set of P-restrictions (conformation rules) and for which there is identity of indiscernibles, will be called a *text,* if (1) every individual constant appearing in the set appears in both a non-relational and at least one relational sentence of the set; and (2) no sub-set of the set fails to contain at least one individual constant which appears jointly in a relational sentence with a least one individual constant not appearing in the sub-set. If we leave aside current technical associations of the term 'connected,' it might be helpful to characterize a text as a connected set of conformable elementary sentences. A text will be

---

[3] In "Realism and the New Way of Words" I have formulated this point more generally as follows: "Since the meaning and the meaningfulness of symbols alike are defined in a purely formal manner, we can say that the *identity of formally indiscernibles* is fundamental to the pure theory of languages. Thus, predicates are differentiated only in terms of conformation rules, individual constants only in terms of the predicates with which they are associated. Formal science makes use of empirical *marks,* but this is an empirical fact about formal science, and it would be a mistake to suppose that the empirical difference of mark from mark is reflected necessarily in a difference of formal status. Thus, in the absence of a formal distinction between 'ϕ' and 'ψ', " 'ϕ' designates ψ" is not formally different from " 'ϕ' designates ϕ". The Leibnitzian conception of identity is merely an application of this insight to individual constants. Where we refuse this identity without explicit formal differentiation, it can be understood to be implicitly assumed."

said to be a *complete text*, if all texts formulable in the calculus which include it are synonymous with it. A *fix* can be defined as a text, all the complete texts containing which are synonymous. A fix will be called a reciprocal fix, if a complementary text which builds it into a complete text, is also a fix.

It is clear that these definitions are at best indicative. We have not attempted to specify the circumstances under which a calculus must permit the formulation of a complete text, or of a text a proper sub-text of which is a fix. These are problems of a highly technical nature in formal science. Our aim is rather to point them out, for their solution is vital to pure pragmatics. We have been preparing for the introduction of the following definitions:

A complete text which includes a reciprocal fix consisting of verifiable sentences, and which also includes for each verifiable sentence the sentences which make up its empirical tie, will be called a *story*.

A reciprocal fix consisting of verifiable sentences will be called a *verification basis* of the story in which it appears.

A verifiable sentence belonging to a Story, S, will be said to be *verified-in-S*.

A calculus in which a story can be formulated will be said to be a *language*.

Any sentence formulable in a language L which is neither analytic nor self-contradictory, will be said to be a *confirmable* sentence of L.

A confirmable sentence belonging to a story S, will be said to be *confirmed-in-S*. A sentence which is confirmed-in-S *may* also be verified-in-S, but need not be as far as these definitions are concerned.

In comment on these definitions, the first thing to note is that if a calculus permits the formulation of one story, it normally permits the formulation of a set of non-synonymous stories. .Consequently, it could no more be determined with respect to a language alone whether or not a given sentence was in the privileged position implied by the terms 'confirmed' or 'verified,' than it can be determined with reference to a language alone whether or not a given sentence is factually *true*. Consider, however, the predicates we have defined above, namely, 'verified-in-S' and 'confirmed-in-S.' *These predicates are decidable on formal grounds.*[4] Sentences assigning these predicates to expressions in an object-language, are either analytic or self-contradictory. It is for this reason,

---

[4] Since writing the above, I have come to the conclusion that the terminology of the argument can be improved as follows: A calculus with resources which permit the formulation of expressions E_i with respect to which the function 'world-story (E_i)' is decidable in view of the conformation rules of the calculus, will be called an *empirical language form*. As we have pointed out (note 3 above) the predicates of a calculus have determinate meaning (in a non-psychological sense) only by virtue of the conformation or combining rules relating to them. But an empirical language must be determinate in meaning not only with respect to its predicates but also with respect to its individual constants. This determinate meaning involves the functioning of these constants in one story. Thus we shall define an *empirical language* as an empirical language form, the formal status (and hence the 'meanings') of the individual constants of which is fixed in relation to one of the world stories formulable in it. This definition clarifies in a non-psychologistic way the notion that the primary non-logical expressions of a language must have determinate meaning. In terms of these definitions, where I use the expressions 'verified-in-S', 'true-in-S' etc., I could also say, 'verified sentence of L', 'true sentence of L' etc., where S is the meaning basis of L.

and this reason alone, that these concepts, *and the family of concepts that are definable in terms of them*, are *philosophical* concepts. Consider, now, the semantic predicate 'true.' In semantics this concept is defined by means of the formal equivalence, "'p' is true if and only if *p*." Note that the predicate 'true' is not decidable with respect to an object-*calculus* (though the predicate 'true or false,' *i.e.*, 'factual' is so decidable), because 'p' and its designatum *p* have no privileges over 'not-p' and its designatum *not-p*. This, however, is not the case with respect to a *story;* the predicate 'true-in-S' is a decidable predicate. Consequently, it is only in pragmatics that the concept of truth receives the final installment of the philosophical clarification initiated in existing semantic analysis. *A philosophical concept must be decidable on purely formal grounds.* If it be asked, "How can a concept which is decidable on formal grounds be the clarification of the concept of factual truth?", the answer must be postponed until we have discussed the relation of stories as we have defined them to "the language we actually speak." Perhaps it will temporarily soften the paradox if we say that philosophical concepts must be *in principle* decidable on formal grounds. The expression 'in principle' has proved soothing on other occasions.

Another question may well be raised at this point. "Does not the above account so merge the concepts *confirmed, verified*, and *true*, that it is difficult to see what distinction, if any, remains?" Thus let us consider the following two theorems in pure pragmatics:

(1) "'p' is verified-in S" entails "'p' is **true-in-S**."
(2) "'p' is confirmed-in-S" entails "'p' is true-in-S."

These two propositions bring out the fact that *verified-in-S* and *confirmed-in-S* are properties that do not admit of degrees. To say this, however, is not to say that a concept *confirmed-to-degree-n-with-respect-to-S* cannot be introduced as a formally decidable concept in pure pragmatics. What we are saying is that such a concept would be a defined pragmatic concept of considerable complexity relating to the clarification of the concept of probability, whereas we are using the terms 'verified' and 'confirmed' to clear up the epistemological contrast between "sentences checked against the facts they assert" (verified sentences) and "sentences checked only indirectly" (confirmed but not verified sentences), where in both cases the sentences in question concern particular states of affairs. A derived pragmatic concept *confirmed to degree-n-with-respect-to-S* might be introduced as a predicate applicable to expressions in a language L, and defined in terms of the ratios in which the individual terms (appearing in a story S formulated in L) which fulfilled one propositional function, also fulfilled other (specified) propositional functions. Such a predicate would admit of mathematical treatment, tying in with statistics and the theory of samples. It would be formally decidable with respect to expressions in L, but "'p' is confirmed-to-degree-n-with-respect-to-S," unlike "'p' is confirmed-in-S," would not entail "'p' is a sentence of S" and hence "'p' is true-in-S." Note, however, that this pragmatic concept of degree of confirmation would have nothing to do with the P-restrictions of the language, though it might apply to universal propositions in L.

It will come out as we proceed, that the concepts of language and story, as we are defining them, are in some sense ideal frames of reference, in terms of which our choice of a "language" can be criticized. From this point of view, whether we choose to regard a given generalization as empirical, or as a consequence of a metalinguistic P-restriction on our "language" is an open matter, to be decided in terms of the ideal standard of a calculus defined by P-restrictions sufficient to constitute it a language. In the present paper, we are concerned with pragmatic concepts which first make it possible to define the framework within which derived pragmatic concepts (*e.g.*, *degree of confirmation*) can receive formal, that is, philosophical, treatment. Let us therefore return to the problem with which we began the preceding paragraph. If neither *verified-in-S* nor *confirmed-in-S* admit of degrees, and if both entail *true-in-S*, where is the difference? Once worry about degree of confirmation has been side-tracked, it is clear from the definitions of the corresponding terms that the distinction rests on the formal circumstance that a sentence that is verified-in-S is one that has an empirical tie in S, whereas a sentence that is confirmed-in-S *need* not have an empirical tie in S, its being confirmed-in-S consisting merely in the fact that it occurs in S, that is to say, in a complete text with a verification base.

A theorem that will be of assistance in claryifying a familiar epistemological controversy[5] is the following:

(3) "'p' belongs to a verification base of S" entails " 'p' is true-in-S."

The clarification rests in part on noting that

(4) " 'p' is *any* sentence in S" entails " 'p' is true-in-S."

The only kind of indubitability that plays a role in epistemology is *analyticity*, and in this respect (3) above is on a par with any tautology. The only kind of indubitability that language behavior has as behavioral fact, would be that designated by 'indubitable' as a predicate of empirical psychology; such a predicate, if there is any need for it, would be an object-language predicate, having as such no relation to the predicate 'true'.

We shall now introduce two additional concepts which belong to the foundations of pure pragmatics. The first underlies the clarification of the family of pragmatic terms relating to *meaningfulness*.

(5) To say that 'Pr' is meaningful-in-S is equivalent (definition) to saying that S contains at least one sentence involving 'Pr.'

Before commenting on this definition, it must be pointed out once more that all the predicates, which appear in a story as we have defined this term, are *primitive* predicates, and that meaningfulness in the fundamental sense we are now considering relates to primitive predicates alone. Let us classify the predicates which appear in a story, S, into those which occur at least once in sentences which are verified-in-S, and those which do not; the former being called 'predicates verified-in-S,' and the latter, *if there can be such*, 'predicates (merely) confirmed-in-S.' It is essential not to confuse the following: 'primitive predicate in S,' 'predicate meaningful-in-S' and 'predicate verified-in-S,' even if one

---

[5] I refer to the debate concerning the indubitability of protocol sentences or *Konstatierungen*. See below, pp. 200

hopes to show either that these terms *must* be co-extensive, or, more modestly, that they are "in point of fact" co-extensive "with respect to the language we speak."

The Lockean principle that simple ideas are formed by abstraction from particulars with which we are acquainted, and that all other ideas are compounded from them, was a distinct gain for empiricism in so far as it was an attack on innate ideas; but the gain consisted in replacing one form of psychologism by a less obnoxious form. The Lockean principle lingers on in current empiricism under the guise of a 'principle of acquaintance.' In our terminology, this principle amounts to giving verified primitive predicates a privileged status with respect to primary meaningfulness. To justify such a status, one would either have to prove that all predicates appearing in a story must appear in at least one verifiable sentence belonging to the story; or else argue that such a restriction is characteristic of "the language we speak." I have argued elsewhere[6] that the current insistence on the epistemological priority of sense-datum predicates, that is to say, of a sense-datum language, rests on a confusion between two propositions, (1). The primitive predicates of a meaningful language *must* be datum-predicates (which is false, since there is no such theorem in pure pragmatics) and (2). A meaningful language is such in relation to a sentence-system formulated in that language which includes a verification base consisting of datum-sentences (which is true, as being a theorem in pure pragmatics). Our interest in the present paper will be focused on the fact that if (1) is not a theorem in pure pragmatics, then the question as to whether the primitive predicates of "the language we speak" are without exception datum-predicates, would seem to be in some sense a factual one. But how can philosophy as a formal science make factual statements? Is there such a thing as the *philosophical* criticism of the language we speak? (Is there such a thing as the *mathematical* criticism of the calculations of Jones, age 6?)

The closest, then, that pure pragmatics comes to a principle of acquaintance is in its requirement that a story have a verification base. It is this requirement that constitutes empiricism as a proposition in philosophy, for it is in this sense that *empiricism as a meaningfulness-criterion is a formal truth in pure pragmatics.* If, in addition, it is an analytic truth that a story contains both sentences which are *confirmed-in-S* and sentences which are *verified-in-S*, this does not mean that a story *must* contain sentences which are not *verified-in-S*, since verifiable sentences are a sub-class of confirmable sentences.[7] Whether or not a story contains such sentences, and if so, whether it contains predicates which are *merely confirmed-in-S*, depends on the conformation rules of the language in which it is formulated. Consequently, whether or not a given language permits or requires a story, S, formulated in that language to include primitive predicates not ap-

___

[6] "Realism and the New Way of Words."

[7] If it were a theorem in pure pragmatics that a story must contain at least one sentence that is confirmed in S but not verified in S, then an essential though minimal thesis of realism would be a philosophical tautology. If, on the other hand, it could be proved that a story can contain no such sentence, realism would be a self-contradictory position in philosophy.

pearing in sentences *verified-in-S*, 'predicate verified-in-S' and 'predicate (merely) confirmed-in-S,' that is, (roughly) 'primitive *datum* predicate' and 'primitive non-*datum* predicate,' would be on a par with respect to 'meaningful' as a *philosophical* term.   This need not be the case with *psychological* terms that can easily be confused with the above.   The philosophical distinctions we are drawing are not those of genetic psychology.

The second fundamental concept to be introduced is that of *existence* as a pragmatic concept.   As we shall see, pure pragmatics permits a clarification of the term 'exists' which supplements the fruits of the Russellian analysis. Part of this clarification comes with the account that remains to be given of logically proper names.   Now we are concerned with the existence of classes.   Thus

(6) The class *Pr* will be said to exist-in-the-world-designated-by-S, if 'Pr' is meaningful in-S.

The concept of a *world* is one that will be introduced later in the argument. For this reason the above definition is necessarily provisional.   As the formulation itself suggests, it claims to be a clarification of the platonizing demand for the 'real' existence of classes; a clarification which grants the demand, but not the Platonism.[8]   The existence of a class is, of course, to be distinguished from the existence of members of a class.   This distinction is necessary even in the case of the primitive predicates appearing in a story (which are all that are covered by the above definition), even though in their case each corresponding class must have at least one member in the world designated by the story.   *Defined* object-language predicates are in a different position.   The primary problem involved in the pragmatics of the latter, it is interesting to note, is that of clarifying the nature of *defined factual predicates*, and correspondingly, of *complex individuals*.[9]   Our concern in this paper is with the most general topics that arise

---

[8] In "Realism and the New Way of Words" I have formulated this point more generally as follows: "By the enlarged conception of the formal mode of speech as including pragmatic statements, we are enabled to clarify certain perennial problems relating to *existence*.   The term 'exists' as ordinarily used has a sense consisting of syntactical, semantical *and pragmatic elements*.   The last of these is the key to the Platonism issue, for it is to Platonism that a factualistic interpretation must lead.   The pragmatic element is suggested by the statement, "to say that an individual or class exists is to say that the corresponding individual or class term is meaningful."   Since existence in this sense is (on our interpretation) as non-factual a notion as the syntactical sense that was clarified at Cambridge, one can admit, nay, insist, that classes exist without swallowing a two-storied world.   Needless to say, the question as to the existence of the *class* lion, is to be distinguished from that as to the existence of lions.   For the latter, given a meaningful language, the analysis of Russell is adequate.   It is essential to note that the pragmatic sense of existence applies only to the *designata* of the factual terms of the object-language, (e.g. *a exists* is equivalent to '*a*' *designates a and* '*a*' *is meaningful*; *red exists* is equivalent to '*red*' *is a class term*, '*red*' *designates* RED, *and meaningful* ('*red*')."

[9] An exploration of this issue would lead to an examination of the pragmatic structure of temporal stories; to an analysis of the substance-mode relationship, and of the concept of dispositional property; that is to say of the syntax of thing, property and event words.   I have sketched the direction such an analysis might take in the "Realism" paper.

PURE PRAGMATICS AND EPISTEMOLOGY   195

at the very foundations of pure pragmatics, that is to say, with the formal features common to all languages the expressions of which qualify for characterization by pragmatic predicates and in the present context it is important to note that existence in the pragmatic sense applies only to classes designated by object-language predicates. *In the pragmatic sense of existence, formal systems as formal systems do not exist. The distinction of the pragmatic from the syntactical sense of 'exists' is thus a definite gain for empirical philosophy.*

III

We have pointed out that the sentences appearing in a verification base of a story, and indeed all the sentences of a story must have the logical characteristics of sentences "about individual states of affairs." In the languages we have been considering, such sentences are formed by joining individual- and predicate-*constants*. What of the use of variables and definite descriptions? Let us consider two types of object-calculi in relation to the pragmatic predicates we have been considering, (1) calculi of which the variables (individual and predicate) are defined in terms of explicit lists of constants (individual and predicate), and (2) calculi the variables of which do not have cash value in terms of such lists. Since the calculi with which pragmatics is concerned are languages, we shall call the first type *languages proper*, and the second, language *schemata*. Although schematicity can, and usually does, concern predicate terms as well as individual terms, the fundamental difference between these two types of calculi comes out most clearly when we consider the relation of general statements to statements "about individuals." In a language proper, general statements are equivalent to *explicit* and *specified* conjunctions or disjunctions of statements that do not involve individual-variables. In a language schema, this is not the case, and the concept of a general-statement (and therefore of a variable) is given content not within the system, but through the non-formal fact that an eye is kept on a *miniature language* proper, the role of general statements within which serves as a model for the role of general statements within the language *schema* that is being considered. This function is usually performed by the use of a short string of disjunctions or conjunctions involving the early letters of the alphabet. On the other hand, the fact that this function is performed by these strings is then promptly obscured by following them with 'etc.' or '&' or '. . .' for these suggest that instead of a non-formal reference to a *model*, a formal definition of general operators in their relation to individual statements is being given.

A language *schema*, then, is a language proper with blanks instead of individual constants and/or blanks instead of predicate-constants. This gappiness is overcome, to the extent that it can be overcome, by the use of two devices, (1) a device for indicating which blanks would be filled by the same constant if it were a language proper, and (2) a device for indicating which blanks could be filled by only one constant, if it were a language proper. The latter device is that of the *definite description*. It is of particular interest to pragmatics. The general moral to be drawn at this time is that *language schemata and statements within language schemata are intelligible only with reference to model languages proper, and statements within model languages proper.*

Let us introduce the predicate 'logically proper name.' An individual constant in a language proper, LP, will be said to be a logically proper name in a story, S, formulated in LP, if it appears in a sentence of S. Now a language proper can make use of variables and definite descriptions, but the pragmatic predicates we have been considering are decidable with respect to such statements by virtue of their translatability into sentences involving no variables, but only logically proper names and predicate-constants. In a language proper, then, pragmatic predicates are decidable with respect to sentences involving definite descriptions by virtue of their relation to a story, a structure for which P-indiscernibility entails semantic identity. (In this respect a story can be compared to a Leibnitzian world.) Now we have noted that statements involving definite descriptions are the closest one can come with the resources of a language schema to statements "about individuals." How close is that? Under what circumstances would the pragmatic predicates we have been considering be decidable with respect to statements involving definite descriptions in a language schema? They would be decidable only if these statements belonged to a system of statements which had this Leibnitzian property. In other words, they would be decidable only with respect to statements belonging to such a set as one would have if one began with a story in a language proper involving the same predicates and P-restrictions, and transformed every statement involving logically proper names into a statement involving definite descriptions. A moment's reflection on the complexity the latter statements would have shows that these predicates would be decidable only with respect to a set of sentences which do in a complicated way that which could be done in a simpler way with the same resource of explicit symbols, by the use of logically proper names in a language proper. This makes it clear that a language, which is schematic with respect to individual constants, has exactly the same motive for being schematic with respect to the formal devices for circumventing this schematicity, that is to say, for indicating and manipulating its variables. In general, schematicity is a pervasive feature of a language system. Schematicity in an object-language penetrates the hierarchy of meta-languages of which it is the base. We shall return to this point later on.

These considerations make it clear that the type of calculus, that would be the (re)constructed model or norm of our empirical symbol behavior, is a language schema, and a crude and incomplete language schema at that. It seems natural, then, to say that as language *schema*, its nature is to be clarified and criticized with reference to the standard provided by a language *proper*; and as *language* schema, its nature is to be clarified and criticized with reference to *languages* proper, that is to say, calculi proper which are object-calculi of pragmatic meta-languages. *We are tempted to say that the formation, transformation, and conformation rules governing the language schema which is the model of our empirical language behavior are such in so far as they belong to the same class as do rules which relate to the construction of a story in a language proper.* But such a statement, though of great clarificatory value, is misleading. It suggests that to criticize the empirical language is to confront it with a language proper. *But it is quite obvious that we are not in a position to construct a miniature language proper to the expressions of which pragmatic predicates are applicable.* The only thing we can confront the empirical language with, it would seem, is another language schema. But what of the notion of a story in a language proper, which we have been at such pains to develop? Haven't we just admitted that it is beyond our power to formulate a story in even a *miniature* language proper? Is not pragmatics, on our own testimony, limited to *schematic* statements, and is it not a formal contradiction to speak of a *schematic* language (of whatever level) being about *non-schematic* subject-matter? Then how can schematic propositions be about "stories in languages proper?" Here is indeed something to be cleared up before we can explain what is meant by "philosophical criticism of the empirical language."

Let us raise the question, "In what language does the statement 'L is a language schema' belong?" If 'language-schema' and 'language proper' are formal predicates, it is clear that they do not belong in L. Do they belong to the meta-language which constitutes L? No, for in view of what we said at the time of introducing these terms, it is clear that if they concern formal features of language, it is the rules relating to language-schemata and languages proper that are being compared. We are thus forced to the conclusion that if these predicates are formal predicates, they belong in a language two levels above their ostensible subject-matter. They must be disguised versions of predicates applying to rules. But the latter predicates must surely be 'schematic rule' and 'rule proper,' and a moment's reflection shows that the same difficulty breaks out all over again. *'Language schema' and 'language proper' are not formal predicates, and 'language' as a term with which they can be associated is a psycho-sociological term, rather than one belonging to formal science.* The problem we were worrying about in the final sentences of the preceding paragraph is a pseudo-problem. *To talk about a story consisting of a P-complete set of atomic sentences is formally consistent even though from the standpoint of behavioral science the person so talking is talking a language-schema.* It is an important psychological fact that the formal devices of language-schemata regarded as spatio-temporal facts, function as *adequate* cues for symbol-formation and -transformation behavior, for which the *complete* cues would be given only by devices belonging to a language proper. It is this psychological fact and what it involves that makes any other than the most rudimentary formal manipulations possible, and hence makes possible mathematical *activity* and philosophical *activity*. From the standpoint of behavioral science, all but the most trivial and miniature formal systems are *schemata*.

IV

Returning, then, to formal considerations (even though from the standpoint of behavioral science we are talking schematically), we must come to a final reckoning with naive realism.   This reckoning will consist in a clarification of the relation between an object-language and "the world it is about."   The usual temptation has been to argue that if a language is *meaningful*, then its expressions mean items and classes of items in *the* world; while if the language is meaningless, then there is no problem as to *what* its expressions mean.   Reasoning of this type is a perfect illustration of the way in which a factualistic interpretation of 'meaningful' inevitably leads to factualism in semantics, for it implies that all semantic statements are *false* except those relating to "the empirically meaningful language."

Let us approach the matter from a different direction.   Reflection shows that any statement concerning the relation of a language *as formal system* to "the world" must be a metalinguistic statement.   The question immediately arises, "How can a statement have as its subject-matter two such disparate areas as (1) a language as formal system, and (2) *the* world?"   It would appear that it can have either but not both, and that if its subject-matter falls in (1) it is in the meta-language; while if the subject-matter belongs in (2) the statement is in the object-language.   Must we then say that it is impossible to talk about the relation of a language as formal system to *the* world?   Would not such an admission constitute a surrendering of the fruits of semantic analysis?

The answer to the first of the above questions is 'yes'; but to the second 'no'!   It is impossible to talk about the relation of language to *the* world, for the simple reason that 'designates' is not an object-language predicate.   *It must be understood once and for all that talking about the designata of object-language expressions is, and is only, an essential ingredient in the formal devices which specify the decidability of semantic and pragmatic predicates with respect to these expressions.*   Thus, in the sentence " 'p' designates p," the letter *p* without quotes, and the letter p with quotes belong to the same frame of reference; the predicate 'designates' and the letter *p* without quotes (in this context) have as their be-all and end-all the gearing in with semantical and pragmatic rules relating to the decidability of " 'p' is true," " 'p' is verified-in-S," and so on.   There is thus no sense to the notion of one privileged language or group of languages "really designating" whereas other ("meaningless") languages somehow "merely go through the motions."   All *languages* (in the formal-pragmatic, as opposed to the factual behavioral sense of the term[10]) are formal systems, the expressions

[10] One of the central theses of this paper concerns the terms 'language' and 'meta-language.'   We have insisted that two irreducibly different usages of the term 'language' must be distinguished, namely, the *factual* and the *formal*, or, more suggestively, the *descriptive* and the *constitutive*.   In the factual-descriptive usage, a language is a set of socio-psycho-logico-historical facts.   In this context, the concepts in terms of which we describe a language are factual concepts, such as *goal-behavior*, *substitute stimuli*, etc., together with a strong dose of statistics.   The "meta-language" in terms of which we describe a language thus understood is a "meta-language" in a purely factual sense; from the formal standpoint it is no more a meta-language than is language about *non-linguistic* socio-psychologico-historical states of affairs.   As long as we are dealing with languages in the factual sense, we are not making use of the concepts of the formal theory of language, even when we talk

PURE PRAGMATICS AND EPISTEMOLOGY 199

of which designate if and what the meta-language constituting the language says they do. *To put it bluntly, there are, from the standpoint of pragmatics, as many designated worlds as there are designating stories.* For (1) the constitution of a story involves the use of designation sentences; (2) "Story S designates world W" is a suitcase way of saying " 'p' designates p, 'q' designates q . . ., and Story ('p,' 'q,' . . .)"; and (3) "S_1 designates W_1" is quite compatible with "S_2 designates W_2."

Thus any collection of expressions which is formulated in accordance with the requirements which define a story is "about a world," for this is merely another way of saying that designation sentences are part of the mechanism of constructing a story. Furthermore, pragmatic predicates are decidable with respect to the sentences of *any* story, and on purely formal grounds. *Thus, epistemological predicates, even 'verified' and 'confirmed' have no intrinsic tie with any single world, with "THE" world. They are purely formal predicates, and do not discriminate among formal systems (stories) provided that all the systems alike conform to the rules which make these predicates applicable.* This principle of indifference could be discarded only if something analogous to the ontological argument could be formulated in pure pragmatics.

---

about *sentences*, *meaning*, and *having the same meaning as.* In such a context, the latter concepts are purely factual.

What, then, would it be to talk *formally* about an historical language such as French? To talk about a language, in the formal sense of the term 'language' is, as we have seen, to *posit* the language, that is to say (schematically) to constitute the language-cum-story-of-a-world-in-which-it-is-used. It is nonsense, however, to talk about positing French as an historical language. Does this mean that one who is talking formally about (positing) a language, *cannot* be talking formally about, say, French? The answer consists in drawing a distinction; or, better, in introducing a new sense to the expression "talking about a language." The schematic formal language-behavior (positing) of a logician Jones will be said to be about the French language, if a stratum of that behavior conforms to the verbal habits of French speaking people. This account is clearly an over-simplification; yet in terms of it we are able to clarify the customary distinction between 'pure' and 'applied' semiotic. After one has made the fundamental distinction between *formal linguistics* and *socio-psychologico-historical linguistics*, we turn our attention to the former, and classify the activities of the formal student of language according to whether or not a stratum of his utterances gears in with our own language habits, or those of a recognizable historical group of individuals. Although the activities are equally formal and pure in both cases; it is useful, though misleading, to refer to the case where there is this gearing in as "applied semiotic." *The important thing is to avoid confusing "applied semiotic" in this sense with socio-phychologico-historical linguistics.* The following analogy may be helpful; The theory of chess is a branch of the pure theory of "capture" games; as such a branch it must be carefully distinguished from the descriptive study of historical chess games.

Note that the pragmatic formal mode of speech of whatever metalinguistic level clarifies the relation of the factual to the formal elements in a "world." *In this sense, the formal mode bends back on itself.* As fact, a metalanguage of this level can be described in psychological terms. However, *as formal mode of speech*, it must "itself" be constituted in a more complex metalanguage. This new constituting is *autonomous*, and is "about" the former only in this factual-descriptive sense that the manipulations of the former are glimpsed in its manipulations. See also footnote 11 below.

We are now in a position to characterize the pragmatic concept of a story in a way which brings out the status of this concept as a regulative idea. Using the terminology we have just introduced, we can see that the requirement that a story contain a verification base amounts to the requirement that the world designated by the story include items which are tokens of sentences in the story, which tokens are co-experienced with the items designated by the sentences they token, which latter items they themselves also designate as being tokens of these sentences. These tokens are the clarified equivalent of the *Konstatierungen* or *Protokolsaetze* of that stage of Logical Positivism which came as close as can any theory of psychological *evidenz* to the view that epistemological predicates have the same type of decidability as do those of pure mathematics.

The constituting of a story, S, thus involves (a) the story as type; (b) the world designated by the story (no naive realism, please!); and (c) items in (b) which token the sentences *verified-in-S*. Consequently, the constituting (by what from the behavioral standpoint is schematic symbol behavior) of a *story-cum-world*, is the constituting of a *story-cum-world-in-which-the-verification-bases-of-the-story-are-tokened*. This means that we have made some progress in our attempt to formalize the notion of a *language* as the sort of thing that is about the world in which it is used. That it is only a beginning will be emphasized in a moment. What concerns us now is the fact that in the case of certain sentences in a story it is an analytic proposition that such and such items in the world designated by the story are tokens of them, and as such qualify for the same syntactical, semantical, and pragmatic predicates as do the types of which they are tokens. (Note that a type expression is not a class of token expressions; the difference in status between type and token goes back to the difference between the left hand and the right hand sides of the designation sentences involved in constituting the story.)   If we look at the matter from the other end, we see that to characterize certain items in a world in terms of meta-linguistic predicates is to talk in a pragmatic meta-language about them as *tokens* of sentences in a story designating that world; or, more accurately, since this would be true only of the most elementary pragmatic predicates, as tokens of expressions in the language in which the story is formulated, which expressions are related in certain formally defined ways to sentences of the story.

The importance of the above analysis consists in the fact that it enables us to clarify the notion of one *fact* in a world being *about* another fact in the same world, *in a formal as opposed to psychologico-factual sense of 'about.'* But we must clarify also the notion of a "world in which statements are made attributing pragmatic (hence also semantic, syntactic) predicates to empirical language expressions."

We are led to distinguish between *stories-cum-worlds* belonging to higher and lower constitutive levels, for the above notion turns out to be that of a world which includes not only items which are tokens of first-level sentences, but also items which are tokens of pragmatic meta-sentences. Such a world cannot be constituted in a pragmatic meta-language. It must be constituted in a meta-meta-language which *pictures* both a pragmatic meta-language and its first-level language, just as a pragmatic meta-language contains the picture of a first-level language.[11]   It may not be too misleading to say that the concept of a *story-cum-world* as constituted in such a meta-meta-language is the schematic (from the psychological stand-point) concept of a *story-cum-world-containing-at-least-one-confirmer-of-the-story*, that is to say, of a story about a world *containing an omniscient knower of the world designated by the story.*[12]   It is in terms of such a structure that the "attribution of metalinguistic predicates to language as fact" (see p. 184f) is to be clarified.   Notice, again, that what can be clarified is the notion of one item in *a* world being in a formal sense about another item in the *same* world, which in turn has some direct or indirect relation to the *same* world. It is a matter of *the same world as,* and not of *the* world *tout court.*

If it is asked, "are you not suggesting an infinite hierarchy of pragmatic structures?", the answer consists in pointing out the following: (1) Pragmatic predicates (and hence semantic predicates in the full sense in which they gear in with pragmatic predicates and concern the relation of empirical language expressions to a world) make sense only with the names of expressions in an empirical language.   It makes no sense to speak of a pragmatic meta-meta-language if by it is meant a meta-meta-language in which pragmatic predicates (e.g. 'verified') are applied to pragmatic meta-sentences.   It is, however, permissible to characterize a meta-meta-language which contains a picture of a pragmatic meta-language as itself pragmatic, provided this confusion is avoided. (2) Above the levels in which we clarify the use of an empirical language in its world, and the use of pragmatic (and hence semantic, syntactic) predicates in the same world, the constitutive hierarchy becomes trivial.   It is the tokening of sentences involving the "same" *syntactical* predicates which is clarified in higher and higher constitutive levels.   Thus, the statements of Pure Pragmatics itself are statements in which the predicates are 'theorem', 'analytic', etc., and in considering the occurrence of philosophical statements in a world, we pass to the general problem concerning the place of analytic systems in a world of fact.

If philosophical propositions are propositions in the pure theory of languages (the pure syntax of pragmatic meta-languages), in what sense is there a philo-

---

[11] The point we have been making concerning the nature of a meta-language (see p. 200 above) can be generalized.   All the expressions of a language of whatever level belong to that level, even should they be, for example, meta-meta-language expressions "about the relation of its immediate object-language (a meta-language) to a first-level language."   It is clear that this irreducible stratification of languages can be transcended only by abandoning formal categories and talking in psychological terms regarding symbol-behavior, and symbol-behavior "about" symbol behavior, where only psychological categories are involved, and even "about" (not to be confused with the semantic term 'designates') is a factual predicate.   There is no formal elevator that takes us from one meta-linguistic level to another.   Each level formally "reconstructs" the lower levels.   It is clear from this that the notion of *reconstruction* is a *factual* one, as is the notion of *levels* in this context.

[12] As a first approximation, the notion of a world which includes a confirmer of the designating story (which, of course, has no theological implications) can be characterized as a set of co-experiences which token (1) all sentences of the story, as well as (2) the meta-sentences which assign pragmatic predicates to the type sentences making up the story.   The next step would be the clarification of the notion of a world which contains items which are tokens of sentences characterizing the assignment of pragmatic predicates as analytic or self-contradictory.

sophical criticism of "the empirical language?" We have seen that from the stand point of formal analysis, there is no such thing as *the* language. Consequently, if it consists of philosophical *statements*, philosophical "criticism" could only be the formulation of theorems in the pure theory of language, and could not be in a formal sense about "the empirical language". Such "criticism" would be comparable to criticizing Johnny's "2 plus 2 equals 5" by demonstrating that "2 plus 2 equals 4". On the other hand, from the standpoint of behavioral science, the philosopher is one who, like the mathematician, has developed a highly integrated system of formation and transformation *habits*,—habits which stand over and against the habits which are the various strata of the empirical language. From this standpoint, to say that a philosopher is philosophizing about the empirical language is to make factual statements to the effect that the habits, which *are* the empirical language from the standpoint of psychology, are embedded in his philosophical habits of symbol-behavior. *The concept of philosophical criticism and clarification is a factual concept.* Notice that we are now talking about *habits* and *behavior*, rather than about *rules*, *types* and *tokens*. In this frame there is confrontation of habit with habit; of a confused set of habits relating to the assignment of pragmatic predicates (the pragmatic meta-language of commonsense) with the corresponding habits of the philosopher; of a confused set of habits with respect to "known for certain" with the formalist's use of "theorem". The habits of any formal scientist, like those of the mathematician in particular are tautology-habits.[13] We can urge their adoption; we can point to the practical consequences of not adopting them. The same is true of *justification*. Thus, a "justification of induction" is either a tautology in pragmatics; or else it is a recommendation of a set of tautology-habits for "law," "confirmed-to-degree-n," "evidence," etc.

"Are you not saying that, after all, the pragmatist has the last word?", I shall be asked. In a sense this is true. But the pragmatist must take the bitter along with the sweet; for the "last word" is not a philosophical proposition. Philosophy is pure formalism; pure theory of *language*. The recommendation of formalisms for their utility is not philosophy. Hume's scepticism was a consequence of his mistake in supposing that the *philosophical* questions he asked *in the study* were sweeping questions of fact, and that therefore *outside the study* he took an unquestioning attitude towards factual propositions questioned in the study. The truth of the matter, and I speak in the tradition of Hume, is very opposite. There are no factual statements which become philosophical in the study (though there are non-factual statements which are philosophical outside the study); and *in philosophy*, scepticism is a self-contradictory position. *University of Minnesota, Minneapolis*

---

[13] The term 'tautology-habit' is clearly not a term in formal science. As I am using the term, it stands to the 'tautology' of formal science as the 'language' of descriptive to the 'language' of formal linguistics (see footnote 10 above). As a descriptive term, 'tautology-habit' is a dispositional term corresponding to 'tautology-behavior', (roughly) behavior which has the consequences characteristic of "It is raining or it is not raining."

SECTION I

(645.1,.2) The development of the pure semantic phase of "logical empiricism" has made "the formal-linguistic approach to epistemological and metaphysical issues" a potential alternative to more traditional views. But, in addition to the study of syntax and of semantics, philosophy is in need of further resources, i.e., ones which would make it clear that philosophy is "the pure theory of empirically meaningful languages."

(645.3) "Pragmatics," as this is presently done (i.e., in 1947), does not qualify as the additional "resources" since "pragmatics" is presently a "socio-psychological" subject and thus not one suited to bring out the distinctive nature of philosophical propositions.

(646.1,.2) Both "classical rationalism" and "classical empiricism" treated philosophical statements as one sort or another of "factual statements." Much of the conflict between rationalism and empiricism stems from the confusions brought about by the "factualizing" of philosophical statements.

(647.1) The resources necessary to save philosophy from these confusions and to augment pure syntax and pure semantics are a treatment of a group of "epistemological predicates" (e.g., 'verified,' 'confirmed,' 'type,' 'meaningful,' 'world-story'). This treatment is approached through a discussion of a "perfect language," to be understood as the language of an "omniscient being."

SECTION II

(647.2; 648.1) In discussing epistemological predicates, we must keep in mind that a language, "adequately tailored to a world" provides a "mirroring" of the world "by a one-to-one correspondence of designations with individuals." Since it is clear that, in one way, our language does not in fact have such a "mirroring" of the world, we shall consider the language of an "omniscient" being, Jones. We shall approach the features of Jones' language by investigating the obvious fact that Jones' language enables him to formulate false sentences and thus world-stories that are different from the true world-story. How does Jones make a "well-founded" choice among these world-stories?

(648.2) Since Jones' world-story speaks about everything, it also speaks about Jones and his "immediate experiences." This fact suggests to the Platonist that Jones selects as true those sentences who "meaning" and whose "data" (i.e., the immediate experiences the sentences designate) appear for "comparison" in his "immediate experience." Such a route is not open to an "empiricist" for whom "meaning" (e.g., propositions) are not "data."

(649.1) But though an empiricist cannot have "meanings" appearing in Jones' experience, he can note that "tokens" of sentences of Jones' language do appear in Jones' experience. Thus, there can be an "experiential confrontation" of tokens of sentences with the "designata" of the sentences.

(650.1) A "verified" sentence is one "a token of which is co-experienced with its designation." Jones' "well-founded" choice of a world-story can be seen to depend on his making a "rational connection" between "verified" sentences and other true sentences which are not verified. What sort of rational connection can be made between "verified" sentences (which are atomic) and other non-verified (but atomic) sentences?

(650.2,.3) A rationalist suggestion on this matter involves "logical" connections among atomic sentences through "synthetic *a priori*" connections among "universals" (i.e., properties and relations) which are expressed by the predicates of the atomic sentences. The problem is to decide what use an empiricist might be able to make of the doctrine of synthetic *a priori* truth.

SECTION III

(651.1; 653.1) The first step in accommodating a correct view of the "synthetic *a priori*" is to gain the proper understanding of 'the world,' 'a world-story in a language means a world,' etc. This understanding requires an account of the term 'means.' In particular, the term 'means' is a term of the "formal" theory of empirically meaningful languages and is closely connected with other terms of this theory such as 'story,' 'conformation rule,' 'token,' 'type.'

SECTION IV

(654.1) However, the complete explication of the concept of an empirically meaningful language requires the explication of further restrictions on anything which is to count as a language. These restrictions can be stated with the help of a relation for which the term 'coex' is used.

(655.1) What has been said about predicates and their meaning has an analog for the (undefined) individual constants; they too, like the predicates, are distinguished by their (formal) roles in the language. The role for an individual constants is specified by the "world-story" of the language: *"The meaning-base of the individual constants of an empirically meaningful language must be a complete world-story formulated in that language...."*

(656.1) The term 'coex' is essential in the definition of a "confirmed" world-story and, in particular, in the definition of 'sentence verified in a story.'

(657.1) Given the definitions of the previous paragraph, we can see that "every world-story in every empirically meaningful language designates a world."

(658.1) Further definitions of epistemological predicates are presented; among these predicates are 'empirically meaningful language' and 'confirmed in a story.'

(658.2; 659.1) Sentences in which ''epistemological predicates'' are predicated of expression of an empirically meaningful language are, if true, ''logically true'' and, if false, ''logically false.'' The reason for this can be found in the fact that epistemological predicates are part of the theory of empirically meaningful language and presuppose *all the restrictions* laid down in the definition of an empirically meaningful language.

(659.2,.3; 660.1) We cannot, of course, produce, as human language users, a whole world-story. There is a sense in which we speak a ''language schema.'' Yet these facts do *not* show that the theory of empirically meaningful languages does not illuminate the structure of our language and our use of epistemological predicates.

EPISTEMOLOGY AND THE NEW WAY OF WORDS [1]

I

THE general perspective of the present paper can best be indicated by saying that the author is a rationalistic realist who has deserted to the camp of logical empiricism; but who feels that in doing so he has not so much rejected one set of philosophical propositions in favor of another, as come to a clearer understanding of what philosophical propositions *are*. This change of allegiance has been made possible by the development of the semantic phase of the pure theory of languages; for only with the achievements of pure semantics did the formal-linguistic approach to epistemological and metaphysical issues begin to appear *relevant*, let alone adequate.

Today it is generally recognized that the tools of the syntactical phase of logical empiricism were not up to the task of dealing with all genuinely philosophical issues. That the situation has been improved by the addition of the semantic dimension to the pure theory of languages, is clear. Yet to the question, "Are we yet in possession of the tools necessary for a systematic clarification of philosophical issues?" the answer, as I shall indicate, must be in the negative. I shall argue that philosophy is properly conceived as the *pure theory of empirically meaningful languages*, and that pure semantics, as it now exists, is but a fragment of such a theory.

It is hardly necessary to point out that the additional tools for which we are looking are not to be found in the development which has come to be known as "pragmatics," for this is, on the whole, a branch of empirical science, a focusing of psychology and sociology on the phenomena subsumed under the empirical concept of language. I say "on the whole," because philosophers who work in this field often adumbrate certain issues of a genuinely epistemological character which can not be handled in terms of current syntactic or semantic categories. Unfortunately, since these issues are adumbrated in a socio-psychological context, they are inevitably falsified and confused with empirical problems. Even more unfortunate is the fact that because the felt need for a *philo-

[1] A revised edition of a paper read at the meeting of the Western Division of the American Philosophical Association at Iowa City, May, 1947.

sophical supplementation of semantic categories is thus finding expression along empirical-psychological lines, there is occurring a psychologistic infection of these semantic categories themselves. The result is a blurring of the sharp distinction between philosophical and factual propositions which was a primary value of the syntactical phase of logical empiricism, whatever its shortcomings in other directions. It is by the proper supplementation of contemporary semantic categories that this infection is to be overcome. This supplementation, then, must serve two functions: (1) It must make possible the development of a system of concepts in terms of which all genuinely philosophical questions can be given an adequate formulation. (2) It must lead to a clarification of the very distinction between philosophical and empirical concepts, so that we can understand what it means to say that questions involving philosophical concepts are answered on *a priori* rather than empirical grounds.

The present paper amounts to the contention that classical rationalism, in so far as it was concerned with genuinely philosophical issues, made explicit the grammar of epistemological and metaphysical predicates, but—owing to certain confusions, particularly with respect to *meaning* and *existence*—came to the mistaken conclusion that philosophical statements were factual statements, albeit of a peculiar kind. Classical empiricism, on the other hand, argued that these statements were common or garden variety factual statements, and usually put them in the psychological species. Rationalism gave the grammar, but contaminated it with platonizing factualism. Classical empiricism threw out the platonizing, but continued to factualize, and confused the grammar of philosophical predicates by attempting to identify them with psychological predicates. In many cases the grammar was so seriously confused that certain of the more consequent empiricists can hardly be called philosophers.

It is now time to realize that classical rationalism was essentially sound as a naïve syntax of philosophical predicates, and not only can but must be absorbed into the empiricist camp if the latter is to be a philosophy. As a matter of fact, such a process of absorption has been going on for some time, and is proceeding, according to all indications, at an accelerated rate.[2] The essential task is to rob rationalism of the illusion that it is making factual statements. But in order to do this, empiricism must first recognize that a certain group of concepts which, when they are recognized at all to fall within the province of the philosopher, are

─────────

[2] These lines were written before the appearance of Carnap's *Meaning and Necessity,* which constitutes an excellent example of this trend.

hurled into the psychologistic dump known as pragmatics, are as genuinely philosophical and non-factual as those of pure syntax. Empiricism, too, has its factualistic illusions to lose. Thus the conflict between rationalism and empiricism is a conflict of illusions, and must cease when these factualistic illusions are dispelled. *An empiricism which recognizes that empiricism is not an empirical thesis will be identical with a rationalism which recognizes that rationalism is not a factual thesis.*

The central thesis of this paper can be put by saying that the system of predicates involved in the pure theory of empirically meaningful languages is inadequate so long as it fails to include a family of predicates among the elder members of which are "verified," "confirmed," "type," "token," "meaningful," "world-story." Our aim will be to sketch a grammar which throws new light on these terms by explicating their relation to one another and to the predicates explored in recent semantic and syntactical studies. In attempting to make explicit the syntax of epistemological predicates, we shall make use of the Wittgensteinian device of speaking in terms of a perfect language. For reasons which will become apparent as we proceed, we shall conceive of this language as the language of an omniscient being. If, in illuminating the concept of omniscience, we can show that epistemological predicates, particularly those which are almost invariably given a psychologistic treatment, play a purely formal rôle, then it would remain to draw the implications for the grammar of these predicates of the distinction between perfect and imperfect languages. *That this distinction has no consequences whatsoever for the grammar of epistemological predicates is, from the standpoint of philosophy, the most illuminating insight of all.*

II

In exploring the grammar of epistemological predicates, one of the most fruitful reference points is the fact that it makes sense to say that our language permits us to speak not only about this or that individual, but also about *all* individuals. Thus it makes sense to say that the sentence "All swans are white" says of each item in the universe that either it is white, or else it is not a swan. It is not always realized that this train of thought leads to the conclusion that it makes sense to say that the language in which "All swans are white" is formulated contains a designation for every constituent ingredient of the world to which it refers. In other words, if we permit ourselves to be guided by the grammar of the term "all," we are led to the notion of this language as mirroring the world by a one-to-one correspondence of designations with individuals. A similar train of thought applies to the case of universals or classes. While it is obvious that the English language as belonging to the empirical class determined by the socio-psychological concept of language does not have such an omni-mirroring character, it is equally clear that when we view language in the perspective of epistemological predicates, we treat it as though it were adequately tailored to a world.

Let us call our omniscient being Jones, his language the Jonesean language, and the body of logically simple (atomic) sentences which constitute the story of the universe in which he lives, the Jonesean world-story. Now it is a direct implication of the omniscience of Jones that the sentences of the Jonesean world-story *mean* states of affairs in the world,[3] and are *true*. Instead, however, of exploring at this point the syntax of "meaning" and "truth," we shall take a roundabout way which, as in the adage, will prove the shortest way home. Thus, we note that the Jonesean language permits the formulation of *false* sentences, that is to say, of sentences which are incompatible with sentences belonging to the Jonesean world-story, and indeed, *it would seem*, of a whole set of alternative world-stories, only one of which is true. The concept of the omniscience of Jones involves not only that of a discrimination on his part between the true and the false sentences of the language, but also the notion that this discrimination is *well-founded* or *justified*.[4]

Let us take another look at the Jonesean world-story. It occurs to us that since it speaks about everything, it must mention Jones. That is to say, it must include sentences which constitute the biography of Omniscient Jones, and, in particular, the biography of his immediate experience (hereinafter called the Jonesean datum-biography[5]). This suggests that the justifiability of the selection

[3] Until we become clear about the grammar of the term "world" in such a context, we shall sometimes speak of *the world of Jones,* and sometimes of *the world* without qualification. In general, our use of any philosophical term will be tentative and dialectical until the group grammar of all fundamental terms shows forth, at least in outline.

[4] I share the conviction that all justification in the epistemological sense of the term is ultimately analytic in character. That the justification of which we have begun to speak is epistemological, and hence analytic, it is the specific purpose of this paper to establish.

[5] In order to explicate the grammar of epistemological predicates, we need to consider them in use, that is to say, as applied to the expressions of an object language. Omniscient Jones is merely a device for blowing up our ordinary use of epistemological predicates into their use in the context of a perfect language. Since one of our conclusions will be that there is no epistemological problem of realism, we shall be begging no epistemological issues if we operate on the assumption that the Jonesean world-story includes other sentences than those belonging to the Jonesean datum-biography.

by Jones of certain sentences in the language as true, and as constituting the story of the world, rests on the fact that the selected group of sentences includes the Jonesean datum-biography, *includes*, that is to say, *sentences the meanings of which are exemplified in his immediate experience.* In other words, if it made sense to say that Jones's experience includes both the *meanings* of datum-biographical sentences, as well as the data which embody those meanings, then we might well be satisfied that it is in the notion of a direct comparison of datum-biographical meanings with the data themselves that is to be found the basis for an account of the justification of the selection of certain sentences in the language as the *true* sentences of the language. This is the line taken by the modern platonist, for whom ''immediate experience'' has a broader sense in which it includes universals and propositions as well as the customary narrower sense in which it is limited to certain particular states of affairs. This line, however, is not open to the empiricist, for whom meanings are never data.[6]

As empiricists we must fall back at least temporarily on the fact that if meanings are never data, this is not true of *linguistic expressions.* Indeed, since the use of a language involves the occurrence in the world of tokens [7] of expressions belonging to the language, it occurs to us that the immediate experience of Jones must include tokens of the sentences of the Jonesean language, and, in particular, tokens of the sentences which make up the Jonesean world-story. This leads to the conclusion that Jones's immediate experience must include tokens of the sentences which make up the Jonesean datum-biography. Thus, while we do not have an experiential confrontation of the meanings of these sentences with

---

[6] That meanings in the sense defined by empirical psychology are not data is obvious. (For an account of meaning as psychological fact which brings out the dispositional character of the psychological concept of meaning, see Charles Stevenson's *Ethics and Language*, Chap. III, particularly sections 4 and 5.) However, we must also recognize a use of ''meaning'' which is distinct from that of empirical psychology, even if in some sense it is a ''reconstruction'' of it. This is the sense which is relevant to the semantic analysis of epistemological predicates. It is the recognition of this sense which leads only too often to Platonism. The contention that it is nonsense to speak of meanings in this sense as data constitutes the essential difference between an empiricism which reformulates the insights of Platonism, and Platonism itself. The characteristic tenets of Platonism, as opposed to a sound logical or epistemological realism with respect to universals and propositions, spring from the nonsense of speaking of apprehending universals and propositions.

[7] We shall distinguish below (pp. 653–654) between a linguistic token, a class of linguistic tokens, and a linguistic type (that is to say, between *token, token-class,* and *type*). For the moment it will be sufficient to think of a token as a member of a class of marks as having meaning.

the realizations of these meanings, we do have an experiential confrontation of certain tokens of the sentences with the states of affairs to which they refer.

Let us define a *verified* sentence as *a sentence a token of which is co-experienced with its designatum.* We can then suggest that the notion of the justifiability of the selection of certain sentences in a language as constituting the story of the world [8] rests on the notion that certain sentences in the language are verified sentences. But since *ex hypothesi* [9] not all the true sentences of the language are verified sentences, *the notion of such justifiability presupposes the notion that there is a rational connection between the verified sentences and the other true sentences making up the Jonesean world-story such that the verified character of the former entails the truth of the latter.* Can we make sense of the concept of rational connection in this context?

We have suggested that classical rationalism may yet have a contribution to make to an empiricist epistemology, provided that factualistic illusions are set aside. How then would the rationalist verbalize on this point? Somewhat as follows (if we pick and choose from the history of rationalism). He appeals to an *a priori* principle of supplementation, the principle of sufficient reason, which is bound up with the existence of a realm of universals so related to one another that they constitute a system which can be viewed in one light as a system of necessary connections, and in another as a system of compossibilities. (It is this system which underlies the concept of the laws of nature.) Thus, in answer to the question we raised in the preceding paragraph, the rationalist might be expected to say, ''Omniscient Jones justifies his selection of a group of sentences as those which are true of his world and constitute its story, by reference to the fact that this group includes a sub-set of verified sentences,[10] the meanings of which are propositions known to require supplementation by reference to the principle of sufficient reason, and which, given the structure of the domain of universals meant by the predicates of the language, can be supplemented in only one way to make a complete world story.'' We are suggesting that a de-phlogisticated verbalizing along these lines may find a place in an adequate empiricist epistemology.

But the empiricist would seem to be confronted by a dilemma at the very beginning of an attempt to speak along these lines. In order to hold that one set of *atomic* sentences can be compatible

---

[8] See footnote 3 above.

[9] See footnote 5 above.

[10] For the rationalistic account of a verified sentence we must return to the approach we formulated, only to reject, on p. 649 above.

EPISTEMOLOGY AND NEW WAY OF WORDS   651

(and it is logical, not psychological, compatibility that is in question) with only one set of additional *atomic* sentences, he must make sense of the notion of *a priori* (that is, for the empiricist, *logical*) restrictions on the manner in which atomic sentences can combine—restrictions which are functions of the predicates appearing in these sentences. On the other hand, the notion of such restrictions is repugnant to the contemporary empiricist, for whom no two atomic (and therefore affirmative) sentences can be incompatible.[11] We notice that on the rationalistic position, universal propositions which correspond to a connection of universals are synthetic *a priori* truths about a world exemplifying those universals. Our problem, then, amounts to that of determining what concessions [12] can be made within the framework of empiricism to the notion of synthetic *a priori* truth. Needless to say, any concessions along these lines must be made by showing that the notion of the synthetic *a priori* is the confused notion of an *a priori* that is *analytic*. The terms of our problem, however, prohibit a solution along traditional empiricist lines, for it follows from the above that the universal sentences which express, for the rationalist, eidetic intuition on the part of Omniscient Jones, are synthetic in the usual syntactic sense. If an analytic *a priori* is involved, it can only be on condition that it makes sense to say that *the statement that certain synthetic universal sentences are true of the world, is itself analytic.*[13]

III

How can it be an analytic proposition that certain synthetic universal propositions are true of the world? Here is where empiricism must abandon its naïve realism. The first step consists in

[11] He reluctantly makes an exception for atomic sentences in which determinate predicates falling under the same determinable are predicated of the same individual. This concession, however, does not touch our problem, which concerns the compatibility of atomic sentences about different individuals. To say this, however, is not to say that in so far as additional types of restrictions on the combining of atomic sentences must be recognized, they are unrelated to that which is so reluctantly conceded.

[12] To add, as we must, that in the final analysis we have to do not with concessions, but with a necessary ingredient in an empiricist epistemology, is to restate our contention that the rationalism-empiricism issue is a pseudo-problem.

[13] It is worth noting that for the Platonist it is an analytic truth that synthetic universal propositions corresponding to connections of essences are true of the world embodying those essences. Is it silly to ask, "Might there not be other worlds embodying other realms of essence, so that the synthetic *a priori* propositions actually lived up to by the first world would be only vacuously satisfied by the others, and vice versa?" *Autre pays, autres moeurs?* Here we have a hint as to the direction our argument will take.

examining the rôle of the definite article in the expression "*the* world." Since the very function of the definite article is to imply a set of entities from which one is distinguished, must we not say that the distinction between *the* world and the other worlds is a descriptive one? "But surely," it will be said, "the others don't exist!" Here is the germ of the ontological fallacy. It is now time to realize that every world-story means a world; that the basic grammar of the term "world" is brought out by the statement, "A world-story in a language means a world." It is in terms of this matrix that the expression "the world" is to be understood: "the world meant by. . . ." Thus, to understand the notion of *different worlds,* we must understand those of *different stories* and *different languages.* But it is best to begin with the simpler question, "In virtue of what are two predicates of one and the same language different?" Clearly, the difference has to do with a difference of meaning. At this point the danger is psychologism, the confusion of the *epistemological* predicate "means" with the predicate "means" which belongs to the vocabulary of empirical psychology.[14] We are arguing that statements about the meaning of terms are, in epistemological contexts, non-factual statements which are true or false in a purely formal sense, and decidable (in principle) on purely formal grounds. Not merely is a language characterized by a set of formation rules; we must also add that the primitive predicates of a language are distinguished from one another by *conformation* rules; rules which restrict the formation of compound sentences out of atomic sentences which involve these predicates. I have put the matter elsewhere [15] as follows:

. . . consider the question: in virtue of what are two different predicates "ϕ" and "θ" different? We might be tempted to say either (1) because they are empirically different marks, or (2) because they have different meanings. The first answer is obviously inadequate. The second is more satisfying. But once we have drawn a sharp distinction between *meaning* as a concept of

[14] It is not denied that "means" in certain contexts is an empirical predicate. We are merely insisting that the epistemological and the psychological uses of the term be sharply distinguished. We shall follow current practice below and use the term "designates" in epistemological contexts, unless the context makes it clear which sense we have in mind. We are suggesting that "designates" is a purely formal term which no more stands for a feature in a world than do "implies" or "and." No one, today, would make the mistake of supposing that syntactical predicates are empirical or factual predicates; that "or," for example, stands for a feeling of "or-ness." Perhaps it is safer to say that no one should make such a mistake. If psychologism in syntactics shows some signs of rising from the dead, it is because psychologism in semantics has not been properly buried.

[15] "Realism and the New Way of Words," *Philosophy and Phenomenological Research,* forthcoming.

empirical psychology and *meaning* or *designation* as a concept of epistemological semantics, we see that though the second answer is true it does not clarify. The question asked above can no longer be characterized as a psychological side-issue, *but must be answered in terms appropriate to the conception of meaning or designation as a purely formal concept.* The conclusion at which we are arriving is that from the standpoint of epistemological analysis, the predicates of a language are differentiated from one another in terms of the formal roles they play in the language. Using the term ''syntax'' in a broader sense than is current, we could say ''different syntax, different predicate; same syntax, same predicate.'' We shall prefer to say that predicates are differentiated only by the conformation rules which specify their combining properties. The concept of combining properties of predicates . . . concerns the relation of predicates to individual constants in the following way. It involves (1) the concept of a ''skeletal'' relational predicate (there may be more than one provided they are syntactically related) which signifies the fundamental type of order in which the individuals to which the language can refer must stand; (2) the concept of restrictions on the non-relational predicates which can be associated with given individual constants where the restrictions are a function of (a) the predicates, (b) the (skeletal) relational sentences in which these individual constants are making an appearance. . . . We have here a coherence theory of meaning characterized in purely syntactical terms. . . . It is in terms of such conformation rules that predicate families are formally specified (determinates under common determinables) and different predicate families are distinguished and related.

Thus, the formal concept of *designation* is essentially bound up with that of *conformation rule.* The identity of formally indiscernible predicates (we shall discuss individual constants in a moment) is part of the grammar of formal science, and, in particular, of the predicate ''designates.''

A further clarification of this point is contributed by the type-token distinction. Here it may be helpful to think of a linguistic type as a *nexus* of formal functions. The fact that in *mentioning* a linguistic type we must *use* an empirical mark makes it seem inevitable that the notion of a linguistic type is the notion of an empirical class as designating. Yet empirical classes belong to a world; and, as we have seen, the concept of a world is the correlate of the concept of a language semantically interpreted. For this reason, the concept of a language can not be identified with the concept of empirical classes as bearers of the designation relation. Empirical classes must be conceived as designators in a derivative sense.[16] The notion of such derivative designators is an essential ingredient in the concept of an empirically meaningful language as one that is used in the world it is about. We must thus distinguish between (1) types, (2) token-classes, and (3) tokens. The

---

[16] In the case of *meaning* as a psychological concept, on the other hand, the primary sense has to do with the empirical functioning of particular empirical marks in a constituted world.

metalinguistic predicates "type" and "token" presuppose "designates," and can be explicated as follows:

> The predicate "token" is used properly when it is said that the *designatum* of one expression in a language is a token of another (perhaps the same) expression in the language. The formal significance of the concept of *token* is brought out by the following: If "*p*" designates *p*, and *p* is a token of "*q*," then all the metalinguistic predicates which apply to "*q*" apply also to *p*; thus, " '*q*' is true" entails "*p* is true." In other words, we have here a grammar according to which metalinguistic predicates can be associated in specifiable circumstances with the expressions belonging on either side of the predicate "designates." If *p* is a token of "*q*," then "*q*" is said to be the *type* of which *p* is a token.

It is involved in the notion of an empirically meaningful language that tokens be specified for the type expressions which make up the language. This is done by specifying for each type expression in the language the class (or classes [17]) of items in the world of the language which is to be the token class (or classes) for that expression.

IV

The ingredients we have so far introduced into the grammar which is to clarify the concept of an empirically meaningful language are essentially familiar, and, except for certain implications we have drawn, do not take us beyond the scope of the formal theory of languages as at present conceived. In order, however, to give a formal account of the predicates "verified," "confirmed," "meaningful," and, consequently, in order to complete the grammar of "truth," we must characterize a further restriction on the language to the expressions of which these predicates can apply. Such languages must contain a reflexive, symmetrical, and transitive two-place predicate for which we shall use the term "coex," but which must no more be confused with the predicate "co-experienced with" as a term of empirical psychology than "designates" with "means" as a psychological expression (though in each case it is proper to say that we are dealing with a "formal reconstruction" of language as empirical fact). The formal significance of "coex" lies (1) in its relation to the concept of *token*, linguistic tokens in a primary sense falling in the domain of the relation *coex*, and (2) in its relation to the concept of *verified sentence*, which will be defined below.

---

[17] Thus, from the standpoint of the pure theory of empirically meaningful languages, "different languages used in the same world and which mean that world" are to be understood as different sets of token-classes for the type expressions which constitute one and the same empirically meaningful language. (I note that Rynin, in the interesting essay which accompanies his edition of Johnson's *Treatise on Language*, arrives at a similar conclusion.)

We have argued that the meanings of the (primitive) predicates of a language are formally specified in terms of conformation rules which discriminate between them in terms of the structures of relational sentences (involving the "skeletal" or basic ordering relations of the language) in which individual constants must function in order for these predicates to be properly applied to them. What are we to say about the meanings of the individual constants of a language? *Once again the rejection of psychologism forces us to say that the difference in meaning of individual constants must rest on syntactically characterizable differences in their rôles in the language.* Is it sufficient to say that the individual constants of a language are differentiated in terms of a structure of basic order sentences which might be called the meaning-base of the individual constants of the language; a different individual constant (as type) corresponding to each place in the net-work?[18]   This, however, would be a dangerous half-truth. It makes the relation between the individual constants and the primitive one-place predicates of a language a purely external one; it regards the individual constants (given the skeletal relations) as semantically self-sufficient. That the relation is not a purely external one we have already seen from the side of the one-place predicates. That the dependence is reciprocal is indicated by the following train of thought: (1) It will be granted that it doesn't make sense to speak of individuals which stand in relations, but have no qualitative character. Consequently the semantic aspect of individual constants does involve a reference to one-place predicates. (2) It follows (given our syntactical approach to semantic meaning) that for an individual constant in a language to have meaning involves that it be formally specified as belonging with a one-place predicate. (3) The only alternative to admitting that the semantic determinateness of the individual constants of a language presupposes a specific assignment of one-place predicates as defined by conformation rules, is to postulate one or more one-place predicates which belong to all individual constants, which one-place predicates are independent of the spectrum of one-place predicates defined by conformation rules. (4) This alternative (besides being open to all the classical objections to absolute space and time and to the ether) is incompatible with the fact (which I shall not argue in this paper) that the primitive individual constants of a logically perfect language can be connected in a true sentence with only one primitive, determinate, one-place predicate.[19]

[18] This is the approach suggested by Carnap in *Meaning and Necessity.*
[19] A developed theory of language must draw a clear distinction between primitive individual constants (simple individuals) and defined individual

The sum and substance of these contentions is that the meanings of
the individual constants of a language must be specified in terms
of a specific assignment to them of one-place predicates in conformity with the conformation rules relating to these predicates.
*The meaning-base of the individual constants of an empirically
meaningful language must be a complete world-story formulated
in that language, rather than a pure structure of skeletal relations.*
We must now rebuild this notion from a different perspective.

Let us return to the notion of a world-story, and, in particular,
to that of a world-story the characterization of which as true is
rationally warranted by the fact that it includes a sub-set of verified sentences which uniquely determine the world-story as a
whole.[20] Let us call such a story a *confirmed* [21] world-story, and any
sentence of such a story, a confirmed sentence. We can explicate
the concept of such a world-story as follows:

A confirmed world-story is a set of sentences which, given the conformation rules which specify the meanings of the predicates of the language in
which it is formulated, and given a semantically determinate battery of individual constants, contains a sub-set of sentences (1) which can be built into
only this one complete story, (2) the *designata* (see paragraph which follows
this explication) of which sub-set constitutes a set of items mutually related

---

constants (complex individuals, "things"). Not even complex individuals
can be members of more than one class or (*which is the same thing*) instances
of more than one universal. "(*x*) *x* ε White → *x* ε Circle" says "Each member of a *thing-class* including the note White is a member of a *thing-class* including the note Circle."

[20] The conception that, given the syntax *including conformation rules* of
the language in which they are formulated, a set of verified sentences can
formally entail and be entailed by a complete world-story, and thus be *logically equivalent* to that story, *without the story being translatable into*—or
"reducible" to—*the set of verified sentences*, is what distinguishes my position from positivism. Compare the discussion of a *reciprocal fix* in my
article "Pure Pragmatics and Epistemology," *Philosophy of Science*, Vol.
14 (1947), pp. 189 ff.

[21] This root sense of "confirmed" is not one that admits of degrees. Its
function is to clarify the contrast between sentences "checked against the
facts they assert" (verified sentences) and sentences "checked only indirectly" (confirmed but not verified sentences). A predicate "confirmed-to-
degree-*n*" relates not to this distinction, but to the clarification of statistical
and probability assertions. Such a predicate might be introduced as one
applicable to expressions in a language *L*, and defined as a matter of the
ratios in which the individual terms (appearing in a story *S* which is the
meaning-base of *L*) which satisfied one sentential function, also satisfied other
sentential functions. The employment of such a predicate would always presuppose a constituted world. Therefore it would be nonsense to speak of the
confirmation of natural laws (which correspond to the very meaning-rules of
the language to the expressions of which the predicate "confirmed-to-degree-
n" is applied).

by the relation *coex*, (3) which sub-set consists of sentences *verified in the story.*

Sentence "*p*" will be said to be a *sentence verified in story S* if *S* includes a sentence "*q*" and a sentence "*r*" such that "*q*" designates *r coex p*, where *r* is a token of "*p.*" Sentences "*q*" and "*r*" will be said to be the experiential tie of "*p,*" and *r* the verifying token of "*p.*" Each sub-set of verified sentences as characterized above will be called a *verification base* of the story *S*.

The references to *designata* in these definitions make it necessary to come to a final reckoning with naïve realism. We have already pointed out that the expression "the world" must be interpreted in such a way as to avoid the ontological fallacy. We suggested that the expression contains an implicit reference to a language, and has the sense of "the world meant by . . . a given language." Are we saying that the rejection of the ontological fallacy involves the notion that there are many *real* worlds? Indeed not! The final abandonment of naïve realism comes with the realization that "talking about the *designata* of sentences" is an essential ingredient in "characterizing these sentences in terms of epistemological predicates." The "right-hand side" of designation sentences together with the predicate "designates" and the quotation marks on the "left-hand side" are all alike formal devices belonging to the grammar of epistemological predicates; their function is the purely formal one of hooking up with the rules relating to the assignment of such predicates as "true sentence of (language) *L*," "verified sentence of *L*," etc. If we introduce the term "world" as a collective term for the designata of a world-story, then it is a purely formal truth that every world-story in every empirically meaningful language designates a world. The pure theory of empirically meaningful languages as formally defined systems which are about worlds in which they are used, has no place for *the* world, but only for the world designated by the story which is the meaning-base of a given language.[22]

[22] Once we appreciate the fact that epistemologically it makes no sense to speak of *the* world, it becomes possible to explore certain traditional controversies with the hope of discovering what, if anything, is at stake. Different languages are characterized by different conformation rules; different conformation rules are reflected in differences in the structures of stories formulated in these languages, and of the worlds these stories are about. Epistemology, or the pure theory of empirically meaningful languages, can develop the formal properties of languages with different conformation rules, but can not "choose" *the* story or *the* language. Epistemology can show, or expose the formal confusion that underlies attempts to show, that one or other type of story or language is internally inconsistent. In this sense, and in this sense alone, can it defend or attack "realism," "idealism," or some other epistemological "ism."

A few definitions by way of crystallizing certain expressions we
have used in the course of our argument follow:

A calculus (with specified conformation rules) which permits the formulation of expressions which conform to the defining requirements of a confirmed world-story, will be called an *empirical language form*. The notion
here is that as far as the predicates of a language are concerned, there can be
a family of world-stories involving those predicates (a family of worlds involving the same qualities-laws, but different ''initial'' conditions).

An empirical language form pinned down to one of these world-stories,
and hence for which the formal status (and hence the meanings) of its individual constants is fixed, will be called an *empirical* (or *empirically meaningful*) *language*. The world-story which fixes the individual constants will be
called the *meaning-base* of the language.

The individual constants and (primitive) predicates of empirical language L will be said to be *meaningful expressions of L*, as will (atomic)
sentences constructed of them. The *designata* of meaningful individual constants and predicates will be said to *exist* in the world of the language. This
sense of existence in which individuals and classes exist is to be distinguished
from the sense in which it is said that *lions* (as opposed to the *class* lion) exist.
The former is correlated with ''meaningful,'' the latter with ''true.''

A meaningful sentence of L which belongs to the story S which is the
meaning-base of L will be said to be *confirmed in S*, and to be a *confirmed
sentence of L*.

A meaningful sentence of L which belongs to a verification base of S, will
be called a *verified sentence of L*.

A predicate which appears in at least one verified sentence of L will be
called a *datum-predicate* of L. A meaningful predicate of L which appears
only in confirmed sentences of L, will be called a *non-datum predicate* of L.

The notion that the primitive predicates of an empirically meaningful
language *must* be datum-predicates, and that its basic sentences *must* be
verified sentences, is psychologism pure and simple, and not even good psychologism at that. The psychologism which is classical pragmatism (Dewey)
has sounder instincts than the sensationalistic pragmatisms which have listened
to Hume, Mach, and some of the earlier tales from the Vienna Woods. It is,
however, an analytic truth that an empirically meaningful language is empirically meaningful as resting on a verification base, a set of verified sentences which uniquely determine the language in the complicated way we have
indicated.

The conclusion to which we have come is that since, from the
standpoint of the pure theory of languages, the notion of an empirically meaningful language includes the notion of a confirmed
world-story which is the meaning-base of the language, *sentences
assigning epistemological predicates to the expressions of an empirically meaningful language are either analytic or self-contradictory.* Thus, the sentence '' 'p' is a (*factually*) true sentence
of L'' is itself *logically* true (or false). To say this, is not to
identify semantic truth with syntactical or logical truth. It is
only to say that (in principle) the semantic predicate '' (factually)
true'' is formally decidable. The predicate '' (factually) true''

is characterized by the formal equivalence " '*p*' is true if and only if *p*." But *that the world designated by the story which is the meaning-base of L includes (or fails to include) state of affairs p* is a matter of logical truth (or falsity). Just as the notion of *the* world is a mistake, so is the notion of *the* set of true sentences. To see that "(factually) true" as well as "designates" is *in principle* formally decidable, is to take the final step away from both naïve realism and psychologism. Clearly, however, we must explain our frequent use of the expression "in principle." We shall use it once more, and then make the explanation of it the final point on our agenda.

We have been contending, in general, that where *E* is a linguistic expression, and "ϕ" an epistemological predicate, the sentence "$\phi(E)$" entails "*E* belongs to language *L* of which the meaning base *S* designates world *W*," and that the truth or falsity of "$\phi(E)$" is formal truth or falsity, decidable, in principle, on purely formal grounds. Speaking loosely but suggestively, we would say that the "attribution" of epistemological predicates to an expression implies that the expression belongs to a formal system constituted in such a way that the sentence making this attribution is either analytic or self-contradictory. This is what we mean when we say that the use of epistemological predicates involves (*logically* involves) *presuppositions*.

"But surely," it will be said, "the construction of world-stories and the deciding with respect to them that sentences of the kind ' "*p*" is (factually) true' are analytic or self-contradictory, lies completely beyond our powers! What possible connection can there be between such a mathematician's dream, and our humble use of epistemological terms?" The answer (like the answer to all good philosophical questions) is hidden in the question, and concerns the distinction between "perfect" and "imperfect" languages, and its implications for the sense of formal predicates.[23]

The most fruitful way of looking at this distinction is to consider the rôle of variables in these languages. A perfect language is one which includes no variable (individual or predicate) for which it does not contain an explicit domain of values. Thus, a perfect language is one in which a universal proposition can be translated into a logically equivalent conjunction of singular propositions. An imperfect language is one in which universal propositions can not be so translated, but must make use of ampersands and dotted lines; in it, therefore, universal propositions are *schemata* rather than shorthand for specifiable logical sums and

[23] At this point the closing sentences of section I and the opening sentences of section II should be re-read.

products. Let us call a perfect language a *language proper,* and an imperfect language, a *language schema.* We should admit that human beings speak a language schema.

Now the contention I wish to make is that the distinction we have been drawing between language schemata and languages proper is a *factual-psychological* rather than a *formal-epistemological* distinction. As I have put it elsewhere,[24]

[this distinction] belongs to the psychology of formal *manipulations,* and can no more be formulated in terms of formal concepts, than can the concept of *mistake.* If this is the case, then our factual inability to construct complete world-stories no more entails an inability to give a formal account of a complete world-story, or of a language proper, or to presuppose structures of this kind, than our inability to construct an infinite series entails an inability to give a formal account of infinity, or, indeed, of particular infinite series. Our everyday use of epistemological predicates is *formally* sensible, even though we cannot turn it into petty cash.

It is in view of these considerations that we can understand how it is that as formal scientists we must say that the use of epistemological predicates presupposes a complete world-story in a perfect language, while yet recognizing the blundering status of the human animal.

WILFRID SELLARS

UNIVERSITY OF MINNESOTA

24 "Realism and the New Way of Words," *Philosophy and Phenomenological Research,* forthcoming. See also "Pure Pragmatics and Epistemology" in *Philosophy of Science,* Volume 14 (1947), pp. 195–197.

(In this outline, paragraphs in small type in RNWWR are accounted separate paragraphs if and only if they are not preceded by a full colon.)

SECTION I

(424.1,.2,.3) A significant part of philosophy is the clarification of mistakes based on confusion. One prominent source of confusions in philosophy is factual ignorance due to the lack of a developed psychology of "higher processes."

SECTION II

(425.1,.2) The purpose of this paper is to deal with "realism" as this view is formulated in "the new way of words" and to assess "naive realism" and various epistemological views that reject naive realism.

SECTION III

A Claim of Language. (426.1) Our language "claims to mirror the world by a complete and systematic one-to-one correspondence of designations with individuals" though "our language does not *explicitly* contain such designations."

Epistemology Writ Large: The Language of Ominiscience. (426.2; 427.1) The language of an ominiscient, though not transcendent, being is adopted as a methodological device for posing epistemological questions. The feature of the language of omniscience of primary concern is that it enables its user to formulate all the atomic sentences "which together constitute the story of the universe" in which the user lives.

Omniscience and the Universal Proposition. (427.2) The omniscient being, "Jones," has a language with sufficient individual constants to eliminate any quantification. The problem, then, is why Jones settles for a language with a given list of individual constants rather than a language with a different list.

A Pragmatic Step. (428.1,.2) The solution to the above problem requires an investigation of "semantics" since questions of the "meaning" of the individual constants of Jones' language are pertinent and an investigation of "pragmatics" since the adequacy of Jones' language somehow involves *his* "use" of it.

Language and Language Schema. (429.1) We, as non-omniscient language users, have only a language "schema."

(429.2) It will be necessary to distinguish two senses of 'pragmatic' in connection with language schema.

SECTION IV

The Meaning of 'Meaning': Psychologism. (429.3; 430.1; **431.1**) A common view of meaning treats meaning as a "psychological" relation between signs and items with which we can be acquainted; such a view underlies both "Platonism" and "Humean nominalism."

Behavior, Norm and the Semantic Metalanguage. (431.2,.3) Part of the way in which the confusion of psychology and epistemology is to be avoided is to distinguish between a "descriptive" sense of 'language' and a "normative" sense of this term and, in general, to distinguish between an epistemological ("formal", "normative") study of language and a "socio-psychologico-historical" ("factual," "descriptive") study of language. "The New Nominalism takes 'means' or 'designates' to be a purely formal term, that is to say, a term which as little stands for a feature of the world as 'implies' or 'and'. It has nothing to do with psychological acts, intuitions, or, indeed with experience of any kind."

SECTION V

The Use of Language: Background to Pragmatics. **(432.1)** The language of Jones permits the formulation of different world-stories. In order for one of these world-stories to formulate part of Jones' knowledge, Jones' selection of this world must be "in some sense *justified.*" How is this to be explained?

(432.2) Jones' world-story speaks about everything, including Jones. The world-story that is the story of *his* world is the one such that "*tokens of (Jones) sense-biographical sentences must be co-experienced with the sense-data those sentences mean or designate.* That is, Jones' "immediate experience" *includes* sentence tokens which are *about* his "immediate experience."

(433.1) Since world-stories do not employ "meta-linguistic terms," the world-story Jones has selected does not contain the sentences which formulate Jones' recognition that the story he has selected is the story of *his* world. That is, for Jones to appreciate that he has selected the appropriate world-story, he must be able to "meta-talk about himself."

Meaning, Meaningfulness and the Pragmatic. (433.2) A review of the main stages in the paper thus far.

SECTION VI

Verification and the Confirmation. (434.1, 2) Some of the sentences of the Jones world-story are ones that "confront their designata": i.e., tokens of these sentences are "co-experienced" with the experiences they designate. However, the world-story also contains sentences which are not "confronting" sentences in this sense. What connection is there between the "confronting" sentence and the "non-confronting" sentences such that they can all be said to belong to one "system"? That all the sentences be part of the same syntactical system (generated by the same formation rules) is not enough.

(435.1) Let us call the confronting sentences of Jones' world-story "sentences verified (by Jones)" and the non-confronting sentences of Jones' world-story "sentences confirmed (by Jones)". Then our problem can be stated: "In order for a world-story to contain sentences which are *confirmed* but not *verified,* the atomic sentences which constitute the story must have a unity over and above that of satisfying the syntactic requirements (formation rules) of the language."

(436.1) It is not sufficient to require that every individual constant in the world-story appear in a relational sentence with every other individual constant so that the world-story is "about a spatio-temporal system." Though this requirement will prove insufficient (see 438.2), it is crucial that the verified sentences of Jones' world-story and the confirmed sentences of Jones' world-story "make up *a whole which is about a spatio-temporal system in which every item has its place.*"

Verification and Time. (436.2,.3,.4; 437.1) The application of the Jonesean world-story takes place a time. Thus verification and confirmation are relative to a time. With respect to a given time, "the greater part not only of the world-story as a whole, *but also of the Jonsean sense-biography,* has the status of merely confirmed."

The Relation of the Confirmed to the Verified. (437.2; 438.1) Our problem, given the above remarks on verification and time, can now be seen to be the following: If there is to be one confirmed Jonesean world-story, then one "moment slice of the Jonsean sense-biography" must "require" all the rest of the confirmed sentences (including those that are verified at another time). But how can one such sub-set of sentences "require" all the rest if all the (atomic) sentences of the world-story are "logically independent" of each other?

SECTION VII

The Syntax of Temporal Predicates (438.2) That the Jonesean world-story is about a coherent spatial-temporal structure is not sufficient to solve the problem since a "given biographical slice can form a world-story with any set of sentences so long as it has the proper background of sentences" involving appropriate temporal terms and the individual constants of the world-story. The only way to avoid this result is to insure that predicates other than temporal ones (e.g., 'before') in the world-story "conform" to certain requirements.

Meaning and Syntax. (438.3) At this point, we should remember that 'means' (or, 'designates') is a "nonfactual" ("f ormal") term (see Section IV). In light of this point, let us inquire in virtue of what two different predicates are different. The only answer (consistent with the 'formal' status of 'means') can be in terms of rules ("conformation rules") that specify the "combining properties of predicates." It is only by such formal "restrictions" that predicates can be differentiated. "The concept of the combining properties of predicates......**concerns the** relation of predicates to individual constants in the following way. It involves (1) *the concept of a "skeletal" relational predicate (there may be more than one, provided they are syntactically related) which signi-fies the fundamental type of order in which the individuals to which the language can refer must stand;* [9] and (2) the concept of restrictions on the non-relational predicates which can be associated with given individ-ual constants where the restrictions are a function of (a) the predicates, (b) the (skeletal) relational sentences in which these individual con-stants are making an appearance. These restrictions constitute the conformation rules for the predicates of the language."

The Pragmatic Metalanguage. (440.1) Our next step is to note that such terms as 'verified,' 'confirmed' and 'meaningful' appear in a "pragmatic metalanguage," i.e., a metalanguage "the central concept of which is that of a confirmed world-story."

(440.2,.3) The resources of a pragmatic metalanguage include in addi-tion to syntactical and semantical concepts, "the concepts of *symbol-type* and *symbol-token.*" These concepts presuppose the concept of designation in that this latter concept is the central part of the apparatus which allows us to characterize tokens by means of metalinguistic predicates of types. Finally, a pragmatic metalanguage must have a formal relation (for which the term 'coex' is used) which allows the formulation of sentences that correlate tokens and the states of affairs the tokens designate as tokens of types that desig-nate these states of affairs. These resources are **sufficient for** defini-tions of such terms as 'meaning base,' 'confirmed world-story,' 'verified sentence,' 'empirical language,' etc. Given our present concerns, the essential points are the following: a confirmed world-story is a unity because a confirmed world-story is a story which has a subset of sentences verified in the story that (in addition to meeting certain other restrictions) "can be built into only this complete story in view of the conformation rules (natural laws) of the language." The predicates of a language have determinate meaning and are differentiated from one another by the con-formation rules of the language; similarly, "the individual constants of a language are formally determinate only with respect to that single world-story which is the meaning-base of the language."(**see ENWW,** pp. 655ff).

(442.1; 443.1) The predicate 'true sentence of L' is a formal predicate applicable to any empirical language L; each such language, through its "story S which is its meaning base," has a set of true (atomic) sentences.

(443.2,.3) That the present **view** has no place for "Naive Realism" is shown by the fact that, given the term 'world' introduced as a "collective term for the designata of a world-story," it is a truth in the pure theory of empirical languages that "every story in every empirical language desig-nates a world." Thus no epistemological predicate has any "intrinsic tie with any single world."

(444.1) A discussion of two concepts of existence, one of which is a "pragmatic concept" defined in terms of the pragmatic concept of meaningfulness.

No Predicaments. (445.1) Confirmation is "intersubjective."

Type and Token Again. (445.2) Types should not be confused with classes of tokens: "one and the same language as type may have two or more sets of tokens..... The identity of language as type is not an empirical identity, but rather a formal distinctness bound up with its formation and conformation rules."

(445.3) It is part of the account of empirically meaningful languages that "linguistic tokens conform to rules of language."

Pure Pragmatics and the Uniformity of Nature. (446.1) The present view has an historical parallel in Kant: Built into the notion of an empirically meaningful language is the concept of conformation rules involving temporal predicates and thus the concept of the temporal coherence of characteristics of the events in the world the language is about.

First Thoughts on Realism. (466.2; 447.1; 448.1) In terms of **'world-story'**, ' verified' and 'confirmed,' epistemology as the pure theory of languages can distinguish between "realistic" and "non-realistic" languages but it "cannot choose THE conformation rules or THE language." However, a non-realist (e.g., an idealist) is still faced with the task of building a non-realistic language that would recommend itself in terms of the clarification it brings.

Sense-Data Again. (449.1; 450.1) Some considerations against "phenomenalistic" reduction.

SECTION VIII

The Pragmatics of 'Now'. (450.2; 451.1) The temporal distinctions of "past, present and future" are made with respect to the "meaningfulness" (the application, i.e., tokening, of the language (see 433.2)) rather than with respect to the "meaning" of the language. (See *Verification and Time* in Section VI (436.2ff).) That is, these "distinctively temporal predicates" ('past,' 'present,' and 'future') are explicated with reference to the occurrence (tokening) of language in time and thus "belong in a pragmatic metalanguage."

(451.2,.3) A skeletal predicate such as 'before' is temporal only through its connection with the metalinguistic predicates 'past,' 'present', and **'future'** and thus "its complete character as *temporal* transcends its object-language status." This view is, in one way, analogous to McTaggart's.

(451.4) The sentence 'Now(p)' is a "pragmatic meta-sentence." Such a sentence, to be true, must be tokened simultaneously "with the state of affairs" that 'p' designates and, as a metalinguistic sentence, must mention a token of the sentence 'p'. Moreover, the pragmatic metalanguage must say of 'p' that it is tokened with the state of affairs that 'p' designates.

(452.1) No attempt to account for "past, present and future" on the basis of "relative position in a linear series" can account for the ego-centric element "involved in genuine temporal distinctions."

SECTION IX

The Mind-Body Problem in the New Way of Words. (452.2,.3,.4; 453.1) Since the world-stories we are interested in will contain "physical event sentences as well as sense-biographical sentences " (see 446.2ff), "we must inquire about the relationship of the latter sentences with those physical event sentences that are the physical history of Jones' neurophysiology. The crux of the matter is in whether an "ideal" psychology of the future will furnish us with true(material)equivalences of mentalistic sentences with "physicalistic" sentences. (Compare SSMB .)

SECTION X

Ideal Language and Language Schema. (454.1,.2; 455.1) The main point of this section is that the distinction between "perfect" languages and "imperfect" languages is "not an epistemological distinction." The schematic nature of our language appears "at all linguistic levels." The distinction between the "schematic" and the "proper" is one that cannot be drawn in epistemology but only in "the psychology of formal *manipulations*." Consistent with the pervasiveness of schematicity in our actual language behavior, is the fact that all epistemological predicates, whether they are the primary ones we have discussed or ones that are defined in terms of these primary ones, require the total linguistic structure discussed in this paper and, in particular, require that there be "a complete world-story in a language with given conformation rules." However, "our factual inability to construct complete world-stories" does not entail "an inability to give a formal account of a complete world-story"...any more than "our inability to construct an infinite series entails an inability to give a formal account of the infinite.... Our everyday use of epistemological predicates is formally or epistemological sensible even though we cannot turn it into petty cash."

(456.1) For an unconfused appreciation of the difference between the "factual" and "formal" approach to language, we must firmly fix in our mind the difference between behavioral habits which are "schematic" and the formal discussion of "complete" linguistic "structure."

Conclusion. (456.2) In one sense, a basic theme of this paper is idealistic: an "empirical *language* can only be understood as an incoherent and fragmentary schema of an ideally coherent *language*."

Realism and the New Way of Words

WILFRID SELLARS

I

It has been said that a system of philosophy is not refuted, but becomes ignored. This is true. It is equally true (and for the same reason) that a clash of systems in the philosophical drama ends not in victory and defeat, but in a changing of the scene. Put from a somewhat different point of view, the historical development of philosophy is more truly conceived as the periodic formulation of new questions, than as a series of attempted answers to an enduring body of problems. Although the new questions which appear in this process can be regarded, for the most part, as revisions or reformulations of earlier issues, the fact of revision and reformulation is of the essence of the matter, making new questions out of old. Put in these terms, a system dies when the questions it seeks to answer are no longer asked; and only where the questions are the same can there be a genuine clash of answers.

An essentially similar point of view which, however, cuts a bit deeper, argues that in philosophy, as opposed to the factual sciences, the answer to a properly formulated question must, in the nature of the case, be obvious. It suggests that the evolution of philosophical thought is accurately ·conceived neither as a series of different answers to the same questions, nor as a series of different sets of questions, but rather as the series of approximations by which philosophers move toward the discovery of the very questions they have been trying to answer all the time. This conception of philosophy as a quest of which the goal is the obvious, is, I believe, a sound one. It is the problems and not the answers that are difficult; and a genuine advance is constituted by the replacement of a confused by a less confused question, where the two are in some sense the same.

We have suggested that philosophy as an ongoing enterprise depends for its existence on lack of clarity; that the mere occurrence of philosophical dispute entails that at least one of the parties is tangled in a confused formulation. This thesis is by no means novel, yet many who subscribe to it conceive of philosophical confusion as confusion the removal of which leaves nothing *philosophical* behind unless it be the score for a repeat performance, so that philosophy *becomes* and never *is*. I have implicitly rejected this view by speaking of philosophical questions and answers. Yet clarification is the significant element in philosophical activity, however its nature be conceived. In what, then, does philosophical confusion consist? I doubt that it is a proper or unique species. It appears, rather, to be common or garden variety confusion flowering in an unusually fertile field. It is bad reasoning aided and abetted by factual ignorance. It is asking questions which imply answers to prior questions which have not even been raised. It is using terms now in one sense, now in another. In short, it is making mistakes. The factual ignorance which has assisted philosophers in making mistakes has been, and still is, primarily in the field of psychology. The undeveloped state of the science of the higher processes has thrown philosophers on their own resources in an intricate factual field. The absence of a structure of scientific law in which such key terms as 'conscious', 'concept', 'abstracting', 'knowing', 'believing', etc., are firmly held in place, has made it easy to the point of inevitability to pass from one question to another which only appears to be the same. In particular, this lack has tended to result in a failure clearly to distinguish epistemological from psychological issues. While much has been accomplished in the way of securing this distinction, it is still unfinished business. Here is confusion to be clarified.

II

It was long the custom in systematic discussions of epistemology, to ask the man in the street certain questions concerning what, after all, he *knew* (which questions, being a man in the street, he had never asked himself), and from the answers construct the invaluable dialectical foil called Naïve Realism. Thus arrived at, this construction inevitably appeared in the light of a conviction we all share, appeared to be *common sense*, to be something we all wish were true; and the process whereby subsequent examination first raised doubts, then finally pressed it to humiliating collapse tended to take on the character of a tragedy akin to the loss of our childhood faiths. The inevitable stages in the argument which, initiated by this manner of posing the question, dissolved the grim, but comfortingly substantial, world around us in the dialectical acids of the schools left those who stayed to the bitter end convinced, but uneasy. Somehow the magic was gone. The acts of the tragedy (though not always performed in this order) were Naïve Realism, New Realism, Critical Realism, Idealism, Pragmatism and Epistemological Solipsism of the Present Moment.

It has become increasingly clear, in the course of the past decade, that this particular tragedy was based on a mistake; on an asking of the wrong, or better, of a confused question. This suggests immediately, in view of considerations advanced in the first section of this paper, that the curtain

426   DATA, REALITY, AND THE MIND-BODY PROBLEM

is being rung down on this particular cluster of controversies, and that new *dramatis personae* are moving to the center of the stage. This is true; but those considerations also suggest that while the new questions may be clearer, they will none the less be in essence the same, and that consequently the new play will be the old, cut and adapted to modern dress. The empirical and the formal, the psychological and the epistemological will be more clearly distinguished, yet the competing points of view will be found capable of translation into the new frame of reference, if only to be curtly dismissed. In the remainder of this paper I propose to indicate how the realism issue becomes transformed when translated into the new way of words.

III

A Claim of Language. One of the most striking features of the language we use, from the standpoint of epistemological analysis, is the fact that it enables us to speak not only about this or that individual occurrence in space and time, but also about *some* individuals and about *all* individuals. Thus, it makes sense to say that while 'All swans are white' does not entail 'There are swans', and consequently is not in the technical sense an existential proposition, it does none the less talk about *everything* that *is* and about *nothing* that *is not* and says of *each* item that either it is white or else it is not a swan. It has not always, however, been realized that this train of thought leads directly to the conclusion that our language claims somehow to contain a designation for every element in every state of affairs, past, present and future; that, in other words, it claims to mirror the world by a complete and systematic one-to-one correspondence of designations with individuals. If it is obvious that our language does not *explicitly* contain such designations (and it would hardly be illuminating to say that it contains them *implicitly*), it is equally clear that our language behaves as though it contained them. We shall begin our epistemological examination of language by considering the nature and status of general propositions. But first we shall introduce a methodological device that will be used throughout this paper as an aid to the formulation of epistemological issues.

Epistemology Writ Large: The Language of Omniscience. Philosophers have on occasion found it useful to stand back and essay a God-like vision of the universe; to attempt to see things as they would be seen by an omniscient being. Translated into the new way of words, this endeavor becomes the attempt to envisage the language of omniscience. A consideration of the larger writing may assist us in our argument as it did Socrates in the *Republic*. To be of value, however, the omniscient being whose language we have in mind must be no transcendent Deity with vaguely specified though omnivorous cognitive powers, but rather one who shares, apart from his omniscience, our human lot through being immersed in time, and limited to our characteristic ways of confronting the world. The notion of such a being will be used as a device for suggesting statements to be clarified. We shall begin with no other characterization of omniscience than that offered by common sense. It is not a question of using a clear notion of omniscience and the language of omniscience to clarify a confused notion of human cognition and language. It is rather a matter of writing the latter confusion large so that it may more easily be clarified.

The feature of the language of an omniscient being with which we shall primarily be concerned in this paper is the fact that it permits him to formulate a body of completely unpacked or logically simple sentences which together constitute the story of the universe in which he lives. In the previous section we permitted ourselves to be puzzled by the fact that it makes sense to say that our language enables us to *speak about everything* though it does not enable us to *list each thing*. Since it is involved in the notion of the language of omniscience that it is able to do both, an examination of the status of general propositions in this language should prove fruitful.

Omniscience and the Universal Proposition. When our hypothetical omniscient being (we shall call him, for convenience, Jones) makes the statement 'All A's are B', he makes no claim which he cannot back up with an explicit use of language. Thus he can also say:

> (1) 'i_1 is B or not-A and i_2 is B or not-A . . . and i_n is B or not-A . . . .'

where the dots serve only to indicate the unreproducible magnitude of the statement Jones would actually make. Such a device would play no rôle in the Jonesean utterance. But can we say that (1) even as formulated by Jones would be equivalent to 'All A's are B'? Would he not have to add a further statement,

> (2) '$i_1, i_2, . . . i_n, . . .$ are all the individuals'

where the dots, again, would not appear in the Jonesean formulation? But (2) as it stands is misleading. Individuality is not a quality, or, to put it more technically, in the language in which (1) and (2) are formulated, the term 'individual' has the status of a reflection of the syntactical predicate 'individual constant of the Jonesean language.' Thus (2) must be understood as the reflection ("quasi-syntactical" expression) of something like

> (2') ''i_1,' 'i_2,' . . . 'i_n,' . . . are all the individual constants of the (Jonesean) language.'

This step brings with it a considerable clarification, for it is clear that the question as to what individual constants a language contains is a purely linguistic question which as such involves no reference to the extra-linguistic. Its truth rests on what we shall take to be an analytic truth, namely,

428   DATA, REALITY, AND THE MIND-BODY PROBLEM

(2″) 'An individual constant of the (Jonesean) language is either
'i_1' or 'i_2' . . . or 'i_n' or . . .'

Thus we see that doubts concerning the adequacy of a given conjunction
as a translation of a sentence beginning with 'all' in the Jonesean language
are resolvable by appeal to the battery of individual constants included in
the resources of that language. We are now in a position to give our problem a more accurate formulation:

Granted that in the syntactical dimension the core of "all-ness" in the language
of omniscience is to be found in the battery of individual constants which make
up one segment of the resources of the language, *what makes the Jonesean language with its battery adequate to Jones' world so that as an omniscient being he
uses it?* Or, to put it somewhat differently, what is the non-syntactical core of
the reach of the language of an omniscient being?

A Pragmatic Step. If the question were so phrased as to read, "What
criterion enables Jones to select a language which contains a just adequate
supply of individual terms?" we should be tempted to reply by formulating a thesis to the effect that the world is directly present to the Jonesean
mind, and that consequently he can compare his language with the world.
Not only, however, would such a notion be out of keeping with the restrictions we have imposed on our omniscient being; it could not in any
case begin to give the explanation demanded of it. Even if Jones could
confront all the individual items in his language with items directly present
to his mind, it would not follow that this set of terms was adequate to the
'totality of existence', for no *collection* of objects of awareness could give
the required assurance of totality. As a last resort, we might claim that
the items directly present to the Jonesean mind form a system one of the
characteristics of which is that it is *incompatible with the existence of
anything more.* There may be some sense to the notion of such a system,
but as thus formulated it makes the mistake which underlies the ontological argument. Properly formulated (as will be brought out later) it is as
much a "quasi-linguistic" concept as that of *individual.* We are thus forced
to the conclusion that if it makes sense to speak of a one-to-one correspondence of the individual constants of the Jonesean language with the
constituents of his world, this correspondence cannot be ascribed to a
direct comparing of language with world.

Now to say that a battery of individual constants is adequate to the world, is
to say that each constant *means* an item in the world, and each item in the world
is *meant* by an individual constant of the language. Thus we can at least say that
the concept of adequacy must be clarified in terms of a meta-language involving
semantic resources (for semantics gives us a logic of *meaning*). Furthermore,
in spite of the failure of the above attempts, this clarification must involve some
relation of the language to Jones who uses it, and whose omniscience it embodies.
In this latter respect, it is clear that our account must involve a *pragmatic* element, for the term "pragmatic" in current semiotics refers to language *as used.*

REALISM AND THE NEW WAY OF WORDS   429

Language and Language Schema. If the situation stands so with respect to the concept of the language of omniscience, how stands it with us? We have said that our language *claims*, as far as its reach is concerned, to be an omniscient language. We are now in a position to reformulate this idea. If by 'language' is meant a symbolic system in which all individual constants and predicates are explicitly listed without the use of such devices as '....' or 'and so on', a system, that is, in which the expressions which are substitutable for variables are explicitly listed, then it is clear that we do not speak a language, but rather the schema of a language. Only an omniscient being could effectively use such a language. As a matter of fact, to say that a being effectively uses such a language seems to be at least part of what is meant by calling him omniscient. The symbolic structure we employ resembles a language (in the sense above defined) reasonably well as far as predicates are concerned, but is almost completely schematic as far as individual constants are concerned. We are obliged to make use of general propositions in talking about the world. We rarely, if ever, make a statement which when clarified is not, at least in part, general in form. *But general propositions as we use them are not the full-blooded general propositions of a language proper.* The variables in the latter are genuine (even if bound) variables. The language contains individual and predicate constants which are the domains of these variables. The symbolic structure we use contains *schemata* of general propositions. These we use as though we spoke a complete language proper to which they belonged. *They serve as pragmatic devices which enable us to get along somewhat as though we spoke a language proper.*

We can sum up our line of thought as follows:

The adequacy in reach of even an omniscient language is to be pragmatically construed. The language of a non-omniscient being is therefore doubly pragmatic. It enables him to get along to some extent as though he spoke the adequate language of an omniscient being. *These two uses of the term 'pragmatic' need not have the same sense. Indeed, we shall see that they do not, for the former sense turns out to be a purely formal one belonging to pure pragmatics; the latter, on the other hand, is empirical or factual, belonging to empirical pragmatics.*

IV

The Meaning of 'Meaning': Psychologism. It has until recently been a characteristic assumption of philosophers of both nominalistic and, in the medieval sense, realistic persuasions, that *meaning* in epistemological contexts is a psychological fact involving self, sign and *designatum*. Perhaps the most explicit expression of this notion is to be found in Russell's *Problems of Philosophy.* He writes, "We must attach some meaning to the words we use, if we are to speak significantly and not utter mere noise; and the meaning we attach to our words must be something with which we are acquainted" (p. 91). It needs but a moment's reflection to realize that this conception of the meaning of symbols leads directly to Platonism.

430   DATA, REALITY, AND THE MIND-BODY PROBLEM

A nominalist who commits himself to this account of meaning is committing himself to nonsense. For if the meaning of a symbol must always be something with which someone is or can be acquainted on the occasion of a significant employment of that symbol, then either there are subsistent essences and propositions with which we can be acquainted, or else the meanings of symbols are restricted to *sensa* and *introspecta*, so that indeed symbols must be radically ambiguous, meaning different data on each occasion of their use.[1] But the latter (nominalistic) alternative not only reduces the scope of what can be meant to an extent which makes it equivalent to a denial of meaning by limiting meaning, it would appear, to exactly what does not need to be meant; it actually makes even this limited scope of meaning impossible, for even sentences about *sensa* and *introspecta* involve universal terms, the meaning of which clearly transcends the hard data of the present moment.

It has become the fashion to accuse nominalism of this type of psychologism. The charge is a sound one *if correctly interpreted*. If, however, the charge is taken to mean that these philosophers limit what can be meant to psychological facts, then a consequence of nominalistic psychologism is confused with the psychologistic blunder itself. For the essence of the latter consists *not* in any assertion as to what can be meant, *but in taking meaning to be a psychological fact*.[2] To be guilty of it is to suppose that the term 'means' in such sentences as " 'A' means B" stands for a psychological fact involving the symbol 'A' and the item B, whether the psychological fact be analysed in terms of *Schau*, acquaintance or just plain experience. Psychologism underlies both Platonism and Humian nominalism, not to mention the conceptualistic attempt at compromise.[3]

---

[1] I leave out of consideration the conceptualistic approach which substitutes for subsistent essences a special class of mental item called 'concepts' in which *abstracta* have 'objective' or 'intentional' being, and for propositions a class of mental phenomena called 'judgments' which have more complex intentional objects.

[2] The appearance of extreme paradox presented by this statement can be removed by drawing a distinction, implicit in our discussion, between two uses of the term 'meaning', (1) that which occurs in distinctively philosophical (epistemological) contexts, (2) that which occurs in psychological statements concerning symbol behavior. Our contention can be summarized by saying that the epistemological sense turns out to be purely formal, and sharply to be distinguished from the empirical or psychological sense, though it is, in a sense that is difficult to analyse, a "reconstruction" of it. Once this is seen, the latter loses its metaphysical aura, and becomes a less mysterious subject for empirical analysis. An equally important gain in the opposite direction is the elimination of one of the most persistent sources of confusion in epistemology.

[3] Thus under the broader heading of *psychologism* as the confusion of epistemology with psychology, we can distinguish two sub-forms according as epistemology or empirical psychology predominate in the confusion. If the former, epistemological content appears in the guise of psychological acts and objects *sui generis* (*Wesensschau*, universals as apprehendable objects, intentional acts, intentional objects, etc.). These are ranged alongside the facts of empirical psychology, which persist in the confusion. This first sub-form can be called *epistemologism* (Plato, Aristotle, Kant). On the other hand, if empirical psychology dominates, we have *psychologism* in the narrower sense attacked by Husserl (who was himself guilty of epistemologism). Here the episte-

REALISM AND THE NEW WAY OF WORDS   431

The essentially *new* feature of the New Way of Words is that it does not commit this mistake. Epistemologism leads to *ontological realism* with respect to classes and universals. Psychologism in the narrower sense leads to the absurdities of *logical nominalism*. The New Nominalism avoids both, and defends instead *logical or epistemological realism* with respect to universals and classes. As we shall see, the New Way of Words does justice to the Platonic insight, while avoiding its supposed factual implications. (See pp. 444 ff. and footnote 14 below.)

Behavior, Norm and the Semantic Meta-Language. The psychologistic blunder with respect to "means" is related to another fundamental error, that, namely, of confusing between (1) language as a descriptive category for which symbols are empirical classes to which certain events belong (and hence are symbol-events) by virtue of performing an empirical function, with (2) language as an epistemological category for which the relation of type to token is not that of empirical class to member. We shall develop and explain this contrast in the course of this paper. *For the moment* it will help clarify the epistemological distinction between symbol-types and symbol-tokens, if we think of the former as norms or standards, and the latter as events which satisfy them. We can therefore, *for the moment* at least, contrast the above two senses of 'language' as the descriptive and the normative respectively. Making use of this distinction, we argue that 'meaning' or, better, 'designation' is a term belonging to language *about* languages in the second sense. Its primary employment is therefore in connection with linguistic expressions as norms, and consequently cannot concern a psychological relation of language expressions to objects of acquaintance (even essences). It is only symbol-events which could enter into such a psychological transaction. If this is the case, it is hard to see what kind of a factual relation 'designates' could be. The New Nominalism takes 'means' or 'designates' to be a purely formal term, that is to say, a term which as little stands for a feature of the world as 'implies' or 'and'. It has nothing to do with psychological acts, intuitions, or, indeed, with experience of any kind. It refers to no psychological act, intuition or transaction of any sort.

If this is the case, then the *limitations of meaning* can no more be settled by an "appeal to experience," than can the limitations of (mathematical) *addition* or *logical deducibility*. To say this, however, is not to say that experience imposes no limitations on the meaning of empirically meaningful language, so that we have magically been saved from a solipsistic account of such language. It is merely to say that if epistemology has anything to say about the relation of *meaning* to *experience*, then the term 'experience' as used by the epistemologist must belong to the same frame as 'meaning' and 'implication.' 'Experience' in this

---

mological (which has less survival power) tends to be reduced to a descriptive study of *how we think*. Epistemologism has the virtue of preserving philosophical content, though at the expense of constructing a fictitious psychology. Psychologism in the narrower sense lacks merit as philosophy, although the philosopher and psychologist can join hands in approving its avoidance of pseudo-psychology.

432   DATA, REALITY, AND THE MIND-BODY PROBLEM

use must be contrasted with 'experience' as a term of empirical psychology, just as we have already contrasted 'language' as an epistemological term with 'language' as an expression in socio-psychologico-historical linguistics. Our discussion will lead us to the conception of a type of meta-language in which a family of expressions among which are 'experience' and 'meaningful' supplement customary semantical and syntactical predicates in such a way that the theory of such meta-languages is the pure, *a priori*, in short non-empirical, theory of empirically meaningful languages.

V

The Use of Language: Background to Pragmatics. If the language of our omniscient being permits the formulation of a world-story which, in a sense to be clarified, constitutes knowledge of the world in which he lives, the language also permits the formulation of sentences which are incompatible with sentences included in the story, and indeed, *it would seem*, of alternative world-stories. Thus we can hardly say that one of these bodies of sentences constitutes knowledge on the part of Omniscient Jones, unless we can also say that his selection of this set of sentences is in some sense *justified*. Now the problem we are attempting to formulate does not belong to empirical psychology. We are not concerned with the psychology of belief. *Our goal is a pragmatics which avoids psychologism as rigorously as does semantics as we have conceived it.* Until, however, we can make our problem stand out, we must be content with a blurring of distinctions, and wander for a time between pure pragmatics and psychology.

Before we ask concerning the *justification* of the selection of a set of sentences by Jones as the story of his world, let us seek to understand what such selection involves. In the first place, this selection would seem to involve that tokens of the sentences of this world-story occur in the immediate sense-experience of Jones. But while this would constitute a *sine qua non* of such selection, it would hardly seem to be a sufficient condition; for while such tokening might conceivably constitute Jones' selection of a story of *a* world, the fact that the world is *his* world would not have been clarified. Let us take another look at the Jonesean world-story. It occurs to us that, since it speaks about everything, it must mention Jones *who uses it*. That is to say, it must include sentences which constitute the biography of Omniscient Jones, and, which is more important, sentences which constitute the sense-biography [4] of Jones. Combining this train of thought with the above, we have the notion that for the world-story which Jones selects to be the story of *his* world, Jones' immediate experience must include tokens of sentences which constitute the sense-biography of Jones. In other words, Jones' immediate experience must include items which are tokens of sentences which *designate* the contents of that immediate experience. Tersely put, *tokens of (Jones-) sense-*

[4] The phrase 'sense-biography' will be used as short for 'immediate-sense-experience-biography'.

REALISM AND THE NEW WAY OF WORDS   433

biographical sentences must be co-experienced with the sense-data which these sentences mean or designate. Thus, if i_n is a Jonesean sensation of green, the world-story includes the sentence 'i_n is co-experienced with a case of the sound *eye-sub-en-iz-grēn*,' where the case of *eye-sub-en-iz-grēn* is a token of the sentence 'i_n is (a sensation of) green.' We must say, then, that in one aspect these tokens are *included in* Jones' immediate experience, while in another aspect they are *about* Jones' immediate experience.

It is clear that since 'type', 'token' and 'designates' are meta-linguistic terms, what we have been saying about the relation of Jones to the Jonesean world-story *cannot be said in the language in which the story itself is formulated.* The world-story cannot characterize any feature of the world it is about as a token of a type. This means that insofar as Jones himself "recognizes" that the story is the story of his world, the sentences in which this recognition is "formulated" belong at a higher linguistic level than the sentences which describe his world. This higher level in the epistemological analysis of Jonesean cognition will occupy our attention later on when we shall be concerned with the notion of demonstratives. For the time being we shall meta-talk about Jones, ignoring the fact that Jones must meta-talk about himself.

Meaning, Meaningfulness and the Pragmatic. Let us review briefly the course of the argument. Apart from the introductory comments, it has consisted in the following steps:

(1) A consideration of the use of general propositions by common sense led us to the notion that our language behaves as though it were an ideal language which contained a designation (involving a coördinate system) for every constituent in every state of affairs, past, present and future; as though, in other words, it contained a map which represented in complete detail the history of the world, and mapped nothing not contained in that history. Though it was obvious that our language is not a language in this ideal sense, we concluded that such a language would be our language writ large, and that an investigation of the way in which epistemological predicates geared in with it would throw light on the significance of "normative" statements relating to cognition. We thereupon introduced the figure of Omniscient Jones who has succeeded in formulating a body of sentences constituting the complete story of the universe in which he lives, a body of sentences worthy of the term 'knowledge'. In examining the notion that his coördinate system contains an adequate and no more than adequate number of individual constants, we concluded that such adequacy is not to be explained in terms of a direct comparison of language with the world (naïve realism). We tentatively concluded that it is a pragmatic feature of the language in a sense to be clarified. (2) A preliminary discussion of meaning found us adopting the notion that the term 'meaning' as used in such statements as " 'a' means b" is properly to be understood as a purely formal term in a language whose business it is to be about language, as it is the business of the Jonesean language to be about his world. To say that 'means' is a formal term in such a language is to say that 'means' or 'designates' is one of the bones of the skeleton of the language, enabling it to contain a logic of meaning and truth, just as logical words enable a language to contain a logic of implication. *Meaning* in this sense is no more to be found in the world than is a referent for 'or'. (3) This leads to the conclusion that whether or not a language is *used*, there corresponds

434   DATA, REALITY, AND THE MIND-BODY PROBLEM

to it a meta-language which contains (formally) true meaning-statements about the expressions of the language. In this sense, then, the expressions of any constructible language designate or mean. Consequently, the difference between an applied and a non-applied language has nothing to do with the *meanings* of its expressions. (4) On the other hand, it is obvious that a language that is not applied is, in a sense to be clarified, *empty*. At the present stage in our argument we are considering the possibility that the opposite of empty is *meaningful*, and that a language is meaningful (as opposed to *has meaning*—in the semantic sense) by virtue of being *applied*. We are talking about meaningfulness in terms of the language used by Omniscient Jones, and are suggesting that to say that such a language is applied is to say that *a world-story formulable in it is applied*. (5) We are therefore looking for a pure theory of the application of a language; for a non-empirical theory of the relation of a meaningful language to experience. This we must find if epistemology is to be something more than the empirical psychology of how we use language. Pure semantics, today, studies meaning in abstraction from the being used of a language. In it, therefore, neither the realism nor the solipsism issue can be formulated. Students of pure semantics turn the study of the use of language over to empirical linguistics. There also neither the realism nor the solipsism issue can be formulated. On the other hand, pure pragmatics *is* concerned with the relation of language to experience. It is here that these issues can be formulated and solved. But this is getting ahead of our story.

VI

Verification and Confirmation. Let us return to the analysis of the idea that Jones knows his world through the application of a world story. We had arrived at the notion that the application by Jones of the world-story as a whole involves that tokens of the (Jones) sense-biographical sentences are co-experienced with the (Jones) sense-data which these sentences designate or mean. Thus while all the sentences are *ex hypothesi* tokened in the immediate experience of Jones, only sense-biographical sentences have tokens which *confront* their *designata*. To this account, however, the objection naturally arises that according to it only the sense-biographical sentences, for which this confrontation obtains, are *applied*, as opposed to merely being *tokened*, whereas we have been purporting to give an account of the application of the world-story as a whole. The challenge, thus, is as follows: Can we say that for a sentence system as a whole to be *applied* is for it to be *tokened as a whole* in the immediate experience of a user, and for a sub-set of the sentences to be *sense-biographical sentences*, that is to say, *sentences tokens of which confront their designata?* Let us call sense-biographical sentences "confronting sentences". The objection, then, can also be put in the form of a question. What is the connection between the confronting sentences and the non-confronting sentences belonging to the world-story which enables it to be said that they belong together to *one* sentence *system?*

Let us be quite clear that the mere fact that a group of sentences illustrate a common set of *formation* rules does not suffice to make them one system in the sense that is relevant when speaking of a group of sentences as applied. Unless

REALISM AND THE NEW WAY OF WORDS   435

they have some further relation to one another, the sentences are like the windowless monads of Leibnitz. We are thus forced to the conclusion that we can answer 'yes' to the first question only if we can specify a way in which sentences can constitute a system which is more than a heap of which the only unity is the fact that they conform to the same syntactic specifications. For if the world-story we are considering were such a heap, the fact that the *Jones-biographical* sentences were *confronting* sentences would be of exactly no significance for the *remaining* sentences of the 'system', and we should be forced to admit that even though 'meaning' does not mean confrontation with a datum, the only expressions that are *meaningful* are in point of fact those which have tokens which do confront data, because these are the only sentences which are *applied* [5] as opposed to merely tokened. Should this be the case, we should have defended ourselves against the contention that the nature of *meaning* forces the new way of words into a nonsensical solipsism, only to fall into a solipsistic account of *meaningful* language.

Let us now introduce two terms which will be of great assistance in clarifying our problem. Let us rebaptize the sense-biographical sentences which we have called "confronting sentences" by the phrase "sentences verified (by Jones)", and let us call the tokens of these sentences which are co-experienced with the states of affairs designated by the verified type sentences, "verifying tokens". *A verified sentence is a sentence, a token of which is co-experienced with its designatum.*[6] Let us also characterize each sentence of a world-story about a world which contains an omniscient knower of that world, that is to say, which contains a sub-set of sentences verified by that omniscient knower (in the case of our example, Omniscient Jones) as a "sentence confirmed (by Jones)." The story as a whole as the conjunction of these sentences would also be confirmed (by Jones). Our problem as we posed it above can therefore be rephrased as follows:

In order for a world-story to contain sentences which are *confirmed* but not *verified*, the atomic sentences which constitute the story must have a unity over and above that of satisfying the syntactic requirements (formation rules) of the

[5] The frequently encountered locution which speaks of the "application" of concepts to the given is surely a mistake. The following is a loose formulation of some threads which can be disentangled: (1) The confusion of a token of a sentence "$\phi(o)$" —"object o is of kind ϕ"—on the occasion of the presentation p, with a token of the sentence "$\phi(p)$". The appropriate sentence involving "p" would be something like "p is a presentation of o, and o is of kind ϕ." (2) The confusion of the relevant token of "$\phi(o)$" with an utterance of "$\phi!$" on the occasion of o, that is to say, a confusion of tokens of subject-predicate sentences with utterances of nouns and adjectives in the presence of states of affairs. But whatever the difference between an utterance of the kind "Fire(o)" and an utterance of the kind "Fire!" from the standpoint of descriptive pragmatics, there is none from the standpoint of epistemological analysis. The important thing is to realize that particulars as well as universals belong to the "realm of the conceptual", that it is *sentences* and not *predicates* which are, in any genuinely epistemological sense, "applied."

[6] It might seem more natural to say that a verified sentence is one whose *meaning* is found to be realized in directly experienced fact. This approach, however, is permissible only to the platonist for whom it makes sense to speak of apprehending, finding, intuiting, grasping meanings. See "Epistemology and the New Way of Words" (ENWW), *The Journal of Philosophy*, Vol. 44, no. 24, 1947, especially pp. 648 ff.

436   DATA, REALITY, AND THE MIND-BODY PROBLEM

language. The status of being confirmed but not verified requires a criterion of togetherness in one sentence-structure; *conformation rules* as well as *formation rules*.

But have we not implicitly specified such a principle in describing the sentence-system in terms of which we have set out our problem, as a *world*-story? As the history of a *universe*? Would not the principle be one to the effect that in order for a group of sentences to constitute a system capable of being confirmed, every individual constant must participate in *relational* as well as *non-relational* sentences; and, indeed, that every individual constant must participate in either an atomic-relational or a relational-product sentence with every other individual constant in the sentence-system? Do spatial and temporal relations suffice to constitute such a structure? In terms of the specific problem we are considering, can we say that in order for the world story to be *confirmed* (by Jones), the *remainder* of the sentences must cohere with the *verified* (by Jones) segment to make up *a whole which is about a spatio-temporal system in which every item has its place?* We shall, of course, see that this suggestion is inadequate, but that the concept of such a structure is essential to our argument.

Verification and Time. We must now take into account a most important fact which we have hitherto kept out of the argument. Not only is the Jonesean world-story *about* a temporal world; its application can only be its application *at a time.* Verified sentences fall into sets which are about momentary slices in the Jonesean flow of experience. Each slice contains the verifying tokens for the corresponding set of verified sentences.

If we speak of such a set of verifying tokens as a *verification*, we can say that both *confirmed* and *verified* are relative concepts, relative, that is to say, to a verification. Consequently, in relation to a given verification, the greater part not only of the world-story as a whole, *but also of the Jonesean sense-biography,* has the status of the merely confirmed.

Let us comment briefly on the relation of the world-story and its confirmation to time. As world-story it can characterize its universe of discourse as a serial order by means of a predicate designating a transitive asymmetrical relation, *before.* By the use of this predicate, each event mentioned in the story is characterized as earlier than, simultaneous with or later than, each other event.[1] Each of these events would have corresponding to it three classes of events, those earlier than it, those simultaneous with it, and those later than it. Each set of three classes would constitute candidates for the positions of Past, Present and Future, respectively. But the world-story as such could not *elect* such a set to these positions any more than it can contain demonstratives, and for the same reason.

[1] Complexities in the account of time made necessary by relativity theory are not relevant to our problem, and will be ignored.

REALISM AND THE NEW WAY OF WORDS   437

To speak of the universe of discourse of a story as dividing into a past, a present and a future, is to speak (and detailed analysis must be postponed) of the story *in relation to a verification*. Consequently, the distinction between past, present and future relates not to the *meaning* of a world-story, but to its *meaningfulness;* for, as we have proposed to show, it is the latter and not the former that is tied up with the confirmation of a sentence-structure. If the universe of discourse of a world-story as confirmed includes items which are *before* the verified items and items which are *after* the verified items, then it necessarily consists of a past, a present and a future. To put it bluntly, statements about the past mean the past, just as statements about the present mean the present and statements about the future mean the future, *just because these distinctions are irrelevant to meaning*. But this has been denied in a curious way in recent philosophy: I refer to Ayer and Lewis [8] on the meaning of statements "ostensibly about the past".

The Relation of the Confirmed to the Verified. The discussion of the relation of verification to time in the preceding paragraphs leads us to reformulate our problem. We have been asking: Granted that there is such a thing as the confirmation of sentences that are not verified, what is the relation between the verified sentences and the confirmed but not verified sentences such that the verification of the verified sentences make a difference to those which are merely confirmed? In terms of our illustrative material we were asking: What is the relation between the verified sentences and the merely confirmed sentences of the Jonesean world-story in virtue of which the latter can be said to be confirmed? We are now led to ask:

[8] A. J. Ayer, *Language, Truth and Logic;* C. I. Lewis, *Mind and the World Order.* The above was written in the summer of 1946 before Professor Lewis' important Carus lectures were available. There he *suggests* an analysis of statements about the past with which I am in essential agreement. As I would like to interpret him (but see Stace's acute comments in his review of Lewis in *Mind,* 57, 1948, especially p. 80), he now distinguishes between the *semantic reference* of historical statements to the past, and the *necessary equipollence* which these statements must have to statements about future experiences if they are to be *empirically significant*. His new account recognizes that this necessary equipollence must be given a far more subtle analysis than the "translatability of statements *ostensibly* about the past into statements *genuinely* about the future" which I have taken, perhaps unjustly, to be the crux of his earlier account. If I have misinterpreted that position, my plea is that in it *(semantic) reference to the past* was so overshadowed by *logical equivalence to the future* that it could scarcely be seen—particularly by one who failed to notice that Lewis' harsh words about *transcendent reference* concealed a warm friendship for what only wanted a name to become the *semantic dimension of meaning*.
But while Lewis hints at such an account, he does not give it; nor does he explicate unambiguously his conception of the relation of objective statements to terminating judgments. Here also he havers between an identification of the *semantic reference* of an objective statement with its *sense meaning* (a thesis which corresponds to the complete translatability approach to statements about the past mentioned above) and the conception that an objective statement must be *equipollent* with a set of sense meanings in order to have experiential significance. His stress on real connections is in the right direction, but, unfortunately, he *tacitly* presupposes that real connections are limited to connections between phenomenal given-nesses which fall within the same specious or epistemological present.

438   DATA, REALITY, AND THE MIND-BODY PROBLEM

What is the relation between a verified moment-slice of the Jonesean sense-biography and the remainder of the world-story *including the other segments of the Jonesean sense-biography, in virtue of which the latter can be said to be confirmed?*

At this point in our argument we seem to be confronted with a dilemma. *On the one hand*, if we consider all the world stories formulable with the individual constants and predicates of the Jonesean language, which stories include a given momentary sense-biographical slice, the verification of that slice would seem equally to confirm, and hence equally not to confirm, all these stories. *To say otherwise would surely be to claim that the slice requires one specific context of sentences: but are not the sentences that make up a world-story logically independent of one another? On the other hand*, unless the verification of the moment-slice *picks out* for confirmation *one* of the infinite number of formulable world-story contexts, there is no such thing as confirmation. This clash or antinomy boils down to the following:

(A) *A confirmed sentence-system must be one in which a sub-set of sentences (a sense-biographical slice) requires all the others;* and (B) *No factual sentence requires another factual sentence that is not logically contained in it.*

VII

The Syntax of Temporal Predicates. It will be remembered that in our first attempt at characterizing the type of system formed by the sentences making up the world-story confirmed by Jones, we suggested that the unity of the system might be constituted by the story's being about a coherent spatio-temporal structure. This suggestion looked promising, but an examination of the world-story as time structure has led to the above impasse. Perhaps, however, from this impasse we can gain a clue as to how our analysis should proceed. We have spoken of the individual constants of the world-story as having subscripts indicating that they belong to a coördinate system. They do so as constituting the field of the relational predicate 'before'. In other words, the story involves a set of sentences illustrated by 'i_7 is before i_8'. Now the term 'before' is the relational term it is because of its syntax. This syntax involves the familiar postulates of serial order. In these terms we can formulate our problem as follows:

Unless the syntax of the term 'before' is geared in with the factual predicates of the story in such a way that 'i_n' and 'i_{n+m}' can belong to the story only if the predicates other than 'before' conjoined in it with these individual constants also conform to certain order requirements, *then a given biographical slice can form a world-story with any set of sentences so long as it has the proper background of sentences involving the predicate 'before', necessary in order for it to constitute a story at all, and confirmability flies out the window.*

Meaning and Syntax. We have arrived above at the notion that the predicates of a language in which a confirmed world-story can be formulated must stand in certain "order-relations" to one another. This is a vague concept, and would be of very little assistance were it not for the fact that it dovetails with certain considerations we advanced some time ago. We argued [in Section IV] above that 'means' or 'designates' is a non-factual term. This can be elaborated into the notion that semantic sentences are non-factual sentences which are true or false in a purely formal sense, that is to say, are decidable on purely formal grounds. Thus, consider the question: In virtue of what are two different predicates 'ϕ' and 'θ' different? We might be tempted to say either (1) because they are empirically different marks, or (2) because they have different meanings. The first answer is obviously inadequate. The second is more satisfying. But once we have drawn a sharp distinction between *meaning* as a concept of empirical psychology, and *meaning* or *designation* as a concept of epistemological semantics, we see that though the second answer is true, it does not clarify. The question asked above can no longer be characterized as a psychological side-issue, *but must be answered in terms appropriate to the conception of 'means' or 'designates' as a purely formal concept.* The conclusion at which we are arriving is that from the standpoint of epistemological analysis, the predicates of a language are differentiated from one another in terms of the formal rôles they play in the language. Using the term 'syntax' in a broader sense than is current, we could say "different syntax, different predicate; same syntax, same predicate". We shall prefer to say that predicates are differentiated only by the conformation rules which specify their combining properties. The concept of the combining properties of predicates (and it must be remembered that in this paper we are concerned only with primitive predicates) concerns the relation of predicates to individual constants in the following way. It involves (1) *the concept of a "skeletal" relational predicate (there may be more than one, provided they are syntactically related) which signifies the fundamental type of order in which the individuals to which the language can refer must stand;* [9] and (2) the concept of restrictions on the non-relational predicates which can be associated with given individual constants where the restrictions are a function of (a) the predicates, (b) the (skeletal) relational sentences in which these individual constants are making an appearance. These restrictions constitute the conformation rules for the predicates of the language. *We have here a coherence theory of meaning characterized in purely syntactical terms.* Rather, we have here the germ of such a theory, the working out of which must be reserved for another occasion. *It is in terms of such conformation rules that predicate families are formally specified ("determinates under common determinables") and different predicate families are distinguished and related.*

[9] These skeletal relations are, to use Hume's phrase, "relations of matter of fact" in the world to which the language applies. Putting the matter crudely, and with the aid of Hume's terminology, we can say that "relations of ideas" can only be 'defined' by reference to "relations of matter of fact." See also footnote 13 below.

440   DATA, REALITY, AND THE MIND-BODY PROBLEM

The implication of such an approach to *meaning* for the concept of a *natural law* will be touched on later in the paper.

The Pragmatic Meta-language. The next step in the line of thought we have developed in this paper is to see that 'verified', 'confirmed' and 'meaningful' are to be understood as predicates belonging in a type of meta-language the central concept of which is that of a confirmed world-story. As a matter of fact, meta-languages of this type alone are meta-*languages* in the complete sense of the term, for they alone deal with languages *as languages*, that is to say, as *meaningful* symbols. Syntactics and semantics as epistemological rather than empirical disciplines are abstractions from pure pragmatics, and are misunderstood in a way which leads directly to psychologism when their fragmentary character is overlooked. It is with some hesitation that I speak of these meta-languages as pragmatic, for they have nothing to do with language as expressive or persuasive, or with such other concepts of empirical psychology as have come to be characterized as the subject-matter of a science of pragmatics. Pure pragmatics or, *which is the same thing,* epistemology, is a formal rather than a factual area. In addition to the concepts of pure syntactics and semantics, pure pragmatics is concerned with other concepts which are *normative* as opposed to the factual concepts of psychology, as 'true' is normative as opposed to 'believed', or 'valid' is normative (again, remember that our use of the term "normative" is tentative) as opposed to 'inferred'. These other concepts round off a system of concepts which undercuts the dispute between Rationalist and Empiricist. Psychologism is to be as carefully avoided in the treatment of specifically pragmatic concepts, as in the partial areas of semantics (Plato, Hume), and syntactics (J. S. Mill).

In addition to the resources of syntactics and semantics, a pragmatic meta-language involves the concepts of *symbol-type* and *symbol-token*. These presuppose the concept of designation. Thus, 'token' is a metalinguistic predicate, and is used properly when it is said that the state of affairs designated by one expression in a language is a token of another (perhaps the same) expression in the language. The formal significance of the concept of token is brought out by the following: If 'p' designates p, and p is a token of 'q', then all the metalinguistic predicates which apply to 'q' apply also to p. In other words, we have here a grammar in accordance with which metalinguistic predicates can be associated with certain expressions belonging on the "right hand side of designation sentences". We shall consider the concept of *token* in more detail at a later stage in our argument.

Finally, a pragmatic meta-language requires its object language to contain a predicate designating a reflexive, symmetrical and transitive relation, R, which, whatever its *factual* rôle, plays an additional formal rôle as the *coex* relation of the pragmatic system (cf. ENWW, p. 654). 'Coex' appears in expressions of the form 'p coex q'. The *factual* correlate would be 'aRb';

REALISM AND THE NEW WAY OF WORDS   441

(sentence) 'p' being true of *a* and 'q' of *b*. These resources enable the following definitions:

The meaning base of a language is a world-story formulated in that language. A world-story can be semantically characterized as designating a world consisting of a connected system of atomic states of affairs which conform to a set of natural laws (the status of which will be explained in a moment).

Languages come in families. The languages of a family have primitive descriptive predicates and skeletal relational predicates in common, but not individual constants. The predicates of a language family are differentiated from one another by conformation rules. These latter specify certain formal implications which hold in all world-stories which are meaning-bases of languages in the family. Hence they specify the natural laws of the worlds designated by these stories.

It is a necessary condition of an empirically meaningful language that every universal designated by a primitive descriptive predicate of the language either (1) be exemplified in the worlds of the language only by states of affairs which belong to the domain of *coex*, or (2) function in a law with such universals.

A confirmed world-story is a story which contains a sub-structure of sentences, (*a*) which can be built into only this complete story in view of the conformation rules (natural laws) of the language, (*b*) the *designata* of which sub-structure constitute a set of items mutually related by the relation *coex*, and (*c*) which sub-structure consists of sentences *verified in the story*.

A sentence 'p' will be said to be a sentence verified in story S, if *p* (the *designatum* of 'p' in the world of S) stands in the coex relation to a state of affairs which is a token of 'p'. This token of 'p' will be said to be the *verifying token* of 'p'. Each sub-structure of verified sentences as characterized in the preceding paragraph will be called a *verification base* of S.

A set of conformation rules which defines a class of languages at least one member of which has a meaning base which permits of pragmatic characterization as a confirmed world-story, will be said to constitute an *empirical language form*. It will be remembered that the conformation rules of a language determine the meanings of its predicates. Thus, an empirical language form defines a class of languages involving the same predicates. However, while the languages of a family have their predicates in common, they do not have individual constants in common. The individual constants of a language are formally determinate only with respect to that single world-story which is the meaning-base of the language.[10] Now, not all the languages associated with a given empirical language form will have a meaning-base consisting of a *confirmed* world-story

[10] I have expanded this point as far as individual constants are concerned in "Epistemology and the New Way of Words," *The Journal of Philosophy*, Vol. 44, no. 24, pp. 655 ff.

The conclusion at which we have arrived in the above paragraph can be summed up by saying that the world designated by the meaning-base of a language is the 'actual world' of that language. Needless to say, while the world-story which is the meaning-base of a language occupies a privileged position with respect to that language, the latter permits the formulation of false statements about its 'actual world.' Consequently, Carnap's distinction (*Meaning and Necessity*, pp. 8 ff.) between 'possible states of the universe' (expressed by false state descriptions), and 'the actual state of the universe' (expressed by the true state description) *is relative to a language*. The world designated by the meaning-base of any language is the *fundamentum* of a set of state descriptions, and is 'the actual state of the universe (of that language)' in relation to which one of the state descriptions (the meaning-base) is true.

442   DATA, REALITY, AND THE MIND-BODY PROBLEM

(i.e., be correlated with a world which is completely 'known' by 'minds' contained in that world). Thus, while any language of the family will have predicates which appear in a confirmed world-story, only those languages whose meaning-base is itself a confirmed world-story will have individual constants appearing in a confirmed world-story. Since we are explicating the linguistic implications of omniscience, we shall be concerned only with languages of the latter type. Thus, we shall define an *empirical language* to be a language whose meaning-base is a confirmed world-story. The study of languages which are empirical only in the weaker sense that they belong to a family of languages which includes at least one empirical language in the stronger sense we have just defined, must be deferred to a later occasion.

Any atomic sentence in an empirical language L will be said to be a *confirmable sentence of L*. A confirmable sentence of L which belongs to the story S which is the *meaning base* of L, will be said to be *confirmed in S*, and will be called a *confirmed sentence of L*. Similarly, a sentence verified in story S will be called a *verified sentence of L*.[11]

It is a direct implication of our argument that the predicate '(factually) true sentence of L' is decidable on purely formal grounds. (It must be constantly born in mind that we are discussing epistemological issues in the frame of reference of "perfect languages" and omniscience. The implication of our discussion for the significance of epistemological predicates in relation to "imperfect" languages will be drawn toward the conclusion of the paper.) With respect to language L resting on story S which is its meaning base, it is decidable that $\phi(i_n)$ is the case rather than $\theta(i_n)$.[12] The concept of factual truth is a semiotic concept appropriate to a certain type of calculus, namely empirical languages. The notion of an empirical language is itself a purely formal notion. To suppose that it makes sense to speak of THE set of factually true sentences, is to cast aside painfully acquired insights, and to return to the metaphysics of Meinong and the New Realists. Semantic truth is not "absolute truth". To say this is not to say that truth is relative to psychological facts whether needs, convictions or satisfactions. It is, however, relative to appropriately constituted calculi; that is, as long as an expression in a calculus of a certain kind has the ap-

[11] If we asked a classical rationalist to verbalize about the confirmation of the Jonesean story through the verification of a segment of the story, the answer would be instructive. As I have since formulated it in "Epistemology and the New Way of Words" (see note 6 above) . . . "He appeals to an *a priori* principle of supplementation, the principle of sufficient reason, which is bound up with the existence of a realm of universals so related to one another that they constitute a system which can be viewed in one light as a system of necessary connections, and in another as a system of compossibilities. (It is this system which underlies the concept of the laws of nature.) Thus in answer to our question the rationalist might be expected to say, 'Omniscient Jones justifies his selection of a group of sentences as those which are true of his world and constitute its story, by reference to the fact that this group includes a sub-set of verified sentences the meanings of which are propositions known to require supplementation by reference to the principle of sufficient reason, and which, given the structure of the domain of universals meant by the predicates of the language, can be supplemented in only one way to make a complete world-story.' " For the rationalistic account of verification, see note 6 above.

[12] Compare ENWW, pp. 658-659.

REALISM AND THE NEW WAY OF WORDS   443

propriate characteristics, it is properly characterized as a factually true sentence of the calculus.

The semantic analysis of factual truth, as well as the semantic analysis of factual meaning is incomplete as long as it fails to do justice to the claims of *coherence*. Not that coherence is the *definition* of truth. The point is rather that the Idealistic conception of coherence has its contribution to make to the theory of meaning, confirmation, and truth.

The final abandonment of Naïve Realism comes with the realization that the right-hand side of designation sentences together with the predicate 'designates' and the semi-quotes on the left-hand side are all alike formal devices belonging to the grammar of epistemological predicates; that is to say, their function is the purely formal one of hooking up with the rules relating to the assignment of such predicates as 'verified sentence of L', 'true sentence of L', 'meaningful predicate of L' (see below) and many derivative epistemological predicates that would have to be introduced in a complete discussion. This means that "talking about the *designata* of sentences" is an essential ingredient in "characterizing these sentences in terms of epistemological predicates". If we introduce the term 'world' as a collective term for the designata of a world story, then it is a purely formal truth that every story in every empirical language designates a world.

The pure theory of empirical languages as formally defined systems which are about worlds in which they are used, has no place for THE world; but only for the world designated by the story which is the meaning base of a language. A given set of conformation rules defines a family of empirical languages, *or, which is the same thing, a family of possible worlds which have the same laws.* An understanding of the completely non-factual character of epistemological statements rests on the insight that not even the predicates 'verified' and 'confirmed' have an intrinsic tie with any single world, with "the REAL world". They are purely formal predicates and no properly constructed world-story stands in a privileged position with respect to them. This principle of indifference could be discarded only if something akin to an ontological argument could be formulated in the pure theory of empirical languages; if it could be shown, for example, that only one set of conformation rules is possible which enables a story to be constructed in the language form of which they are the rules; and if only one story could be constructed in that language form.[13]

---

[13] We are now in a position to point out an important sense in which the connections of meaning specified by conformation rules are truth-functional in character. "Surely," it might be objected, "matters of meaning can hardly depend on what is the case!" Yet from the standpoint of Pure Semantics the meanings of the expressions of a language *do* depend on what is the case, though not in "*the* actual world" but rather (1) in the family of worlds which is the family of the language form to which the language in question belongs, as far as its predicates are concerned, and (2) in that world of this family which is *the world of the language in question*, for its individual constants.

Put in this context, the formal characterization of the primitive one-place predicates of a language involves the following: (a) the specification of one or more basic relations, (b) the specification of a set of worlds consisting of all possible relational arrays of atomic states of affairs exemplifying the qualitative universals designated by these

444   DATA, REALITY, AND THE MIND-BODY PROBLEM

A comment is relevant at this point concerning the term 'existence' which is beginning to cause trouble again. The syntactical dimension of 'exists' has been clarified. This clarification is exemplified in the translation of 'Lions exist' into 'Something is a lion'. There is, however, a further usage of 'exists' which is a more restricted one, since it is used appropriately only in connection with factual expressions, whereas the syntactical sense is not so restricted. I am referring to the usage in which the term 'exists' is associated with either (1) empirical class terms, as in the sentence '(the class) *Lion* exists' (as opposed to 'Lions exist'), or (2) logically proper names, as in the sentence 'i_n exists' where 'i_n' is a logically proper name. Let us introduce the root pragmatic sense of 'exists' as follows:

Let us say that the primitive factual expressions (predicates and individual constants) of an empirical language L are (empirically) *meaningful* expressions of L. We shall then say that the class ϕ exists in the world designated by the meaning base, S, of L, if 'ϕ' designates ϕ and 'ϕ' is a meaningful expression of L; similarly, that i_n exists in the world designated by S, if 'i_n' designates i_n and 'i_n' is a meaningful expression of L. In the case of primitive classes and individuals, the corresponding expressions must appear in S in order to be meaningful, and indeed to belong to L at all. The existence of complex classes and individuals is defined in terms of the existence of primitive classes and individuals.

Since existence in this sense is a "quasi-pragmatic" concept corresponding to 'meaningful,' to say that universals or classes exist is not to lump them together with lions. The sense in which lions exist corresponds rather with '(factually) true.' Thus one can admit that classes and individuals exist without swallowing a two-story world.[14] Note that the pragmatic concept of existence applies only to the designata of the factual expressions of the object-language. It does not make sense to say that verification exists, or that truth or entailment exists, in this pragmatic sense. That verification, truth, entailment, and, in general, formal "facts" or systems *do not exist* in either this "quasi-pragmatic" sense or the (closely related) sense which correlates with '(empirically) true' is the final clarification and destruction of the rationalism-empiricism issue.

---

predicates, subject only to the condition that, (*c*), certain formal implications (synthetic in the kantian sense) involving these predicates and relations are true of all these worlds, such that, (*d*), each predicate can be distinguished from the others in terms of the rôle it plays in these formal implications. The specifying of such a set of formal implications is exactly what is accomplished by a set of conformation rules. For a more complete discussion see my article, "Concepts as Involving Laws and Inconceivable Without Them," in *Philosophy of Science*, October, 1948.

[14] The solution of the problem of universals thus consists exactly in showing that the following statements are all true: (1) "There are universals." (2) "Some mental events *mean* universals." (3) "It is nonsense to speak of any psychological relationship between mental events and universals." The solution involves, as we have seen, *first* a making explicit of the ambiguities of the term 'existence'; *second* a distinction between "meaning" as a term belonging to the framework of epistemological or logical analysis, and "meaning" as a descriptive term in empirical psychology relating to habits of response to and manipulation of linguistic symbols. The classical conception of mind as apprehending universals and propositions is based on a confusion of these two frames of reference. To deny that universals exist *when speaking in the logical frame*, is as mistaken as to assert that universals exist when speaking in the framework of the psychological description of thought. We must, and can, avoid both *logical nominalism* and *ontological realism*.

REALISM AND THE NEW WAY OF WORDS   445

No Predicaments. The pragmatic meta-language we have been considering characterizes the meaning base, S, of its object language as confirmed
in relation to many verification bases, those, namely, which concern successive momentary experiences on the part of Jones. That a pragmatic meta-
language should be thus neutral with respect to successive Jones-experi-
ences does not startle. Can it be similarly neutral as between Jones and his
neighbor Smith? The principle is exactly the same. Demonstratives do not
belong in the object language. They are not to be confused with proper
names—e.g., 'i_3', 'i_9'—either as types (which is obvious) or as tokens. They
belong, rather, to the pragmatic meta-language, and, indeed, are to be construed in terms of (certain) *tokens* of expressions of this meta-language.
The trivial fact that *tokens* are localized in a world entails no provincialism
on the part of language *types*. Indeed, the concept of such provincialism is
self-refuting.

Type and Token Again. In introducing the meta-linguistic predicates
'type' and 'token', we pointed out that it would be a mistake to conceive
of type as classes of tokens. The distinction between type and token being
traceable to the difference between the left and right hand side of designation sentences, there is a difference of semantic level incompatible with
such a conception. On the other hand, while a type expression is not a
class of tokens, the tokens of a given type expression are specified in terms
of one or more empirical classes. It is essential for the discussion of the
mind-body problem below to realize that empirical difference of symbols
relates in epistemological contexts to language only as token. One and
the same language as type may have two or more sets of tokens.[15] (Thus,
from the epistemological standpoint, English and German as empirically
meaningful languages constitute two sets of token-classes for the same type
expressions.) The identity of a language as type is not an empirical identity,
but rather a formal distinctness bound up with its formation and conformation rules. Same formal rules, same language as type; though it may be
represented in its world by many empirically different sets of token classes
which bear its meaning.

All our argument up to date is the unpacking of the notion that meaningful language is language about a world in which it is used. This means
that in the idea which defines the what-it-is to be a meaningful language,
it is an analytic truth that linguistic tokens conform to the rules of the language. If we look at the matter from the opposite side, we may say that
to characterize certain items in a world as true, verified, meaningful, etc.,
is to talk in a pragmatic meta-language about designata of sentences in a
story being tokens of other sentences in the story.[16] Now we do not speak

[15] Since writing the above it has been called to my attention that Professor D.
Rynin, in the essay which accompanies his edition of Johnson's *Treatise on Language,*
makes a similar distinction. See also ENWW, pp. 653 f.

[16] Consider an item in the world designated by a world-story, where the item is a
token of a sentence which designates another item in that world. Thus (1) the first
item *qua* token designates the second item. Now (2) consider the relation of the first

446   DATA, REALITY, AND THE MIND-BODY PROBLEM

a language proper. It is because of this that there is a sting in the pragmatic concept of meaningful language. *It is this which leads us to confuse the necessary formal harmony between type and token with factual relationships of utterances to standards or norms.* For it is the whole pragmatic mode of speech with its (among others) 'type', 'token', 'verified', 'true', 'world-story', and, to sum up, 'meaningful language', that shames our language behavior, and consequently carries on the philosopher's traditional task of "criticism". Behind the therapeutic activity of the modern Socrates lies the medicine kit of a more or less fully developed pure theory of empirically meaningful languages. The task of philosophy today is to determine the specifications of such kits, and make them generally available.

Pure Pragmatics and the Uniformity of Nature. The above account of pure pragmatics and pragmatic meta-languages is a tentative account of an intricate and highly technical area. It would be foolish for me to pretend that I have done more than grope in the right direction. Before we turn to comment on the specific problem of Realism, let us sum up our results to date by pointing out an historical parallel. Kant argued that conformity to the causal principle (the temporal *schema* of the principle of sufficient reason) is a necessary condition of the possibility of temporal experience. We argue that conformity of its expressions to conformation rules built upon the skeletal predicate 'before' (the temporal form of the coherence theory of meaning) is a necessary condition of the possibility of a meaningful temporal language. *Put in the quasi-pragmatic mode of speech*, this amounts to saying that a necessary condition of the meaningfulness of a temporal language, is that the temporal order of the events occurring in the world it is about, be reflected in a necessary and systematic coherence of the characteristics exemplified by these events. Other parallels to Kant might be drawn. We note only that the truth of Kant's conception of Space and Time as *pure* manifolds is contained in the pragmatic conception of skeletal relations in terms of which the primitive one-place predicates of a language are distinguished, and hence, in a sense, defined. This latter also underlies the insight contained in definitions of causality in terms of a space-time indifference of the laws of nature.

First Thoughts on Realism. We must now examine another aspect of the Jonesean world-story in terms of which we have been formulating epistemological issues. We have contrasted not only a slice of Jones' sense-

---

.qua item in the world to the second item. (Thus, consider the relation of p to aRb where 'p' designates p, 'aRb' designates aRb and p tokens 'aRb'). In considering this relationship, we are still operating in the formal mode of speech. We see that p must be a complex fact, consisting of, say, q, r and s, where q tokens 'a', r tokens 'R' and s tokens 'b'. In this respect, p as fact in the world must *map* aRb. The ineffable mapping of which Wittgenstein speaks is thus capable of characterization in pure pragmatics, for it is a confusion of *token-designation* as in (1) and the mapping characterized in (2).

It might be pointed out here that the *epistemological* concept of *objective reference*, is that of *psychological events* in perception as *tokens of sentences about physical objects.*

REALISM AND THE NEW WAY OF WORDS   447

biography with his sense-biography as a whole, but also the latter with sentences which do not belong to the Jonesean, or indeed to any other sense-biography belonging to the story. We have spoken as though physical event sentences belong to such an idealization of the sentence structures we use, in exactly the same way as do sense-biographical sentences. If asked to justify this assumption, our answer would probably be that a human sense-biography is not by itself coherent, in that causal considerations inevitably take us beyond it. In schematic metalinguistic statements we speak of the laws of psycho-physics, implying that it makes sense to speak of a language proper the conformation rules of which tie together predicates appearing in the verification base of the story with predicates which do not. Two questions arise: (1) Does this make sense? (2) What justification can be offered for saying that our language is to be understood in terms of such a structure?

As to the first question, the answer is surely "yes". The concept of an empirically meaningful language rests on that of a verification base, but by no means presupposes that every sentence of the story which is its meaning base is to be found in that verification base. That the Jonesean world-story and the language in which it is formulated are, as we have characterized them, *realistic*, is clear. It is essential to note, however, that this realistic character is conceived of as a consequence of specific conformation rules, and that if it is possible for an empirically meaningful language to be realistic, it also makes sense to speak of non-realistic empirically meaningful languages. If it is a theorem in pure pragmatics that a meaningful language must be defined in terms of conformation rules, the only requirement that the conformation rules of a given language must fulfil is that they be sufficient to permit the definition in that language of a confirmed world-story. The difference between 'realistic' and 'non-realistic' languages is to be defined in terms of differences in the formal properties of different sets of conformation rules. Thus it seems possible to conceive of stories of the following different types:

1. Stories which consist entirely of verified sentences.
2. Stories which include some sentences which are confirmed but not verified. These can be divided in turn into two types:
   a. Stories all the predicates of which appear in the verification basis of the story.
   b. Stories some of the predicates of which appear only in sentences which are confirmed but not verified.

If we introduce the term 'datum predicate' for predicates which appear in the verification base of a story; and 'non-datum predicate' for those that do not, then the three possibilities listed above become: I. All sentences verified sentences, all predicates datum predicates; IIa. Some merely confirmed sentences, all predicates datum predicates; IIb. Some merely confirmed sentences, some non-datum predicates. As far as I can see, I. would

448   DATA, REALITY, AND THE MIND-BODY PROBLEM

be what is meant by a non-realistic story. II*a* is a realistic story of the type proposed by Neutral Monism. II*b* is that proposed by common or garden variety realism.

What concerns us here is that epistemology as the pure theory of languages can develop the formal properties of languages with different conformation rules; can compare realistic with non-realistic languages; but as a purely formal discipline cannot choose THE conformation rules or THE language. It is a mistake to look for a formal (epistemological) justification of "Realism" or "Idealism", etc.

If, on the other hand, we turn from epistemological to factual statements, we make use of *language* as a factual (psychological) category. In this context a language is a set of causally related events and habits, and the distinction between language and meta-language a factual distinction between habits of different levels, the latter being, in *a causal sense* built upon the former. It is a task of empirical psychology to characterize the factors leading to the adoption and abandonment of language habits. Further, "formal" (here used as a *factual* predicate) meta-languages might be characterized, tentatively, by empirical psychology as habits relating to the "clarification" or "unpacking" of linguistic phenomena. From the empirical standpoint, the linguistic behavior of an epistemologist is evaluated in terms of the clarification it brings, by doing more adequately what is done by metalinguistic activity at the common-sense level. This suggests that the only way to recommend a "non-realistic epistemology" of a certain sort is to give a formal account of a language which combines the following features: (*a*) its conformation rules require a confirmed world-story to include no atomic sentence not appearing in the verification base of the story (type I above), and (*b*) the language is such that from its conformation rules via introduced defined terms one can derive rules which would be *recognized by one observing the epistemologist as echoing the language habits of scientists.* It is something along these lines that the conventional realist is asking for when he demands that the idealist or positivist "come across" with the "sense-datum language" to which he is always referring.[17]

[17] We have been insisting that epistemological predicates, whether they appear in the mouth of the philosopher or the common sense man, have the same formal status as logical predicates in the narrower sense. (I should not object to the term 'transcendental logic' in place of 'pure pragmatics'). We shall see in Section VIII below that from the formal or epistemological standpoint a "here-now" sentence is such only as a token of a pragmatic meta-sentence, and as such *presupposes* a confirmed world-story. Thus the idea that the term 'protocol sentence' is a factual one belonging to the language of psychology, rests on a confusion between *psychological indubitability* and the *formal status of verified sentences in an empirically meaningful language.*

From the standpoint of pure pragmatics, the meaningfulness of expressions involving variables depends on their relation to a complete world-story. This applies also to Russellian descriptions. Furthermore, a world-story as a whole is logically prior to its parts. "How can it be that in the formal mode of speech we can speak of objects (languages-proper, world-stories) which transcend humanly possible experience?"

REALISM AND THE NEW WAY OF WORDS   449

Sense-Data Again. That human sense-biographies are incomplete, and would require supplementation in order to yield the story of the world in which we live is hardly a matter for debate. Yet what would be the nature of this supplementation? If one answers, "physical event sentences", one is likely to meet the contention that sentences about physical events make sense only as translatable into sense-biographical sentences.[18] Let us introduce the term '*verificatum*' as a means of referring to the *designatum* of a verified sentence in a world-story. Could it seriously be proposed that human sense-biographies require completion by sentences about physical events, where the latter are conceived to be translatable into sentences about *verificata?* Hardly, for then physical event sentences would not perform the work of *supplementing* the sense-biographies which are *ex hypothesi* incomplete. *What must be meant is that the physical event sentences are translatable into a set of alternative sense-biographies, only one of which consists of verified sentences,* that is to say, designates *verificata.* This won't work. The incompleteness with which the argument began was a *causal* incompleteness and (1) *possibilia* are not causes; (2) the problem of incompleteness would break out for each of the alternative sense-biographies. I suspect that in addition to the semantic psychologism which underlies the demand for the translatability of physical event sentences into sentences about actual or possible sense-data, there is an additional confusion which adds to its plausibility. This is the confusion between physical *object* sentences and physical *event* sentences. Physical object sentences themselves involve a reference to sets of *possibilia* [19] and if these *possibilia* are confused with possible sensa (a confusion which involves the mistake of taking *actual*

The question is a confused one. It must be clarified by a distinction between *factual* statements about the utterance limitations of formal scientists, and formal sentences about meta-linguistic tokens in a constituted world. See Section VIII below.

[18] In "Epistemology and the New Way of Words" I point out (p. 656, note 20) that "(the) conception that . . . a set of verified sentences can formally entail and be entailed by a complete world-story . . . without the story being translatable into—or 'reducible to'—the set of verified sentences, is what distinguishes my position from positivism." The use of the term 'entail' in this passage obviously rests on our analysis of causal necessity in terms of logical necessity.

[19] Object- or thing-sentences are clearly more complicated than event-sentences. Thus they involve a special class of predicates, namely *dispositional predicates.* These are to be understood in terms of the concept (which they help define) of *alternative* event sequences which involve (1) the same functional correlation of non-dispositional predicates (laws) and (2) the same *things.* As for (2) it is clear that a language which includes dispositional predicates must also include a special class of individual constants (said to designate *things* or *substances*) which combine with these predicates to constitute sentences. Since the syntax of these individual constants will not admit of their combining directly with spatio-temporal predicates, a relational predicate 'is an event happening to' must also be introduced. The syntax of substance terms, dispositional predicates, event-terms and event predicates would define the meaning of such expressions as "would have happened to the same thing if . . ." It would also clarify such terms as 'change', 'interaction', etc. For an excellent account of the perplexities which arise when one forgets that sentences about substances are derived expressions in a language which is about a *single* world of *states of affairs*, see the selection from Broad's *Examination of McTaggart's Philosophy* below, pp. 472 ff.; also note 10 above.

450   DATA, REALITY, AND THE MIND-BODY PROBLEM

sensa to be external physical events—see next paragraph), the phenomenalist position gains an unjustified appearance of dovetailing with common usage. It is clear, however, that it is physical *event* sentences and not physical *thing* sentences which the phenomenalist must translate into sentences about possible sensa.

As for the notion that the predicates of physical-object sentences in a world-story must be definable in terms of sense-predicates, the following comment is sufficient. The pragmatic meta-language of L distinguishes predicates of L by means of conformation rules; thus *predicate of L* and *law of S* are correlative notions, as are *quality manifested in W* and *natural necessity in W* (*Law of W*, where 'law' does not refer to a linguistic expression)—where W is the world meant by S. *It is nonsense to speak of the same qualities obeying two different sets of laws in different contexts. To say that physical events are complexes of sense qualities, is to say that physical laws are analysable into psychological laws.* It is perhaps more plausible to say that sense qualities are complexes of physical events. If so, Neutral Monism is plausible only as physicalism. These are issues that cannot be settled by a mere appeal to epistemological concepts. The usual argument rests on the psychologistic blunder of supposing that only predicates appearing sometimes in verified sentences can be meaningful. But psychological meaning must not be confused with either designation or meaningfulness. A third sense of 'sense-datum language' is bound up with the contention that the verification base of a language cannot be formulated in physicalistic terms. This question is discussed below in the section on the mind-body problem in the new way of words.

VIII

The Pragmatics of 'Now'. We noted above (p. 437) that ". . . to speak of the universe of discourse of a story as dividing into a past, a present and a future, is to speak . . . of the story in relation to a verification," and that "consequently, the distinction between past, present and future relates not to the *meaning* of a world story, but to its *meaningfulness*." In terms of the arguments which followed, this means that temporal distinctions are bound up with the specifically pragmatic concepts of verification and confirmation. Indeed, as we shall see, *the distinctively temporal predicates belong in a pragmatic metalanguage.* Since the applicability of pragmatic predicates to the expressions of a language presupposes that the language is "about a coherent world," and since the coherence of a temporal world is "causality", we are in a position to de-psychologize Kant's argument and show that *the use of distinctly temporal predicates logically presupposes the framework of a causally ordered world.* Furthermore, the following discussion lays the foundation for a general theory of egocentric expressions and demonstratives.

REALISM AND THE NEW WAY OF WORDS   451

That the language of common sense involves a pragmatic stratum is clear from its use of epistemological predicates. The radical pervasiveness of this stratum is easily overlooked in the absence of an analysis of distinctively temporal utterances in the framework of the pure theory of languages. In this connection we must abandon the assumption that the immediate experience of Omniscience Jones need only token object-language sentences in order to be a model adequate to the clarification of all epistemological issues. In doing so, however, we shall raise questions that take us beyond the scope of the present paper.

It will have been noticed by the student of McTaggart that the world designated by the Jonesean world-story constitutes, as we have characterized it above (pp. 436 ff.), a *B-series*. That is to say, it is a series of items which are the field of the relation *earlier than* or *before*. What he calls an *A-series*, namely a division of the items into a past, a present and a future, has been stated by us to be bound up with a confirmation of the story in relation to a given set of the verified sentences of the story (those which designate a momentary set of co-experiences). Our analysis needs further refinements.

McTaggart, speaking as a naïve realist with respect to the events which the object-language is about, puts our claim that the A-predicates ('past', 'present', and 'future') are bound up with the pragmatic metalanguage into ontological terms when he says that an A-series is a matter of *appearance* rather than *reality*. He argues that the relation *earlier than* is a temporal relation only by virtue of its connection with the A-characteristics; but that it cannot be defined in terms of them for as a transitive, asymmetrical relation it underlies the distribution and redistribution of the A-characteristics. It is as such a non-temporal relation, and gains the appearance of being a temporal relation through the appearance which is presentness. The constituents of reality as related by this non-temporal relation, which as such should not be called 'earlier than', make up what he calls the *C-series*. Our distinction between world-story sentences and pragmatic meta-sentences corresponds to his distinction between reality and appearance. The world designated by a temporal world-story contains a skeletal relation which corresponds to his non-temporal C-relation in that its complete character as *temporal* transcends its object-language status. To call it 'earlier than' or 'before' is to view it in another context.

Statements making a particular assignment of A-predicates are interpreted by McTaggart as *factual* statements which, however, are about *apparent*, as opposed to *real*, facts. Our claim is that an utterance "Now (. . . .)" is to be interpreted as a token of a pragmatic meta-sentence. But this is just a beginning, for the utterance, if valid, must be simultaneous with the state of affairs (. . . .), and, if meta-linguistic, must involve the sentence designating the state of affairs (. . . .). *What we must actually do is reconstruct the notion of a world containing tokens of pragmatic meta-sentences* to the effect that certain items are *verificata*—a *verificatum*

2   DATA, REALITY, AND THE MIND-BODY PROBLEM

being defined as the *designatum* of a verified sentence—where the pragmatic tokens and *verificata* are not only co-experienced, but the pragmatic tokens *say* they are co-experienced. This we do as follows:

Consider the sentence 'p' which belongs to a set of verified sentences N about a momentary set of co-experiences C. '*Verificatum(p)*' is a type sentence in the pragmatic meta-language. Consider an experience *r*, belonging to C, which plays the rôle of a token of the pragmatic meta-sentence '*r* coex *p* · *verificatum(p)*'. This token is the reconstruction of an utterance "Ecce(p)", and provides the key to the understanding of all derived "ego"-centric expressions. (This revision of my earlier account was stimulated by reflection on tantalizing § 50 of Reichenbach's *Elements of Symbolic Logic*.)

Two remarks are relevant: (1) The above analysis clearly makes it necessary to distinguish sharply between "here-now" statements and what we have called "verifying tokens". (2) The above analysis involves the notion of the constitution of *empirical-language-cum-world* in a meta-meta-language, and suggests of a hierarchy of such constitutions.[20]

Apart from such an analysis as the above, the distinction between time merely as serial order, and time as involving the contrast between past, present and future simply cannot be made; for any attempt to clarify this contrast solely in terms of relative position in a linear series cannot bring out the 'ecce!' element involved in genuine temporal distinctions. *On the other hand, our account does not involve the vicious regress found by McTaggart*, since temporal distinctions do not apply to the pragmatic *as pragmatic*. "Now (verified ('p'))" is nonsense. Only the names of empirical language sentences make sense with pragmatic predicates.

IX

The Mind-Body Problem in the New Way of Words. Since we have been led to the conclusion that in the type of world-story relevant to a clarification of our employment of epistemological predicates, there belong physical event sentences as well as sense-biographical sentences, it is clear that the meeting place of these two sets of sentences in such a structure requires analysis. The problem as to the coherence of these two sets of sentences must be distinguished from the psychologistic pseudo-problem of "perceptual epistemology".

As containing the above two types of sentences, the Jonesean world-story *apparently* will contain the following two sets of sentences: (1) the set of verified sentences constituting the sense-biography of Jones; (2) the set of physical event sentences constituting the biography of the sensory centers of the Jonesean brain. It is in terms of these two sets of sentences that the hook-up of *verified sense-biographical sentences* with *confirmed physical event sentences* must be analysed.

It is frequently claimed that psychological advances are pointing toward

[20] For an elaboration of this point see the concluding pages of my "Pure Pragmatics and Epistemology" in the July, 1947, issue of *Philosophy of Science*.

REALISM AND THE NEW WAY OF WORDS   453

the truth-value equivalence of mentalistic sentences with sentences in the language of an, as yet, ideal neuro-physiological psychology. What would be the implications of such a claim for the structure of the ideal world-story we are envisaging? One's first line of thought might be that it points towards a world-story which contains, in connection with each sentient being described in it, two isomorphic sub-sets of sentences, (*a*) a mentalistic sense-history, and (*b*) a selection from a physicalistic brain history. Once started on this line of thought, one would be troubled by the question, "How is *identity* to be distinguished from *parallelism?*" But to initiate this train of thought presupposes that one has given an affirmative answer to a prior question, namely, "Can a world-story contain such isomorphic sub-sets *and still have that coherence which makes it confirmed?*" In an older parlance, the corresponding question was, "Is parallelism compatible with the (self-evident) principle of sufficient reason?" If the question as we have formulated it is answered in the negative, as it must be, then we might be led to say that to the extent that psychology "points toward the truth-value equivalence of mentalistic sentences with sentences in the language of an as yet ideal neuro-physiological psychology," it is pointing toward the truth value equivalence of *two world stories*, one of which is in completely physicalistic terms, whereas the other contains a sub-set of mentalistic sentences in place of what in the first are selections from brain biographies. Reflection shows, however, that *formally* the "mentalistic language" would be indistinguishable from a section of the physicalistic language. Furthermore, they are *ex hypothesi* about the same world. The proper interpretation of this situation would be to say that in the sense in which the mentalistic "language" and the segment of the physicalistic "language" were *two* they are to be understood as different *token classes* of the *same* type language. A genuine difference of the "mentalistic" and "physicalistic" expressions must be traced to a difference in the conformation rules relating to the predicates of these expressions; in other words, *same laws, same qualities; different laws, different qualities.* (See pp. 438 ff., *Meaning and Syntax*, and 445 ff. *Type and Token Again.*)

   If the expectation of such a "truth value equivalence" is doomed to disappointment, then some form of dualism is the alternative to the above approach. Such dualism would take the form either of minds and bodies as *interacting things*,[21] or of different kinds of events taking place in the *same* thing (the emergence form of the identity approach). May I express my (inherited?) predilection for the latter approach, while insisting that

---

[21] If we leave out of account those arguments which rest on the epistemologistic fallacy, and which seem to be invalid even if one grants the fruit—intentional acts, awareness of propositions, intuitions of square roots, etc., etc.—of this fallacy, the only reasonable basis for accepting a dualism of mind and body as two interacting things would be a general acceptance by scientists—the Psychical Research Society?—of the separate existence of mental events.

454   DATA, REALITY, AND THE MIND-BODY PROBLEM

emergence has nothing to do with indeterminism or Bergsonian *elan?* Emergence is one form taken by a negative answer to the question: "Could a world which includes minds be described with the same primitive predicates (and laws) as a mindless universe?" Needless to say, the dates at which emergent qualities occur has nothing to do with the case. The history of the universe could be as Aristotle conceived it.

X

Ideal Language and Language Schema. Our aim in the present paper has been to explore the group grammar of epistemological predicates, and particularly to bring out the relation of the concepts of verification, confirmation and meaningfulness to the concepts of semantic analysis as practiced by Carnap and Tarski. In attempting to make explicit this grammar, we have made use of the Wittgensteinian device of speaking in terms of a perfect language; that is to say, the language of an omniscient being. We have written the grammar of epistemological predicates large in order better to see it. We pointed out that after a discussion conducted in this framework, the problem next in line would be that of drawing the implications of this discussion for the grammar of these predicates in connection with "imperfect languages". It is now my aim to indicate that the difference between "perfect" and "imperfect" languages cannot be drawn in epistemological contexts, that is to say, is not an epistemological distinction.

But before we elaborate on the above contention, let us point out that the epistemological predicates with which we have been concerned are those which are primary, and apply for the most part to atomic sentences belonging to a world-story, or to the individual constants or primitive predicates appearing in these sentences. But it is clear that derivative pragmatic predicates can be defined in terms of these fundamental predicates. 'Confirmed,' as we have used this term, applies to atomic sentences in a world-story, and entails 'true'. Now, a predicate 'confirmed-to-degree-n' can be introduced in terms of the primary syntactical, semantical and pragmatic predicates which has neither of these limitations. Similarly, a family of predicates can be introduced which rests on the predicate 'meaningful' as we have defined it. All these defined pragmatic predicates will (1) *presuppose* the notion of a complete world-story in a language with given conformation rules; (2) be such that their applicability is (in principle) determinable on purely formal grounds. The application of such a predicate to an expression implies that the expression belongs to a formal system defined in such a way that the sentence making the application is either analytic or self-contradictory. This is what we mean when we say that the use of epistemological predicates involves presuppositions. Was Bosanquet so far wrong when he suggested that "Reality" is the subject of all judgments? We make the concept of *reality* a purely formal one,

REALISM AND THE NEW WAY OF WORDS   455

and say that each empirical language speaks about its own "Reality" or world.

Since our discussion of epistemological predicates has been in terms of what we called (pp. 429 ff.) languages proper as opposed to language *schemata*, we must end with a review of this distinction. The first thing to note is that it is one which breaks out at all linguistic levels. We can say that a pragmatic meta-schema claims to be a pragmatic meta-language proper, just as we have said that a language schema claims to be a language proper. Now it is clear from this very formulation that the whole distinction between the schematic and the proper is a factual-psychological rather than a formal-epistemological distinction.[22] It relates to the psychology of formal *manipulations*, and can no more be formulated within formal science itself then can the concept of *mistake*. If this is the case, then our factual inability to construct complete world-stories no more entails an inability to give a formal account of a complete world-story, or of a language proper, than our inability to construct an infinite series entails an inability to give a formal account of infinite, or, indeed, of particular infinite series. Our everyday use of epistemological predicates is formally or epistemologically sensible even though we cannot turn it into petty cash. Furthermore, the *psychological* contrast between language schema and language proper must not be mixed with *formal* distinctions between different formal predicates. Thus, the difference between 'confirmed' and 'confirmed-to-degree-n' must not be confused with a difference between "confirmed" as appearing in a meta-language, and "confirmed" as appear-

---

[22] Cf. "Pure Pragmatics and Epistemology," pp. 195–197, also notes 10–13. The fact that the distinction between language proper and language schema is a factual-psychological one also throws light on the "puzzle" of the fruitfulness of deduction. When as logicians we characterize an argument as *valid*, we are "reconstructing" it as a token of an expression in a language in the formal sense of the term. We *take it* (to use a metaphor) as a token of an expression in a language which is *posited* as a complete and exhaustive structure in which everything that is formally involved in the language is "given." On the other hand, when we characterize an argument as *fruitful*, we are making empirical statements about a series of linguistic events in the psychological sense of "language".

The higher mental processes as *empirical facts* can be described without reference to the categories of pure semiotics. This is the proper task of a psychology of "knowing," "believing," etc. The puzzles which lead to epistemologism arise when we confuse this task with the formal reconstruction of "knowings," "believings," etc. as tokens of linguistic expressions in the formal sense of "language." Our sense of human dignity focuses our attention on empirical description when we are concerned with Fido's belief that he has a bone. In the case of Smith's belief that he has a penny, we are prone to confuse.

It must be emphasized that over and against the formal theory of languages, there is the empirical theory of languages which includes empirical concepts relating to "formal" language behavior. (Put a psychologist to watching a mathematician.) We must admit that just as there is a formal distinction between the "empirical" and the "formal," so there is an *empirical* distinction between the "empirical" and the "formal" aspects of language as an empirical category. See also H. Feigl, "Operationism and Scientific Method," *Psychological Review*, 1945, included in this volume, pp. 498–508 below, especially p. 500.

456   DATA, REALITY, AND THE MIND-BODY PROBLEM

ing in a meta-schema. Confusions of this kind give comfort to psychologism in pragmatics, and stimulate attempts to connect meaningfulness in a primary sense with probability.

According to our argument, it is a tautology to say that a meaningful language is about a causal world. The predicates of a meaningful language are such only by virtue of the conformation rules which differentiate them.[23] In these statements, the expression "language" appears as a formal predicate. On the other hand, as we have seen, the expression "language" also functions as a factual predicate relating to behavioral habits. This ambiguity of significance brings with it the danger of confusing the *psychological* factors leading to the discarding of one set of *habits* in favor of another with *formal* considerations of *probability, evidence* and *truth*. In speaking formally we "posit" a subject-matter which is *complete* within the scope of its presuppositions in that it doesn't make sense to say that the domain of this subject-matter is *incomplete*. On the other hand, the behavior which posits this domain is legitimately characterized as schematic. The English language as an anthropological fact may grow and change with the times. But the formal positing of a linguistic structure which clarifies (rationally reconstructs) the English language at a given time is the positing of a *complete* language (indeed, reflection would show, a *class of complete languages*).

Conclusion. This paper represents a meeting of extremes. The echoes of Leibnitz, Hume and Kant are no less obvious than those of Wittgenstein, Carnap and Tarski. But as a matter of historical justice long due, I like to think that we have reformulated in our own way a familiar type of Idealistic argument. It has been said that human *experience* can only be understood as a fragment of an ideally coherent *experience*. Our claim is that our empirical *language* can only be understood as an incoherent and fragmentary schema of an ideally coherent *language*. The Idealism, but not the wisdom, disappears with the dropping of the term 'experience'. Formally, all languages and worlds are on an equal footing. This is indeed a principle of indifference. On the other hand, a reconstruction of the pragmatics of common sense and the scientific outlook points to conformation rules requiring a story to contain sentences which are confirmed but not verified. In this sense the ideal of our language is a realistic language; and this is the place of Realism in the New Way of Words.

[23] The conformation rules of an empirically meaningful language determine the *necessary* elements in the structure of the world in which it is used. Here is the key to the concept of *causal law* and the *causal modalities*. A study of the requirements which conformation rules must fulfil in order to permit the construction of a confirmed world-story in the language of which they are the rules, as well as of the different properties of different sets of such rules, is the primary task of Pure Pragmatics.

SECTION I

(287.1(288); 289.1) C. I. Lewis in *An Analysis of Knowledge and Valuation* argues that a law of nature of the form 'all F is G,' which he now understands to involve a "real connection", can be construed neither as 'every actual particular which is F is also G' since this sentence would not have the appropriate implications for "circumstances contrary-to-fact" nor as 'every possible particular which is F is also G' since this sentence, "according to Lewis, must be analytic in order to be true." Because he thinks that the first construal is what is captured by "material implication" and the second construal, by "strict implication or deducibility", Lewis introduces an implication for construing laws of nature, an implication which is neither of the above two.

(289.2) Lewis attempts to obtain "real connections" without sufficient reflection on the notions of "actual (existing) particular" and "possible (thinkable) particular."

SECTION II

(289.3) Two groups of three propositions the first and second of which "the empiricist would like to maintain, while the third provides *prima facie* evidence of the mutual incompatibility of the first two:"

Ia) Laws of nature are properly formulated as generalized material or truth functional implications.
Ib) Laws of nature are not restricted in their scope to actual happenings.
Ic) The *fundamentum* of material or truth functional implication, generalized or not, is the actual world, for only with respect to it is there truth or falsity.

IIa) Laws of nature are not analytic.
IIb) Laws of nature are not restricted in their scope to actual happenings.
IIc) Propositions about all possible particulars must be analytic if true.

(290.1) A sketch of some ways of dealing with these groups of propositions that are, perhaps, open to the empiricist.

(290.2) With respect to group I, Lewis now denies Ia; but it is "not so
clear, however, what line, if any, he takes with respect to" group II. The
main concern of this paper is group II.

(291.1,.2; 292.1,.2) The approach to group II will assume that it is satisfactory
to "retain, at least provisionally, the distinction between actual and possible
particulars" and "to explore our naive conceptions relating to possibilities
in the hope of clarifying the relations which obtain between *possibilities*
and *real connections*, thus laying a foundation for a sophisticated understanding of both." For a sophisticated understanding of both "we should
have to abandon the traditional or naively realistic frame of reference. . . .
and reformulate our conclusions *in terms* of the contemporary empiricists
apparatus of formal linguistics."

SECTION III

(293.1,.2) A "history" is "a spatui-temporal structure of atomic states
of affairs which exhibits uniformities of the sort we have in mind when
we speak of the laws of nature." Each atomic state of affairs is a particular (in fact, an event) "exemplifying a simple qualitative (as opposed
to relational) universal." Histories come in a family, one history of
which is "the actual and possible history." "Every possible particular
belongs to one or other of the possible histories" of the family.

(293.3 (294) A symbolism for the various items that have been mentioned: This symbolism reflects the condition that particulars come "in
world-sized packages." It is assumed that there is "truth and falsity
with respect to histories". Moreover, there are false statements to be
made about any history; such false statements formulate states of
affairs which are possible, but not actual, "relative to" a history. "In
another sense," such false statements do not formulate what is possible.

(295.1) The symbolism permits an attempt at rewriting the two construals
of 'all F are G' (see section I). Let 'U1' and 'U2' be expressions for
non-relational universals and history O be the actual history. Then 'every
actual particular which is F is also G' becomes

> B. if 'x' is restricted to the particulars of history O, then
> (x) (x exemplifies U1 $\supset$ x exemplifies U2).

If we assume that

> (i) 'all possible particulars' is the same as 'all possible particulars
> belonging to the family of possible histories which includes the
> actual history,'

'every possible particular which is F is also G' becomes

    E. if 'x' is restricted to the particulars of the histories of the family
        (of possible histories) which includes history O, then
        (x)(x exemplies U1 ⊃ x exemplifies U2).

(295.2) Is (i) correct? Is E satisfactory? To answer these questions, an
investigation of the notion of "a family of possible histories" is needed.

SECTION IV

(295.3) The discussion thus far tacitly assumes that the possible histories are a family because the universals exemplified in them are the universals exemplified in"the actual history". It is the purpose of this
section to show that the universals are the same throughout this family
of histories if and only if all the histories of this family "conform to the
same laws as the actual history."

(296.1) Two related mistakes are characteristically made: (1) to take
"for granted" a list of universals "whose difference from one another"
is "not clarified"; (2) to assume that, though talk about actual particulars and merely possible particulars makes sense, attempts to talk
in such a way about universals does not.

(297.1) How is the difference of one universal "from its fellows" to
be explicated?

(297.2; 298.2,.2) Several attempts at answering this question fail, but
do suggest that the differentiation of universals *"cannot be understood
without taking particulars into account"* and not just actual particulars
but all possible particulars.

(299.1) An example in which possible particulars must be taken
into account is that of explicating the "ordering relations" of "most
determinate universals which fall under a common determinable."
Consider determinate pitch universals. Since "being higher-in-pitch-
than" relates items which have a pitch, these items must be the
exemplifications of pitch universals and not the pitch universals
themselves. Thus, to say that two determinate pitch universals are
ordered by the relation being higher-in-pitch-than is "shorthand" for
saying that "all particulars which exemplify one universal stand in
the relation in question to particulars which exemplify the other universal." However, in such a case it is clear that "the exemplifications
in question must be all possible exemplifications, and not merely all
actual exemplifications."

(299.2(300)301.1) The general thesis is that *"the diversification of the
most determinate qualitative universals is to be understood in terms of
relations which obtain between all particulars, actual or merely possible,
which exemplify these universals. This thesis will lead us to the
conclusion. . . .that a family of possible histories exemplifying the same
universals is ipso facto a family of possible histories conforming to the
same laws, differing only in their "initial conditions."* Note first, that a
universal, A, is different from a universal, B, if and only if they differ in
their properties. Second, since *"the properties of a universal as universal concern that which is involved in its being exemplified"*, the properties that are distinctive of that universal, i.e., the properties that
together distinguish it from other universals, are those it has with respect
to its exemplifications "in all possible histories in which it is exemplified". A universal has such distinctive properties only if *the family* of
possible histories in which are the exemplifications of the universals of
the domain to which this universal belongs *does not* "consist of all
"logically possible" arrays of exemplifications of the universals by
sets of particulars". *If the family were of this nature, then each universal would function "symmetrically" with all the others in relation to
the family, and hence would have no distinctive property with
respect to its exemplications in the family."* The non-logical
restrictions on the arrays of exemplifications allowed into the
family of possible histories are the laws; these laws must also involve
the basic relations of the family.

SECTION V

(301.2) A summary of the argument thus far: "The basic unit of possible
existence is a family of possible histories. *A set of universals depends
on a set of sets of possible particulars, just as much as a set of possible
particulars depends on a set of universals.* In exemplifying a common
domain of universals, the histories of the family exhibit certain common
invariancies involving the relations in which particulars stand and the
qualitative universals they exemplify. Since these invariancies necessarily obtain of the family, being bound up with the fact that the universals
exemplified by the family are the universals they are, and since these invariancies restrict the family to less than what we referred to as the
"logically possible arrays of exemplifications of the universals"--and are
therefore not the invariancies which are exhibited in the formulae of logic--
we may call them *material invariancies.* We have thus found that the notions
of a *domain of universals*, a *family of possible histories* and a *set of material invariancies* are correlative, being internally related, that is, essentially
bound up with one another."

(301.3;302.1,.2; 303.1,.2) An objection that leads to a broadening of our
view of histories: Histories, which are arrays (structures) of exemplifications of universals, are only a sub-group of all arrays; arrays which
are not histories are, of course, distinguished from histories by not conforming to material invariancies. A completely satisfactory exposition
of this broader domain of arrays and of histories as a certain sort of
array cannot be given within the intentionally "naive" framework of
this paper.

SECTION VI

(304.1) Though an assumption of our discussion was the traditional one
(mentioned in 296.1) that "the contrast between actual and possible
doesn't apply to *universals*," our argument has led "to the conception
of *alternative systems of universals characterized by other sets of co-
exemplification properties or material invariancies, and exemplified in
other families of possible histories.*" With a family of possible systems
of universals comes "*a family of families of possible histories.*"

(304.2) In addition to alternative systems of material invariancies, it
must also be noted that alternative systems of basic relational structures
are possible. Thus far consideration has been given only to a fixed
system of structural relations that were assumed to be spatio-temporal
relations.

(305.1) A satisfactory discussion of the resulting totality of families of
possible histories would require a better terminology ("concrete system"
instead of "history") and a delineation of kinds of concrete systems
(such as "empirical systems" which are concrete systems that include
beings "which "know" the system in which they are embedded"). The
study of empirical systems, i.e., self-knowing concrete systems, is
"epistemology."

(306.1,.2; 307.1,.2) Though each particular belongs to only one history
and each universal to only one family, our symbolism must be changed
to reflect the additional possibilities, both possible particulars and
possible universals, that the recent reflections have introduced. This
symbolism is to be used under the restrictions that no particular "from
one family exemplifies a universal from another family" and that no
particular "from one possible history is related to a particular in another possible history."

SECTION VII

(307.3; 308.1) In the beginning (sections I and II),it was pertinent to
the discussion of "real connection" to discover whether sentences of the
form 'every possible particular which is F is also G' would be "analytic
if true". According to the above account of possibility, there really is
no such problem: A universal combines not with all possible particulars,
but only with those particulars of the family of histories to which the
universal belongs. Let the term for the family of possible histories
which includes history O (i.e., the actual history) be '*a*'. Then 'every

actual particular which exemplifies U1 also exemplifies U2' becomes

    F. If U1 and U2 are in family *a* and 'x' is restricted to the particu-
       lars of history O of family *a*, then
       (x)(x exemplifies U1 $\supset$ x exemplifies U2).

In addition,

    G. if U1 and U2 are in family *a* and 'x' is restricted to the particulars
       of the histories of family *a*, then
       (x)(x exemplifies U1 $\supset$ x exemplifies U2)

says (what is perhaps misleading said by) "every possible particular in any
history of family *a* which exemplifies U1 also exemplifies U2". But *no* sentence says "every possible particular in any history of *any* family which exemplifies U1 also exemplifies U2", for this putative saying is ruled out by
the restrictions developed in the discussion of universals and material invariancies. However, it can be asked of sentence G whether it is "analytic"
even though G is not about all possible particulars.

(308.2) Note that there are sentences which are about all possible particulars:

    H. if 'x' is restricted to the particulars of the histories of any family and
       'U' and 'V' are restricted to the universals of any family and, in addi-
       tion, in each instantiation to the family which includes the history to
       which the instantiation of 'x' belongs, then
       (x) (U) (V) (x exemplifies U $\supset$ (x exemplifies U or x exemplifies V)).

Sentence H says (what is perhaps misleadingly said by) "every possible
particular in any history of any family which exemplifies a universal of the
family of its history also exemplifies that universal or another universal
from the same family". "A system of "true" statements having such unrestricted generality would constitute the theory of concrete systems."

SECTION VIII

(309.1) "*A natural law is a universal proposition, implicative in form, which
holds of all histories of a family of possible histories; as such it is distinguished from "accidental" formal implications which hold of one or more
possible histories of the family, but do not hold of all.*" How can a law of
nature "hold of all possible histories which exemplify the universals involved
in the law, and hence be a necessary truth with respect *to* those histories,
without being an "analytic proposition?"

(309.2; 310.1) The laws of nature are material invariancies. These, it was
argued above (section IV), are a necessary condition of a family's having a
system of universals and yet are "non-logical invariancies common to all"
the histories of the family.

(310.2) Consider a simple case of a material invariancy for a family *b*:

    K. If U1, U2 and R are in family *b* and 'x' and 'y' are restricted to
       to particulars of the histories of family *b*, then
       (x) (y) ((x,y) exemplify R and x exemplifies U1 $\supset$ (y exemplifies U2)).

Since K is part of the definition of family *b*, the relation between

(ii) U1, U2 and R are in family b and 'x' and 'y' are restricted to particulars of the histories of family b

and

(iii)   (x) (y) ((x,y) exemplify R and x exemplifies U1 $\supset$ (y exemplifies
        U2))

is "necessary" since (ii) could not be true and (iii) false "without b being
a different family than it is".

(311.1,.2) Consider next

L. if U1, U2 and R are in family b and 'x' and 'y' are restricted to the
    particulars of history 2 of family b, then (iii)
    (x) (y) ((x,y) exemplify R and x exemplifies U1 $\supset$ (y exemplifies
    U2))
and

M. if U3, U4 and R are in family b and 'x' and 'y' are restricted to the
    particulars of history 2 if family b, then (iii)'
    (x) (y) ((x,y) exemplify R and x exemplifies U3 $\supset$ (y exemplifies
    U4)).

Sentence "L is a logical consequence of K"; but let us suppose that M is
not the logical consequence of any material invariancy of the family b.
Though L is a special case of a law and M is "accidental", the relation of

(iv) U1, U2 and R are in family b and 'x' and 'y' are restricted to the
     particulars of history 2 of family b,

to (iii) and the relation of

(v) U3, U4 and R are in family b and 'x' and 'y' are restricted to the
    particulars of history 2 of family b

to (iii)' are exactly the same. Indeed, both are necessary since history 2
cannot be the history it is if either L or M is false. Thus the difference between L and M is not to be indicated in a symbolism by using one symbol
for the connection between (iv) and (iii) and another symbol for that between
(v) and (iii)'. The appropriate means of indicating that what L says of history 2 of family b holds of all histories of family b (and is thus materially
invariant over the histories of family b) is by writing L with, say, an arrow
in place of the horseshoe. The arrow, or "nomic implication", is simply
material implication except that, while the appearance of the horseshoe in
its position in M does not entitle us to infer that M is a consequence of a
material invariancy, the appearance of the arrow in the rewriting of L does
entitle us to infer that L is a consequence of a material invariancy.

SECTION IX

(312.1) Three objections: (1st) Is it not a consequence of the above view

that any truth about anything concerning a history is a necessary truth?
For example, if we suppose

> N. Given that U9 is in family *b* and x7 is in history 3 of family *b*,
>   then x7 exemplifies U9

is a truth about history 3 of family *b*, then is not N a necessary truth since,
if N were false, history 3 of family *b* could not be the history it is (namely,
a history in which N is true)? (2nd) Since this paper provides an "a
priori science of possible histories", is there not *a fortiori* an "a priori
science of the actual history"?   (3rd) On the argument of this paper is
it not "impossible to be acquainted with universals without *ipso facto*...
being acquainted with laws involving these universals?"   And since we
are acquainted with universals, it follows, absurdly enough, that we are
acquainted with the natural laws which are necessary to these universals.

(313.1,.2,.3) To the 1st and 2nd objections: It is correct that all truths
about possible histories, such as N, are necessary truths. But this point
simply reflects the "neutrality" of talk about possible histories: All
are on equal footing and the science of families of possible histories
does not pick out one family or one history as "privileged". The distinction between what is possible and what is actual is *"relative to"*
each history. "Any special privileges which belongs to one history
must be a status which stems from outside the Conceptual Realm and
which consequently cannot be penetrated by the a priori science" of
families of possible histories.

(314.1) To the 3rd objection: This objection requires an abandonment
of the framework of naive realism, which lends "aid and comfort" to
mistaken talk of being acquainted with universals, in favor of an appropriately "pragmatic" understanding of the results of this paper within
the framework of the "pure theory of empirically meaningful languages."

CONCEPTS AS INVOLVING LAWS AND INCONCEIVABLE WITHOUT THEM

WILFRID SELLARS

Formal implication is usually represented by symbolization such as '(x) ϕx $\supset$ Ψx,' which may be read, "for all values of 'x', ϕx (materially) implies Ψx." If the values of the variable 'x', in 'ϕx' and 'Ψx' be 'x₁' 'x₂' 'x₃', etc., then . . . 'ϕx' formally implies 'Ψx' if and only if, whatever values of 'x', 'xₙ', be chosen, 'ϕxₙ' materially implies 'Ψxₙ' . . .

However, this still leaves it doubtful which of two possible interpretations of expressions having the form '(x) ϕx $\supset$ Ψx' is to be taken as correct. . . . It means one thing to say, "Every *existent* having the property ϕ . . . has also the property Ψ," and it means quite a different thing to say, "Every *thinkable* thing which should have the property ϕ must also have the property Ψ." *The second of these holds only when having the property ϕ logically entails having the property Ψ; when 'Ψx' is deductible from 'ϕx'.* . . . The first of them, however, holds not only in such cases . . . but also in every case where among *existent* things, one property is *universally accompanied* by another. (C. I. Lewis, *An Analysis of Knowledge and Evaluation*, pp. 217–8. I am responsible for the italicizing of the sentence, otherwise the italics follow Lewis.)

I

The passage I have quoted above sets the stage for Lewis' discussion of the implicative relation involved in the contrary to fact conditionals in terms of which, in his new book as in *Mind and the World Order*, the concept of the independent reality of the objects of knowledge is to be clarified. In his earlier account he was satisfied to point out that, for obvious reasons, this implicative relation cannot be material implication, and to refer the curious reader to his logical writings for an account of strict implication.[1] That Lewis is no longer satisfied with this hasty identification of the required implication with strict implication as developed in his logical writings is a distinct advance. The latter conception could hardly be equated with *real connection*, and it is real connection which he now finds to be indispensable to an account of the contrary to fact conditionals which play a decisive role in his pragmatic empiricism. His argument is characterized by a frank recognition that, "as Hume correctly maintained, the only alternative to admission that . . . real connections genuinely obtain, is scepticism." (p. 228). I am in complete agreement with this thesis, if not with Lewis' explication of it, and I have a general sympathy with the epistemology he builds upon it. Furthermore, I find that in addition to new insights, many long neglected truths are to be met with in the pages of his important book, though I am not too happy about the psychologistic garb in which they tend to appear. On the other hand, where I do disagree, the sources of my disagreement strike deep. Differences with a philosopher of Lewis' stature, who is furthermore a logician, almost inevitably concern the basic premises

---

[1] *Mind and the World Order*, p. 142n. It is interesting to note that Lewis doesn't come right out and say that the implication involved in the contrary to fact conditionals with which it is concerned is strict implication. His turn of phrase is a curious one, indicating, I should like to think, some degree of uneasiness.

and presuppositions of his argument, rather than its systematic elaboration. Now the passage I have quoted at the beginning of the paper involves in one way or another certain presuppositions, by no means peculiar to Lewis, which are not examined in the course of his argument, and which, as I see it, are the source of much confusion and perplexity in contemporary epistemology. It is these presuppositions which are the subject matter of the following discussion, and the quoted passage which embodies them will serve as our text. Let me summarize the gist of the quotation as follows:

If the values[2] of 'x' are *actual* particulars, then '(x) $\phi x \supset \Psi x$' means that every actual particular which is ϕ is also Ψ. On the other hand, if the values of 'x' are *possible* particulars[3] then '(x) $\phi x \supset \Psi x$' means that every possible particular which is[4] ϕ is also Ψ. On

---

[2] For simplicity of expression, I shall adopt the following convention with respect to the values of an expression. Instead of saying that the values of, say, 'x' are 'x₁', 'x₂', . . ., I shall say that the values of 'x' are $x_1, x_2, \ldots$. Similarly, I shall mean by 'particulars' not the individual constants of a language, but rather the *designata* of these constants.

[3] I shall use the expression "possible particulars" instead of Lewis' phrase "thinkable things" for two reasons: (1) The word "thing" is dangerous as suggesting dispositional properties—for these are at the core of the everyday meaning of the word—and hence as making for a superficial, because merely verbal, solution of the problem of possibility and counterfactual conditionals. (2) The term "possible" has the advantage, which "thinkable" does not, of making it clear that our problem has nothing to do with empirical psychology. Furthermore, little would seem to be gained by substituting "what possible acts of thought are about" for "the possible."

It is important to understand that I am not offering the phrase "possible particular" as a philosophically more luminous phrase than "thinkable thing." Philosophical clarity comes only with system and structure, and not with the substitution of one isolated phrase for another. The value of the terminology we have selected will become apparent only at the end of our argument, where it will be clear that to have followed Lewis' terminological signposts would have meant taking the wrong road.

We are going to be as deliberately naïve throughout most of our argument with respect to the contrast between "thinkable things" and "existing things" (though in our own terminology) as Lewis is for a passing moment. Thus, we shall assume that in some sense of "exist" there exist *possible* particulars as well as *actual* particulars. The fruitfulness of this assumption can only emerge in the course of our argument, and I ask the suspicious reader to bear with me.

[4] Lewis writes, "every thinkable thing which *should* have the property ϕ *must* also have the property Ψ," however the "should" and the "must" are ill-considered. (1) There is no obvious reason why the "thinkable things" interpretation should require a "should," when a "should" would clearly be out of place in the "existing things" interpretation. It is dangerous to take for granted that when dealing with thinkable things the indicative mood should be dropped in favor of the subjunctive, for to do this is to *take for granted* that no implication relating to thinkable things can be a material or formal implication. Is Lewis, perhaps, confusing together "every *thinkable* which *has* the property ϕ . . ." and "every *existing* thing which *should have* the property ϕ . . ."? (2) The same caution applies to the use of the term "must". While its use *may* be warranted by the extension of the scope of 'x' to include things which are thinkable but do not exist, its introduction is unwise until the statement with the extended scope has been explicated in such a way as to make this clear.

These remarks are not captious. It will turn out that I am not criticizing Lewis for a mere failure to justify what is in point of fact a correct introduction of "should" and "must" at this point. We shall find, indeed, that his introduction of these terms embodies a most serious mistake.

this second interpretation, Lewis claims, '(x) ϕx $\supset$ Ψx' can only be true if 'Ψx' is deducible from 'ϕx'; in other words, if the property Ψ is logically included in the property ϕ so that the statement is analytic.

Now it does not take Lewis long to show that, if all this be granted, laws of nature cannot be understood in terms of either of these interpretations of statements of the form '(x) ϕx $\supset$ Ψx'. The import of a law of nature cannot be represented by "Every actual particular which is ϕ is also Ψ," for, as Lewis correctly points out, the latter kind of sense cannot have the implications for circumstances contrary to fact which are part and parcel of the import of a law of nature. On the other hand, since the laws of nature are not analytic truths, they can hardly be represented by such a statement as "Every possible particular which is ϕ is also Ψ," for the latter, according to Lewis, must be analytic in order to be true. Having reached this conclusion, Lewis introduces the notion of an implication which is neither that expressed by '$\supset$' (material implication) nor by his symbol '$\prec$' (strict implication or deducibility).

Let it be understood right from the beginning that I am equally convinced that something of the sort must be done. This conviction that real connections of universals must be recognized in epistemology has been the most abiding of my philosophical prejudices. I am disturbed, however, by the ease with which Lewis gets what he wants. One would have expected real connections to be a bit more expensive, and the cry of "This or nothing!" does not convince. In surveying the ground, I notice that although Lewis leads us to the idea of an implication which, as expressive of real connections, "is independent of the truth or falsity of the antecedent or hypothesis" (p. 223) without being logical or strict implication, by exploiting a distinction between *existing* and *thinkable* values of 'x'; once he has introduced this implication, he makes use of its symbol '$\rightarrow$' in universal statements without so much as raising the question as to the range of values of individual variables which is appropriate to such implication. To be sure the characteristic individual variable now becomes 'o' (for occasion) instead of 'x', but the problem is the same, and Lewis doesn't worry about 'o' as he had worried about 'x'. Does Lewis wish to restrict the values of 'o' to "existing occasions" when '$\rightarrow$' is being used? Or does 'o' then take into account all "thinkable occasions"? If the former, then Lewis must be prepared to hold that all statements about "thinkable but non-existent" occasions, are properly understood as contrary to fact conditionals about "existing" occasions. If the latter, must we not ask how a statement, even with an '$\rightarrow$' in it, can hold of all thinkable occasions and not be analytic? Perhaps Lewis regards his contrast between "existing" and "thinkable" things as an heuristic device or nonsensical ladder which can be thrown away once one has scaled the heights of Real Connection. I have found it more valuable, and shall argue that it is only by taking seriously and, indeed, expanding the Leibnitzian conception of possible worlds that the concept of natural necessity can be given an adequate explication.

II

The plight of the philosopher who is suspicious of Real Connections is a difficult one; much more difficult, indeed, than would appear from the relative ease with which the Humean tradition has come to dominate recent philosophies of science. His situation can be brought to a focus by considering the following two groups of propositions, each of which contains two propositions which the empiricist would like to maintain, while the third provides *prima facie* evidence of the mutual incompatibility of the first two. The first group of propositions consists of the following:

Ia) Laws of nature are properly formulated as generalized material or truth functional implications.

Ib) Laws of nature are not restricted in their scope to actual happenings.

Ic) The *fundamentum* of material or truth functional implication, generalized or not, is the actual world, for only with respect to it is there truth or falsity.

The second group of propositions is made up as follows:

IIa) Laws of nature are not analytic.[5]

IIb) Laws of nature are not restricted in their scope to actual happenings.

IIc) Propositions about all possible particulars must be analytic if true.

While the contemporary empiricist would like to stick by the first proposition in each group, he is increasingly sensitive to the force of the second, and here the third proposition, in each case, stands in the way by (apparently) making it impossible to accept the second without discarding the first. The temptation which confronts him today with respect to the first group of propositions is to get out of the hole (though at a cost not easily measured) by denying Ia, introducing a special non-truth-functional implication for laws of nature. Indeed, it is difficult to see what else can be done but abandon Ia if Ib is to be accepted while Ic is retained. On the other hand, with respect to the second group of propositions, the prevailing temptation is to "reinterpret," rather than deny, one of the propositions, in this case IIb, by insisting that empirical propositions *ostensibly* about possible-but-not-actual particulars are properly understood as contrary to fact conditionals (involving a special implication introduced for laws of nature) about *actual* particulars. Possible happenings thus become the possibilities that actual happenings might have been differently characterized, or, to use the language of the New Realists, false propositions (*in rebus*) which involve actual happenings as constituents.

I mention these temptations, not because they are the only lines along which contemporary empiricists are attacking the problem, for this is not the case, but because they seem to be exerting the most attraction. Thus, as we have seen, Lewis follows the course charted above with respect to the first group of propositions. It is not so clear, however, what line, if any, he takes with respect to the second group. It is, however, the latter group which I plan to

---

[5] The minimum content of this statement is that laws of nature are not analytic in the "Kantian" sense according to which '(x) ϕx $\supset$ Ψx' is analytic if Ψ is either identical with or a constituent of ϕ. However, even if the scope of the term 'analytic' is broadened to include logical necessity which is not of this simple form, so that statements can be analytic without being analytic in the Kantian sense, it is *prima facie* highly improbable that laws of nature are analytic even in this broader sense.

explore in this paper, for I am convinced that here, rather than in the first group, is the nub of the problem of real connections. Since my aim is systematic rather than historical, I shall not comment directly on any approach, including that which has been sketched above, unless the occasion to do so arises naturally in the course of the argument.

Turning, then, to the second group of propositions, the two basic alternatives would seem to be the following:

A) Reject as nonsense the whole distinction between actual and possible particulars except in so far as "merely possible" particulars can be interpreted in terms of contrary to fact conditionals about "actual" particulars. This approach would involve either the abandonment or a radical reinterpretation of IIc; and IIb could be retained only if interpreted as sketched in our account of the prevailing temptation with respect to the second group of propositions.

B) Retain, at least provisionally, the distinction between actual and possible particulars.

On alternative B, the available lines of defense for IIb would seem to be as follows:

B1) The scope of laws of nature is restricted to actual particulars, empirical statements about possible happenings being interpreted as in A.

B2) The scope of laws of nature includes possible as well as actual particulars, but either

B21) this scope does not include *all* possible particulars, but only some characterizable sub-set of possible particulars, so that we can also assert both IIa and IIc, or

B22) this scope includes all possible particulars so that in order to assert IIb we must either

B221) abandon IIc in order to retain IIa, or

B222) abandon IIa in order to retain IIc.

We shall assume that of the two basic alternatives, the second, or B, is the correct one. In other words we shall continue to operate on the assumption that in some sense of "exists" there exists both a narrower set of values for the 'x' in '$(x) \phi x \supset \Psi x$', the *actual* values, and at least one broader set of possible[6] values. As we have already pointed out, we shall continue throughout our constructive argument to take the naïvely realistic view of possibility with which Lewis was willing to work only while getting his argument under way. Instead of lapsing into a silence (which need not be construed as sophistication) about "real possibilities" the moment we get a glimpse of "real connections", we are going to continue to be explicitly naïve about them. We are not going to assume that the idea of Real Connection has an intrinsic sophistication which the idea of Possible Particular lacks. The trouble with philosophical naïveté, if I may speak metaphorically, is not so much that it is naïve, as that it is isolated, fragmentary. Philosophical sophistication is achieved not by atomistic leaps from this naïve idea and that, but rather by a change of perspective which rests on

---

[6] If the reader is impatient of the notion that material or truth-functional implication is appropriately used in connection with statements about possible particulars ("Surely there is truth and falsity only with respect to the *actual*!"), I urge him to hold his fire for a page or two, as the usage will be justified shortly.

adding the naïve to the naïve, on systematizing the naïve, drawing it out. The former process is rather seduction, and in thought as well as in the world one can be seduced many times without becoming sophisticated.[7]   Accordingly, I propose to explore our naïve conceptions relating to possibilities in the hope of clarifying the relations which obtain between *possibilities* and *real connections*, thus laying a foundation for a sophisticated understanding of both.

The free exploration and elaboration of the framework of naïve realism is, however, more suited for reflection *in foro interno*, than for the argument of a paper. Here I must indicate the lay of the land as I have discovered it to be.   I have not traveled alone, for it is in the philosophy of Leibnitz that one finds the most plausible and complete systematization of one level of our common sense notions about possibility.   Thus, I shall begin with a restatement of the Leibnitzian framework.   However, as our purpose is not historical, we shall have to disregard much that he said, and add much that he didn't say.   A number of factors, among the more important of which were his confusions concerning substance and relation, make his account less straight-forward and easy to follow than it otherwise would have been.   Of greater significance is the fact that his account of possibility is radically incomplete, and must be considerably added to in order to provide (even on the level of naïve realism) a solution of our problem.   Yet even here we shall be following his lead, for the supplementation his account requires is not only thoroughly in keeping with the Leibnitzian philosophy, but is even, as we shall find, demanded by it.

One final point remains to be made before we begin our constructive argument. To verbalize in the Leibnitzian manner about possibility involves saying that in some sense of "exists" there *exists* a family of possible spatio-temporal worlds, one of which is the *possible-and-actual* world, the others being *merely possible* worlds.   We shall assume that it makes sense to say this, and we shall make no attempt to explicate either this sense of "exists" or this contrast between the possible-and-actual world and merely possible worlds.   Though a complete account of possibility and real connections would demand such an explication, we shall be able to go a long way without it.   Furthermore, in order to provide this explication we should have to abandon the traditional or naïvely realistic frame of reference in which we shall be operating—in Carnap's phrase, the *material mode of speech*—and reformulate our conclusions in terms of the contemporary empiricist apparatus of formal linguistics.   I have indicated elsewhere[8] the lines along which, to my way of thinking, such a reformulation is to be made.

---

[7] If it is pointed out that this sounds like Bosanquet and the Neo-Hegelians, I can only say that much is to be learned from this movement.   I have indicated elsewhere ("Realism and the New Way of Words," *Philosophy and Phenomenological Research*, June, 1948) the extent to which the coherence theory of meaning and truth must be absorbed—after proper translation—into an adequate empiricism.

[8] For a brief account, see "Epistemology and the New Way of Words," *The Journal of Philosophy*, Vol. XLIV, No. 24, November 20, 1947.   A longer and more complete account is to be found in "Realism and the New Way of Words," *Philosophy and Phenomenological Research*, Vol. VIII, No. 4, 1948.

III

In speaking of a family of possible worlds, what are we to understand by a "world"? Let us begin with the following: A world is a spatio-temporal structure of atomic states of affairs which exhibits uniformities of the sort we have in mind when we speak of the laws of nature. In this characterization, an atomic state of affairs is a particular exemplifying a simple qualitative (as opposed to relational) universal. Such a state of affairs is mentioned in language by a sentence of the form "Ux" where in place of "U" is the name of a simple qualitative universal, and in place of "x" is the name of a particular. Three comments are in place. (1) Our assumption that every possible world is spatio-temporal is a temporary one, and will be revised later in our argument. (2) I have deliberately avoided any commitment concerning the nature of a law, for it is by exploring other aspects of possibility that we hope to gain insight into the distinctive character and force of the laws of nature. (3) The term "world", which our discussion has inherited from Leibnitz, must be abandoned. It is as dangerous and misleading as the word "thing" which we have already decided not to use.[9] Like the latter, it suggests substances or continuants with their dispositional properties. Our particulars, on the other hand, are events, or, better, states of affairs, rather than substances. Dispositional properties are not among the naïve data of our argument. Yet if we can succeed in clarifying the concept of real connection, we shall have prepared the way for an analysis of contrary to fact conditionals, and this in turn would be the threshold of an understanding of dispositional properties and continuants. We shall not, however, embark on such an analysis in the present paper. The sum, and, if I may say so, substance of these remarks is that in the argument to follow we shall discard the term "world" in favor of "history". We shall speak of possible histories where Leibnitz spoke of possible worlds, the term "history" being used, of course, in that sense in which it refers not to statements, but to events.

Our basic framework is thus a family of possible histories, one of which is the actual and possible history. We shall now make the assumption that there are no unattached particulars; that is to say, we shall assume that *every possible particular belongs to one or other of the possible histories making up this family.* In Leibnitzian terms we are assuming that both actual and merely possible existence comes in world-size packages. Looking at the matter from a slightly different point of view, we shall assume that Leibnitz's principle of the identity of indiscernibles applies not only to actual particulars but also to all possible particulars. Thus, every possible particular is the possible particular it is by virtue of being an ingredient in a possible atomic state of affairs which occupies a certain place in a spatio-temporal net-work which is a possible history.

Let us now develop a system of symbols in terms of which the resources we have brought together can be readily mustered in discussion. We have assumed

I. a set of simple non-relational universals.

$U_1, U_2, U_3, U_4, \cdots$

---

[9] See note 3 above.

II. basic spatial and temporal relations with their characteristic properties. These can be symbolized as needed.

III. a family of possible histories,
H^0, H^1, H^2, $\cdots$
of which the first, H^0, is "the actual history".

IV. the sets of possible particulars which are ingredient in these possible histories,

K^0 consisting of x_1^0, x_2^0, x_3^0, $\cdots$ ingredient in H^0;
K^1 consisting of x_1^1, x_2^1, x_3^1, $\cdots$ ingredient in H^1;
K^2 consisting of x_1^2, x_2^2, x_3^2, $\cdots$ ingredient in H^2;

. . . .

. . . .

V. for the corresponding variables we shall use 'U' ('V', 'W', etc.); 'H' and 'K'. The variables for possible particulars requires more discussion. I consider only the cases where these variables appear as bound variables in statements having a general form.

(1) Where the scope of the statement is restricted to the particulars of one possible history, we can either

(a) use as our variable the letter 'x' ('u', 'v', etc.) with a superscript indicating the history in question, or

(b) use these letters without superscripts as variables, adding an expression, say, 'x ϵ K^0,' which indicates the restricted scope of the statement; thus, '(x) x ϵ $K^0 \cdot \supset : U_1 x \supset U_2 x$.'

(2) Where the scope of the statement includes the particulars of all the possible histories, we shall use the letter 'x' ('u', 'v', etc.) without superscript together with the bound variable 'K' and the expression 'x ϵ K'; thus, '(x) (K) x ϵ K$\cdot \supset : U_1 x \supset U_2 x$'. This is designed to embody in our symbolism the fact that though the scope of the statement includes all possible particulars, it belongs to the essential nature of particulars to come in sets.

VI. We shall assume that it makes sense to speak of truth and falsity with respect to possible histories. Thus '$U_1 x_1^2$' is either true or false with respect to H^2, true if x_1^2 exemplifies U_1 in H, false if it does not. Accordingly we shall assume that statements involving truth functions (e. g., material implication) are as appropriate to possible histories as they are to "the actual history". Thus, '$(x^2) \cdot U_1 x^2 \supset U_1 x^2$' is both proper and true.

VII. It follows from VI that not only are we operating with a (provisionally) absolute distinction between the possible-and-actual *history* and merely possible *histories*, but we must also draw a distinction between possible-and-actual and possible-but-not-actual *states of affairs* with respect to each history. Thus, if H^2, itself a "possible history", includes state of affairs *Red* x_7^2, we shall say that *Red* x_7^2 is a possible-and-actual state of affairs with respect to H^2, whereas Green x_7^2 is a merely possible state of affairs with respect to H^2. Such a mere possibility is the meaning of a false statement about H^2. We shall speak of possibility and actuality in this sense as "relative to a history".[10] The reader should be prepared to find that although Green x_7^2 is in this sense a possibility relative to H^2, in another sense Green x_7^2 is impossible, given, as above, that in H^2 x_7^2 is red.

Let us now put our symbolism to the test by attempting to translate into it statements of the form '$(x) \phi x \supset \Psi x$', with which we were concerned at the opening of our discussion. In the case of the interpretation of such statements which restricted the values of 'x' to *actual* particulars, there is little difficulty. We have as a translation either

     A. $(x^0) \; U_1x^0 \supset U_2x^0$

or

     B. $(x) \; x \, \epsilon \, K^0 \supset : U_1x \supset U_2x$.

On the other hand, in the case of the interpretation of '$(x) \phi x \supset \Psi x$' which extends the scope of 'x' to all possible particulars, we can only offer a translation into our symbolism if it can be asserted that the expressions "all possible particulars" and "all possible particulars belonging to the family of possible histories which includes the actual history" are strictly equivalent. Should this be the case, then

     C.   For all possible values of 'x', $\phi x \supset \Psi x$

has the same meaning as

     D. ϕ materially implies Ψ in each of the family of possible histories which includes the actual history;

and both would be symbolized by

     E. $(K) \; (x) \; x \, \epsilon \, K \cdot \supset : U_1x \supset U_2x$.

Clearly, however, before we can say whether or not the notion of *all possible particulars* is the same as the notion of *all possible particulars belonging to the family of possible histories which includes the actual history*, and before we can decide whether or not such a statement as E (above) can be true only "if 'Ψx' is deducible from 'ϕx'," we must explore what is meant by the expression (which we have hitherto used without question) "the family of possible histories which includes the actual history," and, indeed, by the very expression "a family of possible histories."

IV

In approaching the task which we set ourselves at the end of the preceding section, we notice that we have been tacitly assuming that what makes a *family* out of the possible histories of which we have been speaking is the fact that they

---

[10] Thus, Carnap's distinction (*Meaning and Necessity*, pp. 8 ff.) between 'possible states of the universe' (expressed by false state descriptions) and the actual state of the universe' (expressed by the true state description) does not correspond to the distinction we are attempting to draw between possible histories and the actual history. In so far as our conception is sound—and we have just begun to expound it—Carnap's distinction must be made with respect to each possible history as well as the actual history. Thus each possible history is the *fundamentum* of a set of state descriptions, and is 'the actual state of the universe' which makes one of these state descriptions true.

all exemplify the universals which the actual history exemplifies. They constitute a family because they exemplify the same qualities and relations. But if we were asked to start from scratch and find another basis for grouping possible histories, we might soon hit upon the following. This time we should collect into one group all those possible histories which conform to the same laws as does the actual history. If we were then asked, "Is the group of possible histories which conform to the *same laws* as the actual history co-extensive with the family of possible histories which exemplify the same qualities and relations as the actual history?" what should we answer? If we followed the usual lead, we should soon answer in the negative; and we should give something like the following ground for our reply. "It is possible," we should claim, "to conceive of other laws than those to which the actual course of events conforms, but surely impossible to conceive of other qualities and relations than those of the history in which we live, move and have our being!" And, indeed, if it is *possible* to conceive of two histories which conform to different laws, but *impossible* to conceive of two histories which exemplify different sets of universals, the negative answer would be justified. *It is now my purpose to show that such an answer would be a mistake, and that universals and laws are correlative; same universals, same laws, different universals, different laws.* Once again, we shall not approach the concept of *law* directly. Instead, we shall tackle that of *universal*. We shall not, however, ask, "Are there universals?" or "What is exemplification?" or any question characteristic of the usual sort of puzzlement about universals. That universals exist, and that they are exemplified by actual and by possible particulars is a presupposition of our discussion. The only significant question relating to the existence of universals concerns the sense in which they exist, the "how" and not the "that", and this does not concern us here.

There are two closely related mistakes which are characteristic of western philosophy as a whole. They are (1) the discussion of philosophical questions in terms of a list of universals which is taken for granted, and which is a list of universals whose difference from one another is taken for granted and not clarified[11] and (2) the assumption that while it makes sense to speak of possible particulars, and to contrast actual with merely possible particulars, neither of these ways of speaking makes sense in connection with universals. Certainly some philosophers have discussed the possibility of there being universals which are not exemplified by the actual history, but the sort of thing they have had in mind is a color which nobody will ever happen to see. Such a universal is not conceived of as a merely possible universal as opposed to actual universals, it is an actual universal (a phrase which is, for them, redundant) which the world doesn't happen to have taken to its bosom. Furthermore, even this idea has been discussed as one might discuss the possibility of there being ghosts, as something unlikely and queer. We, on the other hand, are soon going to assert the existence of domains of possible universals, and not just as a queer speculation to which one should pay one's respects in a systematic discussion, but as an in-

---

[11] Except to a superficial and inadequate extent which will be brought out in the discussion which follows.

tegral part of our naïve conceptions concerning possibility. We shall find here the key to the puzzle of real connections, a key which, when translated into the language of modern empiricism, opens the way for a reconciliation of the rationalistic and empiricist traditions in modern philosophy.

Turning now to the first of the mistakes we have mentioned, we find that it has been dangerously easy to assume a set of universals in terms of which questions relating to possibility, real connections, logical necessity, and so on, are asked without raising the question, "In virtue of what is each of these universals a different universal from its fellows?" The answer to this question is not so easy as it might seem, and far more significant. Even those who worry most about *meaning*, take for granted such universals as Redness, indeed, the usual battery of sensible qualities. "Everybody knows that these universals are different from one another!" Now, while it would be an exaggeration to say that most philosophers have written as though a set of universals were a set of universals regardless of any relation or lack of relation among themselves or between themselves and anything else, it would not be an excessive caricature of some positions. On the other hand, those philosophers who explicitly deny that all relations between universals are "purely external," do not develop the "internal" relations upon which they insist, and which we shall discuss in a moment, into an adequate theory of the differentiation of universals. Yet we need such a theory to stand beside a clarified Leibnitzian conception of the identity of indiscernible particulars.

The simple[12] universals which are exemplified in the course of the actual history are characteristically bunched into families. This situation is often described by saying that the universals which are exemplified are "most determinate" universals, and that they are bunched into families by being specifications of various "determinable" universals, which in turn are specifications of "still less determinate" universals, and so on. Determinables are properly said to be exemplified only in a derivative sense according to which a determinable is exemplified if one of the most determinate universals which is a specification of it is exemplified. Now it might seem that the fact that universals fall into this pattern of determinables and determinates provides us with at least a partial answer to the question, "In virtue of what are two universals different?" If two most determinate universals, ϕ and Ψ, fall under different determinables, of course they must be different! Yet a moment's reflection shows that we cannot rest here. How are we to understand the difference of two determinables? How are we to understand the fact that a most determinate universal is a specification of one determinable rather than another? Redness isn't red; nor is Color a case of Color; ϕ doesn't exemplify ϕ. We thus find it difficult to put our finger on any distinctive contents for ϕ and Ψ other than their

---

[12] Our discussion of the diversity of different universals will proceed, as has our entire discussion to date, on the assumption that there must be absolutely simple universals. This assumption, though it cannot, indeed, be clarified within the naïve frame of reference to which we are restricted, strikes us, within this frame, as a necessary truth. It is the purpose of our argument to discover such "necessities," and explore their inter-relation, not to attempt an isolated explication of each "necessity" as we find it.

relational properties with respect to the determinate-determinable structure. We seem, therefore, to be confronted by the following paradox: *Each universal belongs where it does in the determinable-determinate structure, by virtue of being the universal it is; yet each universal is the universal it is by virtue of belonging where it does in the determinable-determinate structure.*

At this stage, one might be prepared to admit that the differentiation of universals cannot be understood in terms of universals alone, that it involves the relation of universals to particulars. Certainly, a universal is by its very nature the sort of entity that is exemplified by particulars. In this general sense, at least, universals are internally related to particulars, and this fact may throw light on our problem. But the illumination isn't immediate. Thus, one might be tempted to say that while Redness isn't red, it at least has the property of having exemplifications which are red, and that this property, at least, can belong to no other universal. Unfortunately, to say that ϕ is the only universal whose exemplifications exemplify the universal ϕ is to utter a tautology which doesn't throw the slightest light on the difference between ϕ and Ψ. It gives us no basis whatever for ruling out the suggestion that 'ϕ' and 'Ψ' might be synonyms. Nor does it help to say that ϕ is the universal exemplified by x_1^0, x_4^0, x_7^0, $\cdots$ and Ψ the universal exemplified by x_2^0, x_3^0, x_6^0, $\cdots$ for this is compatible with ϕ and Ψ being the same universal and hence does not clarify their difference; nor to say that ϕ is exemplified by x_1^0, x_4^0, x_7^0, $\cdots$ and *not* by x_2^0, x_3^0, x_6^0, $\cdots$ for this *presupposes* that the latter particulars exemplify a different universal and hence takes us no further than we have already gone.[13]

Perhaps desperation may lead us to say that we know that ϕ and Ψ are different universals, because we are acquainted with ϕ and Ψ and apprehend them to be different. Yet even if it is granted that such a remark makes sense, and that universals are objects of acquaintance, it throws no light on what it is that one is apprehending when apprehending ϕ and Ψ to be different. Since the remark can hardly be intended to mean that universals and their difference depend in any way on their being apprehended, nothing new has been added. But perhaps the point of the remark is that the difference of universal from universal is "ineffable," that simple universals have "intrinsic" natures which determine their relative places in the structure of universals in a way which is ultimate and "ineffable," which cannot be characterized in rational discourse, or, which amounts to the same thing, is unintelligible. What fantastic end for the Platonic Realm of Intelligible Being this would be! Fortunately we do not have to take this course, and, indeed, it would seem to be self-contradictory. In the first

---

[13] Indeed, it might seem that since we have accepted the Leibnitzian account of the identity of particulars, any attempt to explicate the diversity of universals in terms of the diversity of particulars must lead to an obvious circle. Three comments are relevant: (1) We have been limiting our discussion recently to the diversity of simple *non-relational* universals. May it not be the case that the diversity of particulars is to be understood in terms of their position in a relational structure? (2) While circularity is indeed to be avoided, we may find a reciprocal dependence of the diversities of universals and particulars. (3) Note that our above discussion takes only *actual* particulars into account.

place "ultimacy" doesn't entail unintelligibility. After all, any understood situation is a matter of ultimately related ultimates. In the second place, I suppose that the closest to the unintelligible one can get would be an "unrelated simple," and whether or not this notion is self-contradictory, it is not applicable to the present circumstance, for here there is no lack of relations. Thus, *ex hypothesi*, the relations of the universals are themselves related to the "intrinsic" natures of the universals. The relation was said to be that of "determining," with the "intrinsic" natures of the universals doing the determining, but it is difficult to find any justification for making the "intrinsic" nature "prior" to the relations. Indeed, we have left the frying pan of unintelligibility only to fall once again into the fire which is the paradox of two paragraphs back. *The truth of the matter is not that the differentiation of universals is unintelligible, but rather that it cannot be understood without taking particulars into account. When we made an attempt along these lines a moment ago, we limited our attention to actual particulars. This time we must take possible particulars into account.*

Before we come to our constructive account, let us consider a suggestion which the reader has probably been impatiently waiting to make, and which, indeed, will help put us on the right track. The suggestion is that in many cases, at least, most determinate universals which fall under a common determinable are distinguishable from one another in terms of an order relationship,—thus the family of pitch qualities and the various shades of red. The point is clearly both relevant and sound. But how are we to understand these ordering relations? Indeed, is it the universals themselves or is it exemplifications of the universals which stand in these relations? Is it pitch universals or particular exemplifications of pitch universals which are the proper terms of the relation *higher-in-pitch-than?* Surely it makes no more sense to say of the most determinate shade of Red which is Red_1 that it is "deeper" than the most determinate shade Red_2 than it would to say that Red_1 exemplifies Red_1 . Must we not say that, to speak of two universals in the same family as related by an ordering relation is to use "shorthand" for a statement to the effect that all particulars which exemplify one universal stand in the relation in question to particulars which exemplify the other universal? *But if statements about the relations of universals (at least of the kind we are considering) are to be understood as statements about the exemplifications of universals, it is clear that the exemplifications in question must be all possible exemplifications, and not merely all actual exemplifications.* How, then, are statements to the effect that all possible exemplifications of one universal stand in a certain relation to all possible exemplifications of another universal to be interpreted?

Before approaching the question we have just raised, I want to advance the general thesis that the *diversification of the most determinate qualitative universals is to be understood in terms of relations which obtain between all particulars, actual or merely possible, which exemplify these universals. This thesis will lead us to the conclusion that universals and laws are correlative; that a family of possible histories exemplifying the same universals is ipso facto a family of possible histories con-*

forming to the same laws, differing only in their "initial conditions." Turning now to the argument, we must first notice that in demanding an account of the difference of different universals we have been tacitly applying the principle of the identity of indiscernibles to universals. To do this is to say that two universals (putting the matter in the usual paradoxical way) which have the same properties are identical. *Now the business of a universal is to be exemplified, just as the business of a particular is to exemplify. Thus, the properties of a universal as universal concern that which is involved in its being exemplified. These properties will be identical with respect to all possible exemplifications of the universal, and together they will be distinctive of the universal.* For convenience of expression, we shall consider the set of properties which together are distinctive of a universal to be a single property which we shall call the distinctive property of the universal. Now in terms of the framework with which we have been working, we can say that the distinctive property of a universal concerns its exemplification in all possible histories in which it is exemplified, and is identical with respect to all exemplifications in all possible histories in which it is exemplified. But in order for each universal to have such a *distinctive* property, the family of possible histories which exemplify the domain of universals to which the universal belongs cannot consist of the relational arrays of states of affairs which would be possible if, *per impossible*, universals were completely indifferent to the context in which they are exemplified. In other words, the family of possible histories which exemplify this domain of universals cannot consist of all "logically possible" arrays of exemplifications of the universals by sets of particulars, where by this is meant the arrays that would be possible if a domain of universals were a sheer multiplicity of *exemplifiables*, as substitutable for one another in any context as pennies.[14] The reason for this is obvious. *If the family were of this nature, then each universal would function "symmetrically" with all the others in relation to the family, and*

---

[14] This sentence can be expanded as follows: It cannot be the case that for each type of relational array of n particulars, where the variety of such types depends solely on the character of the basic relations of the family and in no way on its "qualitative" universals, there are as many possible histories exemplifying the set of m universals associated with the family as mathematically calculable combinations of n elements taken n at a time with the members of another set of m elements, where each element of the first set is paired with one and only one element of the second set, whereas each element of the second set can be paired with any number (from 0 to n) of elements in the first set.

It will be noticed that I am assuming that the basic particulars of a history can each exemplify only one simple most determinate "qualitative" universal to constitute an atomic state of affairs.   It follows from this contention, of course that the values of 'x' in '$\phi \cdot \Psi x$' must be *derived* individual constants. Let us use 't' instead of 'x' for the variable corresponding to derived individual constants. Now such derivation involves a "thing-making" relation. Call such a relation, however complex, 'f'. We then have the schema 't = f $(x_i, x_j, \ldots)$' defining the thing t in terms of the atomic particulars x_i, x_j, ... We next define the relation Ingredience-in-a-thing, symbolized by 'I', as follows: 'I (x, t)' if and only if 't = f $(\ldots, x, \ldots)$'.

Given the atomic predicates 'ϕ_j', 'ϕ_j', ... we define '$\phi_i t$', as short for '$(Ex) I (x, t) \cdot \phi_i x$'. It follows that '$\phi_i \cdot \phi_j t$' abbreviates '$(Ex, y) I (x, t) \cdot I (y, t) \cdot \phi_i x \cdot \phi_j y$'. We consequently see that if 'Ψ' is defined as '$\phi_i \cdot \phi_j$', this definition by no means involves merely the primitive predicates 'ϕ_i' and 'ϕ_j' together with the logical relation of conjunction.

hence would have no distinctive property with respect to its exemplifications in the family. The universals would be indiscernible, and, hence, identical.

We are thus led to the conclusion that each universal of a domain of universals must exhibit a systematic difference from all other universals of that domain with respect to its exemplifications in possible histories involving that domain of universals. One thinks here of Leibnitz's conception of *compossibility*. Unfortunately, owing to certain central confusions, Leibnitz did not develop this idea to its full stature, and fell back on the idea that in the case of simple universals there are no non-compossibilities except logical contradictories. Here his confusions about relations were decisive, for the "asymmetry" of the roles of qualitative universals in a family of possible histories can only be characterized in terms of co-exemplification properties which are invariant with respect to that family, and in which each universal plays a different role; and these co-exemplification functions involve the basic relations of the family, as well as the qualitative universals.

v

If we put together our discussion of universals in the preceding section with our account of particulars in section II, the total picture looks as follows: The basic unit of possible existence is a family of possible histories. *A set of universals depends on a set of sets of possible particulars, just as much as a set of possible particulars depends on a set of universals.* In exemplifying a common domain of universals, the histories of the family exhibit certain common invariancies involving the relations in which particulars stand and the qualitative universals they exemplify. Since these invariancies necessarily obtain of the family, being bound up with the fact that the universals exemplified by the family are the universals they are, and since these invariancies restrict the family to less than what we referred to as the "logically possible arrays of exemplifications of the universals"—and are therefore not the invariancies which are exhibited in the formulae of logic—we may call them *material invariancies*. We have thus found that the notions of a *domain of universals*, a *family of possible histories* and a *set of material invariancies* are correlative, being internally related, that is, essentially bound up with one another.

In spite of the plausibility of the above line of thought as a development of the naïve presuppositions of common sense, there are *prima facie* reasons for denying its claim to be a clarification of the differentiation of universals. I shall say nothing at this time to the charge that in effect all we have been doing is reduce naïve realism to absurdity by drawing out its absurdly rationalistic implications. Although this charge may seem a serious one at this stage, it will have assumed quite manageable proportions by the end of our argument. Of more immediate concern is an objection which might be formulated as follows: "Surely," one might say, "once you start talking about 'possible histories', you must admit even the 'wildest' history to be possible. Is it not a truism to say that all conceivable histories are possible histories? And surely only the 'invariances' of logic, if even these, can set a limit to the conceivable wildness of a history! Did not you yourself speak, a moment or so ago, of the 'logically possible arrays of exemplifications of the universals'? These seem to be what I have in mind in speaking of "all conceivable histories'. To be sure, you went on to argue that the family of possible histories which is correlated with a domain of universals must be smaller than the set of all 'logically possible' arrays, but while your reasoning seemed plausible enough at the time, I am now very uncomfortable. How can the number of *possible* histories be fewer than the number of *conceivable* histories? Perhaps my objection is best formulated as a dilemma. If you take the *first* alternative of this dilemma, (A), you deny that the conceivable arrays which violate your material invariancies are 'really' (possible) histories (*i.e.*, arrays of exemplifications of universals) at all. In terms of an example, if array i includes $\cdots U_1x_m^i$ & $U_2x_n^i$ & $x_m^i R x_n^i \cdots$ which violates an invariancy relating to the universals U_1 and U_2, you deny that either $U_1x_m^i$ or $U_2x_n^i$ or, indeed, any of the *prima facie* states of affairs in the array are 'really' exemplifications of U_1 or U_2 or any other universal, are 'really' (possible) states of affairs at all. But to take this alternative must you not be prepared to assert that although the U_1, U_2, etc. of array i do not function in this array as universals, they are nevertheless somehow identical with ('appear to be') the universals U_1, U_2, etc. which are exemplified in those other arrays which do not violate material invariances? Must you not also assert that the array i itself, though not a (possible) history, is a structure which is so 'continuous' with (possible) histories ('appears to be a history') that in grasping it we can be said to be conceiving a 'wild' history? But are these genuine options? Can something which isn't a universal be identical with ('appear to be') a universal? a structure that isn't a history be 'continuous' with histories? On the other hand, if you take the *second* alternative, (B), you admit that the arrays which violate the material invariancies are possible histories, in which case what becomes of your assertion that in the family of possible histories, in relation to which the domain of universals is differentiated, there are 'invariancies' (other than the purely logical) which no member of the family violates?"

A satisfactory resolution of the above dilemma is not to be found within the limits of the naïve frame of reference in which we are operating. Indeed, at this point the sophisticated empiricist is likely to find his conviction of the necessity for a "linguistic" reformulation of our problem and such insights as we have gained, so strengthened that he has no further patience with the argument. I urge him, however, to bear with us for a while longer, for we have hardly scratched the surface of what is to be learned from an exploration of naïve realism. It is dangerous to become sophisticated too soon, and, after all, if linguistic philosophizing performs the function of clarifying common sense, there can be little harm and possibly much good in organizing and taking the measure of the common sense which is to be clarified. Indeed, can clarification come entirely *ab extra*? Must not an adequate clarification be anchored in a familiarity with the full scope of what is to be clarified?

Let us, then, return to our dilemma, and attempt to resolve it in a way which is continuous with the argument which called it forth. We begin by drawing what seems to be an inevitable distinction between 'logical' and 'physical' possibility. While this distinction is not luminous in and of itself, it may lead us out of our present difficulties. If we make what seems to be proper use of this distinction, alternative B now becomes the notion that 'violating' arrays are *logically* possible histories, and this is quite compatible with the idea that the domain of universals is differentiated in relation to material invariances common to *all possible* histories exemplifying the universals, provided that in this latter context the term 'possible' refers to *physical* possibility.

But if the discovery of an apparent ambiguity of the term 'possible' enables us to feel more comfortable about alternative B, at least on the verbal level, actually little progress has been made. If we were asked, "Which *logically* possible histories are also *physically* possible?" we should reply, "Those which do not violate a material invariancy," If we were then asked, "Do you mean anything more by the expression 'physically possible history' than *history conforming to the material invariancies associated with the universals?*" we should be hard put to it to give any other answer than "No." But then to say that a certain set of structures or arrays divides itself into logically-possible-and-physically-possible histories and logically-possible-but-physically-impossible histories, is merely to say that it divides itself into logically-possible-and-*conforming* histories and logically-possible-but-*violating* histories. This enables the objector to reformulate his difficulty. "If we bear in mind the context in terms of which you introduced your 'material invariancies,' it will be remembered that the latter are bound up with 'coexemplification properties' of the universals. But to say this is surely to say that 'violating' arrays, by not conforming to the 'coexemplification properties', *cannot be arrays of exemplifications*, and therefore cannot be histories." The objection is a telling one. It drives us out of alternative B, and, unless we are going to be able to slip between the horns, we must grapple successfully with A, or begin our argument anew.

Fortunately, certain formulations we have used in the above discussion provide us with a clue to a satisfactory reformulation of alternative A. The original statement repelled us with its use of the terms 'really' and 'appear.' We are now, however, in a position to see that they were actually unwarranted. Properly formulated, this alternative becomes the notion that a certain set of structures or arrays divides itself into structures which are (possible)[15] histories, *i. e.*, arrays of exemplifications of universals, and structures which, though not (possible) histories, are so continuous with (possible) histories that the criterion

[15] The term 'possible' here means logically possible, for on the alternative we are considering, the expression 'physically possible history' is tautologous, a *physically* possible array being by definition a logically possible *history*. In other words, on this alternative there are no logically possible histories which violate material invariancies; there are no histories which are *logically* possible but *physically* impossible. This, however, does not mean that there is a general coincidence of the logically and the physically possible with respect to histories, for we must distinguish (as we have before) between the usage of 'possible' in which *histories* are possible, and that usage which is *relative to a history* and in terms of which Green x_7^2 was said to be a possible state of affairs in history H^2. In the latter usage of 'possible' the *logically* and the *physically* possible do not coincide.

of whether or not a structure satisfies certain material invariancies is sufficient to discriminate between them. *Here the decisive advance is constituted by the notion of structures which belong to the same general domain as arrays of exemplifications of universals, or, to put it somewhat differently, by the notion of a domain of structures which is not exhausted by arrays of exemplifications of universals.* For it is by means of the idea of structures which belong to the same domain as arrays of exemplifications of universals, but which are not such arrays, that we can understand how the 'conceiving of wild histories' can get hold of something existent and possessed, in a broad sense, of logical form, without making such conceiving 'illusory' as in the original formulation of A. While the imagery would be the same in thinking of 'violating' arrays as in thinking of 'conforming' arrays, in the latter case thought would be dealing with universals and exemplifications of universals, whereas in the former case it would not.[16]

VI

The first step in the exploration of this broader domain which includes other structures than arrays of exemplifications of universals, consists in reminding ourselves that although from the very beginning we have taken for granted that possible as well as actual *particulars* exist, we began by assuming that the contrast between actual and possible doesn't apply to *universals*. Our argument, however, forces us to abandon this assumption, for the very notion that the *actual* domain of universals, one of the possible histories exemplifying which is the actual history, is characterized by a set of co-exemplification properties or material invariancies, leads to the conception of *alternative systems of universals characterized by other sets of co-exemplification properties or material invariancies, and exemplified in other families of possible histories.* We are thus led to the notion of a family of possible systems of universals, one of which is the actual system, and therefore to the conclusion that the distinction between the possible-and-actual and the merely possible, whatever this distinction may be, applies not only to particulars but also to universals. Both ingredients of a possible state of affairs are themselves possible; each, universal as well as particular, belongs to one set of possibles out of many. In speaking of a family of possible systems of universals, we are saying that the realm of possibilities consists of *a family of families of possible histories.*

The reader who has caught the contagion of *a priori* speculation, and is beginning to be at home in possible worlds, is likely, by now, to be chiding us for being too earth-bound in our argument. Isn't it about time that we said something about the basic relations which hold between the particulars of the possible histories of a family, and which are essential to the co-exemplification properties of the universals of that family? Indeed, have we not tacitly been assuming that all possible "worlds" or systems of states of affairs are similar to "our world" in their relational (spatio-temporal) structure? These questions are certainly to the point. We are, today, quite accustomed to the idea of

[16] We must be careful to distinguish between "wild histories" as physical impossibilities relative to a conforming array (see concluding sentences of note 15 above) and "wild histories" as non-conforming arrays.

CONCEPTS AS INVOLVING LAWS   305

alternative types of "spatial" structure.   Less has been done with time relations, and as yet there is not even a clear answer to the question, "What is the *structural* (as opposed to *pictorial*) difference between relations (however different among themselves) which we should classify as *spatial* and relations which we should classify as *temporal?*"   Must we not have some structural criterion in mind? If so, cannot the further question be raised as to whether the type of relational structure which is temporal admits of alternative specifications, as does the type of relation which is spatial?   Beyond this lies the question, "Granted that a 'world' of exemplifications of universals must have a *structure*, need this structure be of a sort which we would classify as spatio-temporal at all?!"   These questions confront us with new, and seemingly boundless, horizons to explore.   We cannot do more here than indicate the chief landmarks that are visible from our present position.   One thing is clear; the system of possible "histories" is much more complicated than we have yet acknowledged.   It would be a mistake to move in one leap from the idea of a family of possible histories to that of *the* family of *all* families of possible "histories."   We must recognize that the "family tree" of possible histories involves intermediate families between these two extremes, the intermediate families being differentiated not only by a classification of sets of co-exemplification properties developed in terms of basic relations which have the same structural properties (which is all we have made room for up to now), but also by a classification of the types of basic relations involved.

A discussion which explored these issues would be well advised to drop the term "history" and use instead some such neutral phrase as "empirical system." Indeed, such a discussion would soon move into other territory which we have avoided.   It would be forced to distinguish between a broader and a narrower sense of "empirical system."   The narrower sense would cover only such relational systems as include "minds" which "know" the system in which they are embedded.   The broader sense would cover any systems which could be said to be a system of exemplifications of universals.   With this distinction in mind, one might introduce the phrase "concrete system" to stand for this broader sense, and use the phrase "empirical system" for those systems which are "self-knowing," to which alone the term "empirical" is appropriate.   An exploration of the concept of self-knowing concrete systems would take us into the heart of epistemology, for, indeed, in the material mode of speech, epistemology is nothing other than the pure theory of such systems.[17]   Since we are not concerned in

[17] In the framework of logical empiricism, epistemology is the pure theory of empirically meaningful languages, that is to say, languages which are *about* worlds in which they are *used*.   For a development of this conception, see "Realism and the New Way of Words," *Philosophy and Phenomenological Research*, 1948.

A reader may ask, "Doesn't your whole discussion assume the soundness of metaphysical realism?   Haven't the phenomenalists from Berkeley to Bergmann shown that the only meaningful individual constants are ego-centric particulars"?   But ego-centric particulars like 'this' and 'that' do not belong to the object-language!   They belong in the pragmatic metalanguage.   If a philosopher proposes to concern himself only with such pragmatic systems as involve a one-one correspondence between the ego-centric particulars of the pragmatic segment and the individual constants of the "object-language segment" of the system, he should be quite clear that there is no *sanction* for such a restriction in the pure theory of pragmatic systems (Pure Pragmatics).

this paper with the problem of knowledge, any more than with the nature of the distinction between *possible* worlds and the *possible and actual* world, we shall limit our discussion to concrete systems in the broader sense.

We are now in a position to formulate the insight at which we have arrived as follows: *Within the field of conceivable or ideal systems there are those which can be said to be systems of exemplifications of universals. These latter, concrete systems, constitute the scope of possible states of affairs. Concrete systems come in families, each of which is correlated with a domain of universals and exhibits certain material invariancies involving these universals. Although each concrete system, and each family of concrete systems has its "bias" as confronted by alternative possibilities of existence, this is not true of the totality of concrete systems. No possible states of affairs remain outside this totality. No possible particular transcends the concrete system to which it owes its indiscernibility, and no universal transcends the family of concrete systems in relation to which alone it has its distinctive being.* The analysis of the place of the totality of concrete systems within the realm of conceivable or ideal systems is a task of ultimate importance and extreme difficulty. What concerns us is the fact that, to revert to our earlier terminology which we shall use from now on, the family of families of possible histories is the realm of possible universals and possible particulars. *Here are "all possible values" of the 'x' and the 'U' in 'Ux'.*

Before we turn to consider the light which is thrown on the status and logical character of a "law of nature" by the distinctions to which we have been led, let us consider the modifications that must be made in the symbolism we introduced above in order to make it embody these distinctions. Our symbolism took account of only one of what we now see to be many families of possible histories. Thus, our basic change will be to introduce superscripts which discriminate between the families of possible histories. For this purpose we shall use lower case Greek letters on the left hand side of the symbol which carries the superscript. The letter 'ξ' will be used as the corresponding variable. Furthermore, since we now recognize that universals come in sets, just as we saw before that possible particulars come in sets, we need a symbol to stand for a set of universals such as is correlated with a family of possible histories. For this purpose we shall use the letter 'C' with appropriate conventions, thus '$^\alpha$C' represents the set of universals correlated with family of possible histories α. We must also comment on the use of individual and predicate variables in our extended symbolism. In the case of individual variables, the procedures mentioned under "V" on page 294 become:

(1′) Where the scope of the statement is restricted to the particulars of one possible history, we can either

    (a) use as our variable the letter 'x' ('u', 'v', etc.) with superscripts indicating the history in question, thus '$^\alpha x^0$', or

    (b) use these letters without superscripts as variables, adding an expression, say 'x ϵ $^\alpha K^0$', which indicates the restricted scope of the statement; thus '(x) x ϵ $^\alpha K^0 \cdot \supset$:$U_1 x \supset U_2 x$' where U_1 and U_2 belong to $^\alpha$C.

(2') Where the scope of the statement includes the particulars of all possible histories *of a family*, say α, we shall use the letter 'x' ('u', 'v', etc.) without superscripts together with the bound variable '$^\alpha$K' and the expression 'x ϵ $^\alpha$K'; thus, '(x) ($^\alpha$K) x ϵ $^\alpha$K $\cdot$ $\supset$: U$_1$x $\supset$ U$_2$x' where U$_1$ and U$_2$ belong to $^\alpha$C.

We must now add a third mode of referring to possible particulars by means of a variable. This mode is appropriate to those cases where the import of what we have to say demands an explicit reference to all possible particulars without restriction, that is to say, to all the possible particulars of all possible histories of all possible families of histories. This we do as follows:

(3') Where the scope of the statement includes all possible particulars without restriction, we proceed as in 2' above with the exception that the family superscript now becomes the variable 'ξ' which in turn is bound. Thus such a statement would, in so far as particulars were concerned, begin with an expression of the following kind:

$$\text{`}(^\xi)(x)(^\xi K) \cdots x \, \epsilon \, {}^\xi K \cdots \text{'}.$$

Finally, rules must be laid down for the quantification of variables which take universals as their values. This we do as follows:

(1) If the scope of the statement is restricted to one family of possible histories, then either

(a) the letter 'U' ('V', 'W', etc.) is used with a superscript indicating the family; thus '($^\alpha$U)(E$^\alpha$K)(Ex) x ϵ $^\alpha$K $\cdot$ Ux', or

(b) the letter 'U' ('V', 'W', etc.) is used without superscript together with an expression which indicates the restriction to one family, say 'U ϵ $^\alpha$C'; thus, '(U)U ϵ $^\alpha$C $\cdot$ $\supset$: (Ex)(E$^\alpha$K) x ϵ $^\alpha$K $\cdot$ Ux'.

(2) If the scope of the statement covers all possible families of histories, then the letter 'U' without superscript is used together with the bound variable 'C' (which will usually be bound in the form '($^\xi$) $\cdots$ $^\xi$C') together with the expression 'U ϵ $^\xi$C'. Thus, such a statement would, in so far as universals were concerned, begin with an expression of the kind, '($^\xi$)(U)($^\xi$C) $\cdots$ U ϵ $^\xi$C $\cdots$ '.

It should be borne in mind that our symbolism is designed to make it as impossible to say that a particular from one family exemplifies a universal from another family, as to say that a particular from one possible history is related to a particular in another possible history.

VII

We are now in a position to deal with the question, "Must a statement of the kind '(x) ϕx $\supset$ Ψx' be analytic if true, 'Ψx' being logically contained in 'ϕx', when the values of 'x' are taken to be all possible particulars?" We deal with this question by showing that it is based on a mistake. There are no universals which combine with all possible particulars (without qualification) to constitute possible states of affairs. A universal can combine with only those possible particulars which belong to the family of possible histories in relation to which the universal has its being. Thus, if 'ϕ' and 'Ψ' are to be the names of definite universals (and not variables, in which case we would be dealing with a statement form rather than a statement) they must belong to the set of universals characteristic of one family of possible histories, and the values of 'x' associated with them can only be the possible particulars belonging to that family. This being the case, we can consider the exemplification of the universals by the particulars of one history, or by the particulars of the various sets which make up the particulars of the family, but we cannot consider the exemplification of the universals by particulars falling outside the family. If the superscript 'α' refers to the family of possible histories which includes the actual history, and if we assume that ϕ and Ψ belong to $^\alpha$C, then the assertion that all actual particulars which exemplify ϕ also exemplify Ψ would be represented by

F.   (x) x ϵ $^\alpha$K$^0 \cdot \supset$:ϕx $\supset$ Ψx.

A similar assertion could be made about the particulars of any one possible history belonging to the family α.

On the other hand, the assertion that all possible particulars belonging to the family α which exemplify ϕ also exemplify Ψ would be most conveniently represented by

G.   (x)($^\alpha$K) x ϵ $^\alpha$K$\cdot \supset$:ϕx $\supset$ Ψx.

Here the fact that the possible particulars which can exemplify ϕ and Ψ must belong to the family to which ϕ and Ψ belong is indicated in the symbolism. The very idea that there could be two universals one of which materially implies the other in all possible histories of all possible families of histories is a mistake, and *consequently the question as to whether a statement which makes such a claim with respect to two universals must be analytic if true cannot arise.* On the other hand, the question whether such statements as G above must be analytic if true can now be approached without our being stampeded by the idea that an implication which holds all possible particulars must be analytic if true, *for the claim made by G, while going beyond all actual particulars, does not extend to all possible particulars without restriction.*

Approaching the matter from the opposite end, we note that if the particulars which combine with ϕ and Ψ are not intended to be restricted to the possible particulars of one family, then 'ϕ' and 'Ψ' cannot be constants, but must instead be variables. In this case, in order for '(x) ϕx $\supset$ Ψx' to formulate a statement, a binding of the variables 'ϕ' and 'Ψ' must be understood. There can be no question here of digging up anything which would have the meaning that '(x) ϕx $\supset$ Ψx' was originally intended to have, for there 'ϕ' and 'Ψ' were not variables, but the names of definite universals. The interpretations of which '(x) ϕx $\supset$ Ψx' admits on that condition have been discussed above. I therefore give an arbitrary example of a statement making unrestricted reference to all possible particulars and in which no names of universals appear.

H.   ($^\xi$)(x)(U)(V)($^\xi$K)($^\xi$C) x ϵ $^\xi$K$\cdot$U, V ϵ $^\xi$C$\cdot \supset$:Ux $\supset$ Ux $\vee$ Vx.

This statement is to the effect that if any possible particular exemplifies a universal (of its family) it either exemplifies that universal or another universal (of its family). A system of "true" statements having such unrestricted generality would constitute the theory of concrete systems.

VIII

The conceptual framework in terms of which we have been operating points to the following definition of a natural law: *A natural law is a universal proposition, implicative in form, which holds of all histories of a family of possible histories; as such it is distinguished from "accidental" formal implications which hold of one or more possible histories of the family, but do not hold of all.* The expression "family of possible histories" is used as before, and refers to such possible histories as exemplify a common set of universals. Now it is obvious that a natural law cannot have a wider scope than such a family, for the possible exemplifications of the universals involved in the law do not extend beyond the family. "But," it might be asked, "could not a law hold of a *sub-set* of the histories exemplifying a common set of universals, *so that different sub-sets of such a family might conform to different laws?* The answer is, "Not if it makes sense to distinguish between "accidental" and "lawful" formal implications which hold of a possible history!" The reason is clear: Unless the fact that the supposed law holds of the sub-set is required by the universals exemplified in the sub-set, then the fact that a single history could be such a sub-set would force one to hold that any formal implication holding of a possible history is a law for that history, and the distinction between accidental and lawful formal implications has vanished. On the other hand, if the fact that the implication holds of the sub-set *is* required by the universals exemplified in the sub-set, then the implication must hold of all histories of the family. Clearly, then, if the distinction between lawful and accidental formal implications is to make sense, we must hold to the definition we have advanced above. The important question thus becomes, *must a family exhibit lawfulness?* That the answer to this question must be in the affirmative is part and parcel of our argument to date, requiring only to be made explicit. We want also to understand how a law of nature can hold of all possible histories which exemplify the universals involved in the law, and hence be a necessary truth with respect *to* these histories, *without being an "analytic" proposition, in the sense that the universal or universals appearing in the consequent of the implication are contained in the universal or universals appearing in the antecedent.* Thus, if we suppose for a moment that a law of nature holding of the histories of a family α could have such a simple form as

I. $(x)(^\alpha K)\ x\ \epsilon\ ^\alpha K \cdot \supset : U_1 x \supset U_2 x \qquad U_1, U_2\ \epsilon\ ^\alpha C$

the corresponding question would be: Could I be true without U_2 being contained in U_1 or, rather, since we are dealing only with simple universals, without U_2 being the same universal as U_1?

The answer to both our questions is to be found in the material invariancies which we found to be necessary to the differentiation, and hence to the existence, of a domain of universals. Indeed, such material invariancies are exactly laws of nature. We pointed out that the material invariancies characteristic of a family of histories are bound up with the co-exemplification properties of the universals exemplified in the family. Just how are we to understand the relation of the material invariancies to the co-exemplification properties? How are we to represent these in terms of our symbolism? Now a co-exemplification

property of a group of universals belonging to a domain of universals is a matter
of what obtains of all possible particulars exemplifying universals belonging to
the group, and, indeed, of the relations obtaining between such particulars.
Thus, if we represent a co-exemplification property by such an expression as
'$f(^\alpha U_i, ^\alpha U_j, \cdots ; ^\alpha R_i \cdots)$', then, in a misleadingly simple case we would have

$$\text{J.} \quad f(U_1, U_2 ; R) = \cdot : (x)(y)(^\alpha K)\, x, y\ \epsilon\ ^\alpha K \cdot \supset : xRy \cdot U_1 x \supset U_2 y$$
$$\text{where } U_1, U_2\ \epsilon\ ^\alpha C.$$

Since the expression on the right hand side of the identity sign formulates a
material invariancy, we see that the co-exemplification property which is among
those possessed by U_1 and U_2, and which, with others, constitutes their distinc-
tiveness as universals, is identical with a material invariancy characteristic of
the family α.   Furthermore, since *ex hypothesi* U_1 and U_2 are simple and distinct
universals, we have found the kind of proposition we are looking for.

It takes but a moment to see that not only are the material invariancies bound
up with a set of universals laws of nature which obtain of all histories which
exemplify these universals, they are also the only non-logical invariancies common to all these histories.   This follows directly from the fact that unless such
a non-logical invariancy were rooted in the universals it involves, at least one possible state of affairs in at least one possible history of the family would violate it,
and it wouldn't be an invariancy.   But if it is rooted in the universals it involves,
it is a co-exemplification property of these universals, and hence a material
invariancy.   Thus, material invariancies and only material invariancies as characterized in our earlier discussion of the diversification of universals conform
to the definition of a natural law with which we began this section of our paper.

We are now in a position to understand the nature of the implication involved
in statements of natural laws, as well as the nature of "natural necessity."
Neither of these can be understood so long as we begin our discussion with an
attempt to interpret such statements as '$(x)\phi x \supset \Psi x$' in terms of a sharp di-
chotomy between "actual" and "all possible" particulars.   If we do this, sooner
or later we are going to say, "Since a law applies to possible as well as actual cases,
and since a material implication which applies to all possible cases must be
analytic, we must have in laws a new kind of implication.   Since this new kind
of implication is not material implication, we no longer need to toy with the silly
idea of possible particulars, but can do adequate justice to possible cases by
means of contrary to fact conditionals about actual particulars, for which our
new implication is admirably designed."   Now, I don't mind saying that in laws
of nature we have a "new kind" of implication, but I doubt that, properly understood, this implication is as "new" as has been suggested.   Its "newness" is
rather a result of its postulation without adequate explication.   Let me give
an historical example.   *Principia Mathematica* developed the propositional calculus in terms of material implication.   It was soon noticed that the major
implication of a theorem, though it was a material implication, was certifiable
in a special way.   In a sense it was material implication, and in a sense it wasn't.
It was proposed to represent material implications which were "tautologous"
by a special sign.   Thus, whereas before *Principia* philosophers would have

smiled at the idea that the material implication of the Stoics could be the same implication as logical implication or deducibility and would have insisted on using a different sign for it, *now, though we are willing to use a different sign, we understand just how they are the same and how they are different. The situation is exactly the same with respect to the implication involved in natural laws.* Consider, for example, the following statement which we shall consider to be a law obtaining of the family β:

K. $(x)(y)(^{\beta}K)$ x, y ϵ $^{\beta}K \cdot$implies$:xRy \cdot U_1x \supset U_2y$ $(U_1, U_2$ ϵ $^{\beta}C)$.

This statement, we have seen, can only be true by virtue of being an explication of the distinctive beings of the universals and particulars involved, so that the truth of K is involved in β being the family it is. Such statements as K serve to present the articulation of the realm of what we have called "concrete systems" (systems of "possible states of affairs"), and the dominant implication of K is a "necessary" implication in the Irish sense that it couldn't be false without β being a different family than it is. Using the symbol '$\prec$' to represent such "necessary" implication, we can write:

K'. $(x)(y)(^{\beta}K)$ x, y ϵ $^{\beta}K \cdot \prec :xRy \cdot U_1x \supset U_2y$ $(U_1, U_2$ ϵ $^{\beta}C)$.

Let us consider next the following two statements which concern one single history, $^{\beta}H^2$ of the family β:

L. $(x)(y)$ x, y ϵ $^{\beta}K^2 \cdot$implies$:xRy \cdot U_1x \supset U_2y$ $(U_1, U_2$ ϵ $^{\beta}C)$.

M. $(x)(y)$ x, y ϵ $^{\beta}K^2 \cdot$implies$:xRy \cdot U_3x \supset U_4y$ $(U_3, U_4$ ϵ $^{\beta}C)$.

Notice that L is a logical consequence of K, for it is the assertion with respect to one history of the family β of something which is asserted of the entire family by K. Let us assume that there is no truth about the whole family which stands to M as K stands to L; that what M asserts of the history $^{\beta}H^2$ is *not* true of all histories of the family. Thus, whereas what L asserts of $^{\beta}H^2$ is a *law* with respect to that history, what M asserts is merely an *accidental constant conjunction*.

Now it is clear that we need some way of indicating in our symbolism the difference between L and M in virtue of which the former is the statement of a law of $^{\beta}H^2$, whereas the latter is not. Can a distinction be drawn with respect to the dominant implications of these statements, one being a "necessary" implication, the other not? A moment's reflection shows that no such distinction is to be found. While we may be getting worried about the extent and the significance of such "necessity," it is clear that M as well as L couldn't be false without $^{\beta}H^2$ being a different history than it is. Thus we have,

L'. $(x)(y)$ x, y ϵ $^{\beta}K^2 \cdot \prec \cdot xRy \cdot U_1x \supset U_2y$ $(U_1, U_2$ ϵ $^{\beta}C)$.

M'. $(x)(y)$ x, y ϵ $^{\beta}K^2 \cdot \prec \cdot xRy \cdot U_3x \supset U_4y$ $(U_3, U_4$ ϵ $^{\beta}C)$.

Since, therefore, we cannot distinguish between L and M with respect to the dominant implications, let us consider the subordinate implications. But the subordinate implication is, in the case of all three statements, K, L and M, material or truth functional implication, and there can be no question of finding it to be anything else in any of these cases. Thus, it should be sufficiently obvious that the fact that a material implication holds *necessarily* of that of which it holds hasn't the slightest tendency to show that it "really isn't material implication after all"; and in any case that the generalized material implication (formal implication) of M holds of $^{\beta}H^2$ is no less (and no more) necessary than that the implication of L holds of this history. All that remains for our symbolism to take into account is the fact that whereas the material implication which L asserts of all values of 'x' and 'y' belonging to $^{\beta}H^2$ holds also of all values of 'x' and 'y' belonging to any history of the family β, this is not the case with respect to M. We shall accordingly indicate the difference between a law asserted of a single history, and a constant conjunction which is either accidental or which we do not wish to assert as a law, by using the symbol '$\rightarrow$' where we wish to imply that a formal implication, although asserted of only one member of a family of histories, holds also of all histories of the family, using '$\supset$' where no such commitment is to be made. Thus we would have,

L''. $(x)(y)\ x, y\ \epsilon\ ^{\beta}K^2 \cdot \prec : xRy \cdot U_1x \rightarrow Y_2y$ $(U_1, U_2\ \epsilon\ ^{\beta}C)$.

M''. $(x)(y)\ x, y\ \epsilon\ ^{\beta}K^2 \cdot \prec : xRy \cdot U_3x \supset U_4y$ $(U_3, U_4\ \epsilon\ ^{\beta}C)$.

It is in terms of $\rightarrow$ or *nomic* implication that the "causal" modalities and their relation to the "logical" modalities are to be understood.[17a]   Furthermore, it is in terms of the apparatus we have developed that contrary to fact conditionals and the concept of substance are capable of clarification. But these are subjects for another occasion.

IX

The empirically minded reader who has had the patience to read this far (and I hope there are a few) is undoubtedly ready to explode with something like the following: "*Primo.* If I understand you aright, you have just been saying that what formal implications hold of a particular history is a matter of necessary truth, *law-like* formal implications being distinguished as those which hold of the entire family to which the history belongs. But, shouldn't you go on to say that *any* truth about *any* aspect of *any* history of *any* family is also 'necessarily' true? For these are *possible* histories (if they are anything) and must not any truth about the possible as such be necessary truth? To use an argument of a kind of which you have given us two examples, if we suppose the following to be a true statement about the history $^{\beta}H^3$,

N. $^{\beta}U_9x_7^3$

must we not say that if N were false, $^{\beta}H^3$ would be, in Butler's words, 'another thing,' that is to say, a different possible history?

"*Secundo.* Are you not claiming to be presenting us with insights belonging to an *a priori* science of possible histories or concrete systems, a branch of a still more inclusive Science of Structures? Is there, then, to be an *a priori* science of the actual history? If so, doesn't your argument lead to the most absurd, because most thorough-going Rationalism? If not, why not? I notice that throughout your discussion you have maintained an embarrassed silence about the "possible *and actual*" history.

"*Tertio.* Does not your argument imply that it is impossible to be acquainted

---

[17a] It is, of course, this analysis of *physical necessity* in terms of *logical necessity* which by note 20, page 656, of "Epistemology and the New Way of Words," *The Journal of Philosophy*, Vol. 44, 1947.

with universals without *ipso facto* (in virtue of the "internal" relations you have described) being acquainted with laws involving these universals, and, indeed, without being acquainted with the entire content of the family of possible histories associated with these universals, if not the entire content of the "realm of structures"?! Is not this a *reductio ad absurdum* of your entire line of thought? for surely we are acquainted with universals!"

An adequate reply to this outburst would take us into another paper. We can, however, indicate the path which leads from our conclusions to the recent analyses of meaning and necessity in terms of which they can find their place in a thorough-going Logical Empiricism. The first step on this path is the realization that Platonistic rationalists have not done justice to their own Realm of Ideal or Conceptual Being; they have narrowed their vision by assuming the blinkers of a misplaced empiricism. For, properly grasped, it is the very scope of the Realm of Being, its neutrality, its lack of "factual" bias, which suggests its true status. Thus, as we have seen, it must include not only *a* system of universals, but a plurality of systems of universals; not only universals, but particulars and, indeed, systems of systems of particulars. Furthermore, the basic unit of the Realm of Being, in so far as it involves universals and particulars, is a family of concrete systems (histories).[18]

Returning to the reader's comments, *ad primum*, we must grant the point he is making to be a straight-forward consequence of our argument. We shall not only admit, but insist that any truth about any aspect of the Realm of Being is "necessarily" true. *Ad secundum.* Here we must grant part of the contention, but not all. We are indeed claiming to make statements belonging to an *a priori* Science of Structures, but, all appearances to the contrary, we are not committed to the absurd idea of an *a priori* science of "the *actual* history." The point is a delicate one (if there is an *a priori* science of *all* possible histories, mustn't there be an *a priori* science of the *actual* one?) and the fact that our discussion has developed in an atmosphere of "naïve realism" does not make it more easy to grasp. For the moment we can say that the naïvete consisted in assuming that within the Conceptual Realm is to be found an absolute distinction between the *merely possible* and the *possible and actual*. The truth of the matter, of course, is that within this Realm no concrete system or family of concrete systems has a privileged position. The conceptual distinction between what *is*, and what *isn't* but yet is *possible*, is relevant to *and relative to* each concrete system. This can be brought out by considering statement N above. We can say both that event x_7^3 of $^\beta H^3$ *is* $^\beta U_9$ and that—$^\beta U_9 x_7^3$ is possible. (That in a *different* sense x_7^3 could not have not been U_9 does not impair the truth of this remark.)

At this point the reader will exclaim, "That the distinction between the 'possible' and the 'is' in relation to a given history is relative must indeed be granted as a matter of obvious tautology. But what of the contrast between *two*

---

[18] From this perspective, the main trouble with the Idealistic doctrine of the Concrete Universal was that, like the Platonists, the Hegelians didn't go far enough. Their mistake was to speak of *The* Concrete Universal.

histories where one is spoken of as actual, the other as possible? *This* is what you had to explain, and your remark is pure evasion!" Here we are indeed at a disadvantage, for we cannot answer his challenge in terms of the concepts with which we have been dealing. Only once have we even hinted at the area that would have to be explored to show that even here the distinction between the possible and the actual is relative, and that was when we introduced (above, p. 305) the idea of concrete systems which include "minds" which "know" the system in which they are embedded. In the absence of such an exploration, we shall have to be dogmatic. However, if we are right, then any special privilege which belongs to one history must be a status which stems from outside the Conceptual Realm and which consequently cannot be penetrated by the *a priori* Science of Structures.

It is, however, the third fall which is decisive. *Ad tertium.* Here we must acknowledge the full extent of our naïvete. In speaking of an "exploration" of the Conceptual Realm, we have been making use of a ladder which we must throw away, for to rely on this metaphor is to give aid and comfort to the notion that thinking involves "acquaintance" with universals and other meanings. This notion, however, is a mistake.[19] For an account of thought we must go to the psychologist as a student of the learned language activity with which the human organism responds to internal and external stimuli, and, for the more complicated patterns of language activity, to the social psychologist and anthropologist. (Unfortunately, the study of human language behavior is in its infancy.) Now, among the linguistic activities which can be discriminated are the "explicative" or "analytic" which, to use Ayer's phrase,[20] "elucidate the proper use" of linguistic expressions. Furthermore, the anthropologist (I am using this term in the broad sense in which it is used by Kant) can distinguish within language activity between that which "deals directly with the environment" and that which attempts to mirror, within language itself, the relation of language to the world. In connection with this Fichtean self-diremption, the language user makes use of such words as "means", "true", "verified," and so on. This is linguistic activity as semantic and pragmatic metalanguage. But the language activity of human organisms can achieve an even greater degree of internal complexity, such as comes out most clearly in the "explicative" metalinguistic activity of the logician and epistemologist, but is also to be found, highly confused, in more "practical" organisms. The Realm of Ideal Being is the illusory precipitate of this doubling in (tripling in, etc.) of language upon itself. Thus, under the guise of "exploring" the "realm of possibility" we have been rehearsing explicative metalinguistic activity of the sort which is characteristic of the "analytic philosopher" who is but a few steps removed from common sense. We have avoided some of the pitfalls into which many

---

[19] For a detailed discussion of this point, see my article, "Realism and the New Way of Words," *Philosophy and Phenomenological Research*, Vol. VIII, June, 1948. See also Gustav Bergmann's important articles, "Pure Semantics, Sentences and Propositions," *Mind*, Vol. LIII, 1944, and "A Positivistic Metaphysics of Consciousness," *Mind*, Vol. LIV, 1945.

[20] *Language, Truth and Logic*, (2nd Ed.), p. 17.

have fallen, and reached the point where further "exploration" would soon lead us to explicit recognition of distinctions which would need but a slight twist to become the characteristic apparatus of the "pure theory of empirical languages" that is being developed by contemporary Logical Empiricism. This exploration would give us a clearer understanding of the status of our results, but would not impair their validity.[21]

University of Minnesota

[21] From the standpoint of formal linguistics, one of the most interesting implications of our analysis is the conception of a truth-functional or extensional account of the *prima facie* non-extensional relationships of the primitive descriptive predicates of an empirical language in virtue of which they mean what they do. "Surely the meaning of the expressions of a language doesn't depend on what is the case!" Surprising though it may seem, from the standpoint of epistemological semantics the meanings of the expressions of a language do depend on what is the case, though not in "the actual world" (however this concept be analysed) but *in the family of worlds which are the worlds of the language.*

The formal characterization of the primitive one-place predicates of an empirical language by means of semantic techniques involves (a) the specification of one or more basic relations, (b) the specification of a set of "worlds" consisting of all relational arrays of atomic states of affairs exemplifying the qualitative universals designated by these primitive one-place predicates, where (c) certain formal implications (synthetic in the Kantian sense) involving these predicates and the basic relations are true of all these "worlds," and where (d) each predicate can be distinguished from all the others in terms of the role it plays in this set of formal implications.

(289.1; 290.1,.2; 291.1,.2) The purpose of this paper is to discuss evaluations
in the context of "rule-regulated behavior" with the aim of developing a view
which avoids "rationalistic a-priorism" as well as "descriptivism", i.e.,
"the claim that all meaningful concepts and problems belong to the empirical
sciences." Pragmatism has been guilty of descriptivism in certain areas.

(292.1) The approach to these problems is through a discussion of justification. But since "to justify is to *do* something", it might seem that such
a discussion belongs to scientific study of behavior, i.e., psychology. Perhaps the philosopher's task is to discuss only the "*correctness or validity*"
of justifications.

(292.2; 293.1,.2) The alternatives to which the above suggestions give rise.

(293.3; 294.1,.2; 295.1,.2; 296.1,.2) Examples of justification in some
of which the matter of necessity ("must") appears important.

(296.3; 297.1) If we are to invoke rules to explain (at least part of) what
happens with regard to necessity and justification, we must begin by distinguishing between action which "merely *conforms to* a rule" and that
which "occurs *because of* a rule." Learned "habits of response to our
environment" are reflected in behavior that conforms to a rule, but such
behavior is not necessarily because of a rule. But "rule- regulated"
activity is, in some sense, because of rules. Such rule-regulated activity
is the key to understanding intellectual activity: "To say that man is a
rational animal is to say that man is a creature not of *habits*, but of *rules*."

(298.1) No "adequate psychology of rule-governed symbol behavior exists."

(299.1,.2) A rule is not merely a generalization, but a generalization
accompanied by special expressions (e.g., 'correct', 'proper', 'right') or
cast in a special syntactical form (e.g., 'One ought to tell the truth').
The importance of this feature in the formulation of rules is that they reflect the fact that (roughly speaking) a rule is a generalization that
"tends to inhibit the occurrence of such events as would falsify it"
(the generalization). This view of rules is much like Kant's.

(300.1) The "chief purpose" of the above remarks is to stimulate investigation of the notion of rules, particularly rules of language, so that
"the field of cognitive and moral psychology" is not left to the
"rationalists."

(301.1,.2; 302.1) The proponent of the doctrines of rule-regulated symbol activity, the "regulist", is sometimes misled into thinking that there must be "sense meaning rules" which connect "language with the world". There is, of course, symbol behavior which is "tied" to environmental stimulation, but this symbol behavior is not rule-regulated. However, it is true that in order for rule-regulated symbol behavior and tied symbol behavior to mesh certain items (e.g., "the noise "blue"") must appear both in "tied" responses to "our environment" and in a system of symbol behavior regulated by rules. The "linguistic meaning of a word is entirely constituted by the rules of its use."

(303.1; 304.1,.2) An argument against the regulist's accepting the claim that there are "sense meaning rules"; the likely consequences for a regulist of accepting these rules.

(305.1) We now turn to the account, built on the regulist view, of the "necessities" which appeared in the examples of justification; this account avoids the traditional features of the doctrine of the "synthetic a priori" while preserving "the insights" of this "rationalist doctrine."

(305.2; 306.1) A brief review of the traditional doctrine of "real" (necessary) "connection" as it appears in the rationalist doctrine of the synthetic a priori.

(307.1,.2) Arguments to show that it is not correct for the rationalist to speak of "real connections as possible objects of awareness or intuition."

(309.1) What, then, does the regulist say about "real connections" and "the significance of modal words in logically synthetic sentences"? In brief, the regulist claims that the "use of the term "necessary" in causal as well as in logical contexts is to be traced to linguistic rules."

(309.2) Which rules are the ones in terms of which causal modalties are to be understood? These rules are "conformation rules". They are rules the language has in addition to formation and transformation rules. "For each basic factual word in the language there are one or more logically synthetic universal sentences which, as exhibiting the rules for the use of these words, have the status of "necessary truths" of the language. These sentences are those into which a user of the language would insert the words 'must' or 'necessary'."

(310.1; 311.1; 312.1) Replies to some questions about the account just sketched. These replies include the claim that the history of science provides examples, not only of new terms and new rules to regulate these terms, but also of the use of the same noises or marks with new rules. Such new rules are adopted and old ones dropped in the scientific attempt "to develop a system of rule-governed behavior which will adjust the human organism to the environment."

(312.2,.3; 313.1; 314.1) The rationalist distinguishes between real connections which are "known" and those which are accepted on the basis of "probable opinion." Is there anything in the regulist view to correspond to this distinction? Yes, there are two sorts of rules that the advance of science has not yet considered alternatives for. The one sort or rule is concerned with very general structural features of our language; the other sort or rule is concerned with the connection between predicates (e.g., 'colored' and 'extended') which are caught up in "tied" symbol behavior.   It is in these cases that we are most content to say that we know since we have "no serious alternatives."

(314.1) "Why one set of rules rather than another? How is the a-doption of a set of rules itself to be justified?"   In some sense, "pragmatically"; but there are difficulties about rules that must be investigated more thoroughly before these questions can be answered with confidence.

Language, Rules and Behavior*

by WILFRID SELLARS

MY PURPOSE in writing this essay is to explore from the standpoint
of what might be called a philosophically oriented behavioristic
psychology the procedures by which we evaluate actions as right or
wrong, arguments as valid and invalid and cognitive claims as well
or ill grounded. More specifically, our frame of reference will be
the psychology of rule-regulated behavor, or rather, since such a
science as yet scarcely exists, it will be such anticipations of a psychology of the so-called higher processes as can be precipitated
from common sense by the reagents synthesized by the naturalistic
revolution in psychology instituted within the memory and with
the vigorous assistance of the man to whom this volume is dedi-
cated. Within these coordinates I shall attempt to map a true *via
media* (one which doesn't covertly join up with one or other extreme beyond the next bend in the road) between rationalistic a-
priorism and what, for want of a better term, I shall call "descriptivism," by which I understand the claim that all meaningful con-

*The present paper has grown out of the stimulating discussions with my
friend and colleague, Herbert Feigl, which it has been my good fortune to
enjoy over the past three years. It was precipitated by a reading of an early
draft of his paper, "De Principiis non Disputandum—?" which will appear in a
volume of *Essays in Analytic Philosophy*, edited by Max Black, to be published
in the fall of 1950 by the Cornell University Press. There the reader will find
an exceptionally clear statement of puzzles relating to the justifiability of First
Principles, together with a brilliant and original analysis of the various forms
taken by the "appeal to Reason."

cepts and problems belong to the empirical or descriptive sciences, including the sciences of human behavior.

Those who deny the existence of such a *via media* offer the following argument: "How can one assert the existence of concepts and problems which do not belong to empirical science, without admitting the existence of a domain of non-empirical objects or qualities together with a mental apparatus of acts and intuitions for cognizing them?" The rationalists add a minor premise of the form, "Concepts and problems relating to validity, truth and obligation are significant, but do not belong to the empirical sciences," and conclude, "Therefore a domain of non-empirical qualities and a corresponding apparatus of acts and intuitions exist." The descriptivist, on the other hand, denying, as he does, the rationalists' conclusion while accepting their major premise, finds himself forced to deny the minor premise. Clearly he can do this either by maintaining that the concepts and problems to which the rationalists appeal are pseudo-concepts and pseudo-problems, or by claiming that, though legitimate, they are, after all, included within the scope of empirical science. In the field of moral philosophy, descriptivistically inclined philosophers characteristically divide into those who claim that the concept of moral obligation is a pseudo-concept, such words as "right" and "duty" serving merely to express attitudes and instigate actions, and those who accept some form of the venerable subjectivistic account now widely known as the "autobiographical analysis."

I can now bring my introductory remarks to a focus by supposing a suspicious pragmatist to ask: "Are you, perhaps, leading up to the following argument?

> Pragmatists are descriptivists
> Descriptivism entails Mill's philosophy of mathematics
> But Mill's philosophy of mathematics is absurd
> Therefore pragmatism is absurd

If you are indeed raising this old chestnut, it can be said right away that pragmatism is by no means committed to what it grants is an absurd interpretation of mathematics. The pragmatist merely in-

Sellars—Language, Rules and Behavior   291

sists that there is no aspect of *mathematical inquiry as a mode of human behavior* which requires a departure from the categories of naturalistic psychology for its interpretation. If this is what you call descriptivism, then the pragmatist is a descriptivist, but in that case, descriptivism does not have the absurd consequences with which you threaten us."

Let me reply to this challenge by immediately disavowing any intention of accusing pragmatism of being a descriptivistic philosophy *as a matter of principle*. Indeed, there are clearly certain areas, one of which is exactly the philosophy of mathematics, in which pragmatism has explicitly rejected the descriptivist account, while expressing sympathy with its naturalistic motivation. Notice that our suspicious pragmatist did not say

"The concepts and problems of mathematics belong to naturalistic psychology."

If he had, he clearly would be formulating a descriptivistic philosophy of mathematics. What he actually said was

" . . . there is no aspect of *mathematical inquiry as a mode of human behavior* which requires a departure from the categories of naturalistic psychology for its interpretation."

With this latter statement I am in full agreement. It must by no means be confused with the former. If it entails a descriptivistic philosophy of mathematics, it must be shown to do so by an involved argument of a type familiar to students of the rationalistic tradition. Needless to say, I do not believe that such an argument would be successful.

But if I do not accuse the pragmatist of being a descriptivist as a matter of principle, I do contend that pragmatism has been characterized by a descriptivistic bias. Thus, while it has defended the important insight that to reject descriptivism in the philosophy of mathematics is not to embrace rationalism, it has committed itself to descriptivism in other areas of philosophy (*e.g.* in its interpretation of truth and of moral obligation) with all the fervor of a

Dutch boy defending the fertile lands of Naturalism against a threatening rationalistic flood. Now it will be my contention in this paper that a sound pragmatism must reject descriptivism in all areas of philosophy, and that it can do so without giving one jot or tittle of comfort to what has so aptly been called the new Failure of Nerve. My point of departure will be an examination of the forms taken by our appeals to standards and principles when we *justify* something we have done.

What sort of thing, then, is a justification? Before attempting to answer this question, it will be worth our while to consider a familiar challenge to our right to raise it. Those who are alert to raise their voices on behalf of psychology will insist that to justify is to *do* something, to perform a mental action. To explain mental action is the business of the psychologist, and if he is not yet in a position to give a satisfactory acount, if the truth must wait until he is adequately grounded in the behavior of the *rattus albinus Norvegicus,* the question nevertheless belongs to him. It is not a more legitimate concern of the philosopher than, say, the question, What is gravitation? If the philosopher objects that this same argument would excuse the logician from examining reasoning and the philosopher of science from examining explanation, he is promptly told that these very parallels make it clear that his business is to explicate the *correctness* or *validity* of justifications, and not the causal structure of justifications as matters of psychological *fact.*

But is it so obvious that by concerning ourselves with the correctness or validity of justifications we have moved from one field called psychology to another called philosophy? If validity or correctness is a property of certain mental processes, then does it not fall within the province of psychology to tell us about this property and its opposite invalidity or incorrectness? Or shall we say that psychology deals with some but not all of the properties exhibited by psychological processes? And if not with all, then what distinguishes the properties with which it does deal from those with which it does not? Furthermore, must not the latter fall within the scope, if not of psychology, then of some branch of empirical anthropology?

Has, then, our philosophical problem turned out, after all, to be one of empirical science? Or shall we perhaps say that validity is a non-empirical property, and that, together with other non-empirical properties it falls within the scope of a non-empirical science of thought, a rational psychology? Is, perhaps, epistemology the non-empirical science of such non-empirical properties of thought as validity and truth? Could the propositions of such a science be anything but synthetic *a priori* truths?

How shall we choose between these alternatives? Or perhaps we have already made a mistake in speaking of validity as a property which can be exemplified by psychological processes; so that these alternatives do not even arise. If so, how could this be determined? Clearly we have come to the point where what is required is an exploration of some typical contexts in which the terms "valid" and "correct" appear to be properly, shall I say correctly, employed.

We began by asking "What sort of thing is a justification?" We should also ask "What sort of thing does one who justifies justify? Consider the following exchange:

Jones: I stayed away from the meeting.
Smith (pompously): How would you justify your conduct?

Clearly, then, it is proper to speak of justifying *actions*. How is it done? The above exchange continues:

Jones: One ought to do what is conducive to the greatest happiness of the greatest number, and, as I could readily convince you, staying away from the meeting was so conducive.

We are thus reminded that to justify a piece of conduct is to argue concerning the conduct, and, what is more important, that at least the earlier stages of such an argument consist in subsuming the conduct under what used to be called a moral law. Characteristic of moral laws is the use of the word "ought" in its categorical sense.

Now, I must confess that I find the emotive theory of moral obligation as unacceptable as would be an emotive theory of logical necessity, or (*pace* Hume) an emotive theory of physical necessity. This is not to say that I agree with the intuitionists in finding a non-natural quality or relation to belong to actions over and above their empirical characteristics. As I see it, an inventory of the basic qualities and relations exemplified by this universe of ours, and, in particular, by the mental processes of human beings, would no more include obligatoriness than it would include either logical or physical (that is, "real") connections. Although I have felt ever since making its acquaintance that the intuitionism of Ross, Prichard and Ewing is the only contemporary philosophy of morals which is reasonably faithful to the phenomenology of moral thought and experience, I have been equally convinced that we must look elsewhere for an adequate insight into the nature of the *ought* which they so rightly find to be central to the moral universe of discourse. For a time I thought that this insight was to be sought in the direction taken by emotive theories. I now regard this as a mistake—not because the ethical "ought" isn't *essentially* an expressor and instigator, but because what it expresses and instigates is *the observance of a rule*. To make the ethical "ought" into even the second cousin of the "hurrah" of a football fan is completely to miss its significance. If I have become more and more happy of late about Kant's assimilation of the ethical "ought" to the logical and physical "musts," it is because I have increasingly been led to assimilate the logical and physical "musts" to the ethical "ought." But of this more later.

Let us now examine the process of justification in another type of context. Consider the following exchange:

> Jones: It will rain shortly.
>
> Smith: Justify your assertion.

Clearly it is proper to speak of justifying assertions, which are, in a suitably broad sense, *actions*. It is equally proper to speak of justifying beliefs, which are, at least in part, dispositions relating to assertion. Shall we say, then, that one does not justify a *proposition*, but the *assertion* of a proposition?—that one does not justify a *principle*, but the *acceptance* of a principle? Shall we say that all justification is, in a sense which takes into account the dispositional as well as the occurrent, a *justificatio actionis?* I am strongly inclined to think that this is the case. But if so, is not our new example of justification as much a justification of conduct as was the first? Or can we distinguish within action in the broadest sense, between action which is conduct and action which is not? and if so how?[1]

However this may be, Smith, in the above dialogue, has asked Jones to justify a certain assertion, and Jone's reply to this challenge is certainly relevant to our problem. The exchange continues:

> Jones: Clouds of kind X cause rain, and there are clouds of kind
>   X overhead.

Once again we have before us an argument of a familiar form. I want now to focus attention on three directions the argument might take if continued beyond this point.

(1) The justification will achieve its purpose only if Smith accepts the causal premise. If Smith should ask "Why *must* clouds of kind X be accompanied by rain?" Jones may either say, "Because they must, and that's all there is to it!" or, if he is in a position to do so, he may draw on his knowledge of meteorology in an attempt

---

[1] Certainly it won't do to say that that which is criticized as conduct is overt behavior, an individual's impingement on his environment, so that *public* assertion would be conduct, whereas the *private* assertion that is involved in thinking would not. For surely the mental setting oneself (Prichard) to stab an enemy would be conduct even though paralysis or a stroke of lightning prevented the occurrence of the intended sequence of events. Bearing in mind this obvious connection between conduct and *intention,* shall we say that what the moralist has in mind by "conduct" is basically a matter of the tendency of *thoughts about* sequences of events beginning with the me-here-now to bring about the actual occurrence of these sequences? Do not primitive and pictorial mis-conceptions of desire, motivation and the role of reward and punishment in shaping behavior stand in the way of a recognition of the true scope of "ideo-motor activity?"

to derive this law from other laws relating to atmospheric phenomena which are accepted by Smith. If Smith should challenge these new *musts*, and Jones is willing to continue the argument, but is unable to find still other laws which Smith will accept and from which they can be derived, he may attempt to persuade Smith to accept them (or the original law) by means of an argument from instances.[2]

(2) The justification will achieve its purpose only if Smith accepts the minor premise ("There are clouds of kind X overhead"). If Smith challenges this assertion, Jones, if he is willing to continue the argument, will attempt to find statements of particular matters of fact—let us call them *historical* statements—and causal laws which Smith accepts, and from which it would follow that there were (or that it was probable that there were) clouds of kind X overhead.

(3) Finally, the justification will achieve its purpose only if Smith accepts the logical *musts* embodied in the arguments Jones offers, as when he says "A and B, therefore *necessarily* C." If Smith challenges these, Jones is likely to say "It is necessary because it is necessary, and that's all there is to it!"

Now, when certain contemporary philosophers hear the words "must" and "necessary," particularly in such contexts as "It must because it must," or "It's necessary, and that's all there is to it," they immediately say to themselves, "Aha! Here we have something that is required by a rule of this fellow's language." And I am convinced that this is a very illuminating thing to say, though I am not certain that I know exactly what it means. As Augustine with

[2] In dealing with such situations, philosophers usually speak of inductive arguments, of establishing laws by induction from instances. For reasons which will manifest themselves in the course of my argument, I am highly dubious of this conception. I should be inclined to say that the use Jones will make of instances is rather of the nature of Socratic method. For Socratic method serves the purpose of making explicit the rules we have adopted for thought and action, and I shall be interpreting our judgments to the effect that A causally necessitates B as the expression of a rule governing our use of the terms "A" and "B." But of this, more later.

Time, I knew what a rule was until asked. I asked myself and proceeded to become quite perplexed.

I suspect that my trouble with the concept of a rule is in large part due to my ignorance of the psychology of the higher processes. Yet certain things seem clear. In the first place, we must distinguish between action which merely *conforms to* a rule, and action which occurs *because of* a rule. A rule isn't functioning as a rule unless it is in some sense internal to action. Otherwise it is a mere generalization. Thus, if I train an animal to sit up when I snap my fingers, the animal's behavior conforms to the generalization "This animal sits up when my fingers snap," but we should scarcely say that the animal acts on the rule of sitting up when I snap my fingers. Clearly the type of activity which is rule-regulated is of a higher level than that which is produced by simple animal learning procedures. One way of bringing this out is to say that most if not all animal behavior is tied to the environment in a way in which much characteristically human behavior is not. Certainly, we learn habits of response to our environment in a way which is essentially identical with that in which the dog learns to sit up when I snap my fingers. And certainly these learned habits of response—though modifiable by rule-regulated symbol activity— remain the basic tie between all the complex rule-regulated symbol behavior which is the human mind in action, and the environment in which the individual lives and acts. Yet above the foundation of man's learned responses to environmental stimuli—let us call this his *tied behavior*—there towers a superstructure of more or less developed systems of rule-regulated symbol activity which constitutes man's intellectual vision. It is in terms of such systems of rule-regulated symbol activity that we are to understand an Einstein's grasp of alternative structures of natural law, a Leibnitz' vision of the totality of all possible worlds, a logician's exploration of the most diversified postulate systems, a Cantor's march into the trans-finite. Such symbol activity may well be characterized as *free*—by which, of course, I do not mean *uncaused*—in contrast to the behavior that is learned as a dog learns to sit up, or a white rat to run a maze. On the other hand, a structure of rule-regulated symbol activity, which as such is free, constitutes a man's understanding of *this* world, the world in which he lives, its history and future, the laws according to which it operates, by meshing in with his tied behavior, his learned habits of response to his environment. To say that man is a rational animal, is to say that man is a creature not of *habits*, but of *rules.* When God created Adam, he whispered in his ear, "In all contéxts of action you will recognize rules, if only the rule to grope for rules to recognize. When you cease to recognize rules, you will walk on four feet."

If what I have just said appears to be rhetoric and not philosophy, I can only plead that it ought to be psychology, but that if an adequate psychology of rule-governed symbol behavior exists, I have not yet made its acquaintance. This, however, may well be just another example of the philosopher's characteristic ignorance of the science of his day (as opposed to the science of yesterday, with which he is notoriously well acquainted). But if what we have been saying belongs to psychology, then, once again, we must ask, "How does it concern us, who are philosophers and not psychologists?" What would be the relevance of an adequate empirical psychology of rule-regulated symbol activity to the task of the philosopher? Now, that psychology is neither the whole nor even a part of philosophy is granted. Yet bad psychology may give aid and comfort to bad philosophy. This is most clear in connection with the rationalistic pseudo-psychologies which we shall be criticizing in a moment. I want now to point out that if there is any truth in what we have said, then much of what(among philosophers)passes for tough-minded psychology is an over-simplified extension to the higher processes of the *dog—fingersnap—sit-up—sugar* schema of tied responses to environmental stimuli. Not that I should deny for one moment that animal learning theory provides the key to all psychological phenomena. On the contrary I am convinced that this is the case. And not that I should deny that the laws of animal learning (if we had them) would explain even the mathematician's behavior in developing alternative postulate sets for n-dimensional geometries. I am even prepared to endorse this promissory note. Yet the fact remains that the distinction between tied behavior and free, rule-regulated symbol activity, whatever they may have in common, is a fact of experience, one that the philosopher cannot afford to neglect.

We distinguished above between action which merely conforms to a rule and action which occurs because of a rule and pointed out that in so far as actions merely conform to it, a rule is not a rule but a mere generalization. On the other hand, we must not say that a rule is something completely other than a generalization. The mode of existence of a rule is as a generalization written in flesh and blood, or nerve and sinew, rather than in pen and ink. A rule, existing in its proper element, has the logical form of a generalization. Yet a rule is not *merely* a generalization which is formulated in the language of intra-organic process. Such a generalization would find its overt expression in a declarative sentence. A rule, on the other hand, finds its expression either in what are classified as non-declarative grammatical forms, or else in declarative sentences with certain special terms such as "correct," "proper," "right," etc., serving to distinguish them from generalizations. What do these special features in the formulation of rules indicate? They give expression to the fact that a rule is an embodied generalization which to speak loosely but suggestively, tends to make itself true. Better, it tends to inhibit the occurrence of such events as would falsify it—if it weren't already false, that is, for the generalizations which lie at the core of rules are rarely if ever true, and unless they *could* (logical *or* physical possibility) be false, they could scarcely function as rules. Thus, consider the moral rule, "One ought to tell the truth." The core-generalization on which this rule is built is "People always say what they believe" which is, of course, false.

Now, Kant saw all this quite clearly. He pointed out that moral action is action because of a rule, and said that to say this is equivalent to saying that to act morally is to act "so that I could also will that my maxim should become a universal law."[3] If he had said in-

---

[3] *Fundamental Principles of the Metaphysics of Morals*, p. 18 of Abbott's translation, included in his *Kant's Theory of Ethics*. The historically minded reader will observe that the concept of rule-regulated behavior developed in this paper is, in a certain sense, the translation into behavioristic terms of the Kantian concept of Practical Reason. Kant's contention that the pure consciousness of

stead that to act morally is to act as though the truth of the corresponding generalization depended only on the occurrence of that action, his claim would have been essentially identical with ours. As far as I can see, the basic fault of Kant's ethics is that he attempted (or seems to have attempted) to derive a specific code of rules from the definition of moral action as action because of rules together with a consideration of the basic traits of human nature.

Now, my chief purpose in making the above metaphorical and unscientific remarks about rule-governed behavior is to stimulate those philosophers who are always talking about rules— usually rules of language—to explain more fully what they have in mind. To urge that these are questions for the empirical psychologist to answer, and that we must wait upon his convenience, is to leave the field of cognitive and moral psychology to the rationalists. To content oneself with glib phrases about stimulus-response conditioning is to give the rationalist armor and armament. (In the good old days before the failure of nerve, when the climate of opinion was favorable to empiricism, the empiricist got away with murder. Today, he must use every weapon in his arsenal, and make doubly certain that it is sharp.) It is easy to shape the psychology of the higher processes as embodied in common sense into the direction of intuitionism and rationalism. Philosophers have been doing just that for over two thousand years. But common sense also contains cues which, when combined with the achievements to date of empirical psychology, can be developed into the outlines of an adequate psychology of rational behavior, and to do this is an urgent task for the embattled empiricist. In thus reconstructing common sense psychology, the empiricist will find that the outcome shows more *structural* kinship with the pseudo-psychologies of the rationalist than

moral law can be a factor in bringing about conduct in conformity with law, becomes the above conception of rule-regulated behavior. However, for Kant's conception of Practical Reason as, so to speak, an intruder in the natural order, we substitute the view that the causal efficacy of the embodied core-generalizations of rules is ultimately grounded on the Law of Effect, that is to say, the role of rewards and punishments in shaping behavior. The most serious barrier to an appreciation of Kant's insights in this matter lies in the fact that most discussions in philosophical circles of the motivation of behavior stand to the scientific account (whatever its inadequacies) as the teleological conception of the adjustment of organisms to their environment stands to the evolutionary account.

with much that passes today for psychology among empiricists. But the teeth will have been drawn. It is only by absorbing the insights of rationalism that a pragmatic empiricism can do justice to the facts. There are many signs that this is being done.

I have already indicated how I would approach this reconciliation of rationalism and empiricism in the field of ethics. I want now to turn to the problem of the *a priori* in the field of specifically cognitive activity. Here we note that where the *regulist* speaks of statements which exhibit the rules of the language in which they are formulated, the *rationalist* speaks of intuition or self-evidence. The regulist goes from object-language up to meta-linguistic rule, whereas the rationalist goes from object-language down to extra-linguistic reality. The regulist explains the significance of the word "must," as it occurs in arguments, in terms of the syntactical rules of the language in which it occurs; the rationalist explains it in terms of a non-linguistic grasp of a necessary connection between features of reality.

Now, certain overly enthusiastic regulists have spoken of the "sense meaning rules" of a language, arguing that the hook-up of an empirically meaningful language with the world is a matter of rules of linguistic usage. I am as convinced a regulist as any, and, as I shall indicate in a moment, a far more thoroughgoing regulist than most, but I regard this as a mistake. I have already argued above that the hook-up between rule-regulated symbol activity and the external environment rests on the *meshing* of rule-regulated symbol activity with what I referred to as "tied behavior." Now though this tied behavior is not *rule-regulated* symbol behavior, it is nevertheless customary to refer to certain forms it may take as "symbol behavior." Let us distinguish this symbol behavior by the phrase "tied symbol behavior." Thus we can say that picking up his dish is a tied symbol of food to a dog. Now, what misleads these regulists who speak of the sense meaning rules of a language is the fact that in order for the above mentioned meshing of rule-regulated language with tied symbol behavior to take place, *certain*

302   *John Dewey: A Symposium*

intra-organic events must function as symbols in both senses, as both free and tied symbols. Thus, as children we learn to understand the noise "blue" in much the same way as the dog learns to understand the noise "bone," but we leave the dog behind in that the noise "blue" also comes to function for us in a system of rule-regulated symbol activity, and it is a *word*, a linguistic fact, a rule-regulated symbol only in so far as it functions in this linguistic system. The noise "blue" becomes a mediating link between what can suggestively be called a rule-regulated calculus, and a cluster of conditioned responses which binds us to our environment. Here we should note that the rules which inter-relate these mediating symbols *qua* linguistic symbols must mesh with the inter-relationships of these symbols *qua* tied symbols in the causal structure of tied sign behavior.[4]

Let me nail down the point I have been making as tightly as I am able, even though this means anticipating certain things I shall have to say later on. To think of a system of qualities and relations is, I shall argue, to use symbols governed by a system of rules which, we might say, *implicitly define* these symbols by giving them a specific task to perform in the linguistic economy. The linguistic meaning of a word is entirely constituted by the rules of its use.[5] A scientist who thinks of worlds which exemplify quali-

[4] Linguistic systems of the kind we are considering center around a structure of sentences which is, so to speak, a *map*. Thus, a language enables us to "find our way around in the world." Clearly this involves that in the employment of a language, not only must certain *predicates* in the language play the above double role, so also must certain *individual constants*. It is also obvious that the individual constants which do this must, from the logician's standpoint, be logical constructions from the basic individual constants of the language, since "recognizable individuals" are always "continuants" or "concrete universals." Thus, not only do "green" and "sweet" function both as linguistic symbols proper and as tied symbols, so also do "Jones" and "Picadilly."

[5] At this point, the reader will probably hurl the following challenge: "Are you not confronted by a dilemma? For surely the rules for a linguistic system are themselves linguistic phenomena. Therefore either you must hold that they, in turn, are rule-governed, or else admit that at least one linguistic structure exists which is not "rule-governed" in your sense. You can scarcely be prepared to adopt the latter course. If you take the former, you are committed, surely, to an infinity of rules, meta-rules, meta-meta-rules, etc." A full reply to this challenge cannot be given in the available space. The following remarks, however, may help. The reader is quite correct in predicting that we shall take the former course and grant that the rules are themselves rule-governed He is, however, mistaken in inferring that this "regress" is vicious. It would be vicious if

ties and relations not to be found in this world is making use of symbols which are, or may be, on a par with the symbols we use to think about *this* world *in every rule-regulated respect*. The "artificial" language with which the scientist is speculating does not, however, include— as does the language in which he speaks about the actual world—a sub-set of symbols which mesh in with his tied symbol responses to environmental stimuli.

If there were such things as sense meaning rules (as opposed to verbal conditionings) how should they be formulated? Perhaps: "When I have such and such experiences, I am to use the expression 'I see red' "? Unfortunately, the philosophers who speak of sense meaning rules are the same *moderni* who insist that there is no such thing as cognition unmediated by symbols. Whether or not such a rule as the above would be sensible given the non-symbolic intuitive cognition of the rationalist is another matter, but without it the rule obviously either doesn't make sense or doesn't perform the function for which it was invoked. In order for the rule to be intelligible, the person who is to obey it must already know when he sees red. But to know when he sees red he must, according to these same *moderni*, understand the meaning of either the symbol "red" or a synonym (which need not, of course, belong to any intersubjective language of *overt* utterance). In short, the very symbols whose possession of meaning is explained by these overly enthusiastic regulists in terms of sense meaning rules, must either already have meaning independently of the rules, or else the sole value of the rules is to serve as a means of acquiring synonyms for symbols which have meaning independently of the rules. This is but a sample of the confusion into which one gets by failing to

the infinity of rules which an organism would have to learn in order to exhibit rule-governed behavior constituted an infinity of rules which differed in the full-blooded way in which the rules of chess differ from the rules of bridge. That the hierarchy of rules is in a certain sense repetitious (compare a rule for naming a name with a rule for naming the name of a name) provides the answer to this difficulty. However, even granting this, the regress would still be vicious if in order for a type of behavior to be rule-governed, every instance of the behavior must be accompanied (brought about) by an organic event of which the *text* (to use Bergmann's term) is the core-generalization of the rule. If this were the case, then, obviously, an infinite hierarchy of events with texts would have to occur in order for any case of rule-governed behavior to occur.

distinguish the learning of tied symbol behavior from the learning of rule-regulated symbol activity.[6]

The above discussion enables us to understand why certain regulists who, owing to a failure to distinguish clearly between tied and rule-regulated symbol activity, push the latter beyond its proper limits are tempted to hold that the meaningful use of language rests on an intuitive cognition unmediated by symbols. Action on a rule presupposes cognition, and if confusion leads these philosophers to conceive of all symbol behavior as in principle—that is, parroting aside— rule-regulated, then they are committed to the search for an extra-symbolic mode of cognition to serve as the tie between meaningful symbol behavior and the world. This link is usually found, even by regulists who have been decisively influenced by behaviorism, in a conception of the *cognitive given-ness of sense-data*. It must, of course, be confessed that these tough-minded empiricists rarely formulate such a doctrine of cognitive awareness in so many words—and might even disown it—but the careful student can frequently find it nestling in their arguments.

Here we must pay our respects to John Dewey, who has so clearly seen that the conception of the cognitive given-ness of sense-data is both the last stand and the entering wedge of rationalism. Thus, since anything which can be called cognition involves classification, the conception of the cognitive given-ness of sense-data involves

---

[6] The stress laid by many empiricists on "ostensive definition" is on the one hand a sound recognition of the patent fact that a meaningful language system must tie up with the environment, and on the other hand a sad confusion between learning the *definition* of a word, that is to say, learning to use it in a rule-regulated manner according to socially recognized rules, and learning (being conditioned) to respond with the word-noise to certain environmental stimuli. This confusion is exhibited by the ambiguous usage of the phrase "ostensive definition." Sometimes it is used to refer to procedures typified by teaching a dog to understand the noise "bone." Sometimes it refers to procedures typified by leading an individual to adopt a rule by which he would use a new symbol "X" as an equivalent of the rule-regulated symbol "Y"—where "Y" is usually a complex symbol of the form "U and V and W. . . ." Thus a person might be led to adopt a rule by which he would use "sugar" as an equivalent of what corresponds in his intra-organic symbol economy to the "white and sweet and granular . . ." of the *language of overt utterance* which is English, by pointing to a piece of sugar (which he cognizes by means of this intra-organic symbol economy) and uttering the noise "sugar."

as a necessary condition the given-ness of universals.[7] But once the unwary empiricist commits himself to the given-ness of universals —even if only sense-universals—he has taken the first step on a path which, unless he shuts his eyes and balks like a mule, will lead him straight into the arms of the traditional synthetic *a priori*.[8] After all, if sense universals are given, and if there are real connections between them, must not these real connections be given? And who is so empirically minded today as not to make obeisance to real connections?

It is my purpose in the following pages to sketch a regulist account of real connections and of the "synthetic *a priori*" which preserves the insights of the rationalistic doctrine, while rejecting its absolutism as well as the pseudo-psychology of cognitive givenness on which this absolutism is based.

It is important to note that the classical doctrine of synthetic *a priori* knowledge distinguishes carefully between the *ontological* and the *cognitive* aspects of such knowledge. Ontologically there is the real connection between the universals in question— say, Color and Extension. It is here that the necessity is located. On the other hand there is the cognitive fact of the intuitive awareness of this real connection, the *Schau* of the phenomenologist. Since it is a necessary consequence of the real connection of the universals that any exemplification of the one (Color) must also be an exemplification of the other (Extension), to *see* this real connection is to have rational certainty that the corresponding universal proposi-

---

[7] Let me hasten to emphasize that the difference between the platonist and the nominalistic empiricist with respect to universals (and propositions) does not consist in the platonist's saying "There are universals" and the nominalist's saying "No, there are no universals," but rather in the platonist's speaking of psychological relationships between minds and universals, whereas the nominalist finds this to be nonsense. It is this way of speaking which constitutes the platonic hypostatization of universals, and not the making of triangularity into a super-triangle—which not even Plato seems to have done.

[8] But is this such a horrible fate? Already we find in the younger generation of epistemologically-minded philosophers—particularly among those who have been influenced by C. D. Broad's masterful *Examination of McTaggart's Philosophy*—those who argue that a carefully restricted synthetic *a priori* is not incompatible with the insights of logical empiricism.

tion "All colors are extended" will not be falsified by any future experience—or so the traditional doctrine goes.[9]

Now a philosopher who finds the notion of a real connection between universals to be a sensible one, and who approaches the problem of what is meant by "causal necessity," is likely to say that causal necessity consists in real connections between the universals exemplified by events in the natural order. On the other hand, unless he shares the rationalistic optimism of a Hegel, he will not claim that we are able—even in principle—to have a direct apprehension of these real connections and so achieve an *a priori* knowledge of the laws of nature. He may, however, as we have already suggested, make an exception in the case of certain real connections between sense-qualities and, perhaps, in the case of real connections between universals of a "categorial" nature, universals relating to the most pervasive features of the world. "Science," he will say, "is able to claim with ever increasing rational assurance that such and such *kinds of events* are connected, but with an assurance that is based on empirical evidence and induction, never on self-evidence."[10]

[9] In speaking of the "traditional" doctrine of the synthetic *a priori* I am, of course, referring to the rationalism characteristic of the Platonic-Aristotelian tradition, though only since Descartes and Locke has the distinction between analytic and synthetic necessity been explicitly drawn and given the center of the stage. Kant, who was aware—as his rationalistic predecessors were not—of the pitfalls of conceptualism, and who, in common with the overwhelming majority of the philosophers of the age, failed to see a possible way out along the lines of conceptual realism—later explored by Moore and Russell—gave his own peculiar twist to the notion of necessary synthetic truth. The regulist position we are formulating could equally well be developed against a Kantian background, but that is a story for another occasion.

[10] It must be confessed that it sounds rather queer to say that there are necessary connections between universals (kinds of events) and that we can understand scientific statements referring to these universals—as the rationalist understands "understand"—but that we cannot apprehend the real connections between them. For surely real connections are not so "external" to the connected universals that these can be apprehended without an apprehension of their connection! Sophisticated rationalists have invented plausible ways of circumventing this objection, the most popular of which rests on a distinction between the apprehension of a universal, and the thought of a universal by means of apprehending a definite description of the universal. Sense universals and perhaps a limited class of other universals, instances of which are *given*, can be directly apprehended. Other universals are accessible to thought only by means of descriptions. This approach, however, can only be consistently defended by denying that the universals one can apprehend have any *connection* with universals which one can not apprehend. But surely there are real connections(if we grant real connections

Sellars—Language, Rules and Behavior   307

It takes but a moment to show that if there are real connections between universals, then universals are obviously not the kind of thing one would want to speak of apprehending. In the first place, the philosopher who asserts the existence of real connections can readily be seen to be committed to the existence of non-actualized possibilities. For in saying that all A's *must be* B, he clearly means to say more than that *in point of fact* all cases of A have been, are and will be cases of B. He is, in effect, saying that *there are no possible worlds in which there are non-B A's.* If there were possible worlds in which there are non-B A's, why shouldn't one of them be the actual world?[11]

The following obvious objection to the conception of real connections arises at this point: "If the connection between A and B is synthetic, then it *is* (*logically*) possible that there should be a world in which there are non-B A's. Why shouldn't this logically possible world be the actual one? Must not the rationalist admit that the assumption of a real connection between A and B doesn't *entail* that all actual cases of A are cases of B, and hence that the very concept of a synthetic necessary connection is a self-frustrating one?" Now, as far as I can see, the only reply open to the defender of real connections is that it is a *matter of ultimate fact* that there are no possible worlds which violate the generalization "All A's are B"—though he might explain this fact about A and B to the extent of subsuming it under a more general fact about the realm of the possible, namely, that for *every* universal there is at least one generalization which no possible world violates. A real connection, the rationalist must say, is *identical with* the non-existence of certain possible worlds, of possible worlds answering to a certain de-

at all) between sense universals and physical universals (the laws of psychophysics). Thus, the rationalist who takes this line is forced to underwrite either phenomenalism or neutral monism as an account of the qualities of physical objects.

The other approach is that of Blanshard, who speaks of *degrees* in the apprehension of universals and their internal relations. Induction is necessary for Blanshard, not because we cannot apprehend universals and their connections, but because only a grasp of the place of each universal in the total scheme would be a total grasp of any universal.

[11] For a detailed explication of the logical and physical modalities in terms of possible worlds, see my "Concepts as Involving Laws and Inconceivable without them," *Philosophy of Science,* 15, 1948.

scription. Should he be tempted to put this by saying that where A
is connected with B it *makes no sense* to say "This is A but not B,"
he must hasten to add that this statement makes no sense *because*
there is no possible world which violates "all A's are B." *Within
his framework, the sense-ful reflects the possible and not the pos-
ible the sense-ful.*

If we are right in claiming that the defender of real connections
is forced to hold that a real connection between A and B is identical with the sheer absence from the totality of possible worlds of
worlds which contain A's which are not B, then it is obviously not
open to him to speak of apprehending real connections. Real connections are no more possible objects of intuition or awareness
than are families of actual and possible sense data.

But though it doesn't make sense to speak of intuiting real connections between universals (as this phrase is understood by the
rationalistic philosopher), may not universals themselves be possible objects of awareness? But what would one be aware of in
being aware of a universal? Since no universal exemplifies itself,
to be aware of, say, *redness* is not to be aware of something *red*.
Surely the rationalist is right in claiming that a universal is an item
characterized by its place in a structure of universals and, indeed,
that this structure is a system of real connections. If this is the case,
then it is just as nonsensical to speak (in the philosopher's sense)
of intuiting universals, as it has been shown to be nonsensical to
speak of apprehending real connections.

Am I, then, claiming that it is nonsense to talk about real connections?—that the latest fashion in philosophy is just one more
mistake? Far from it. I shall insist that it is just as legitimate and,
indeed, necessary for the philosopher to speak of real connections,
as it is to speak of universals, propositions and possible worlds. On
the other hand, it is just as illegitimate to speak of real connections
as possible objects of awareness or intuition or *Schau* (as these
terms are used by the rationalist) as it is to speak of apprehending
universals, propositions and possible worlds. I hasten to add that
there is a context in which it is perfectly legitimate to speak of
grasping a possibility or *seeing an alternative* or *apprehending the*

meaning of an expression. This context is correct English usage in non-philosophical discourse. The rationalist makes the mistake of accepting the metaphors of common sense psychology as *analyses* of psychological facts. As Moore has pointed out, common sense knows what it knows, but doesn't know the analysis of what it knows. It is the regulist and not the rationalist who explicates the grammar of assent.

What, then, is the truth about real connections? What is the significance of modal words in logically synthetic sentences? The answer is the twin brother of the regulist conception of the logical modalities. Our use of the term "necessary" in causal as well as in logical contexts is to be traced to linguistic rules. Where Hume charged the rationalist (and before him, common sense) with projecting a subjective feeling of compulsion into the environment, we charge the rationalist with projecting the rules of his language into the non-linguistic world. Where Hume finds an example of the pathetic fallacy, we find the rationalist's (or rationalistic) fallacy, a pervasive mistake which has been bread and butter to the philosophical enterprise. Hume was on the right track, but since he failed to distinguish between rule-regulated mental activity and the association of ideas (an earlier form of the contemporary failure to distinguish between rule-regulated and tied symbol behavior) his account was necessarily inadequate, a fact which comes out clearly as soon as one realizes that he was unable to give even the germ of an account of *logical* necessity. From this perspective, Mill was wiser than most empiricists have realized. He, at least, saw the parallel between logical and causal necessity, and put them in the same category. Given the framework of psychological theory which he learned on his father's knee, what else could this category have been but the association of ideas? And does not his phrase "inseparable association" indicate a groping for a more adequate account?

But these historical asides are delaying the final stages of our argument. Our task is to give an account of the rules in terms of which, we have claimed, the causal modalities are to be understood.

What are these rules? and how do they differ from the formation and transformation rules which we have all come to recognize? I have elsewhere[12] called the rules I am going to discuss "conformation rules" and the phrase seems appropriate. In order to see that a language must have conformation rules as well as the familiar rules of formation and analytic inference, it is necessary to bear in mind the conclusions at which we arrived in the first part of this paper. The meaning of a linguistic symbol *as a linguistic symbol* is entirely constituted by the rules which regulate its use. The hook-up of a system of rule-regulated symbols with the world is not itself a rule-governed fact, but—as we saw—a matter of certain kinds of organic event playing two roles: (1) a role in the rule-governed linguistic system, and (2) a role in the structure of tied sign responses to environmental stimuli. But if the linguistic as such involves no hook-up with the world, if it is—to use a suggestive analogy—a game played with symbols according to rules, then what constitutes the linguistic meaning of the factual, non-logical expressions of a language? The answer, in brief, is that the undefined factual terms of the language are *implicitly* defined by the conformation rules of the language. These specify the proper use of the basic factual expressions of the language in terms of what might be called an axiomatics. Thus, for each basic factual word in the language there are one or more logically synthetic universal sentences which, as *exhibiting* the rules for the use of these words, have the status of "necessary truths" of the language. These sentences are those into which a user of the language would insert the words "must" or "necessary." He would say that what they express is *necessarily* so, as opposed to what *just happens to be so.*

Now it is clear that if the above account is correct, a language is essentially an axiomatic system. Here we run up against an obvious objection. "Is it not clear," it will be said, "that only logicians, mathematicians, and a few theoretical physicists behave in a way which we should call 'manipulating the expressions of an axiomatic system'? How, then, can we say that our ordinary use of language

[12] "Realism and the New Way of Words," *Philosophy and Phenomenological Research,* June, 1948; reprinted in *Readings in Philosophical Analysis,* edited by H. Feigl and W. S. Sellars, Appleton-Century-Crofts, New York, 1949.

is the manipulating of an axiomatic system? Furthermore, if our
language is an axiomatic system, how shall we account for the fact
that although the language has remained the same, yesterday's necessities are today's contingencies, and vice versa? If the language
is the same, must not the rules be the same, and hence the necessities the same? If the rules of the language determine what is recognized as physically necessary, how make sense of the fact that we
can meaningfully ask whether or not two kinds of event are causally related, and spend time and ingenuity seeking an answer? If
what is causally necessary is merely a matter of the implicit definition of the corresponding terms by the rules of the language,
could there be any sense to such a procedure?"

Fortunately, these questions admit of a straightforward answer.
In the first place, knowing a language is a knowing *how;* it is like
knowing how to dance, or how to play bridge. Both the tyro and
the champion know how to dance; both the duffer and the Culbert-
sons know how to play bridge. But what a difference! Similarly,
both you and I, as well as the theoretical physicist, can be said to
manipulate an axiomatic system; but we are clearly at the duffer
end of the spectrum. Again, in answering the second question we
need only note that the identity of the empirical events used as
symbols *is* at best a necessary and by no means a sufficient condition
of the identity of a language. In a perfectly legitimate sense one
language can change into another even though the noises and shapes
employed remain the same. Indeed, modern man is not only constantly introducing new symbols governed by new rules, he is constantly changing the rules according to which old symbols are used.
Thus, as science has progressed, the word "mass" as a class of visual and auditory events has remained, but the rules according to
which it is used in the language of science have changed several
times, and, strictly speaking, it is a new symbol with each change
in rules, though each new implicit definition (conformation rule)
has had enough in common with earlier implicit definitions so that
the use of the same symbol has not seemed inappropriate. Indeed,
the scientist in different contexts uses the term in different senses,
according to different rules. In common sense contexts his language

is of ancient vintage. Thus we can stick to English and yet be said to speak not one language but many.

In ancient time, changes in the rules of language were very slow. Man was content to be baffled. Since the birth of modern science, man has constantly remodeled his language; indeed, from the standpoint of the anthropologist, science consists exactly in the attempt to develop a system of rule-governed behavior which will adjust the human organism to the environment. If there are regularities in the world, it is only by means of regularities in behavior that we can adjust to them. This process of adjustment can be speeded up by the deliberate exploration of alternative linguistic structures. The recognition of this fact is the achievement of the philosophy of science since the Einsteinian revolution.

We have pointed out that most contemporary rationalists distinguish between those real connections which human thought cannot directly apprehend, which cannot, as they say, be *known*— so that we must be content with *probable opinion* concerning their existence— on the one hand, and those real connections (extremely limited in number) which we can directly apprehend and by apprehending gain synthetic *a priori* knowledge of the world. As examples of the latter we are offered such truths as "All colors are (necessarily) extended," "All tones have (necessarily) an intensity and a pitch," etc. The list is a familiar one. What is there, if anything, in our analysis which corresponds to this distinction? That there is *something* is suggested by the fact, which empiricists are surely sophisticated enough by now to recognize, that where there is rationalistic smoke there usually can be empiricist (regulist) fire.

We have interpreted the notion of real connection in terms of the conformation rules of languages. We thus make real connections, so to speak, entirely immanent to thought. They are the shadows of rules. What sense, then, can there be to a distinction between real connections which are *known* and real connections which are *accepted* but not *known?* The answer, as I see it, is to be found along the following lines. Modern man has been constantly modifying the rules of his language, and this resulted in an awareness of *alternatives* which keeps the reflective person from saying that he *knows*. Now, these modifications have occurred chiefly in a mid-region between two extremes which I shall now characterize. On the one hand, at least until recently, certain very general structural features of the axiomatics of our language have persisted through the changes due to the advance of science. Indeed, in spite of the dramatic changes of the past few decades, the axiomatics of the language has retained certain structural features from earlier science and even from common sense. These common features— and the extent to which there are any can easily be exaggerated— represent one portion of that which people are tempted to think of as real connections which are known, and which the rationalist claims to be synthetic *a priori* knowledge. These are features for which most of us have not yet been led to seek alternatives. Yet to the extent that one seriously looks for alternatives, they lose the feel of the "unconditionally known" and acquire a "hypothetical" character which is perfectly compatible with their performance of the *a priori* role which the regulist conceives them to have. As a matter of fact, then, the contemporary philosopher of science sees in this direction only structural features of our language for which we are more or less willing to consider alternatives.

In the other direction, however, we find those rules which even the most startling advances in science have not tempted us to abandon, rules which one who pays out any rope at all to the rationalistic doctrine of cognitive awareness will end by claiming to express insight into objective real connections. I have in mind the rules which concern those symbols which not only function in the language as rule-regulated symbols, but also are elements in the tied sign behavior of the organism, and which, by playing this dual role provide the link between language and the world. Here the rules mirror, so to speak, the structure of learned sensory discriminations and associated tied sign behavior. It is these rules that most forcefully present themselves to us as having no serious alternatives. Here is the locus of the most tempting claims to synthetic *a priori* knowledge.

Now it is one thing to recognize that these rules are *causally* in a privileged position, and quite another to make any concession to pseudo-psychologies of "seeing the universal in the particular" or of "intuitive induction." Here again we find rationalistic smoke which only the empiricist (regulist) can turn into illuminating fire. A useful test of one's thought in this connection is to ask oneself what happens when a person who has been blind from birth gains vision and, *never having heard color words used,* develops his own language about color experiences. Does one think of him as apprehending the universals Red, Green, etc., and as more or less deliberately fitting symbols to these universals and giving these symbols rules which correspond to the structural properties which these universals are apprehended to have? This is the way in which many philosophers would seem to think of the matter. And, of course, there is as much sense to it as there is to speaking of intuiting universals, apprehending meanings, envisaging possibilities, etc. It is a metaphorical way of speaking which, provided it is not taken to provide an *analysis* of the learning of rules relating to the use of sense predicates, is both useful and proper. Taken to be an analysis, on the other hand, it is one more example of rationalistic pseudo-psychology.

In the course of our argument we have analyzed the moral "ought," the logical "must" and even real connections or physical necessity in terms of the concept of rule-regulated behavior. The question arises, in each of these areas, "Why one set of rules rather than another? How is the adoption of a set of rules itself to be justified?" I should like to be able to say that one justifies the adoption of rules pragmatically, and, indeed, this would be at least a first approximation to the truth. The kinship of my views with the more sophisticated forms of pragmatism is obvious. Yet I should like to close on a note of caution. The more I brood on rules, the more I think that Wittgenstein was right in finding an ineffable in the linguistic situation, something which can be *shared* but not *communicated*. We saw that a rule, properly speaking, isn't a rule unless it *lives* in behavior, rule-regulated behavior, even rule-violating behavior. Linguistically we always operate *within* a framework of *living* rules. To *talk about* rules is to move *outside* the talked-about rules *into* another framework of living rules. (The snake which sheds one skin lives within another.) In attempting to grasp rules *as rules* from without, we are trying to have our cake and eat it. To *describe* rules is to describe the *skeletons* of rules. A rule is *lived*, not *described*. Thus, what we justify is never a rule, but behavior and dispositions to behave. The "ought" eludes us and we are left with "is." The skeletons of rules can be given a pragmatic or instrumentalist justification. This justification operates within a set of living rules. The death of one rule is the life of another. Even one and the same rule may be both living as *justificans* and dead as *justificandum*, as when we justify a rule of logic. Indeed, can the attempt to justify rules, from left to right, be anything but an exhibition of these rules from right to left? To learn new rules is to change one's mind. Is there a rational way of losing one's reason? Is not the final wisdom the way of the amoeba in the ooze, the rat in the maze, the burnt child with fire? The convert can describe what he was. Can he understand what he was? But here we are on Wittgenstein's ladder, and it is time to throw it away.

SECTION I

(306.1; 307.1; 308.1.2) "The purpose of this paper is to raise certain issues relating to the concept of predication, and, having done so, to develop a schema for clarifying them." More specifically, this paper discusses the propositional "form", 'f(x)', "in an attempt to show that *expressions of this design are actually used to represent three radically different types of logical structure.* Of these three types of structure, two can be briefly indicated as follows:

(1) Atomic propositions, thus 'ϕ(a)', where 'a' is an *underived* individual constant, and 'ϕ' a *primitive* descriptive predicate, of the language to which they belong.

(2) Propositions which attribute "properties" to "things", thus 'ψ(b)' where 'b' is a *derived* individual constant, and 'ψ' an *undefined*[1] or *defined* (descriptive) *property predicate* of the language to which they belong."

In discussing these topics, the paper will also treat part of the problem of "complex particulars."

SECTION II

(308.1; 309.1) Though "it is common to give the same formal representation, 'f(x)' to" all of

A.1. Fido is a dog.
A.2. It is a twinge.
B.1. Fido is angry
B.2. It (a certain experience) is painful.[1],

"it becomes difficult to avoid the conviction that the statements of each of these groups (A and B) agree with one another, and differ from those of the other group, in a way which is independent of the empirical subject matter of the statements, and which consequently would seem to concern their logical form."

(309.2; 310.1) While it is a "sound" observation that 'dog' belongs to a classificatory system "in which the defining characteristics of terms belonging to such a system are so chosen that two terms (infima species) never apply to the same object" and 'anger' and 'angry-thing' do not, this observation does not settle the logical structure of "thing" statements.

(310.2) Consider A.2. "Would it not be reasonable to say that this statement asserts that its subject item *as a whole* is a *case* of, an *instance* of the concept Twinge?" Apparently, yes.

(311.1, .2,.3; 312.1) In order to ask the corresponding questions of the B-statements, we must decide what concepts are involved. The alternatives are:

   (1) The concepts Anger and Pain.

On (1), it seems false to say of the B-statements "that their subject items *as wholes* are respectively cases or *instances* of Anger or Pain *without doing violence to our (unexplicated) notion of what is involved in something's being a case or instance of a concept.* We should prefer to say that anger and pain are somehow, in a way which would also require analysis, *present in* the subject items." Perhaps, we should also conclude that the subjects of the B-statements "contain an aspect or *ingredient* which is a case or instance of the predicate concept."

   (2) The concepts Angry-thing and Painful-situation.

On (2), it seems plausible to say that Fico is "a case or instance of Angry-thing."

Another way of stating the purpose of this paper is to say that it attempts "to clarify what is meant by statements of the form 'x is an f-thing' where, in our examples of type B, 'f' designates a concept such that we should **deny** that x as a whole is an f, while admitting that as a whole it is an f-thing."

SECTION III

(312.2 (313)) What is meant by 'thing'? Though this question cannot be answered at this point, it is perhaps helpful to say that 'thing' is to be understood as 'complex particular.'

SECTION IV

(314.1) Let us write 'x is a case (or instance) of f' as

    x is a specimen of f

and take that as the way to "read" 'f (x)'. Then "B-statements can only be represented by a simple use of this form if the predicates of these statements are taken to have the structure 'f-thing'," Let us, on an intuitive level, investigate whether it makes "sense to speak of specimens of such concepts."

(314.2) Note that 'Fido is an angry-thing' is "logically equivalent" to 'Fido is angry.' On (1) above, it appeared that 'Fido is angry' should be understood as

    anger is present in Fido

which, in its turn, is understood as

    There is a y such that y is an ingredient of Fido,
    and y is a specimen of anger

For various reasons, this complicated statement of ingredience *seems* like a poor candidate for a satisfactory analysis of 'Fido is an angry-thing.'

SECTION V

(315.1; 316.1) Another approach reads 'f(x)' as

    x exemplifies f

where exemplification is *not* to be taken as a "linguistic relation". The sample statements now are rewritten as

    A. 13 Fido exemplifies Dog
    A. 23 It exemplifies Twinge
    B. 13 Fido exemplifies Anger.
    B. 23 It exemplifies Pain.

SECTION VI

(316.2 (317)(318)) A dialogue between Smith and Jones reaches the conclusion that it does not "make sense to say of a basic particular that it exemplifies more than one non-relational concept." So, where a is a basic particular, the form 'f(a) & g(a)' is "illegitimate."

SECTION VII

(319.1; (320.1) Given the conclusion of Section VI, we are again led to consider Fido as a complex particular "which is analysable into "ingredient particulars" because "it obviously makes sense to say "Fido is angry and hungry"." What are the most general things to say about the relation of ingredience?

(320.2) "I, or Ingredience, is a relation between an ingredient particular and the complex particular of which it is an ingredient. *But prior to I are the relations between a set of items by virtue of which they constitute a whole of which they are ingredients.*" For simplicity, let us assume there is only one such relation called "co-ingredience-in-a-thing." Then

    I (y,x) (i.e., y is an ingredient of x)

is defined by

    x is a co-ingredient set of basic particulars which includes y.

(320.3) Assuming, "for purposes of illustration, that 'Anger' is a primitive predicate", we can give the analysis of 'Anger(Fido)' (i.e., 'Fido is angry') as *(roughly* what was offered in section IV):

    (Ey)I(y, Fido) & Anger(y),

(321.1,.2,.3) There are "four different types of statements representable by the form 'f(x)'."

    Type I: Atomic propositions. These attribute undefined properties
            to basic particulars.

Type II: Those that are reducible to '(Ey)I(y,x) & f(y)'. These
          attribute undefined properties to complex particulars.

Type III: Those that are reducible to

           (Ey)(Ez).....I(y,x).....& g(y) & h(z)...... .

           These attribute defined properties to complex particulars.

Type IV: A special case of III, but which include in addition

          (w) (if I(w,x), then w= y or w = z or......)

          The defined predicates which appear in these statements
          are called ''θ-predicates''.

(322.1,.2) The distinctive feature of θ-predicates as defined predicates
is that ''the definition'' of a θ-predicate specifies a *complete* battery of
primitive predicates for the complex particulars to which it applies......
A θ-concept ''covers'' a complex particular which exemplifies it, as a complex mould, or an engraved plate, fits its product.'' It follows from the definition of a θ-predicate that *no complex particular can exemplify two
(different) θ-concepts.*

(323.1,.2; 324.1,.2) The question remains whether the notions of atomic
proposition, primitive predicate, underived individual constant and
θ-predicate clarify the ''logical structure of our language.'' In order for
them to do so, it is not necessary that in our language we formulate statements with primitive predicates, underived individual constants or
θ-predicates. All that is required is that we speak on a ''level'' that is
''derived from a level of statements'' with primitive predicates, underived individual constants and so on.

SECTION VIII

(325.1) The four sample statements were so chosen that each one fits
''plausibly'' into one of the four types: A.2, into I; B.2, into II; B.1, into
III; and A.1, into IV.

(326.2) But A.1, 'Fido is a dog', is *not* of type IV. If it were, then ''it
would analytically entail a set of statements exhaustively specifying the
intrinsic characteristics of Fido.'' But A.1 does not do this and thus
''tells only part of the story about Fido.'' But, then, how is A.1 different
from a statement of type III such as B.1, 'Fido is angry'?

(326.1; 327.1) ''In order to grasp the difference in logical structure
between ''Fido is a dog'' and ''Fido is angry'', we must first appreciate
their fundamental identity of structure. To do this, we must focus our attention once again on such concepts as ''*Angry-thing*.'' Though ''*Angry-
thing* is not a θ-concept'', the following is an ''attempt'' to understand it
in terms of θ-concepts:

    'Angry-thing' picks out the θ-concept exemplified by Fido which
    has the concept Anger as a ''constituent''.

Thus, 'Fido is an angry-thing' is analysed as

Anger is a constituent of the θ-concept exemplified by Fido

which is written

C(Anger, (theθ)θ(Fido)).

Constituency and Ingrediency are related as follows:

$$(t) \left[C (f, (the\, \theta\,)\, \theta\, (t)) \text{ iff } (Ey) I\,(y,t\,) \,\&\, f\,(y) \right].$$

(327.2) Since both Ingrediency and Constituency are definable in terms of co-ingredience-in-a-thing, the question arises, "What is the advantage of the "language of constituency in θ-concepts"?" The remainder of the paper is devoted to answering this question.

SECTION IX

(328.1; 329.1) Let us use the terms "naming" and "describing" for the ways in which *constants* and *descriptive phrases*, respectively, refer to something. Then our ordinary terms for "kinds of things", e.g., 'Dog', as well as such terms as 'Angry-thing', refer to *"complex concepts by means of descriptions in terms of constituent concepts which they name."* What, then, is the difference between 'Angry-thing' and 'Dog'? Let us say that the class of θ-concepts which is referred to by 'Angry-thing' in virtue of having the constituent Anger has "the *note* Anger." Then 't is an angry-thing' can be equivalently written as 't exemplifies one and only one θ-concept having the note Anger'. The answer to the question about the difference between words like 'Angry-thing' and words for 'kinds of things' like 'Dog' is: *"Words for "kinds of things" are so introduced that every overlap of the classes of θ-concepts specified by the notes* named *by these words, contains only θ-concepts which are unexemplified either as a contingent matter of fact, or because they are physically impossible.* Thus 'Dog (t) & Cat (t)' is ruled out while 'Angry-thing (t) & Hungry –thing (t)' is not.

(329.2; 330.1,.2) The relationship between the present approach in terms of exemplification and the previous one in terms of being a specimen of is to be found in the "intuitive" criterion we used for determing whether a particular is a specimen (a case or instance) of a concept: viz., does the concept "cover" the particular "as a whole"? Only statements of Type I and IV satisfy this criterion; only they cover "particulars as wholes by concepts named rather than merely described."

SECTION X

(331.1) Summary of conclusions at which the previous section have arrived.

(332.1,.2; 333.1.,2; 334.1,.2; 335.1,.2; 336.1,.2,.3; 337.1,.2 (338)) A "model language" with a specified list of primitive predicates is given and the development of this language illustrates the concepts already discussed (particularly, that of θ-concept and of classes of θ-concepts) and related concepts.

II.—ON THE LOGIC OF COMPLEX PARTICULARS

By WILFRID SELLARS

I

THE purpose of this paper is to raise certain issues relating to the concept of predication, and, having done so, to develop a schema for clarifying them. Put somewhat differently, its aim is to show, by an examination of the roles played in contemporary analytic philosophy by the propositional function or form '$f(x)$', that certain persistent confusions have prevented the resources of modern logical theory from providing a full clarification of the logical structure of the language in which we speak about the world. More precisely, after a preliminary dialectical exploration of the terrain, it will gradually focus attention on three roles played by this form, in an attempt to show that *expressions of this design are actually used to represent three radically different types of logical structure.* Of these three types of structure, two can be briefly indicated as follows :

(1) Atomic propositions, thus '$\phi(a)$', where 'a' is an *underived* individual constant, and 'ϕ' a *primitive* descriptive predicate, of the language to which they belong.

(2) *Propositions which attribute " properties " to " things ",* thus '$\psi(b)$' where 'b' is a *derived* individual constant, and 'ψ' an *undefined*[1] or *defined* (descriptive) *property predicate* of the language to which they belong.

The third type of structure, intermediate in complexity between the two we have just mentioned, and resting on the former as the latter in turn rests on it, cannot, for reasons which will become clear in the course of our argument, be fruitfully characterised at this point. It is deeply embedded in our conceptual structure, and is, indeed, the key to the understanding of the thing-property level of language. Yet a rational reconstruction

---

[1] We shall find it most important not to confuse the *undefined property predicates* of a language with the *primitive predicates* of that language. Undefined as well as defined property predicates belong, along with derived constants (said to designate " things "), at a level of language which is built upon the level of primitive predicates, basic particulars and atomic propositions. The grounds of this remark, however, will emerge only at a relatively late stage in our argument.

of the language we use reveals that this third type of structure finds employment only as an element in the more complicated type of structure which we have mentioned under (2) above. Thus, it is as impossible to give a convincing example of it as of an atomic proposition, and for the same reason. On the other hand, such brief abstract characterisations as occur to me raise ghosts, and to offer them would place a burden on the argument which will prove illusory when gradually assumed.

An even more fruitful manner, implicit in what we have just been saying, of indicating the subject matter of this paper, is to say that it will be an essay on the logic of complex particulars. Its scope, however, will be restricted to the analysis of statements which attribute " qualitative " properties to " things ", and with *relations* only in so far as things involve mutually related constituents. Put in these terms, our contention is that in the rational reconstruction of a language in which one speaks about a world, the strongest of distinctions must be drawn between a level of statements involving only underived or primitive individual constants and predicates, and the level on which derived individual constants (" thing-names ") and predicates put in an appearance.   Thus, we shall argue for the following theses (among others) :

(1) Where ' x ' has underived individual constants as its substitution range, ' $f(x)$ & $g(x)$ ' and ' f & $g(x)$ ' are illegitimate forms : that is to say, the range of ' f ' must be restricted to primitive predicates if paradox is to be avoided.

(2) Where ' $f(x)$ & $g(x)$ ' and ' f & $g(x)$ ' are legitimate forms the range of ' x ' must lie among the derived individual constants of the language.

(3) Where ' $f(x)$ & $g(x)$ ' and ' f & $g(x)$ ' are legitimate forms, neither ' f ' nor ' g ' can be underived or primitive predicates of the language. To put the matter in a less startling way, if ' h ' is an underived or primitive predicate, then the " h " of ' $h(x)$ & $g(x)$ ' must be a " thing-level predicate " constructed, in a manner which we shall analyse, out of the atomic level predicate ' h ' and must not be confused with the latter. The same holds, of course, of the " g ". In other words, a careful distinction must be made between the *primitive* predicates of a language, which belong to the atomic level, and the *undefined* predicates of the molecular level which are constructed from them. Notice that it is a direct consequence of (1) that defined one-place predicates belong to the molecular level.

308   WILFRID SELLARS :

Now it is clear that if the above theses can be substantiated, they call for a radical reinterpretation of the logical foundations of the functional calculus. Such a reinterpretation would involve the following steps :

(a) A theory of atomic functions based on the recognition that such formulæ as

$$(x) :. f(x) \supset g(x) . \& . g(x) \supset h(x) : \supset . f(x) \supset h(x)$$

simply have no place in it, which is an obvious consequence of the first of the preceding theses, all such formulæ presupposing the legitimacy of the form ' $f(x) \& g(x)$ '.

(b) A theory of the introduction into a language of derived individual constants, that is to say, a theory of complex individuals or " things ", a theory which does not confuse such derivation with " epistemic reduction ".

(c) A theory of the introduction into a language of " thing-level " predicates.

(d) A theory of the distinction at the thing-level between *defined and undefined* property predicates, that is to say, a theory of definition for descriptive one-place predicates.

(e) An explication of the thing-level form ' $f(x) \& g(x)$ ' which shows why this form is legitimate at that level, in spite of the fact that it is illegitimate at the atomic level.

Before our argument is over, something will have been said on all these points, if only to sketch the course a systematic account would take.

We have now indicated in a number of ways the subject-matter of our paper. *Au travail !*

II

When it is desired to use the language of functions, as contrasted with the language of classes, it is common to give the same formal representation, ' $f(x)$ ' to statements such as

A. 1. Fido is a dog.
A. 2. It is a twinge.

on the one hand, and for statements such as

B. 1. Fido is angry.
B. 2. It (a certain experience) is painful.[1]

[1] It is assumed, both in the case of these examples and throughout our argument, that unless the contrary is explicitly indicated, the predicates with which we are dealing mention *most determinate* concepts. The reader will recognise that the function ' Colour( ) ', where ' Colour '

on the other.   So represented, these statements become,

A. 11.   Dog (Fido).
A. 21.   Twinge (it).
B. 11.   Angry (Fido).
B. 21.   Painful (it).

However, should the question be raised, " Do these four statements have the same logical form ? " it becomes difficult to avoid
the conviction that the statements of each of these groups (A
and B) agree with one another, and differ from those of the other
group, in a way which is independent of the empirical subject
matter of the statements, and which consequently would seem
to concern their logical form.

One way of focussing attention on the intuitively felt difference
we have claimed to exist between these two types of statement
is to point out that whereas we should be quite happy about
translating the former into the language of classes to read

A. 12.   Fido ∈ Dog.
A. 22.   It ∈ Twinge.

*with the same words now functioning as class terms which before
functioned as predicates*, we should feel that statements of kind B
would be more correctly formulated as

B. 12.   Fido ∈ Angry-*thing*.
B. 22.   It ∈ Painful-*situation*.

*where certain suffixes, obscure in meaning and requiring analysis,
have been added to the words which appeared as predicates in the
language of functions.*

Now at this point the reader is less likely to disagree with what
we have said, than to deny its significance.   Thus, he may claim
that ' Fido ∈ Dog ' is only verbally different from ' Fido ∈ Canine-
thing ', and hence that if there is a logically significant difference
between " Fido is a dog " and " Fido is angry " we have not yet
put our finger on it.   Having said this, he would probably be
moved to admit that the difference between ' Fido ∈ Dog '
and ' Fido ∈ Angry-thing ' is not a mere matter of verbal
form, while denying that they differ in logical form.   He would

mentions a *determinable* concept, is not legitimately satisfied by individual
constants.   Thus, ' Colour(x) ', where the range of ' x ' consists of individual
constants, is nonsense.   On the other hand, as Reichenbach has recently
reminded us, ' Coloured(x) ' does make sense, though only as a definitional
abbreviation of ' (Ef) Colour (f) & $f(x)$ '.   It is clear that in claiming in
the previous section that at the atomic level the form ' $f(x)$ & $g(x)$ ' is
illegitimate, we must exclude functions of the type represented by
' Coloured(x) ' from the range of ' f ' and ' g ', for ' Coloured(x) and
Red(x) ' is legitimate, if redundant, at the atomic level.

21

310   WILFRID SELLARS :

probably find the difference to lie in the fact that ' Dog ' belongs
to a classificatory system, whereas ' Angry-thing ' does not.   The
defining characteristics of terms belonging to such a system are
so chosen that two terms (infima species) never apply to the same
object.   It is the fact that ' Dog ' implies such a system which
we are dimly grasping when we feel that statements such as
" Fido is a dog " are different.

Our hypothetical reader's comments are so much to the point,
and, indeed, so sound, that if the sole purpose of this analysis
were to clarify the difference between the two types of statement
represented respectively by " Fido is a dog " and " Fido is
angry ", we might well call it a day.   Since, however, our aim is
the broader one of determining the logical structure of statements
on the thing level, we can hardly rest satisfied with an analysis
which counters our claim that " Fido is angry " translates into
' Fido ϵ Angry-thing ' with the assertion that ' Fido ϵ Dog ' differs
only verbally from ' Fido ϵ Canine-thing '.   In short, we shall be
satisfied with nothing less than a logical analysis of the suffix
' -thing ' which our discussion has served to introduce.   As for
the reader's sound comments, we shall return to them later and
fit them into our analysis.   For the time being, however, we shall
put them out of our mind, and try a fresh, indeed naive, approach
to the felt difference between A and B statements.

Consider A. 2, " It is a twinge ".   Would it not be reasonable
to say that this statement asserts that its subject item *as a whole*
is a *case* of, an *instance* of the concept Twinge ?   In " Fido is a
dog " is it not Fido *as a whole* that is said to be a *case* or *instance*
of Dog ?   These questions are likely to evoke the following two
reactions : (1) " In so far as I grasp the meaning of these questions (if they mean anything) they seem to be *silly*, in that the
answer in each case couldn't possibly be anything but ' yes ! '
After all, the subject of a subject-predicate statement is its subject and not a part of it !   If the concept Twinge were being
predicated of part of something, the statement would be of the
form ' *Part of* x is a twinge ', and not ' x is a twinge ' ".   (3)
" Until you have explicated ' case of ', ' instance of ' and ' as a
whole ' I don't know what I was asked or what I have answered."
As to this second comment, we must grant that the terms in
which our questions were phrased are obscure, and that no analysis
which makes use of them can be complete until they in their turn
have been clarified.   Yet provided this is kept in mind it is quite
permissible to rub one set of unanalysed concepts against another
in the hope of striking fire.   To the first comment we reply : Let
us try these same questions on statements of kind B and see if

ON THE LOGIC OF COMPLEX PARTICULARS   311

here also the answer is so obviously ' yes ! ' as to make the questions ' silly '.

But before we can ask the corresponding questions of B-statements, we must make up our mind as to what concepts are to be mentioned by our questions, as Twinge and Dog were in the case of A-statements.   There are two alternatives.

(1) We select the concepts Anger and Pain.   We ask of " Fido is angry " the question : Does not this statement assert that its subject item as a whole is a case of, an instance of Anger ?   This question and its mate are no sooner asked than a negative answer is seen to be required.   It strikes us as impossible to interpret the examples of B-statements as saying that their subject items *as wholes* are respectively *cases* or *instances* of Anger and Pain *without doing violence to our (unexplicated) notion of what is involved in something's being a case or instance of a concept.*   We should prefer to say that anger and pain are somehow, in a way which would also require analysis, *present in* the subject items.   Thus, our answer to the question concerning the statement about Fido must be in the negative *not, indeed, because Fido as a whole isn't the subject of the statement* (which would be as silly a reason as our hypothetical reader's first comment suggests), *but because the statement does not say of Fido that he is a case or instance of Anger.*
" But ", it will be urged, " this is absurd !   ' Fido is angry ' is a typical subject-predicate proposition, and if it doesn't say that Fido is a case of Anger, what *does* it do ? "

Let us dodge this question, and beat about in the surrounding bushes.   Thus, we note that whether or not it is legitimate to say that Fido (as a whole) is a case or instance of Anger, we must surely admit that in order for " Fido is angry " to be true the world must include at least one case or instance of Anger.   The question, therefore, is not " Does the statement ' Fido is angry ' entail ' *A* case of Anger exists ' ? " but rather " Does this statement entail ' Fido is a case or instance of Anger ' ? "   It is to the latter question only that the answer would seem to be in the negative.   If we are asked, " What, then, could be the case of Anger, if not Fido ? " what can the answer be but " His emotional state " ?   Are we to conclude that statements of type B, interpreted in terms of the relation *case (or instance) of* (whatever this may turn out to be), say of their subjects that they contain an aspect or *ingredient* which is a case or instance of the predicate concept ?   This suggestion has the merit of echoing G. F. Stout's contention [1] that the qualities of a thing are as particular as the

[1] " The Nature of Universals and Propositions ", *Proc. British Academy,* 1921-22 (reprinted in *Studies in Phil. and Psych.,* 1930).

312   WILFRID SELLARS :

thing itself; that, to use our term 'ingredient', the qualities of
a thing are ingredient instances of qualitative universals, rather
than these universals themselves.[1] But regardless of this or
other merits of the suggestion, we can scarcely rest content in it,
given our present lack of a satisfactory analysis of *case or instance
of* and *ingredience*. Furthermore, we remember that this line of
thought arose on the assumption that in interpreting statements
of type B, the predicate concept is to be chosen as, given " Fido is
angry ", we chose Anger. But need it be so chosen ? This brings
us to the second alternative.

(2) We select the concepts Angry-thing and Painful-situation.
The reader may well have muttered in the early stages of the
previous interpretation that the statement " Fido is angry "
jolly well tells us that Fido, and Fido " as a whole " at that, is a
case or instance of something, and that this something is referred
to by the word " angry ". To give us our present suggestion, it
was only necessary for him to argue that the word " angry "
mentions the concept Angry-*thing*, and not, as we took it, to the
concept Anger. While it does not seem sensible to say that Fido
is a case or instance of Anger, what could be more proper than to
say of Fido that he is a case or instance of Angry-thing ? Can
we rest here ? We could if we were in possession of a satisfactory
analysis of such concepts as Angry-thing. This, however, is not
the case.

> *As a matter of fact, the purpose of this paper can also be characterised
> as the attempt to clarify what is meant by statements of the form ' x is
> an f-thing ' where, as in our examples of type B, ' f ' designates a con-
> cept such that we should deny that x as a whole is an f, while admitting
> that as a whole it is an f-thing.*

III

Our frequent use of the term ' thing ', as well as the distinction
we have just drawn between the predicates ' f ' and ' f-thing '
inevitably raise the questions, " What is the meaning of ' thing ' ?
What does the suffix ' -thing ' add to ' f ' that you find the above

---

[1] Indeed, the historically minded reader will notice that if Aristotle
had drawn (or drawn more clearly) a distinction in other categories corresponding to his distinction between primary and secondary substance,
his *predicated of* and *present in* would look very much like our *case or instance of* (or rather its converse) and our *ingredient of*. For such an Aristotle
would not " Fido is a dog " have as its import that the substance-universal
Dog is *predicated of* Fido ? Would not " Fido is angry " be to the effect
that the quality-universal Anger is predicated of a " primary " (particular)
quality *present in* Fido ?

ON THE LOGIC OF COMPLEX PARTICULARS   313

distinction to be so important ?   Unless you are going to introduce a ' metaphysics of substance ' or something of this ilk, must
you not admit that ' x is an f-thing ' is just a redundant way of
saying ' x is an f ' ?   For does not ' x is an f-thing ' break up into
' x is an f and x is a thing ' where the latter conjunct is surely a
tautologous appendage ? ''   These questions may perhaps formulate some of the suspicions which our recent remarks must have
aroused.   We can do little by way of answering them until a
later stage in our argument.   We can, however, allay those
suspicions which the word " substance " above has brought into
the open.   The truth of the matter is that the word ' thing ' as
we are using it—and our usage is close to the grassroots—stands
for a type (or family of types) of logical structure to which the
concept of substance (properly explicated) belongs, but which
the latter concept by no means exhausts.   Perhaps the safest
way of indicating the sense of ' thing ' in which we are interested,
is by saying that it is equivalent to ' complex particular '.   This
sense is broader than that which can be salvaged from the classical
concept of substance, for the latter is essentially that of such
complex particulars [1] as have, or can meaningfully be said to have,
dispositional properties, *capacities, potentialities,* as well as actual
or " occurrent " states and qualities.   We shall have nothing to
say in this paper about the " problem of substance " except in so
far as an investigation of the more general concept of complex
particular may serve to throw light on the topics covered by this
phrase.   Indeed, the generality of this essay in the logic of complex particulars can be brought out in another way.   An examination of the language in which we speak about the world shows it
to recognise complex particulars of widely different structure and
of all degrees of complexity.   These structures involve spatial
and temporal relations, and the various levels of lawfulness,
physical, biological, and psychological exhibited by our world and
embodied in our language.   We shall decidedly simplify this
situation, and with justification.   For this essay is not concerned
with the peculiarities of this world.   Rather, it is a study in the
foundations of logic, and, indeed, is a study of the characteristic
features which must be present in a language about a world of

[1] This characterisation of substances as falling under the general heading
of ' complex particulars ' might appear to rule out the possibility of simple
substances.   Yet that even simple substances, should there be sense to
this notion, would be complex particulars becomes less paradoxical when
it is remembered that classical metaphysicians admitted that their simple
substances were not without internal complexity.   For a sound and
valuable treatment of this whole subject, see C. D. Broad, *Examination
of McTaggart's Philosophy*, Vol. I, pp. 267-278.

314 WILFRID SELLARS :

fact in order for the familiar formulæ of the calculus of functions
to be applicable to expressions belonging to it. Thus, our procedure, by abstracting from the complexities of the conceptual
apparatus we actually use, will amount to the schematic construction of a model or artificial language which will clarify the
general problem, while offering no more than a guiding light as
far as the task of clarifying the logical structure of the thing-level
of our actual language is concerned.

IV

We saw in a previous section that if '$f(x)$' is read "x is a case
(or instance) of f"—which we shall now abbreviate to "x is a
specimen of f"—then while statements of kind A are (or seem to
be) readily symbolisable by this form, B-statements can only be
represented by a simple use of this form if the predicates of these
statements are taken to have the structure 'f-thing'. We then
asked, "What sort of concept is Angry-thing? What is the
sense of the suffix '-thing'?" To which we now add, "Does it
make sense to speak of specimens of such concepts?" If the
answer to this question should be in the negative, then our tentative reading of the '$f(x)$' of the functional calculus as "x is a
specimen of f" must be abandoned; for it is typically B-statements that are represented by this form. We shall answer this
question by a final exploratory use of our vague and intuitive
criteria for deciding when a particular is (or is not) a specimen of
a concept, before beginning a systematic explication of the
different modes of predication.

Our point of departure is the fact that "Fido is an angry
thing" is logically equivalent to "Fido is angry". Now, in our
first analysis of the latter, we decided that if this statement says
of anything that it is a specimen of *Anger*, it does so not of Fido,
but rather his emotional state. We then adopted the term
'Ingredience' for such relations as that of the emotional state to
Fido. This led to the conclusion that statements of type B are
implicitly of a form which we shall symbolise as follows :

$$(Ey)\ I(y,x)\ \&\ f(y).$$

This is read, "There is a y such that y is an ingredient of x, and y
is a specimen of f". Let us define the form '$f/x/$', which we
shall read "f is present in x", as follows,

$$f/x/ = (Ey)\ I(y,x)\ \&\ f(y).$$

Now if we assume that it makes sense to speak of specimens of concepts of the form *f-thing*, so that '*f*-thing(x)' is a legitimate use of the form '- - -(. . .)' as we are tentatively interpreting this latter, we have

$$f\text{-thing}(x) = f/x/ = (\text{E}y)\ \text{I}(y,x)\ \&\ f(y).$$

But if this reasoning is sound, it follows that in so far as it is possible to speak of concepts or universals of the form *f-thing*, these must be recognised to have a most unusual character. They are concepts or universals which require for their analysis the use of existential operators. Now we should surely be surprised to learn that in making common or garden variety statements of kind B we had such peculiar concepts in mind. Furthermore, it seems correct to say that our intuitive criteria require that in order to have cases or instances (specimens) a concept must be of that simpler type which does not involve existential operators in its analysis. Our argument thus forces us to the conclusion that B-statements are not legitimately symbolised by a simple use of the form '$f(x)$' *where this is read "x is a specimen of f"*. But statements of kind B are typical grist for the mill of the functional calculus, and no explication of the form '$f(x)$' can be satisfactory which does not permit them to be represented by a simple use of this form. We must therefore try another approach. Fortunately our exploratory dialectics have not been in vain. Although the specimen-ingredience co-ordinate system (dimly grasped) has not enabled us to reach our goal, it has brought insight into the topology of the terrain, insights which will reappear in the better map we are about to construct.

V

In our new approach, we shall interpret the form '$f(x)$' by reading it as "x exemplifies f", where "exemplifies" is so used as to have the sense *satisfies the one-place descriptive function*, and is compatible with any legitimate degree of complexity in the function exemplified. Notice that in this context *satisfaction* is a relation *in the world* between particulars and "objective" or non-linguistic functions. It corresponds to (in a way which is a topic for analysis in Pure Semantics), but is carefully to be distinguished from the sense in which the individual constants of a language satisfy *linguistic* functions. I mention these two senses of "satisfaction" only to make it clear that the above characterisation of exemplification is not intended to make it a linguistic relation.

316   WILFRID SELLARS :

We shall begin with the assumption that statements of types
A and B alike can be reformulated to become

        A. 13.   Fido exemplifies Dog.
        A. 23.   It exemplifies Twinge.

        B. 13.   Fido exemplifies Anger.
        B. 23.   It exemplifies Pain.

It should be particularly noted that the concepts which are mentioned by B. 13 and B. 23 are not Angry-thing and Painful-
situation, but rather Anger and Pain.   We do not yet know what
in this new context is to be made of concepts of the form f-thing.
However, our account of exemplification suggests that, unlike the
conclusion at which we arrived when operating with *specimen of*,

        B. 14.   Fido exemplifies Angry-thing

is also legitimate.

VI

   We are now in a position to raise one of the decisive issues on
which the argument of this paper turns.   It can be formulated
quite simply as follows : " Does it make sense to say of a basic
particular that it exemplifies more than one non-relational concept ?   In other words, is '$f(a)$ & $g(a)$' a significant form where
'a' is an underived or primitive individual constant of the
language ? "   In answering this question, it will obviously be
sufficient to consider only *primitive* non-relational concepts.   The
argument, curiously enough, takes us into the problem of " negative facts ".   Let us present it in the form of a dialogue, and
begin with a familiar and well-worn dialectical exchange.

Jones : In virtue of what is '$\phi(a)$' true, where '$\phi(a)$' is a basic
      proposition in the sense characterised above ?

Smith : '$\phi(a)$' is true if and only if $\phi(a)$.

Jones : Then in virtue of what is '$\sim\phi(b)$' true, where '$\phi(b)$' is
      also a basic proposition ?

Smith : I suppose, by parity of reasoning, that '$\sim\phi(b)$' is true if
      and only if $\sim\phi(b)$.

Jones : But there are facts of the form $\phi(a)$.   Do you wish to
      maintain that there are facts of the form $-\phi(b)$?   Does '$\sim$'
      stand for a feature of the world ?

Smith : No, I wouldn't want to say that.   Notice that if '$\sim\phi(b)$',
      which is a negative proposition, is true, there must be some

affirmative proposition which is also true of b, for surely there are no bare particulars.

Jones : That is reasonable enough. Suppose that this true affirmative proposition is ' $\psi(b)$ '. Where does this get you ? Are you suggesting that it is by virtue of the fact that $\psi(b)$ is the case that '$\sim\phi(b)$' is true ? But what does something's being ψ have to do with its not being ϕ ?

Smith : Ah ! But it has everything to do with it if ϕ and ψ are incompatible !

Jones : And what does it mean to say of two concepts that they are incompatible ?

Smith : Incompatibility is a relation which exists between determinate universals which fall under the same determinable universal. Thus the various colour qualities are incompatible. Thus '$\sim\phi(b)$' is true by virtue of the fact that $\psi(b)$ is the case, ψ being a quality of the same genus or family as ϕ.

Jones : I remember. But aren't you deluding yourself ? You seem to think that with your $\psi(b)$ you have gotten away from negative facts. But incompatibility doesn't enable you to dispense with facts of the form $\sim\phi(x)$, for to say that ϕ and ψ are incompatible is surely only to say that

(x) $\phi(x)$ entails $\sim\psi(x)$ and $\psi(x)$ entails $\sim\phi(x)$.

Thus the incompatibility to which you appeal can itself only be understood in terms of negative propositions.

Smith : I see that I shall have to cut somewhat deeper. Strictly speaking, once one looks upon the language in which we speak about the world as something more than a calculus, and asks about the *meaning* and *truth* of expressions belonging to it, '$\sim\phi(b)$' is seen to be an abbreviated way of saying " False(' $\phi(b)$ ') ", in other words " $\sim$true(' $\phi(b)$ ') ". Now you yourself are fond of saying that truth is not a factual feature of the world. Well, when we ask these questions about the truth of empirical statements, '$\sim$' is a calculational symbol in the metalanguage, cheek by jowl with ' true '.

Jones : I see what you are driving at, though I am not quite happy about the way in which you have put it. But though you may have established a useful base of operations, have you really gotten anywhere ? Thus, permit me to ask in virtue of what is it the case that $\sim true($' $\phi(b)$ ') ? Because $\sim\phi(b)$? That, however, would put us back where we were before. Because $\psi(b)$ and, therefore *true*(' $\psi(b)$ ') ? But, once again, what does the truth of ' $\psi(b)$ ' have to do with the falsity of ' $\phi(b)$ ' ?

318   WILFRID SELLARS :

Smith : The answer is still in terms of incompatibility, once this
    concept has been correspondingly re-interpreted.   From the
    standpoint of logical analysis our language involves many
    families of primitive predicates, each family consisting of
    determinates under a common determinable.   The charac-
    terisation of each such set involves truth rules.   Thus if we
    suppose a family consisting only of ' P_1 ' and ' P_2 ', deter-
    minates of ' P ', we have the *schemata*,

   True(' $P_1(x)$ ') entails $\sim$True(' $P_2(x)$ ')
   $\sim$True(' $P_1(x)$ ') entails True(' $P_2(x)$ ').

These rules, of which the second is the most interesting for
our purpose, bring out the fundamental contention of the
approach to negation via the mutual exclusion of determinates
under a common determinable.   They are not only rules for
' P_1 ' and ' P_2 ' but also illustrate the fundamental grammar
of '$\sim$'.   Incompatibility is thus a purely linguistic notion,
requiring no such things as negative facts in the non-linguistic
world.

Jones : This is all very interesting.   You are bringing the prob-
    lem into proper focus.   But although I am quite happy about
    the idea that the predicates of a language are specified in
    terms of truth rules, I find two fundamental difficulties in
    your account.   The first of these is that on your account it
    would be impossible to say of a particular that it had fewer
    than N qualities, where N is the number of families of predi-
    cates in the language.   For to say that a certain particular,
    say c, has no quality of family K is to say

   (1) $(f)\, K(f) \supset \sim f(c)$.

but on your account, to say ' $\sim f(c)$ ' where f belongs to family
K entails

   (2) $(\mathrm{E}f)\, K(f)\, \&\, f(c)$.

    Which contradicts (1).

Smith : Hmm.   And what is the other difficulty ?

Jones : One which I take to be even more decisive.   Surely it is
    an empirical and contingent feature of a world that it in-
    volves qualities which come in families !   Yet your account
    makes it a matter of logical necessity, for you make the in-
    compatibility of the predicates of a family the basis for your
    account of falsity.

Smith : And what, if I may ask, are your ideas on the subject ?

Jones : I suggest that where the values of ' x ' are basic particu-
    lars, the form ' $f(x)\, \&\, g(x)$ ' is illegitimate.   This amounts to

ON THE LOGIC OF COMPLEX PARTICULARS   319

saying that ' $\sim \phi(b)$ ' is entailed by ' $\psi(b)$ ' not in virtue of the fact that ψ belongs to the same family as ϕ, should it do so, *but rather merely by virtue of the fact that ψ is a different quality than ϕ.* To use traditional jargon, *otherness* rather than *incompatibility* is the answer.

Smith : And what is your account of incompatibility ?

Jones : Incompatibilities as well as real connexions [1] are specified by the " axioms " or conformation rules of a language, defining its " P-structure ".   Each such rule specifies a formal implication which involves as many individual-variables as (primitive) one place predicates, and which sets forth a relational pattern to which exemplifications of these qualities conform in all possible worlds to which the language applies.

Smith : Does no incompatibility (or real connexion) concern the qualities which may be possessed by one and the same particular ?

Jones : Indeed.   But only if we are now talking about *complex* particulars.   Such incompatibilities and connexions are derived from the incompatibilities and connexions of the atomic level, together with the definitional structure of the complex particulars.   Only confusion can result if the levels of atomic and " molecular " particulars are confused.

VII

Now, if the conclusions to which we have come (for we agree with Jones) are sound, it follows that statements of kind B must be about complex or derived particulars, for " Fido is angry " is a typical example of such statements, and it obviously makes sense to say, " Fido is angry and hungry ".   Once again we are led, this time by a more rigorous train of thought, to consider the subject of statements of this kind as a " complex " particular which is analysable into " ingredient " particulars, and to consider truths about it as analysable into truths concerning these ingredients.   Let us therefore sharpen our account of *Ingredience,*

[1] A detailed exposition of the analysis of *real connexion* and the *causal modalities* adumbrated above, is to be found in my paper, " Concepts as Involving Laws and Inconceivable without Them ", *Philosophy of Science,* October, 1948.   A more epistemologically oriented discussion is to be found in my " Realism and the New Way of Words ", *Philosophy and Phenomenological Research,* June, 1948 (reprinted, with minor changes, in *Readings in Philosophical Analysis,* edited by Herbert Feigl and Wilfrid Sellars, Appleton-Century-Crofts, New York, 1949).

for the idea of relations of this type will play a key role in the analysis to come.

In view of the fact that our purpose is not to analyse the " thing-making " relations of the actual world, but rather to grasp the most general aspects of the logical structure of complex particulars, those, namely, which obtain in any possible world which includes such particulars, explicit mention will be made of only such of the properties of the relation, I, as will enable it to play the role of a paradigm of all such relations. Thus, we shall take for granted that in its empirical aspects, this relation involves spatio-temporal relations and causal (or " real ") connexions. These aspects, however, will guide, rather than appear in, our analysis.

What then is to be said by way of sharpening our account of Ingredience ? The answer is implicit in the first paragraph of this section. I, or Ingredience, is a relation between an ingredient particular and the complex particular of which it is an ingredient. *But prior to I are the relations between a set of items by virtue of which they constitute a whole of which they are the ingredients.* In accordance with our programme of getting down to essentials, let us suppose that there is only one such relation, and let us call it " co-ingredience-in-a-thing ", symbolising it by ' Φ '. Let us exhibit the connexion between ' I ' and ' Φ ' by means of the following schema which constitutes a " definition in use " of ' I ' in terms of ' Φ ',

$$I(y,x) \text{ if and only if } x = \Phi(\ldots, y, \ldots).$$

In other words, y is an ingredient of x if and only if x is a co-ingredient set of particulars which includes y. It is to be noted that the domain of Φ consists of basic particulars only. This is not to say that a hierarchy of levels of particulars cannot be defined such that particulars of level n have particulars of level $n-l$ as ingredients. It is only to remind us that such a hierarchy must rest on a hierarchy of relations of co-ingredience-in-a-thing. It also entails, when taken in conjunction with the results of our dialogue, that the predicates ' f ' of such B-statements as are correctly analysed into statements of the form ' (Ey) I(y,x) & $f(y)$ ' are *primitive* predicates. To put it more carefully, for reasons which will appear shortly, the ' f ' which appears in the statements which form the analysis of such B-statements must be a primitive predicate.

Now according to our account of exemplification, " Fido is angry " is legitimately represented as

B. 1. Anger(Fido).

If we assume, for purposes of illustration, that 'Anger' is a primitive predicate, the general presuppositions which we have sketched above assure us that

$$(\mathrm{E}y)\ \mathrm{I}(y,\ \mathrm{Fido})\ \&\ \mathrm{Anger}(y)$$

is what might be called the *atomic reduction* of " Fido is angry ". Thus we have

$$\mathrm{Anger}(\mathrm{Fido}) = (\mathrm{E}y)\ \mathrm{I}(y,\ \mathrm{Fido})\ \&\ \mathrm{Anger}(y).$$

We are now in a position to distinguish between four different types of statement representable by the form '$f(x)$'. The first (I) consists of atomic propositions. These are not further reducible for the obvious reason that they belong on the ground floor of the language. Type II consists of statements of the kind we were discussing immediately above. These are statements '$f(x)$' which are reducible to '$(\mathrm{E}y)\ \mathrm{I}(y,\ x)\ \&\ f(y)$'. We have already seen that, given our assumptions, 'f' must in such cases be a primitive predicate. It should now be pointed out that where 'f' is a primitive predicate, and 'x' the name of a complex particular—as it must be if it is to be legitimate to say that x has other properties than f—then '$f(x)$' must entail '$(\mathrm{E}y)\ \mathrm{I}(y,\ x)\ \&\ f(y)$'. *Otherwise, by the mere process of eliminating defined terms, one would pass from a statement which entailed the existence of at least one exemplification of f, to a set of statements which did not.* Type II consists of such B-statements as are analysable in terms of one primitive predicate. With an eye on future developments let us refer to them as statements which attribute an *undefined property* to a thing.

For our type III we have statements '$f(x)$' for which there is no atomic reduction of the form '$(\mathrm{E}y)\ \mathrm{I}(y,\ x)\ \&\ f(y)$, not because they have no reduction, but because it is of the more complicated form,

$$\text{'}(\mathrm{E}y)(\mathrm{E}z)\ \ldots\ \mathrm{I}(y,\ x)\ \&\ \mathrm{I}(z,\ x)\ \ldots\ \&\ g(y)\ \&\ h(z).\ \ldots$$

In such statements, 'f' is clearly a highly derived predicate. We shall refer to such statements as statements which attribute a *defined property* to a thing. We shall give an account of such definition at a later stage in our argument.

Type IV presents itself as a special case of type III. It consists of statements '$f(x)$' of which the analysis proceeds as in the preceding paragraph, but which entail, in addition,

$$\sim(\mathrm{E}w)\ \mathrm{I}(w,\ x)\ \&\ (w \neq y)\ \&\ (w \neq z).\ \ldots$$

Now statements of this latter type, and the predicates 'f' which appear in them will play a key role in the following argument. They merit a separate symbolism. We shall call such predicates,

" θ-predicates ", and they will be symbolised accordingly. They will be said to designate θ-concepts. The letter " θ " has, of course, been chosen because of its relation to the initial sound of " thing ".

θ-predicates constitute a special class of the one-place descriptive functions which take thing-names as arguments. Let us introduce the convention of using the letter ' t ' as the variable which has complex particulars or " things " as its extra-linguistic values. We shall also use it as the ambiguous designation of a single complex particular. (As such it would replace the ' x ' of the above analyses, except in the case of statements of type I.) Where necessary we shall use ' t_1 ', ' t_2 ', etc. as derived individual constants (thing-names). Thus, the primary sentences in which θ-predicates appear are of the form ' $\theta(t)$ '. Sentences of this form may, for the time being, be read, " The complex particular t exemplifies the character complex θ ". As this reading suggests, θ-predicates are derived from the primitive predicates of the language, which designate the simple characteristics of the world about which it speaks. The form of such a derivation can be indicated by means of the following schema for the " definition in use " of the predicate ' θ_i ' in terms of the primitive predicates ' g ', ' h ', etc. This schema should be compared with preceding account of type IV statements.

$\theta_i(t)$ if and only if $(\mathrm{E}y)(\mathrm{E}z) \ldots g(y)$ & $h(z) \ldots$ & $t = \Phi(y, z, \ldots)$.

In other words, ' θ_i ' is a logical construction out of ' g ', ' h ', ... of such a kind that to say that t exemplifies θ_i is a " shorthand " way of saying that $g, h, \ldots$ are exemplified by the ingredients of t. Further refinements would have to be introduced into a technically adequate account, but the above will serve to indicate what we have in mind.

Now the schematic character of the above derivation may mislead the reader into overlooking the fact that the " definition " of a θ-predicate specifies a *complete* battery of primitive predicates for the complex particulars to which it applies. Yet this completeness is the very feature by virtue of which θ-predicates or their equivalents play a key role in the structure of the thing level of a language. This, however, will come out in the course of our analysis. For the moment, a crude analogy may be of assistance in grasping the nature of a θ-predicate. A θ-concept " covers " a complex particular which exemplifies it, as a complex mould, or an engraved plate, fits its product. To put the matter somewhat differently, if t exemplifies θ_i, then nothing be truly predicated of t concerning its *intrinsic* character opposed to its relation to particulars not ingredient in it) which is not contained in the sense of ' $\theta_i(t)$ '. *It follows that expressions of the form ' $\theta_i(t)$ & $\theta_j(t)$ ' are no more legitimate at the molecular level, than are expressions of the form ' $f(x)$ & $g(x)$ ' at the atomic. A θ-concept specifies the complete and determinate nature of any complex particular which exemplifies it.*

At this stage the reader may well be moved to expostulate along the following lines : " What are you trying to do ?   Reinstate occult essences ?   If so, you certainly break all records !   Your account implies that if two complex particular differ intrinsically to the slightest degree, they must exemplify different θ-concepts. That means an awful lot of θ-concepts !   And with just how many θ-concepts are you acquainted ?   How many statements of the form ' $\theta(t)$ ' do you make each day ?   What can such concepts have to do with the logical structure of our language ? "

The proper reply to this outburst consists in the actual employment of the notion of a θ-predicate as a tool of logical analysis. The remainder of our argument will be exactly that.   Before we begin, however, a general comment may be helpful.   We have already suggested that in order to be convinced of the decisive importance for the clarification of logical issues of the notions of *atomic proposition, primitive predicate* and *underived individual constant*, it is not necessary to be able to point with confidence at examples of these notions in the language in which we speak about our world.   What a rational reconstruction *is*, is not easy to say. But it should not be necessary to point out that a rational reconstruction of " our language " is *not* an empirical science of language behaviour, nor, in particular, does it consist in a mere rearranging into a preferred order of items painstakingly *selected* from the flow of observed language usage.   That a formal system is a *reconstruction* is extrinsic to its character as a formal system.   In order for a formal scientist to be " reconstructing our language " he must operate *with an eye on* human language behaviour.   But in its *intrinsic* nature, the activity of reconstruction operates in accordance with the procedures and criteria of formal science.   A sweeping statement may be suggestive.   Out of all formally constructible systems, some involve structures of a type which we should characterise as synthetic propositions consisting of predicates and individual constants.   Other and more complicated formal systems (semantic) exhibit such structures in wholes of which part mirrors part to clarify our notion of a language being about a world.   Of all such constructible systems, a limited range of each type would strike a familiar chord.   Those belonging to the first type, we should recognise as possible formal models of

324   WILFRID SELLARS :

our language ; those belonging to the second type would " clarify *our* language's being about *our* world ". Ideally only one system of each type would ' fit '. To say that more than one of each type would clarify, and that of these all would contain features which we could not fit, and between which we could not choose, is but an unfamiliar way of saying that we are ignorant.

Now the reader may be inclined to grant " in principle " what we have just been saying in our flight into the blue, and nevertheless be moved to ask the following questions : " Granting that the formal theory of languages is a purely *a priori* science, this matter of ' fitting ' strikes me as the most important aspect of your account from the standpoint of your argument. Thus, even if I were to grant that your notion of θ-predicates makes formal sense, how do you propose to show that it throws light on *our* language ? Might it not belong to the theory of a type of language which belongs to a different branch of the family tree of possible languages than any which might ' fit ' our language behaviour ? Your notion of θ-predicates doesn't strike me as having any clarifying value. To reformulate a previous challenge, just how many statements do you make each day which you find to be clarified by the form ' $\theta(t)$ ' ? "

To take the last question first, the answer is that it is as doubtful that we ever make statements which a reconstruction would exhibit as having the form ' $\theta(t)$ ', as it is doubtful that we ever make statements which a reconstruction would exhibit as having the form of an atomic proposition. Those who admit the latter would explain it by saying that from a formal standpoint *we speak on a highly derived level of our language as it would be presented by a rational reconstruction. That a reconstruction of our language involves an atomic level does not entail that we ever actually formulate statements which would be reconstructed as belonging to this level.* A failure—undoubtedly due to misplaced empiricist tendencies—to realise this fact is undoubtedly responsible for much current confusion in philosophical analysis. Now the point I wish to make is that not only do we speak at a derived level of our language which is " above " the atomic level, *we speak on a level which is above that of statements of the form ' $\theta(t)$ ' and which is derived from the level of statements having this form in a way which we shall be concerned to analyse.* That the fact that we speak at such a highly derived level gears in with our ignorance, and explains what Waismann has called the " open texture " of our concepts will come out in the course of our discussion. As for the other questions raised above, a few words will suffice. If, as we have argued, the notion of θ-predicates is essential to the theory of any language which contains derived individual constants, that is to say, to any language which admits of the form ' – – –(. . .) & * * *(. . .) ' (for we have shown that in such a form the values of ' . . . ' must be derived individual constants), then this notion is clearly relevant to the clarification of the language in which we speak about our world. Indeed, it is only slightly less fundamental to such clarification than the very notions of *individual constant* and *predicate* themselves, and these are indeed fundamental!

VIII

Let us now consider, briefly, to what extent our original sample statements fit plausibly into the four pigeon-holes which our analysis has led us to distinguish. Clearly, our example A. 2, " It is a twinge " was chosen as a candidate for pigeon-hole I, and it fits reasonably well, if we abstract from complications relating to tense. Again, perhaps B. 2, " It is painful ", can be regarded as a plausible example of type II. We should feel even more happy with B. 1, " Fido is angry " as an inhabitant of pigeon-hole III. Shall we conclude that A. 1, " Fido is a dog ", is an example of type IV ? Certainly a *prima facie* case can be made for such a conclusion. Thus, predicates such as ' Dog ' and ' Cat ' are clearly predicates which apply to complex particulars or things. Again, when we say of a thing that it is a dog, or a cat, we seem, somehow, to have specified its nature as a whole. Indeed, if we ask, " Is it *sensible* to make statements of the form ' $f(t)$ & $g(t)$ ' where both ' f ' and ' g ' are predicates of the same kind as ' Dog ' and ' Cat ' ? " the answer is surely, " No ! " It would hardly be sensible to say ' $Dog(t)$ & $Cat(t)$ '. At this stage we remember that the form ' $\theta_1(t)$ & $\theta_2(t)$ ' is illegitimate, and the suggestion naturally occurs that ' $Dog(t_1)$ ', ' $Cat(t_2)$ ', etc., are θ-statements.

Would it, then, be correct to say that such statements as " Fido is a dog " belong to our fourth type of statement ? It takes but a moment's reflexion to see that this is not the case. For if ' $Dog(Fido)$ *were* of the form ' $\theta(t)$ ', then it would analytically entail a set of statements exhaustively specifying the intrinsic characteristics of Fido. In other words, if ' $Dog(Fido)$ ' were of this form, and if it were true, then nothing could be truly said of the intrinsic nature of Fido—which did not specify his relations to other items not ingredient in him—which was not compendiously said by ' $Dog(Fido)$ '. But if ' $Dog(Fido)$ ' tells only part of the story about Fido, how does it differ from common or garden

22

variety statements of type III ? For in the case of such statements, it makes perfectly good sense to say " Fido is hungry and
angry ". Of course, in a general way we all know the answer to
this question. The reader has even formulated it for us in one of
his earlier objections (p. 280). Our aim, however, is a fully
explicit account of this difference.

In order to grasp the difference in logical structure between
" Fido is a dog " and " Fido is angry ", we must first appreciate
their fundamental identity of structure. To do this, we must
focus our attention once again on such concepts as *Angry-thing*.
For Angry-thing is a thing-concept as is Dog, and yet " Fido is
an angry-thing " is equivalent to " Fido is angry ". Now it is
clear that *Angry-thing* is not a θ-concept. But can it, perhaps,
be understood in terms of the idea of a θ-concept ? An attempt
along these lines might run as follows :

Although the import of ' Angry-thing ' applies to particulars
as wholes (for it is as wholes that they are angry-things), *and
although every complex particular exemplifies a θ-concept* (a
statement which may surprise until it is realised that it is a
tautology [1]), ' Angry-thing ' does not name the θ-concept which
is exemplified by each of the things to which it applies. Yet it
does refer to θ-concepts, *indeed, to a class of θ-concepts. It
specifies the class of θ-concepts which contain the concept Anger
as a constituent.* Not that ' f-thing(t) ' says of t that it belongs
to the class of θ-concepts having f as a constituent (which
would be nonsense). Rather it says of t that it exemplifies one
of the θ-concepts belonging to this class. What is the relation
between a concept such as Anger (which we shall once again
assume, for the sake of the argument, to be a simple concept)
and a θ-concept by virtue of which the former is a *constituent*
of the latter ? As a first approximation, we may say that
*Constituency is the relation between primitive concepts and θ-
concepts which " parallels " the relation of Ingredience which
holds between basic particulars and things.* More accurately,
the relationship between Constituency and Ingredience (given
the fundamental assumptions of our argument) is exhibited
by the following equivalence,

(t) C[f, ($\imath\theta$) $\theta(t)$] if and only if (Ey) I(y, t) & $f(y)$

where this is read, " for every t, f is a constituent of the θ-con-
cept exemplified by t if and only if there is a y such that y is an

[1] The reader should ask himself the corresponding question, " Do all
basic particulars exemplify a quale ? " Is it a contingent truth, or perhaps even false that (x) (Ef)$f(x)$?

ON THE LOGIC OF COMPLEX PARTICULARS   327

ingredient of t and y exemplifies f ". In these terms we can represent " Fido is an angry-thing " by the expression,

$$C[Anger, (\imath\theta)\ \theta(Fido)]$$

which is read, " Anger is a constituent of the θ-concept exemplified by Fido ". In general, a statement of the form ' t is an f-thing ' is explicated by a statement of the form,

$$C[f, (\imath\theta)\ \theta(t)].$$

Now such an approach as we have just sketched would not seem to be illegitimate in principle ; for (1) θ-concepts were legitimately introduced and (2) concepts as well as particulars can be referred to by description. The form

$$(\imath f)\ F(f).\ \ldots$$

makes just as good sense as the form

$$(\imath t)\ f(t).\ \ldots$$

Furthermore, this approach does not claim that the use of θ-concepts enables us to say anything about the world which could not be said without them. θ-predicates are just as eliminable as thing-names. Everything that can be said about the world can be said entirely in terms of atomic propositions. Yet once we choose to take advantage of a molecular level in our language, θ-predicates as constructible functions become available for use. If the reader forgets our earlier polemic so far as to expostulate, " But they are only *in principle* constructible ", it will suffice to point out that this is just as true of the thing-names which he has accepted without protest. θ-functions, whether or not they are used, lie in the molecular level of a language as mathematical functions lie in a number system. Fortunately, to explicate *this* is not our present concern.

The above argument may lead to a refocusing of the objection. " θ-functions may be ' in ' the language, but do they belong to that part of its apparatus of which we avail ourselves ? Did not you speak of Constituency as the ' parallel ' of Ingredience ? Do not your definitions entail that

$$C[f, (\imath\theta)\ \theta(t)]$$

is logically equivalent to

$$(Ey)\ I(y, t)\ f(y)\ ?$$

What is gained by using the language of *constituency in θ-concepts* as opposed to that of *ingredience in things* ? Does not the former presuppose the latter ? " To the last point, it is important to note, the answer is " No ! " Ingredience and Constituency alike are defined in terms of Co-ingredience-in-a-thing. In this respect the " language of Ingredience " has no advantage. But we still face the main issue. What *is* the advantage of the " language of constituency in θ-concepts ", as the objection put it ? This is obviously the kind of question that is adequately answered only by doing. The remainder of the argument is devoted to that task. Yet it is worth-while pointing out that our results should not be surprising. If we put one foot out of the study, do we not find it plausible to say that our intellectual concern with the world is directed at the conceptual structure it exemplifies, and the place of this structure in the domain of possible structures ? Now θ-concepts are the fundamental unities of the molecular conceptual level. This stands out clearly if we note that the simplest logical form of a complete (intrinsic) characterisation of a complex particular *asserted as a complete characterisation* is either of the form ' $\theta(t)$ ' or, *which is the same thing*, its atomic reduction. Such are statements of type IV, the exhaustiveness of the ingredients y, z, etc., which in our account of type IV was specified by means of the clause,

$$\sim (\mathrm{E}w)\ \mathrm{I}(w, x)\ \&\ (w \neq y)\ \&\ w \neq z\ \&\ \dots$$

showing itself in the clause

$$t = \Phi(y, z, \dots).$$

IX

Let us use the terms " naming " and " describing " for the ways in which *constants* and *descriptive phrases* respectively refer to particulars and universals. In these terms, our contention is that *often when to a casual glance we seem to be naming a concept, we are actually describing a complex concept in a way which involves the naming of one or more of its constituents.* The concept or concepts which are the fundamentum of a description are confused with the concept to which the description applies, so that the very fact that a description is involved is overlooked. Thus, it is of the utmost importance to realise that a word which, from the stand-point of a logical reconstruction, *describes* a concept may function in the language of everyday life in a way which is grammatically indistinguishable from that of words which, again from the stand-point of a logical reconstruction, *name* concepts. This similarity of grammatical syntax leads the unwary to attempt a logical reconstruction in which *all* concepts are named. This mistake brings with it a disastrous misinterpretation of the logical syntax of the words we use for " kinds of things ", *e.g.* " Dog ". *Without exception, these words are properly interpreted as referring to complex concepts by means of descriptions in terms of constituent concepts which they name.*

But if ' Dog(t) ' like ' Angry-thing(t) ' is to be clarified in terms of the form ' $C[f, (\gamma\theta)\ \theta(t)]$ ', wherein does the difference lie ? It will be remembered that this difference finds its expression in the fact that while

$$\text{Angry-thing}(t) \ \& \ \text{Hungry-thing}(t)$$

is a sensible remark,

$$\text{Dog}(t) \ \& \ \text{Cat}(t)$$

is not. A first approximation to an answer is found by reflecting that words for " kinds of things " (as opposed to words which end in the hyphenated suffix ' -thing ' or are mere synonyms for such) are so introduced into the language that either the " P-axioms " of the language, or what are accepted as contingent but universally true generalisations formulated in the language rule out the truth of such statements as

$$T_1(t) \ \& \ T_2(t)$$

where ' T_1 ' and ' T_2 ' are words for " kinds of things ". Now our analysis has shown that a thing-predicate refers to the class of those θ-concepts which have certain concepts *named* by the thing-predicates as constituents. Let us call the named constituent concept(s) which is (are) the fundamentum of the description of a θ-concept, the *note(s)* of the thing-predicates which stand for this descriptive reference ; and let us symbolise them by the letter ' N ' with subscripts. Thus, Anger is the note of the class of θ-concepts referred to by the term ' Angry-thing ', and ' Angry-thing ' is a predicate of such a structure that to say " t is an angry-thing " is to say " t exemplifies one and only one θ-concept having the note Anger ". If ' T_1 ' and ' T_2 ' above have the notes N_1 and N_2, respectively, then ' $T_1(t) \ \& \ T_2(t)$ ' has as its analysis,

$$C[N_1, (\gamma\theta)\ \theta(t)] \ \& \ C[N_2, (\gamma\theta)\ \theta(t)].$$

We can now give a more searching answer to our question. *Words for " kinds of things " are so introduced that every overlap of the classes of θ-concepts specified by the notes* named *by these words, contains only θ-concepts which are unexemplified either as a contingent matter of fact, or because they are physically impossible.* They are so chosen, in other words, that

$$\sim(Et) \ C[N_1, (\gamma\theta)\ \theta(t)] \ \& \ C[N_2, (\gamma\theta)\ \theta(t)].$$

We now understand how " Fido is a dog " differs from " Fido is angry " while belonging with it to type II-III.

We are also in a position to clarify the relation of our original

330   WILFRID SELLARS :

approach to the analysis of thing-statements in terms of the
relation *specimen of* to our present approach in terms of *exemplifies*. It will be remembered that we introduced the term "exemplifies " as short for " satisfies the one place descriptive (*i.e.,*
factual, non-logical) function ". In terms of this second approach we have been enabled to distinguish between three types
of case in which a particular can be said to exemplify a concept,

$$f(x) \qquad . \qquad . \qquad . \qquad . \qquad \text{(Type I)},$$
$$\text{N-thing}(t) \qquad . \qquad . \qquad . \qquad \text{(Type II-III)},$$
$$\theta(t) \qquad . \qquad . \qquad . \qquad . \qquad \text{(Type IV)}.$$

It is the first and third of these cases that satisfy the " intuitive "
criteria we were using in determining whether or not a particular
was a case or instance of a concept. For it is primitive functions
at the atomic level, and θ-functions at the " molecular " level
which alone are " adequate " to the particulars which exemplify
them, " covering " them " as wholes " in an explicit and
straightforward way. This " covering of particulars as wholes
by concepts named rather than merely described " was the
criterion in mind we were using for the phrase " case or instance
(specimen) of ".

It might be asked, " What has happened to the form '$f(t)$ '
which you recognised under the guise of '$f(x)$ ' where an atomic
reduction exists of the form ' (Ey) I(y, x) & $f(y)$ ' ? Wasn't this
your type II ? Isn't the 'f ' of such an '$f(t)$ ' a primitive predicate ? Didn't you analyse type III as a conjunctive complex of
type II statements ? " To answer we need only note that in the
formula

$$f(t) = (Ey) \text{ I}(y, t) \& f(y)$$

the 'f ' on the right hand side is indeed a *primitive* predicate, the
'f ' on the left hand side is not, but is rather the *undefined* molecular predicate which is derived from the homonymous atomic
predicate. An adequate symbolism would have distinguished
these predicates by different signs. The 'f ' of '$f(t)$ ' is logically
equipollent with 'f-thing ', and types of statement II and III as
defined in our earlier discussion have the same force as the types
which we have lumped together in the above classification as
type II-III.

Our final remark before the more technical discussion of the
next and last section. Our analysis, by distinguishing between
θ-concepts and concepts of the form *N-thing*, has enabled us to
realise that our concepts of things are *not* θ-concepts. Who
would have said that they are ? The important point, however,
is that ignorance and the practical attitude combine to support

a naive realism which fails to distinguish between these two types of concept. The concepts we actually use are not the sort of function that has *instances* or *cases* as these terms have been used in the paper. Is it, then, proper to claim that ' instance ' and ' case ' have the sense we have given them in their everyday use ? The reader, if he takes a familiar line, may be inclined to say, " As we actually use these terms, they do not have the sense you have given them, for in the great world outside your study, they are so used that it makes perfectly good sense to say ' . . . is an instance of – – – ', where – – – is one of the thing-classifying words you have discussed at such great length." It is important to realise that this is a *non sequitur.* It must be admitted that we do so use these words, yet the confusion we have attributed to common sense requires us to insist that these terms carry with them as a " recessive " trait the sense we have given them in our discussion. Indeed, it is just because of this fact that we chose them. It has been pointed out that it did not take Aristotle to make man rational. No more did it take Tarski to give him the idea of truth, nor any student of Semiotic to give him any notion fundamental to meaning or meaningfulness. At their best, philosophers *clarify* notions which are deeply and actively embedded in our conceptual structure. Thus, in a sense we all " know " the structure of our language, and, if the argument of our paper is correct, it merely gives a clearer formulation to what we have all " known " all along. Often, on the other hand, philosophical systems make muddy crystals of the confusions of common sense. The Scholastic notion of sensible species is a pertinent example. Yet for common sense to confuse two things they must both be present.

X

In this final section, we shall consider the light thrown by our analysis on the logical structure of the functional calculus. Certain conclusions at which we have already arrived can be set down summarily as follows :

(1) ' $f(x)$ & $g(x)$ ' and ' f & $g(x)$ ' are illegitimate forms, where the values of ' x ' are primitive individual constants, and ' f ' and ' g ' are different primitive one-place predicates. Consequently, while there are atomic functions, and while every set of atomic functions must have an axiomatics, there is nothing which could be called a " calculus " of atomic one-place functions.

(2) ' $\theta_1(\iota)$ & $\theta_2(\iota)$ ' and ' θ_1 & $\theta_2(\iota)$ ' are illegitimate forms, where θ_1 and θ_2 are determinate, named, complex concepts, and ι a complex particular. In short, there is no " calculus " of θ-functions.

(3) Statements such as " Fido is a dog " and " Fido is angry " which are obvious grist for the mill of the calculus of one-place functions can be represented by the form

$$\text{N-thing}(\iota)$$

where this is equivalent to

$$C[N, (\gamma\theta)\ \theta(\iota)].$$

It is also equivalent to

$$(E y)\quad I(y,\iota)\ \&\ f(y),$$

but only a mistaken prejudice against the quantification of predicates springing from a naive nominalism could lead one to suppose that this second form is more " proper " or more fundamental than the first.

In what follows we shall sketch a model language in terms of which the derived character of the level of language to which the formulæ of the functional calculus apply can be made explicit. It will also enable us to give a final clarification of the distinction we have drawn between *defined* and *undefined* thing-level predicates. Finally we shall touch briefly on the light thrown by our analysis on the close relationship which exists between the *language of universals* and the *language of classes*.

In constructing our model language, we shall take as our point of departure the fact that the underived predicates and individual constants of the atomic level of a language must satisfy not only *formation* rules of the sort presented in discussions of the logical syntax of language (as modified by (1) above), but also certain *conformation* rules. The latter give " implicit definitions " of the primitive predicates, and in the process of doing so specify the *underived laws* of the family of worlds to one of which the language applies. We shall assume that the primitive predicates of our model language,

$$\phi_1,\ \phi_2,\ \phi_3,\ .\ .\ .,\ \phi_n$$

are properly " defined " by such conformation rules which specify what is physically possible in the world of the language. Next, we shall assume, as we have done through the paper, that there is only one relation in virtue of which a set of basic particulars is recognised by the language as constituting a complex particular. This relation will be called, as before, *co-ingredience-in-a-thing*, symbolised as ' Φ '. We shall now add a further assumption to the effect that this relation is a triadic relation among basic particulars, and that it is physically impossible for two particulars of a set so related to exemplify the same (simple) quality. Now the underived laws of the world of the language, together with the relation Φ determine a set of complex-concepts (θ-concepts) which are the physically possible completely specified and determinate kinds of complex particular in that world. Let us suppose that there are as many physically possible θ-concepts (kinds of thing) as there are combinations of n items taken three at a time, where n is the number of primitive descriptive predicates of the language. Thus, for each combination of three such predicates, say $/\phi_i, \phi_j, \phi_k/$, there will be a θ-concept with ϕ_i, ϕ_j, and ϕ_k as constituent concepts or *notes*. Let us represent this θ-concept by the symbol ' $\theta^{\phi_i \phi_j \phi_k}$.' Given our *schemata* for the definition of a θ-concept, and of the relation C (pp. 322 ; 326) it is clear that

$$C(\phi_i, \theta^{\phi_j \phi_i \phi_k})$$

is a logically necessary proposition. Thus, on the basis of the rules of the language alone (*materialiter*, on a purely *a priori* basis) we can classify θ-concepts into sets in terms of their notes. For example, we can consider the class whose members are the θ-concepts which have ϕ_i as a constituent concept or note,

$$\hat{\theta}\{C(\phi_i, \theta)\}.$$

Let us represent this class by the symbol ' $\hat{\phi}_i$ '.

We shall now assume that in our list of primitive descriptive predicates are to be found ' White ' and ' Sweet ', and ask how ' t is both white and sweet ', where ' t ', of course, is a thing-name, is to be transcribed into our symbolism. As a first step we have

$$C[\text{White}, (\imath\theta)\ \theta(t)]\ \&\ C[\text{Sweet}, (\imath\theta)\ \theta(t)].$$

This, however, is equivalent to

$$(\imath\theta)(\theta t)\ \acute{\epsilon}\ \hat{W}\text{hite}\ \&\ (\imath\theta)\theta(t)\ \acute{\epsilon}\ \hat{S}\text{weet}$$

where an accent has been put on the class membership sign to indicate that the membership of a θ-concept in a class of θ-concepts, specified in terms of a note, is an *a priori* or L-determinate (Carnap) relation.

Let us now consider statements of the kind, " If anything is white, it is sweet ". How are these to be transcribed into our symbolism ? Taking the above as our cue, we should have the following :

$$(t)\ (\imath\theta)\ \theta(t)\ \acute{\epsilon}\ \hat{W}\text{hite} \supset (\imath\theta)\ \theta(t)\ \acute{\epsilon}\ \hat{S}\text{weet}.$$

Notice that the implication sign in this statement is material or truth-functional implication. According to our assumptions, if

334   WILFRID SELLARS :

this general implication is true of the world of the language, it is a contingent truth both logically and physically.

Now at this point, certain conventions of abbreviation suggest themselves which will translate this statement into a form which not only visibly resembles the form we should ordinarily use, but has its characteristic syntactical properties. Our first step consists in abbreviating ' $(1\theta)\ \theta(t)$ ' to ' θ_t '. If we make use of this convention, then the above expression becomes

$$(t)\quad \theta_t \in \hat{\text{White}} \supset \theta_t \in \hat{\text{Sweet}}.$$

If we now abbreviate ' $\theta_t \in \hat{\phi}_t$ ' by ' $\hat{\phi}_i(t)$ ', the statement finally becomes

$$(t)\ \hat{\text{White}}(t) \supset \hat{\text{Sweet}}(t).$$

The difference between this and the conventional way of symbolising " Everything that is white is sweet ", namely

$$(t)\ \text{White}(t) \supset \text{Sweet}(t)$$

will serve to remind us that in statements of the kind we are considering, the functions represented by the words ' White ' and ' Sweet ' have a logical complexity which distinguishes them from the primitive or atomic functions which we should represent in English by the same words. The use of the circumflex will indicate the logical complexity of what is being said.

Let us now turn our attention once again to the classification of θ-concepts into classes on the basis of their constituent concepts or notes. Remembering that we abbreviated ' $\hat{\theta}\{\text{C}(\phi_i,\ \theta)\}$ ' into ' $\hat{\phi}_t$ ', let us introduce ' $\sim\hat{\phi}_t$ ' and ' $\hat{\phi}_i\&\hat{\phi}_j$ ' as follows,

$$\sim\hat{\phi}_i = \hat{\theta}\{\sim\text{C}(\phi),\ \theta_i)\}$$
$$\hat{\phi}_i\&\hat{\phi}_j = \hat{\theta}\{\text{C}(\phi_i,\ \theta)\ \&\ \text{C}(\phi_j,\ \theta)\}$$

These definitions, together with the familiar power of ' $\sim$ ' and ' & ' in the logic of propositions, enable us to specify such L-determinate classes of θ-concepts as the following,

$$\hat{\phi}_1\mathbf{v}\hat{\phi}_2,\ldots\ ;\ \hat{\phi}_1 \supset \hat{\phi}_2,\ldots\ ;\ \ldots.$$

Two such classes, namely,

$$\hat{\phi}_i\&\sim\hat{\phi}_i$$

and

$$\hat{\phi}_1\mathbf{v}\sim\hat{\phi}_1$$

are particularly important for our purposes, as they will be, respectively, the null class ($\hat{\Lambda}$) and the universal class ($\hat{\text{V}}$) of our analysis. The circumflexes will serve to remind us that these are the null and universal classes of θ-concepts, and not of things.

We can now give an account of the definition of a " complex empirical concept " in terms of " simple empirical concepts ". Here the usual blunder is to think of such a definition as having the form

$$Z(x) = \phi(x) \ \& \ \psi(x) \ \ \mathrm{D}f.$$

where ' ϕ ' and ' ψ ' are *primitive* predicates of the language. The truth of the matter, of course, is that such definitions are of the form

$$\hat{Z} = \hat{\phi} \ \& \ \hat{\psi} \ \ \mathrm{D}f$$

which is by no means a definition of a predicate *in terms of two primitive predicates and the logical relation of conjunction*, as the ordinary account has led many logicians to believe. Thus, from the definition as we have formulated it, it follows that

$$(t) \ \hat{Z}(t) = \hat{\phi} \ \& \ \hat{\psi}(t) = \hat{\phi}(t) \ \& \ \hat{\psi}(t)$$

but our very symbolism reminds us that ' $\hat{\phi}$ ' and ' $\hat{\psi}$ ' are not primitive predicates, but rather are derived functions belonging to the molecular level of the language. Now, in order to take such defined terms as ' $\hat{Z}$ ' above into account in our symbolism, let us introduce the variables ' $\hat{P}$ ' and ' $\hat{K}$ ' which take " defined " classes of θ-classes (e.g., $\hat{\phi}_1 \& \hat{\phi}_2$; $\sim \hat{\phi}_1$) as well as " undefined " classes of θ-concepts (e.g., $\hat{\phi}_3$, where ' ϕ_3 ' is a primitive predicate, and hence at the atomic level) for their values.

We must now distinguish more carefully between logically necessary relationships (we shall call them L-relationships) and factual relationships (F-relationships) between classes of θ-concepts. We have been formulating L-relationships in terms of the membership of θ-classes in classes of θ-classes, and the inclusion of one such class in another. Examples of such relationships follow :

$$\theta^{\phi_i \phi_j \phi_k} \ \hat{\epsilon} \ \hat{\phi}_1,$$
$$\hat{\phi}_i \& \hat{\phi}_j \ \hat{\subset} \ \hat{\phi}_1,$$
$$\hat{\phi}_i \supset \hat{\phi}_j \doteq \sim \hat{\phi}_i \lor \hat{\phi}_j,$$
$$(\hat{P}) \ \hat{\Lambda} \ \hat{\subset} \ \hat{P},$$
$$(\hat{P}) \ \hat{P} \ \hat{\subset} \ \hat{V}.$$

The first of these says that a certain θ-concept is included in a specified class of θ-concepts. The remainder say that one class of θ-concepts is included in, or, case three, identical with (reciprocal inclusion) another class of θ-concepts. These statements are all certifiable *a priori* ; they are logically necessary.

336				WILFRID SELLARS :

Notice that the fourth is to the effect that the null class of θ-concepts is included in all classes of θ-concepts; while the fifth says that the universal or omnium class of θ-concepts includes all classes of θ-concepts.

The next point to be made is that all these logically necessary truths can be formulated as implicative propositions. (Once again we use an accent above a connective to indicate the claim that it holds of logical necessity.) Thus we have the following:

$$(t)\ \theta^{\phi_i\phi_j\phi_k}(t)\ \overset{\cdot}{\supset}\ \hat{\phi}_1(t).$$

$$(t)\ \hat{\phi}_i \& \hat{\phi}_j(t)\ \overset{\cdot}{\supset}\ \hat{\phi}_i(t).$$

$$(t)\ \hat{\phi}_i \supset \hat{\phi}_j(t)\ \overset{\cdot}{\equiv}\ \sim\hat{\phi}_i \mathsf{v} \hat{\phi}_j(t).$$

$$(t)\ (\hat{\mathrm{P}})\ \acute{\Lambda}\ (t)\ \overset{\cdot}{\supset}\ \hat{\mathrm{P}}(t).$$

$$(t)\ (\hat{\mathrm{P}})\ \hat{\mathrm{P}}(t)\ \overset{\cdot}{\supset}\ \hat{\mathrm{V}}(t).$$

In this context, we shall speak of the values of ' $\hat{\mathrm{P}}$ ', that is to say all classes of θ-concepts, as *properties*. Indeed, even a θ-concept itself can be considered as a property, since to each θ-concept there corresponds a class of θ-concepts which has only it for a member. Thus, $\theta^{\phi_1\phi_2\phi_3}$ is the sole member, given our presuppositions, of the class of θ-concepts $\hat{\phi}_1 \& \hat{\phi}_2 \& \hat{\phi}_3$, and can be represented by the latter in the calculus of properties. Where we spoke before of logically necessary inclusion and identity between classes of θ-concepts, we now speak of logically necessary implication and equivalence relationships between properties. Thus, the property $\hat{\phi}_i \supset \hat{\phi}_j$ is logically equivalent to the property $\sim\hat{\phi}_i \mathsf{v} \hat{\phi}_j$.

But not only are there L-relationships between properties, there are also F-relationships. Thus, $\hat{\mathrm{K}}$ is an F-implicate of $\hat{\mathrm{P}}$ if it is only as a matter of fact that

$$(t)\ \hat{\mathrm{P}}\ (t)\ \supset\ \hat{\mathrm{K}}(t)$$

is true. A similar account can be given of the F-equivalence of properties. It should be noticed that in order for two properties to be *exemplified* by the same particular, these properties (classes of θ-concepts) must have at least one θ-concept as a common *member*, namely, that θ-concept which is *instanced* by the particular.

We next introduce classes of *things* (complex particulars). To do this we represent such classes by the lower case form of the letter which represents the corresponding property. Using this symbolism, $\hat{p}$ is the class of things exemplifying the property $\hat{P}$, and is introduced by the following definition,

$$\hat{p} = \hat{\imath}\,\{\hat{P}(\imath)\}. \quad Df.$$

The circumflex is retained to distinguish between classes of *things* and classes of *atomic particulars*, just as it has been used to distinguish between *property predicates* (defined or undefined) and *primitive predicates*. Thus, if we assume, as before, that ' White ' is a primitive predicate, and if we abbreviate it to ' W ', we have distinguished between the primitive predicate ' W ' and the undefined property predicate ' $\hat{W}$ '. In a corresponding way we must now distinguish between the class represented by

$$\hat{x}\,\{W(x)\}$$

and the class represented by

$$\hat{\imath}\,\{\hat{W}(\imath)\}.$$

The former is a class of basic or atomic particulars, and should be symbolised by ' w ' to distinguish it from the latter class which is a class of things or complex particulars, and is properly symbolised according to the convention we propose by ' $\hat{w}$ '.

It remains only to introduce the null class of things and the universal or omnium class of things. This we do as follows :

$$\Lambda = \hat{\imath}\{\hat{\Lambda}\,(\imath)\},$$
$$V = \hat{\imath}\{\hat{V}\,(\imath)\}.$$

Since

$$\sim(E\imath)\,\hat{\Lambda}\,(\imath),$$
$$(\imath)\,\hat{V}\,(\imath),$$
$$(\imath)\,(\hat{P})\,\hat{\Lambda}\,(\imath) \supset \hat{P}(\imath),$$
$$(\imath)\,(\hat{P})\,\hat{P}(\imath) \supset \hat{V}(\imath),$$

are all necessary truths, it is not difficult to show that the null property, $\hat{\Lambda}$, as we have defined it is equivalent to every unexemplified property, while the omnium property, $\hat{V}$, as defined is equivalent to every universally exemplified property. The equivalence is in each case factual or logical depending on whether the lack of exemplification or the universal exemplification is a matter of fact, or a matter of logical necessity.

The above, together with the definitions we have given of class terms, serve to put us on the track of conventional developments of the class calculus. It is perhaps worth pointing out that

338   WILFRID SELLARS : LOGIC OF COMPLEX PARTICULARS

corresponding to the distinction between L-equivalent and F-equivalent properties of things, there exists a distinction between L-identical and F-identical classes of things. On the other hand it is both obvious and important that at the atomic level the identity conditions for *classes of atomic particulars* and *universals exemplified by atomic particulars* are the same. It is along these lines that the thesis of the " basic identity of classes and universals " can receive a final clarification. But a further exploration of the relation of the language of universals to the language of classes would take us far beyond the scope of this paper, which is already an unconscionable time a-dying.

SECTION I

(515.1) "In principle," a "scientifically adequate account" of a natural language can be given "without the use of auditory or visual samples." But the present "systems for classifying" sounds and shapes are "inadequate". Thus the display of "samples", e.g., by placing them "within quotation marks", is unavoidable.

(515.2; (516)) How are we to understand the expression
    'chameau'
in ' "Chameau' is often written on Parisian walls"? If it is an "English class term which mentions the class of marks used by Frenchmen to refer to camels," then
    'chameau'
must be understood as equivalent to something which includes a description with an indexical (an "ego-centric particular"); thus

    the shape of which the ink-object }
    to the right is an instance   }   chameau

Such quotes will be called "pragmatic quotes" and will be written with asterisks.

SECTION II

(517.1) Suppose, in constructing "a model language," a logician wrote
    'a', 'b', 'c',.....are individual constants of language L.
Must the quotation in the above be construed as pragmatic quotation? Is there not a sort of quotation in which
    the tokens of 'a' do not exemplify *a*
is consistent?

(517.2) Reasons to think that the quotation in the logician's statement is pragmatic quotation.

(518.1) However, there is a sort of quotation that is not pragmatic. In the logician's statement the two are combined; the "full import" of the logician's statement is:

    'a', 'b', 'c',.....are individual constants of language L;
    let them be tokened respectively by *a*, *b*, *c*,.....

The non-pragmatic quotation marks, called "syntactical" quotes, are "syntactical devices" which form "names" and indicate "that the item named is a linguistic entity."

SECTION III

(519.1.,2) A word is not "a mere class of patterns as such"; it is "a class of patterns *as performing a specific linguistic function*. Furthermore, one and the same linguistic function can be performed equally well by any one of a vast number of visual design.....expressions formed by means of *syntactical* quotes are the names of *linguistic functions*."

(520.1; 521.1) The "linguistic functions named by expressions formed with syntactical quotes" are to be called "the *type* expressions of a language." Token classes, which can be specified by using pragmatic quotes, are stated independently for each linguistic function. Thus we might have

     ten and *dix* are two token-classes of the type 'ten'.

SECTION IV

(521.2; 522.1.,2.,3) Arguments for "propositions" have fallen into two groups: (1) arguments for "sentences....as linguistic functions, types—in our sense— as contrasted with token-classes"; (2) arguments for "meanings" of sentences, i.e., for non-linguistic entities related to sentences.

SECTION V

(522.4; 523.1; 524.1) The two different sorts of entities which arguments for "propositions" attempt to establish can be identified with (1) linguistic functions and (2) possible states of affairs. It is the "blending" of these two sorts of entities which leads to "hybrid entities which are between languages and the world, sentences being *about* them, and they in turn *about* the world."

SECTION VI

(524.2; (525)) The confusion discussed in the last section can be avoided by *not* using the term 'proposition' for states of affairs (of various sorts) and by using it to fill the "need for a term to designate those linguistic functions which are capable of truth or falsity."

QUOTATION MARKS, SENTENCES, AND PROPOSITIONS

3.341   The essential in a proposition is therefore that which is common to all propositions which can express the same sense.
   And in the same way in general the essential in a symbol is that which all symbols which can fulfil the same purpose have in common.
3.3411   One could therefore say the real name is that which all symbols, which signify an object, have in common. It would then follow, step by step, that no sort of composition was essential for a name.

Tractatus

It is a commonplace fact that the student of a living language is coping with a subject matter embedded in the world to which both he and those to whom he communicates his results belong. An Englishman exploring French cannot only characterize the sounds of this language in terms of the qualities they exemplify and the manner in which they are produced, he can also offer *samples*. In the case of written French, he can give a geometrical characterization of the visual shapes employed, or he can print samples. Samples are of particular value in textbooks and gramophone discs designed to teach people to read and speak foreign languages. Yet it is obvious that a scientifically adequate account of the French language can (in principle) be made without the use of auditory or visual samples. On the other hand, the sounds and shapes employed by existing languages are sufficiently complex, and systems for classifying them sufficiently inadequate, to make it convenient and even necessary for linguistic scholars to make frequent use of samples. As a matter of fact, it is customary to use such samples, placed within quotation marks, or set off in some other distinctive way, as designations for the kinds of visual or auditory patterns to which they belong.

Let us consider an example of the procedure described above. A certain English treatise on French contains, we shall suppose, the following sentence:

'Chameau' is often written on Parisian walls.

What is the status in this sentence of the following expression?

'chameau'

One might be tempted to say that it is an English class term which mentions the class of marks used by Frenchmen to refer to camels. Yet it clearly differs from most English class terms by involving an essential reference to the shapes deployed on the occasion of writing it down. Furthermore, it

515

refers to these shapes otherwise than it would if it were merely the defined
equivalent of the geometrical expression designating these shapes. For it is
clear that whereas the defined equivalent of a geometrical expression doesn't
need to illustrate the geometrical properties designated by that expression,
the device used by the Englishman in his linguistics book *had* to illustrate
the shape of the French word in order to serve its purpose. How, then, are
we to understand this device? A moment's reflection leads to the conclusion that

'chameau'

has the force of a type of descriptive phrase of which another example
would be the following:

the shape of which⎤
the ink-object to ⎱ chameau
the right is an   ⎰
instance   ⎦

Now it is clear that an explication of the above descriptive phrase would
show it to involve a demonstrative term, or, in Russell's terminology, an
"ego-centric particular," that is to say, a word such as "this," "here," or
"now." The semiotic analysis of ego-centric particulars is a task yet to be
satisfactorily performed. The path leads straight into the heart of epistemology, a lion's den outside of which there are many bones. It is sufficient
for our purposes to say with Russell that whenever an ego-centric word
is used, "the person using it is attending to something, and the word indicates this something. . . . When a word is not ego-centric, there is no need
to distinguish between different occasions on which it is used, but we must
make this distinction with ego-centric words, since what they indicate is
something having a given relation to a particular use of the word."[1]
If, then, the above interpretation of the expression

'chameau'

is correct, we can say that on each occasion of its use (and notice that
strictly speaking each *reading* is a new use) the expression has the force of
an *ego-centric description*. Consequently, the quotation marks which serve
in the construction of such ego-centric descriptions—though other devices,
italics, spacing, etc., are often used—might well be called "ego-centric
quotes." Since, however, the theory of ego-centric particulars belongs to
pragmatics, I shall call them *pragmatic quotes*. In the following argument,
wherever a given usage of quotation marks is clearly intended to be a case

---

[1] *Human Knowledge, Its Scope and Limits*, p. 92.

of pragmatic quotation, we shall replace the ordinary quotation marks by asterisk. Thus we can rewrite the sentence with which we began as follows:

Chameau is often written on Parisian walls.

II

Let us now consider the case of a logician who constructs, as we say, a model language in terms of which he hopes to clarify some technical point in his field. We find in his book the following statement:

'a,' 'b,' 'c,' . . . are individual constants of language L.

Now it is clear that the logician is *using* instances of the shapes of the early letters of the alphabet in order to *talk about* the individual constants of the language he is "constructing." *Is he also talking about these shapes?* He is if the quotation marks are pragmatic quotes. In that case it is as if he had said, overlooking the dots,

$$\left.\begin{array}{l}\text{The shapes of which the}\\ \text{ink-objects to the right}\\ \text{are instances are individ-}\\ \text{ual constants of language L.}\end{array}\right\} \quad \text{a} \quad \text{b} \quad \text{c}$$

But *are* the quotation marks pragmatic quotes? Let us answer this question with another question. If the individual constants about which the logician is talking are *shapes*, what shapes can they be but the shapes of the letters of the alphabet? And if they are the shapes of these letters, must not the quotes be pragmatic quotes? The situation seems to be that *if* he is talking about shapes, the quotes are pragmatic quotes, and *if* the quotes are pragmatic quotes, then he is talking about shapes. But need we hold either that he is talking about shapes or that the quotes are pragmatic quotes? Suppose that the logician went on to make the following statements:

'a' has tokens exemplifying *a*
'b' has tokens exemplifying *b*
. . . .

would these assertions be tautological? Is it, perhaps, self-contradictory to say,

The tokens of 'a' do not exemplify *a*?

If the ordinary quotation marks appearing in these statements are pragmatic quotes, then the answer to each of these questions is Yes.

"But," it may be said, "it is obvious that these quotes are pragmatic, for after reading the logician's original statement, we know not only how to write down *designations* of the individual constants, by following his example, thus:

'a,' 'b,' 'c,' . . .

but also how to write down *these individual constants themselves*, thus,

a, b, c, . . .

Since the logician clearly intended us to be able to do this, and since he has given us no *geometrical* account of the individual constants, it is evident that he has given us ego-centric descriptions of these individual constants by means of pragmatic quotes."

Unfortunately, while this point is well taken, it does not completely clarify the logician's use of quotes. It does, indeed, convince us that insofar as his intentions are correctly represented, the logician is offering us an ego-centric description of the shapes we are to deploy whenever we wish to use language L, and that in this respect the quotation marks are serving as pragmatic quotes. I wish, however, to suggest that if these are his intentions, then his formulation fails to do justice to the complexity of what he is communicating. There is, I shall argue, a further usage of quotation marks which is not pragmatic, which does not serve to give ego-centric descriptions of sign-designs by means of samples; and I shall argue that our logician is telescoping the pragmatic and this non-pragmatic usage into one set of quotation marks, with the result that the full import of his statement is more explicitly rendered by the following:

'a,' 'b,' 'c,' . . . are individual constants of language L; *let them be tokened respectively by* *a*, *b*, *c*, . . .

But is there such a non-pragmatic use of quotation marks? Why would one use the expression

'a'

unless it was intended to have the force of something like the following?

the class of marks of which the item between these quotes 'a' is a member

unless it was intended, that is to say, to have the sense we have given to the following?

a

The answer is so simple as to seem simple-minded. Quotation marks are also used (by the logician) to form the *names* of linguistic expressions. We must distinguish between the *pragmatic* or ego-centric use of quotation marks, and the non-ego-centric or *syntactical* use. In the case of the former, an explication of their token-reflexive character would show that the quotation marks are *mentioned* as well as *used*. In the syntactical usage, on the other hand, quotation marks are *used* but not *mentioned*, the quotation marks together with the object inside them being used as the name of, for example, an individual constant of language L. In this usage, the quotation marks serve as syntactical devices indicating that the item named is a linguistic entity, that it belongs to the linguistic domain. It follows that where syntactical quotes alone are being used, the linguistic entity cannot— as in the case of pragmatic quotation—be identified, *merely on the basis of the fact of quotation*, with the class of shapes exemplified by the ink marks between the quotes. Any reference to this class must be separately specified.

III

Logicians have used the word "type" to refer to linguistic expressions as *abstracta* in contrast to individual linguistic occurrences. They have failed to see, however, that the linguistic entities which they called "types," and which they contrasted with linguistic events or *tokens*, are, in a genuine sense, embodiments of still more "abstract" linguistic entities which therefore more properly deserved the term. Thus, logicians speak of a certain class of visual patterns as the type word *and*. Members of this class are said to be tokens of this type word. Yet a word, it is clear, is not a mere class of patterns as such. It is surely a class of patterns *as performing a specific linguistic function*. Furthermore, one and the same linguistic function can be performed equally well by any one of a vast number of visual designs. By themselves these remarks are commonplace, but taken together with our previous discussion of quotation marks, they immediately suggest that expressions formed by means of *syntactical* quotes are the names of *linguistic functions*. The fact that in mentioning a linguistic function, a logician encloses a visual pattern within tokens of syntactical quotes must not deceive one into thinking that the logician is mentioning the class of patterns of which he has produced an instance. To be thus deceived is to confuse syntactical quotes with pragmatic quotes.

We argued in the preceding section that the entity named by an expression formed with the use of syntactical quotes must not *ipso facto* be identified with the empirical class exemplified by the pattern occurring between the quotes. Thus, if

'a'

is the name of an individual constant of language L, this individual constant cannot, on the basis of the quotation marks alone, be identified with the empirical class which is the first letter of the lower case English alphabet. But would such identification, in any case, be proper? It takes but a moment's reflection to see that the answer must be No. Thus, consider the statement,

'a' is of zero type.

If the identity,

'a' = the first letter of the alphabet

were significant and true, we should have to infer,

The first letter of the alphabet is of zero type.

This, of course, is nonsense.[2]

It is, then, the linguistic functions named by expressions formed with syntactical quotes which I shall refer to as the *type* expressions of a language.[3] For the customary meaning of "type" I shall use the term "token-class," as indicating more clearly the linguistic status of classes of shapes and sounds. Thus we shall say that

ten and *dix* are two token-classes of the type 'ten'

which would be translated into French as follows:

ten et *dix* sont deux token-classes du type 'dix'

where we have taken the liberty of enriching French with our English technical terminology. Notice that in these two statements the expressions formed with the help of ordinary quotation marks, serving in a syntactical function, are the English and French names of a linguistic function. Notice

---

[2] It is perhaps worth noting that certain puzzles relating to the use of "variable quotes" can be clarified by means of this analysis. Thus, where the quotation marks in question are syntactical quotes, the expression,

'z'

is not the name of the last letter of the alphabet. On the other hand, this letter finds a pragmatic description in

z

[3] This analysis (which was sketched in "Epistemology and the New Way of Words," *The Journal of Philosophy*, 44, 1947, pp 653ff) leads to the conclusion that the *formal* study of a language does not consist in the study of a language *qua* patterns of marks, but rather in what might legitimately be called the phenomenology of linguistic functions. Phenomenology, as I interpret it, is the systematic exhibition of the rules of a language by the *use* of *that same language* for this purpose. The phenomenology of language is the exhibitory use of syntactical and semantical meta-languages, meta-meta-languages, etc. We exhibit the rules whereby we use such words as "sentence," "true," "actual," etc. I have come to realize that my use of the word formal in several papers has been confused and misleading.

QUOTATION MARKS, SENTENCES, AND PROPOSITIONS   521

also that expressions formed with syntactical quotes have a different status with respect to translation than do expressions formed with pragmatic quotes.

It should now be clear that insofar as our logician is making use of syntactical quotes, he is mentioning the components of a system of linguistic functions. Thus, if, using such quotes, he says,

> 'a,' 'b,' 'c,' . . . are individual constants of language L

he is mentioning a set of linguistic functions of zero type belonging to linguistic system L, and is in no way mentioning visual patterns. On the other hand, should he wish to specify token-classes for these linguistic functions, either one of two courses is open to him. (1) He can specify the token-classes which are to embody these functions by the use of ordinary class terms, thus,

> 'a,' 'b,' 'c,' . . . are individual constants of language L; let triangles, rectangles, pentagons, . . . be token-classes for these individual constants.

(2) He can make use of pragmatic quotes, thus,

> 'a,' 'b,' 'c,' . . . are individual constants of language L; let *△*, *□*, . . . be token-classes for these individual constants,

or, more conveniently,

> 'a,' 'b,' 'c,' . . . are individual constants of language L; let *a*, *b*, *c*, . . . be token-classes for these individual constants.

IV

I shall conclude with some remarks on the question, "Are there propositions?" One familiar argument for "propositions" goes as follows:

> The English sentence "Truman is in Washington" and the French sentence "Truman est à Washington" say the *same* thing. The identical entity which they both formulate is the proposition . . .

This argument is probably best interpreted as an argument for the existence of a certain linguistic function or type expression, for it is indeed the case that

> * Truman is in Washington* and *Truman est à Washington* are two token-classes for the identical type 'Truman is in Washington'

or, as a Frenchman would say,

> *Truman is in Washington* and *Truman est à Washington* sont deux token-classes du type identique 'Truman est a Washington.'

A second argument for propositions runs as follows:

> It might be possible to hold that the meaning of a true sentence is a *fact*. But false sentences are meaningful, and their meanings are obviously not facts. The meaning of a false sentence is a proposition . . . .

The traditional development of this argument does not concern us. For our purpose the important thing to note is that if this argument establishes the existence of any entities, they are not *linguistic* entities. The very purpose of the argument is to locate a set of entities which function as the *meanings* of false sentences.

Finally, we note that the first of the two arguments is capable of a different interpretation. It can be interpreted as saying:

> The English sentence "Truman is in Washington" and the French sentence "Truman est à Washington" convey the same meaning. This common meaning is the proposition . . .

which would read, in our terminology,

> *Truman is in Washington* and *Truman est à Washington* are two token-classes which have the same meaning. This common meaning is the proposition. . . .

or, more explicitly,

> *Truman is in Washington* and *Truman est à Washington* have the same meaning by virtue of being two token-classes of 'Truman is in Washington' which means the proposition. . . .

Here, as in the second argument, the propositions sought are to be the meanings of sentences.

We have said enough to indicate that arguments for the existence of propositions have been, in actual point of fact, arguments for two sorts of entities: (a) sentences as linguistic functions, types—in our sense—as contrasted with token-classes; (b) meanings of sentences. Unfortunately, the arguments have been misinterpreted and blended together—a possibility aided and abetted by the ambiguity of the first argument—with the result that the entities to which they point have been confused into one monstrous entity, the proposition.

V

It is obvious that not everything relevant to a given philosophical analysis can be brought under interrogation simultaneously. Thus, I have been speaking without further explication than that afforded by the immediate context of argument, of the existence of *linguistic functions*; and in the following paragraphs I shall speak without analysis of the existence of

QUOTATION MARKS, SENTENCES, AND PROPOSITIONS   523

possible states of affairs, of linguistic entities being *about* non-linguistic entities, of linguistic entities having non-linguistic entities as their *meanings,*—relying on the fact that in some sense it is obviously legitimate to do so. It is the task of the metaphysician and not the logician to clarify the status of the *entia rationis* of semantic analysis. The logician can grasp the immanent structure of the second intentions and second impositions which populate his corner of the philosophical universe, even though he is not able to locate this corner in the total scheme. The best logicians are by no means always the best philosophers of logic.

Leaving, then, to others the task of clarifying the 'ontological status' of linguistic functions and possible states of affairs, I shall make use of these notions in an attempt to analyze the confusions embodied in the classical doctrine of propositions. First, let me state briefly and dogmatically what I take to be the correct interpretation of the phrase, "the meaning of a (factual) sentence." I limit my account to atomic sentences.

> The meaning of an atomic sentence is a possible state of affairs. The sentence is true if the possible state of affairs belongs to the world, otherwise it is false.[4]

If this thesis, at once obvious and most difficult—particularly for the empiricist—to defend, is sound, then the meaning of a true sentence is a *fact,* and not something which "corresponds to" or "accords with" a fact; while the meaning of a false sentence is an entity which differs from a fact only in that it does not belong to the world. Where we are not concerned with the difference between true and false sentences, we can say simply that the meaning of a sentence is a possible state of affairs or a possible

---

[4] Some current misconceptions would be avoided if the general semantical definition of truth (See Carnap, *Introduction to Semantics,* pp 49ff) were stated in a fully explicit manner. Thus, instead of

S is a true sentence of L = Df There is a proposition p such that S designates p, and p

we should write

S is a true sentence of L = Df There is a possible state of affairs p such that S S designates p, and p is actual.

It is important to note that *actuality* and *truth* are correlative semantical concepts. This undercuts Strawson's criticism of "definition by elimination" in his paper on "Truth," *Analysis,* 1949. The balance between the left and right hand sides of this equation comes out still more clearly when it is realized that only the following formulation is completely adequate:

S is a true sentence of L = Df There is a possible state of affairs p such that S designates p, and p is an actual state of affairs of world W which is the world of L.

For a justification of this line of thought I refer the reader to "Realism and the New Way of Words," *this journal,* June, 1948 (reprinted in Feigl and Sellars, *Readings in Philosophical Analysis*), and to "Concepts as Involving Laws and Inconceivable without them," *Philosophy of Science,* 15, 1948.

fact. As far as the meaning of sentences is concerned, there is no place for propositions unless "proposition" is taken to mean *possible state of affairs*.

Let us pull our discussion together. One of the traditional arguments for propositions points to propositions as *entities which are about* (some aspect of) *the world*, true if they correspond to a fact, false if they do not. According to this line of thought, English and French sentences are true if they *formulate* a true proposition. The other argument points to propositions as *what sentences are about*. According to this line of thought, an English and a French sentence have the same meaning if they are *about* the same proposition. The blending of these two senses of "proposition" produces hybrid entities which are between language and the world, sentences being *about* them, and they in turn *about* the world. Here is one source of the unsound correspondence theories which have haunted philosophy since the days of Aristotle.

VI

It will be asked, "Granted that the usual account of propositions is sheer confusion, can we not save the word 'proposition' itself by giving it a clear and unambiguous meaning, perhaps by limiting it to one of the two senses which traditional doctrine blends together?" The answer is Yes. There is, to my mind, no point in using the word "proposition" to mean *possible state of affairs*. Indeed, to use the word in this sense is to court all the confusions of the *tertium quid*. We should speak of the possibility *p* rather than the proposition *p* when we have the *meanings* of linguistic entities in mind.[5] On the other hand, there is a genuine need for a term to designate those linguistic functions which are capable of truth or falsity, and the word "proposition" seems admirably suited to this purpose. It will be remembered that we distinguished between linguistic functions (in our terminology, *types*) and the kinds of visual or auditory pattern (*token-classes*) which embody these functions in historical languages. Now, customarily, what is referred to as a *sentence* is either a token-class or a particular utterance or token. Consequently, if we were to refer to the linguistic function which is embodied in English by the token-class *Truman is in Washington*, and in French by the token-class *Truman est à Washington*,— in short, if we were to refer to the linguistic function 'Truman is in Wash-

---

[5] This proposal, however, will not do as it stands. It may be satisfactory to speak of the possibility *a-being-red* as the meaning of the atomic descriptive sentence 'red(a)'; but what of the meaning of 'red(a) and not red(a)'? If it were agreed to use "state o affairs" in such a way that "actual state of affairs" was not redundant, then we could speak of the meanings of sentences as *impossible*, *possible but not actual*, *actual but not necessary*, and *necessary* states of affairs.

QUOTATION MARKS, SENTENCES, AND PROPOSITIONS   525

ington' as a *sentence*, we should have to add the hyphenated modifier "-type" in order to preserve the distinction between "sentences" which were linguistic functions and "sentences" which were token-classes. It would therefore seem reasonable to use the word "proposition" for such linguistic functions as 'Truman is in Washington', while continuing to call such token-classes as *Truman est à Washington* sentences.

WILFRID SELLARS.

UNIVERSITY OF MINNESOTA.

SECTION I

(45.1) A central part of the mind-body problem is the question "whether facts about the mind are "reducible" to facts about the body or vice versa , or whether both are "reducible " to facts which are neither mental nor somatic. If we assume for the time being that the "reduction" in question is explicit definition", then there are (at least) four different major views on this reduction:

Dualism--"neither mentalistic nor somatic concepts are definable in
            terms of the other, nor is either definable in terms of a
            more basic set of concepts;"

Materialism--"mentalistic concepts can be defined in terms of somatic
            concepts;"

Mentalism--somatic concepts can be defined in terms of mentalistic
            concepts;

Neutral Monism--"both mentalistic and somatic concepts are definable in
            terms of concepts which are neither."

(46.1) A provisional and traditional characterization of mentalistic concepts: they are concepts of items having "intentionality or aboutness".

(46.2,.3) Mental acts are "the basic mental realities according to this tradition, and all mental acts, elementary or complex, are characterized by intentionality, as are the mental dispositions and tendencies definable in terms of them." Sensory items and characteristics as such are not, by this provisional characterization, mental.

SECTION II

(47.1) For the purposes of this paper, "the mind-body problem is the problem whether mental-acts can be reduced to items which are not mental acts, whether sense characteristics of physical events or both, and, if so, in exactly what sense of "reduced." " A similar problem is the controversy over the "reduction" of "Ought" to "Is".

(48.1) Taking the "ought-is" problem as one concerning "the definability of Ought in descriptive terms, we find a clash between Ethical Naturalism which claims that it is and Ethical Non-naturalism ("Intuitionism") which claims that it is not." But turning from logical reducibility, we can ask about the "causal reducibility" of Ought to Is: "For our present purposes, a concept will be said to be *causally reducible* to descriptive concepts if (roughly) it is either definable in descriptive terms (the trivial case), or occurs in the antecedent of a properly constructed causal explanation only as a subordinate element in a descriptive mentalistic context (e.g., as 'entails' occurs in 'Jones believes that responsibility entails determinism')....If we use "ethical assertion" in such a way that "Jones ought to pay his debt" is an ethical assertion, but "Jones feels that he ought to pay his debt" is not, then we can say that to claim that Ought is causally reducible to Is is to claim that one can give a causal explanation of the history of moral agents without making ethical assertions."

(49.1,.2) Intuitionists (one sort of Ethical Non-naturalists) have rejected both the logical and the causal reducibility of Ought to Is.

(50.1) Ethical Naturalists and such Ethical Non-naturalists as the Intuitionists have agreed that there is logical reducibility of Ought to Is and only if there is causal reducibility of Ought to Is. Sellars holds that one can have the latter without the former.

SECTION III

(51.1,.2,.3; 52.1) As a preliminary to a discussion of mind-body reduction, expressions are divided into three categories. (1) logical expressions in the narrow sense (truth-functional connectives, variables, quantifiers); (2) non-truth-functional "connectives" (e.g., modal expressions, 'believes'); (3) descriptive terms.

(52.2,.3; 53.1) Consider primitive descriptive predicates, logical expressions in the narrow sense and all the expressions constructible and definable from these by the rules of Principia Mathematica. Let us call these "PM" expressions. Are there any terms in (2) which are ultimately *not* definable by terms from the other two categories? That is, are there any terms in (2) that are ultimately not PM expressions? Are mentalistic terms (e.g., 'believes') which *appear* to be non-truth-functional connectives *not* definable by terms from the other two categories?

(54.1) We shall say that "Philosophical Behaviorism" is the view that mentalistic terms are PM expressions.

(54.2; 55.1) Must someone who rejects Philosophical Behaviorism accept some form of "Dualism"? The discussion of the Ought-Is problem suggests that Philosophical Behaviorism should be contrasted not with Dualism, but with positions that hold to the "logical irreducibility" of mentalistic terms to PM terms. Such a position may not be, in any traditional sense, a "Dualism" since it may reject an assumption common to both (most) Dualisms and their opponents: viz., the claim involved in the Ought-Is problem, that there is logical reducibility if and only if there is causal reducibility.

(55.2) If "our solution of the mind-body problem is to take the form, *mentalistic expressions are causally reducible but logically irreducible to PMese,*" then Epiphenomenalism, which is a view of this sort, must be discussed and the definition of causal reducibility must be altered.

SECTION IV

(56.1,.2; 57.1,.2) A discussion of kinds of "behaviorism" other than
Philosophical Behaviorism: in particular, "Scientific" (or "Psychological") Behaviorism (see 59.3) which does not require the logical reducibility of mentalistic terms.

(58.1,.2,.3; 59.1) The Philosophical Behaviorist and the Scientific
Behaviorist agree that there are true beconditionals, one side of which
predicate an intentional mental term of a mind and the other side of which
predicate of the appropriate body a PM term, i.e., a term which does not
in any way involve intentional mentalistic terms. But the Philosophical
Behaviorist holds that these biconditionals are "logical necessary"
since they follow from logical truths and the definitions of mentalistic
terms while the Scientific Behaviorist, as scientist, merely maintains
that these beconditionals express (at least) "material equivalences." The
Scientific Behaviorist, as scientist, does not commit himself on the question of whether these biconditionals are stronger than material equivalences.

(59.2,.3) Since Scientific Behaviorism expresses the claim that mentalistic
terms are causually reducible, we can inquire, assuming that Scientific
Behaviorism is tenable, whether it is possible to hold a philosophical interpretation of Scientific Behaviorism which denies the logical reducibility
of mentalistic terms while not committing oneself to "Epiphenomenalism."
That is, "can the joint thesis of the causal reducibility but logical
irreducibility of the mental be held in any other form than epiphenomenalism?"

SECTION V

(60.1) Further discussion of Scientific Behaviorism through a small dialogue the main points of which are: (1) The sentences about bodies in
the material equivalences (discussed in the previous section) assert, in
some cases, the existence of tendencies of a body ("b") to utter linguistic expressions; (2) in such a case, the material equivalence cannot, e.g.,
in the case of a German speaker, be of the following sort

<blockquote>

m has thought that   iff   .....and b tends to utter
it is raining   'es regnet'.......,

</blockquote>

but must be of the following sort

<blockquote>

m has thought that   iff   .....and b tends to utter
it is raining   'es regnet' and 'es regnet'
                                      means it is raining........;

</blockquote>

(3) finally, "means" would appear to be a non-truth-functional "connective" which has good claim to being considered a mentalistic term.

(61.1) So, in order to have causal reducibility in the sense of Scientific
Behaviorism, there must be true material equivalences which have such
sentences as

<blockquote>

'es regnet' uttered by b means it is raining

</blockquote>

materially equivalent to sentences that say "of b that it has certain habits relating its utterances of "es regnet" to other utterances, to other habits, and to sensory stimuli."

(62.1) If we have, for a Frenchman, that

"il pleut" uttered by b means *it is raining,*

then "il pleut" and "es regnet" have the same meaning and the Scientific Behaviorist is committed to the claim that the French speaker's habits and the German speaker's habits "share a common generic feature" (perhaps very complex). Thus, in general we have:

"..." uttered by b means *it is raining* iff K ("...", b)

where 'K ("...",b), says that b's habits with respect to "...." have the appropriate generic feature.

(63.1) The unquoted 'it is raining' in

"It is raining" uttered by b means *it is raining*

is a "manifestation" (or, "exhibition") of the habits (specified generically) by

K ("it is raining",b).

Thus equivalences of the form

"...." uttered by b means **** iff K ("....",b)

are true only if "utterances of them are "pragmatically consistent", i.e., only if "the component utterance of "****" on the left hand side is a manifestation of the kind of habit mentioned on the right hand side."

SECTION VI

(64.1; (65)) The dialogue continues with the following main points suggested for clarification: (1) that sentences which fit the pattern

"...." uttered by b means ****

mention "no state or disposition ' of b, "whether of his body or of his mind;" (2) that, however, it is reasonable to object that since such sentences do "convey" the fact that b's habits with regard to "...." are the same as the speaker's with regard to "****", it is appropriate to include that these habits encompass "habits of mind as well as habits of body"; (3) that the crux of the response to this objection is to admit that meaning is "a mental phenomenon," in fact, to admit that "of every mental state it can be said that it either is or includes a state which "means **** "," and yet to maintain that being "mental" in this sense (i.e., "meaning****") is not incompatible with being a "bodily" state (though not just any bodily state).

(66.1) The above exchange includes something not in the original dialogue: an "identity" thesis that to say that a mind has engaged in a mental activity or is in a mental state is to say that a body is engaged in a bodily activity or is in a bodily state which activity or state "means****".

(67.1) The "identity" thesis of the preceding paragraph, i.e.,

m has A (0) = b has S and S means 0

(where 'm' is a term for a mind, 'A (0)' a term for a mental act with object 0, 'b'
a term for the appropriate body and 'S' a term for a state of that body b) is
stronger than Scientific Behaviorism but weaker than Philosophical Behaviorism;
to get Philosophical Behaviorism one would have to accept the additional claim
that sentences about items "meaning ****" can be *reduced* to sentences which
are about bodily states and contain neither mentalistic terms not semantical terms.

SECTION VII

(67.2; 68.1,.2) Let us assume, in keeping with a substantial part of the psychological and philosophical traditions, that all mentalistic terms are definable by
means of the terms 'act of thought' and 'about' (i.e., an act of thought is "an
event which is about something"), then "we cannot rule out *ex vi terminorum*"
the possibility mentioned above, namely, that items which are about something
are "bodily states (though not *mere* bodily states)." The identity thesis (of
Section VI) can now be reformulated as:

...... y has x, and x is about 0 = b has S and S means 0

"where the omitted segment of the left hand side contains the information that
y is a mind--a matter, according to this approach, of its ability to have still
other states characterized by aboutness."

(69.1) It should be noted that one can hold that thoughts are identical with
bodily states without claiming that people, in general, are aware of or know of
this identity.

(69.2; 70.1) A similar and more important point can be made about the part of
the reformulated identity theses which involves an "equation of the
"about 0" of the mentalistic language with the "means 0" of the right hand side.
...... the language of the right-hand side is the language of behavior supplemented
by statements of the form "S means ****", where S is a bodily state, and where to
say of S that it means **** is not to *mention* additional facts about the body, nor
even to mention states of another object called the "mind", but rather to convey,
without mentioning the information that S plays a role in the economy of Jones of
the same kind as that played by utterances of "****" in the economy of the
speaker." If "Scientific Behaviorism is true", then there are true equivalences
(discussed in Section V) relating 'means' on the one hand and bodily habits on
the other. But the identity theorist need not hold that we now know such equivalences or that we can even, at the moment, characterize these habits except
indirectly by use of ' "...." means ****'. Such equivalences are formulable only
in an "ideal" behavioral psychology which has not yet been worked out.

(71.1,.2) Indeed, we simply do not have the appropricate behaviorial terminology
for expressing these biconditionals; our present behavioral terms and semantical
terms are dependent on mentalistic discourse. Thus the identity theorist "must
be interpreted as asserting not that our mentalistic vocabulary has the same
meaning as available expressions in behaviorese supplemented by semantical
clauses of the form "S means ****", but rather that in the language of an ideal
behavioristic psychology it would be possible to define semantico-behavioral
functions of the form "b has S, and S means ****" which could be used where we

now use ''m thinks about O'' and which would enable us to say everything which we now say by means of our mentalistic vocabulary.''

SECTION VIII

(72.1,.2) A consideration of a possible alternative to the ''identity'' theory which claims that images are mental.

(73.1) Another objectio· to the identity theory which insists that our ''awareness'' of colors (and such like) is ''more intimate'' than ''mere aboutness.''

(73.2) One reply to this objection which is rejected.

(74.1) Sellars' (tentative) reply is that awareness is to be distinguished from aboutness because awareness is a complex notion which includes aboutness and much more: ''Thus, it seems to me that ''m is aware of y'' can be defined in terms of a tendency of m to have thoughts which (a) are *about* y, (b) are direct responses to y, and (c) are, by virtue of the manner in which the tendency to have these responses is learned, extremely likely to be true.''

(74.2) Such a reply may merely prompt the objector to insist on the fact that a machine can have events which are correctly said to be about something and thus, according to the above reply, be ''aware'', but yet not be conscious as human beings are.

(74.3 (75); 76.1) The reply to this is to admit that human beings are conscious in a sense distinct from ''aboutness'' or ''awareness''. But such consciousness (e.g., having sensations) is not mental.

(76.2; 77.1) The question of whether such states of consciousness as sensations and images are ''bodily states'' is a difficult one which is not to be decided here.

(77.2) However, it should be noted that even if such items as sensations and images must be admitted to be not bodily states, ''the resulting dualism would not as such be a mind-body dualism, even though in one sense of ''consciousness'' it would be a *consciousness*-body dualism. It would be appropriate to call it a mind-body dualism only if it went on to hold that aboutness is directly predicable only of sensations and images, and predicable of bodily states only as symtoms of sensations and images *qua* having aboutness (i.e., qua correctly said to be ''about****'').''

(77.3) To be plausible Scientific Behaviorism must recognize that ''its category of 'bodily states' includes items'' such as sensations and images ''which are, in a familiar and legitimate sense of the phrase ''states of consciousness''.'' Thus the equivalences proposed by the Scientific Behaviorist pertain only to 'm has mental state M', not to 'm has state of consciousness C'.

(78.1) A review of the major steps of the argument concerning logical reducibility and causal reducibility. A major point of this review is that since the identity theorist accepts

m has A(O) = b has S, and S means O

(see sections VI and VIII), the theory is, in a clear sense, truly an
identity theory; but, on the other hand, the identity theorist, while accepting the thesis of Scientific Behaviorism (see section II) and thus "the
causal reducibility of the mentalistic language to PMese about bodily
behavior", "refuses to assert the *logical* reducibility of the mentalistic language to PMese about behavior." Of course, mentalistic language
for the identity theorist is really "ideal Semantico-behaviorese"
(see Section VII).

(78.2; 79.1) "The logical irreducibility of the mentalistic language to
Behaviorese....turns out, if our argument is sound, to be exactly the logical
irreducibility of semantical metalanguages to PMese" in the sense of
'logical reducibility' discussed in Section III.

(79.2; 80.1) There is a sense in which meaning (and aboutness) enter "into
the causal order only via facts of the form, *Jones thinks that X is about y,*"
and "in this respect," they "resemble Ought."

SECTION IX

(80.2; 81.1,.2; 82.1,.2) It has been an assumption of this paper "that
scientific discourse can dispense with the modalities. Thus, we have
assumed that our ideal Behaviorese is an extensional or PM language."
Our conclusions, however, "in no way depend on that assumption": "the
semantical discourse which we found to be the heart of mentalistic
discourse is no more reducible (logically) to a PMese", "enriched with
the logical and causal modalities", "than it is to PMese pure and
simple." Thus, another major point of the paper is that the rejection of
the "extentionalist" program (i.e., the program of reducing all discourse
to extensional discourse) for normative, semantical and modal discourse
can be accomplished "without falling into the traditional dualisms."

45

A SEMANTICAL SOLUTION OF THE
MIND-BODY PROBLEM*

WILFRID SELLARS

Dept. of Philosophy
100 *Wesbrook Hall,*
University of Minnesota,
Minneapolis 14, *Minnesota*
(*U. S. A.*)

It is perhaps not too much of an over-simplification to say that whatever else philosophers may be proposing to do when they raise "the mind-body problem" (and it is notoriously a tangle in which all the major puzzles of philosophy can be found) they are at least asking whether facts about the mind are "reducible" to facts about the body or vice versa, or whether both are "reducible" to facts which are neither mental nor somatic ([1]). If we assume for the time being that the "reduction" in question is explicit definition the following list of alternatives (which is intended to be suggestive rather than exhaustive) comes to mind: (*a*) neither mentalistic nor somatic concepts are definable in terms of the other, nor is either definable in terms of a more basic set of concepts (e.g. concepts relating to sense data); (*b*) mentalistic concepts can be defined in terms of somatic concepts, or vice versa; (*c*) both mentalistic and somatic concepts are definable in terms of concepts which are neither. Perhaps without too much violence, these alternatives may be identi-

---

*) An earlier version of this paper was read in a symposium on the mind-body problem at the Ann Arbor meeting of the American Philosophical Association, May 1952.

[1]) The term 'somatic' is used in the familiar sense of 'pertaining to the body'. It is closely related in meaning to two other terms which will be used in this paper, --namely 'behavioral' and 'physical(istic).' It is not to be taken for granted that all somatic concepts can be defined in terms of physicalistic concepts. Behavioral concepts are a subclass of somatic concepts, though the term 'behavior' is often so broadly used that these two terms are practically synonymous.

fied with the historical positions known respectively as Dualism, Materialism, Mentalism and Neutral Monism. Neutral Monism has in common with Materialism the claim that mentalistic concepts are capable of definition in terms of non-mentalistic concepts. The Neutral Monist, however, makes the additional assertion that physicalistic concepts can be defined in terms of concepts relating to sense-data, a thesis the rejection of which is a defining trait of Materialism. Neutral Monisms differ from one another according to their account of the logical form appropriate to definitions of mentalistic and physicalistic concepts. These differences, however, lie beyond the scope of this paper.

To get our discussion off the ground, we must come to at least a provisonal decision concerning the meaning of the phrase "mentalistic concept". Fortunately, this can be done with some hope of general agreement. It is sufficient to specify the classical thesis, whose most familiar representatives are Descartes and, more recently, Brentano, that the distinguishing feature of mental facts is intentionality or aboutness. The frame of reference we acquire by evoking this tradition is, I believe, essentially sound. Indeed, I shall argue that when reinterpreted in the light of contemporary developments, it leads directly to a radical clarification of the mind-body problem.

According to the tradition to which we are making appeal, the following items typify the sphere of the mental: belief, doubt, desire, choice, expectation, fear. This list obviously makes no pretense of completeness. Nor, which is more important, does it claim that these items are equally ultimate. Some mental items are clearly more basic than others, the latter being definable in terms of them, though not necessarily in terms of them alone. Mental dispositions are definable in terms of mental acts, and, it may be, some kinds of mental act in terms of others more elementary. Acts, however, are the basic mental realities according to this tradition, and all mental acts, elementary or complex, are characterized by intentionality, as are the mental dispositions and tendencies definable in terms of them.

Now it is clear, as was implied above, that instances of the various sense characteristics are not as such mental. They are neither intentional acts, nor are they complex objects including intentional acts as components. Instances of red, or sweet, or C# or adjacency in a visual field are not as such *about* anything, nor do they as such *refer* to anything, though, of course, they are *referred* to physical objects in what Professor Price has called 'perceptual consciousness'.

On the other hand, it would seem impossible (though the point is a most difficult one to which we shall return later) to explicate the meaning of "red datum" [2] without referring to some kind of mental act or disposition or tendency to have mental acts. To come to the heart of the matter, Redness is not a mentalistic concept, but Givenness is. If this is the case, then when Neutral Monists claim that mentalistic concepts are definable in terms of concepts "relating to sense-data" they must be using the latter phrase to mean concepts of sense qualities and relations and their instances as such (and not *qua* given) if they are to avoid the objection that their supposedly "neutral" entities are already mental. In terms of our frame of reference, then, Neutral Monism is the thesis that both physical events and intentional acts can be defined in terms of instances of sense characteristics as such.

II.

For our purposes, then, the mind-body problem is the problem whether mental acts can be reduced to items which are not mental acts, whether sense characteristics or physical events or both, and if so, in exactly what sense of "reduced". Now it is often wise to draw back *pour mieux sauter*. We shall be following this advice if we glance at the dialectics of a problem in moral philosophy, the familiar one of the "nature" of obligation and its relation to matters of fact. For there are two important similarities between the "ought--is" problem, and the mind-body problem. In both cases one asks about the reducibility of one concept or type of concept to another.

---

[2] I am using the terms 'given', 'sensed', and 'datum' to refer to that "direct presence to consciousness" which the colors you are now seeing have and the Straits of Bosphorus do not have. These terms are not intended to carry the weight of any theory, but rather to suggest distinctions which "sense-datum theories" are attempting to clarify.

There is a sense, of course, in which all objects of which we are conscious are "directly present to consciousness". Consciousness of objects is not consciousness of representations of objects. Consciousness of an object is sometimes said to be "indirect" when it is consciousness of an object as *the such-and-such*, and there is a current view which (roughly) equates the notion of *not* being (in this sense) *indirectly* present to consciousness, with that of being directly present to consciousness in the sense suggested by the terms "given" and "datum". To make the same point in the context of language, they correlate the distinction between objects which *are* and objects which *are not* "given" with the distinction between logically proper names on the one hand, and descriptive phrases on the other. Indeed, it is claimed by some that "x is a datum" is to be reconstructed (roughly) as "x is designated by a logically proper name". We shall touch on this and related issues in a closing section of this paper.

48

And in both cases the concept whose reducibility is in question has the logical character of non-extensionality. Thus, just as "Jones believes it is raining" is not a truth function of "It is raining", so "Jones ought to pay his debt", is not a truth function of "Jones pays his debt".

Now, if we so interpret "reducible" that the "ought-is" problem concerns the definability of Ought in descriptive terms, we find a clash between Ethical Naturalism which claims that it is, and Ethical Non-naturalism ("Intuitionism") which claims that it is not. Let us put this by saying that for the former Ought is logically reducible to Is, while for the latter it is not. Although it is not to my purpose to weigh the merits of either contention, it is relevant to the argument of this paper to express my agreement *on this precise point* with Ethical non-naturalism. Yet there is another sense in which "reducible" can (not implausibly) be used, according to which Ought may well be "reducible" to Is even though not *logically* reducible to Is. I shall speak of reducibility in this new sense as *causal* reducibility, as it has to do with the relation of the concept of which the reducibility (in this sense) is in question to causal explanation. For our present purposes, a concept will be said to be *causally reducible* to descriptive concepts if (roughly) it is either definable in descriptive terms (the trivial case), or occurs in the antecedent of a properly constructed causal explanation only as a subordinate element in a descriptive mentalistic context (e.g. as 'entails' occurs in 'Jones believes that responsibility entails indeterminism'). Thus, a Non-naturalist who holds that the only way in which moral obligation can enter into the causal explanation of human history is *via* facts of the form *Jones thinks (feels) that he ought to pay his debt*, would be holding that Ought is, in the above sense, causally reducible to Is. In traditional terminology he would be claiming that obligation enters into the causal order only as an element in the intentional object of a mental act. It is important to note that the above definition of the causal reducibility of a concept to descriptive concepts is one which has been tailored to meet the requirements and plausibilities of the Ought-Is problem, and that we shall be using the phrase "causal reducibility" in a different (if related) sense at a later stage of our argument. If we use "ethical assertion" in such a way that "Jones ought to pay his debt" is an ethical assertion, but "Jones feels that he ought to pay his debt" is not, then we can say that to claim that Ought is causally reducible to Is is to claim that one can give a causal explanation of the history of moral agents without making ethical assertions.

Now the thesis that Ought is causally reducible to Is, interpreted as in the preceding paragraph, would seem at first sight to be a matter of common agreement, almost a truism. Even if this were the case, the concept of causal reducibility might still be a valuable tool for clarifying controversies in other areas. That it is *not* the case; indeed, that Non-naturalists have, by and large, committed themselves to the causal *irreducibility* of Ought to Is-can, I believe, be shown in a simple and straightforward fashion. To do this we need only turn our attention from the causes of conduct to the causes of belief. It is indeed (almost) universally granted by Non-naturalists that the motive (cause) of conscientious action is never an obligation as such, but either (according to some) the *thought* that one ought to act in a certain way, or (according to others) the *desire* to do what one ought, i.e. act in a certain way. To this extent their views are consistent with the causal reducibility of Ought to Is. On the other hand, when it comes to the causes of ethical beliefs, Non--naturalists have surely committed themselves over and over again to the view that ethical facts play an essential role in both the genesis of ethical concepts and the development of moral codes. Human thinking on ethical matters is, as they see it, ultimately grounded in and controlled by objective values and obligations. The existence of moral concepts and beliefs in the human mind cannot be accounted for in purely naturalistic terms. In short, it is impossible, according to the moral philosophies of Sir David Ross, Prichard, and Ewing, to give a causal account of ethical thoughts without, at some stage, making ethical assertions (³). And this, of course, is incompatible with the causal reducibility of Ought to Is.

It is important to note that in discussing the commitments of Non-naturalism with respect to the causal reducibility of Ought to Is, I have made it clear that I have in mind the group of philosophers known as "Intuitionists". Now, if one should use the term "Non-naturalism" to cover any view, whether historically espoused

---

(³) Their awareness of this commitment may well be a partial explanation of the curious fact that in their desperate attempts to clarify the contrast between natural and non-natural characteristics, Intuitionists have on the whole avoided attempts to explicate this distinction in terms of causality, or to draw it in any manner which would clearly entail causal reducibility, --this in spite of the fact that it must have been tempting to identify the natural order with the causal order.

50

or not, which holds that ethical terms have a cognitive meaning (⁴) which is not definable in descriptive terms, then, no doubt, it is possible to be a Non-naturalist and yet accept the causal reducibility of Ought to Is. If, on the other hand, one uses "Non-naturalism" to designate such *historical* movements as have denied the logical reducibility of Ought to Is, then Non-naturalism is indeed incompatible with the causal reducibility of Ought to Is. And it can safely be said that a Non-naturalism which accepted the causal reducibility of Ought to Is would of necessity be radically different in key respects from historical Non-naturalisms.

We have indicated that one source of the strong attachment of Non-naturalists to the causal irreducibility of Ought to Is, was a sense that only if this were the case could Ought be logically irreducible to Is. We may also suspect that the strong attachment of Naturalists to the thesis of logical reducibility was grounded in a conviction that only on the latter assumption could the thesis of causal reducibility reasonably be maintained. In effect, then, Naturalists and Non-naturalists alike have shared a common presupposition, namely, Causal Reducibility of Ought to Is if and only if Logical Reducibility. Naturalists argue "Causal Reducibility therefore Logical Reducibility"; Non-naturalists, "Logical Irreducibility therefore Causal Irreducibility". Elsewhere (⁵) I have questioned this common presupposition and sketched a position which agrees with the Non-naturalist that Ought is logically irreducible to Is, and yet agrees with the Naturalist that Ought is causally reducible to Is. Although this position would be a variety of Non-naturalism according to our original definition of this term, it would be difficult to decide whether it should be classified with historical Naturalisms on the ground that it shares with them the thesis of causal reducibility, or with historical Non-naturalisms on the ground that it shares with them the thesis of logical irreducibility. Traditional terminology becomes inadequate and misleading once this new alternative is taken into account.

(⁴) I have avoided defining Non-naturalism as the view that ethical *characteristics* are not definable in descriptive terms, since I wish to leave open the possibility that while "ought" has cognitive meaning in that it is not a mere sympton or instigator of emotion, it nevertheless does not stand for a "characteristic" (at least in any usual sense of this term).

(⁵) "Obligation and Motivation", in *Readings in Ethical Theory*, edited by Wilfrid Sellars and John Hospers, and published by Appleton-Century-Crofts, New York, 1952.

III

Let us now return to the mind-body problem. By way of anti-cipation, however, let me say that not until the very close of our argument shall we make use of a distinction relating to the mind--body problem which corresponds with any degree of exactness to that drawn above in connection with the relation of Ought to Is. And even then the distinction we draw will be seen to be relevant to the mind-body problem only by virtue of the argument we are about to develop. Yet, in spite of this caveat, it must also be said that the above review of the apparently unrelated debate between Naturalist and Non-naturalist in ethics exhibits in brief compass the general philosophical tone of this paper as a whole.

To begin with, some general considerations of a logical charac-ter. In this context it will be appropriate to speak of *terms* rather than *concepts*, to discuss the logical properties of "...believes..." rather than the status of the concept of Belief. But before we explore the logic of mentalistic terms, let us make a brief and infor-mal survey of the categories made available by modern, recent lo-gical investigations. In the first place we have the category of lo-gical expressions in the narrow sense. This includes such terms as "is" (in its familiar variety of senses), "or", and "not", as well as expressions having the effect of variables and general operators. It does not include such terms as "entails" or "possible" in spite of the fact that they are legitimately characterized as logical terms. Within this first category we find a sub-category of *connectives*. In their basic use, connectives are expressions by means of which sen-tences can be made into parts of larger sentences. Thus, "It is rain-ing" can be built into the larger sentence "It is raining or the garden hose is hitting the window" by means of the connective "or", and into "It is not raining" by means of the connective "not". Connec-tives belonging to this first category are, in a familiar sense, *truth functional.*

As our second category, we shall take connectives which are *not* truth functional. This category includes (to mention for the mo-ment only the more obvious items) the logical and causal modalities, and normative expressions such as "ought" and "may". Thus, "It is necessary that all giants be tall" contains, but is not a truth function of "All giants are tall"; and "It ought to be the case that Jones be paying his debt" contains, but is not a truth function of, "Jones

52

is paying his debt". Much, much more would have to be said to give
an adequate explication of this category, let alone justify our bare-
faced identification in the above examples of subordinate clauses
in the subjunctive mood with the corresponding indicative sentences. I believe, however, that enough has been said to characterize
the second category sufficiently for our purposes.

As our third category we shall take the class of descriptive terms,
of which the most important sub-category for our purposes consists
of descriptive *predicates* and, indeed, descriptive predicates which
designate properties of, or relations between, individuals, as contrasted with those of higher order. Now, descriptive predicates in
artificially constructed languages can be neatly classified into defined and primitive descriptive predicates. If we assume (as we have
been assuming throughout the last few paragraphs) that the distinctions of logic illuminate natural languages to the extent that they
are capable of being illuminated (as opposed to causally explained),
we can say that the same is true of the descriptive predicates of
ordinary English usage. Of particular interest is the distinction
between those defined descriptive predicates of which the definiens
contains in addition to primitive descriptive predicates only expressions of the first of our three categories, and those defined descriptive predicates of which the definiens contains also expressions
from our second category. An example of the latter would be the
term "moral agent" which, for our purposes, can be treated as a predicate.

Consider, next, the class of expressions consisting of (a) primitive descriptive predicates; (b) logical expressions in the narrow sense;
(c) expressions, in particular sentences, constructable from (a) and
(b) in accordance with the formation rules (explicit or tacit) characteristic of the language developed in *Principia Mathematica*;
(d) descriptive predicates defined in terms of (a), (b) and (c). Let us
agree to call expressions belonging to this class "PM expressions",
and a language consisting exclusively of PM expressions a "PM
language".

Now, it has been a widely held conviction in empiricist circles
influenced by *Principia Mathematica*, particularly as interpreted
by Russell and the early Wittgenstein, that the language we speak
can be "reconstructed" as a PM language, -- in other words, that
everything which can be said in the natural language of everyday
usage can be said, and said more clearly, in a systematically cons-

tructed symbolism consisting exclusively of PM expressions as defined above. Clearly a proper evaluation of this convinction would
call for a careful analysis of our second category of expressions.
It will have been noticed that in illustrating the non-truth-functional
character of modal connectives, we pointed out that "It is necessary
that all giants be tall" is not a truth function of "All giants are tall".
If we replace "...all giants be tall" by "...all great pianists have fewer
than twelve fingers" in the modal sentence, the result is false, though
"All great pianists have fewer than twelve fingers" has the same truth
value as "All giants are tall". But this is not by itself sufficient to
establish the non-truth-functional character or *non-extensionality*
of modal sentences in the more searching sense which is philosophically significant. Thus, it can readily be seen that the sentence "It
is unusual that John is coming down the street" is equally not a
truth-function of "John is coming down the street". Nevertheless,
this sentence is truth-functional in the deeper sense that is can be
equated without loss of meaning to a conjunction of sentences which
have the logical character of extensionality, and are PM sentences
as characterized above. In short, the connective "unusual" can be
given a contextual definition (a definition in use) in purely extensional terms.

Our second category of expressions must, therefore, be carefully scrutinized and all connectives eliminated which, in spite of
an "immediate" non-truth-functional character, prove on examination to be definable in PM terms. The question thus arises, Do
any connectives remain in this category once the weeding out process has been completed? Now I do not know of any successful
attempt to define the logical modalities, the causal modalities or
normative expressions in purely extensional terms, and (as already
indicated) I do not think it can be done. To use our earlier terminology, modal and normative expressions are not *logically* reducible
to PM expressions, and insofar as our language contains such expressions it is not a PM language. But what of the mentalistic verbs
which lie at the heart of our problem? Can they be construed as PM
expressions? The class of mentalistic verbs is a large one, and the
grammar of mentalistic sentences as variegated as *Finnegan's Wake*.
Yet it is clear that in some uses some mentalistic verbs are, in the
sense in which we have been using the term, connectives. Just as
"It is raining" is built into the sentence "It is raining or the gar-
denhose is hitting the window" by means of the connective "or",

54

so it is built into the sentence "Jones believes that it is raining" by means of the connective "believes". And it will be noticed that in at least the "immediate" sense, "believes" is not a truth-functional connective. This characteristic of "believes" is a symptom of what traditional philosophers refer to as the "intentionality" of the mental. And, in view of the fact that some mentalistic verbs are definable in terms of others (together with non-mentalistic expressions), it is not impossible that a minimum list of mentalistic verbs adequate to define all others might consist entirely of connectives of this (at least "immediate") non-truth-functional character. In any event, it is clear that unless such mentalistic verbs as are conne tives are definable in PM terms, our language, in so far as it contains these expressions, cannot be a PM language.

Let us use "Philosophical Behaviorism" (⁶) to stand for the thesis that mentalistic terms are definable either in terms of PM expressions alone, or in terms of PM expressions together with modal expressions should these be regarded as both indispensible and logically irreducible to PM expressions. Fortunately, to explore the question at hand, it is not necessary to commit oneself concerning the indispensibility and logical irreducibility of modal connectives, and I shall therefore assume in the argument which follows that the requirements of scientific discourse, even the introduction of disposition terms, can be met by a truth-functional logic. In short, I shall assume that the major part of the "extensionalist" program can be carried out, and focus attention on that part of the program which concerns the mind-body problem. For our purposes, therefore, Philosophical Behaviorism will be the thesis that mentalistic terms are definable by PM techniques in terms of PM expressions, and are therefore themselves PM expressions.

Now, if we leave aside the (dubious) possibility of constructing a position according to which reality consists of mental acts (the non-mental having at best "intentional inexistence" as the "con-

---

⁶) It will doubtless strike many readers as absurd to define "Philosophical Behaviorism" in a way which makes no reference to behavior, even though it is being introduced as a technical term with a stipulated meaning. I would urge, however, that the controversy in the post-Watsonian period over 'Behaviorism' in psychology, in so far as it went beyond purely methodological considerations and touched on the logic of psychological concepts, is more fruitfully viewed as a clash between those who thought that the intentionality of the mental could be *reduced* to facts lacking intentionality (whether overt behavior, neuro-physiology or what have you) and those who denied this possibility, rather than as a clash between those who did, anad those who didn't, think that psychological concepts could be reduced to behavioral concepts.

tents" of these acts), it would seem reasonable to suppose that a philosopher who rejects Philosophical Behaviorism as defined above is committed to some form of mind-body dualism. However, before we decide that "Dualism" is the effective alternative to Philosophical Behaviorism, let us take a warning from our critique (pp. 48 ff. above) of the conventional terminology for discussing the Ought-Is problem. Let us allow for the possibility that although the historical positions which have insisted on the logical irreducibility of the mental can appropriately be called "Mind-Body Dualism" (whether of the "Interactionistic", "Parallelistic" or "Epiphenomenalistic" varieties), the paths of correct analysis lead rather to a view which, though its cornerstone is the logical irreducibility of mentalistic expressions to PMese, is in no sense a dualism of Mind and Body. Instead, therefore, of contrasting Philosophical Behaviorism with Dualism, let us contrast it, less elegantly with the thesis of logical irreducibility.

Now, the whole tenor of our argument to date suggests that we are about to propose a solution of the Mind-Body problem which parallels our brief treatment of the Ought-Is problem. We can sum up the latter as follows: Naturalists and Non-naturalists alike have presupposed that causal reducibility if and only if logical reducibility; the truth of the matter, however, is causal reducibility but logical irreducibility. Turning to the Mind-Body problem, we find that Dualists (with the exception of Epiphenomenalists, to whose views we shall turn shortly) combine the logical irreducibility of the mental with the claim that a causal account of the world must make use of mentalistic terms; while opponents of Dualism have argued that (Epiphenomenalism aside) if the world is to be causally explainable in PMese, mentalistic expressions must be logically reducible to PMese (Philosophical Behaviorism). The pattern seems to be the same, --a common presupposition that causal reducibility if and only if logical reducibility, and hence the possibility of undercutting the traditional argument by its rejection.

It is clear, however, that things are not quite so simple. In the first place, there is already a view of this general type on the market, namely Epiphenomenalism. In the second place, and of more immediate importance, we cannot make use in the present context of our previous definition of "Causal Reducibility". According to that definition a concept is causally reducible to descriptive concepts if it is either definable in descriptive terms (the trivial case) or occurs in the antecedent of a properly constructed causal explanation only as a subordinate element in a descriptive mentalistic context. To begin with, we are now asking whether there is a sense in which certain concepts which we already know to be *descriptive* (and hence to be causally reducible to descriptive concepts according to the trivial alternative of the above definition) can be said to be causally reducible to descriptive concepts of a PM character. And it would be not only false but self-frustrating to hold that "believes", for example, occurs in causal explanations only in such contexts as "Jones believes that he believes it is raining". It is clear, therefore, that if our solution of the mind-body problem is to take the form, *mentalistic expressions are causally reducible but logically irreducible to PMese*, we must define the relevant sense of causal reducibility along radically different lines.

IV

Let us take another look at the behavioristic revolution in psychology. From the standpoint of methodology, its root insight is the idea that if and only if the concepts, laws and theories of the psychologist enable him to understand the mind of the other fellow, has he attained his goal; and that his concepts, laws and theories cannot enable him to understand the mind of the other fellow unless they so connect with his bodily behavior that statements about his behavior imply statements about his mind, and vice versa. Many methodologist went on to conclude from this that mentalistic concepts must be explicitly definable in terms of (i.e. logically reducible to) behavior; just as their phenomenalistic contemporaries were claiming that since it is only by seeing colors, hearing sounds etc. that we can confirm statements about physical objects and their properties, the latter must ("in principle") be explicitly definable in terms of sense qualities. Of those who put forward the thesis of logical reducibility to "behavior", some insisted that definitions of mentalistic terms must ultimately be in terms of overt behavior; others denied that overt behavior provided an adequate basis for the definition of mentalistic terms and borrowed terms from physiology, in particular the physiology of the nervous system.

Other methodologists denied that the confirmability of psychological statements requires the logical reducibility of mentalistic terms to either overt behavior or overt behavior supplemented by physiology. Of these some, influenced by the work of C. A. Campbell in the methodology of physics, took a complex line which involved (*a*) distinguishing between the *undefined* terms of psychological theory and the *basic* terms of the science of psychology, (*b*) agreeing with the first of the above two schools that the basic terms ("observation terms") of psychology relate to overt behavior, (*c*) agreeing with the second school that the language of psychological theory cannot be explicitly defined in terms of expressions relating to overt behavior, (*d*) agreeing with the first school that psychologists should develop their own hypothetico-deductive theoretical structure without any *initial* identification of any of their theoretical expressions with those of, say, neurophysiology, and (*e*) requiring only that certain expressions (defined or undefined) in the theoretical language be "co-ordinated" with expressions relating to overt behavior.   Important for our purposes is the fact that these methodologists took for granted that the primitive or undefined terms of the theoretical language would have the logical characteristics of PM expressions, and combined a rejection of any *initial* identification of these primi- tive terms with definable concepts of physiology, with a conviction that when both physiology and psychology had reached maturity, such identifications would not only be possible, but would leap to the eye.

More conservative methodologists drew from the conception of psychology as the psychology of the other fellow the more modest requirement that mentalistic and behavioral concepts be so connected in a system of definitions and laws that statements about what is going on in a mind either logically *or at least causally* imply statements about behavior, and vice versa.   In other words methodologists of this variety (who might equally be granted the designation "Methodological Behaviorists" if Behaviorism consisted merely in taking seriously the notion of a psychology of the other follow) viewed with equanimity the possibility of a dualistic psychology.

Now it is clear that there was more to Behaviorism than a methodological proposal, or at least that Behaviorists regarded their methodological proposals as having consequences of a substantive character.   In effect, they took themselves to be committed to a rejection of the dualistic conception of the subject matter of scientific psychology.   And it is with this aspect of the behavioristic program that we are primarily concerned.   It is essential to note, in this connection, that we are *not* attributing to the behavioristic psychologist a monistic interpretation of common sense psychology, of everyday mentalistic language, though it must be confessed that those behaviorists who professed to derive the substantive program of Behaviorism from its methodological orientation often transformed this methodology into an epistemology and drew this conclusion.

But while we are not attributing to the psychological behaviorist as such the view that our familiar mentalistic concepts are but common sense anticipations of the behavioristic psychology of the future, in other words, while we are not identifying Psychological Behaviorism with the logical reducibility of the mental, it will be convenient to work up to a formulation of the distinction between Psychological Behaviorism and what we have called Philosophical Behaviorism by considering how a successful realization of the behavioristic program would appear to a Philosophical Behaviorist. Behaviorism triumphant would mean to him that in principle every sentence stating that a mind is in a certain state (using 'state' in a very broad sense to cover anything that can be attributed to a mind) is logically reducible by means of a chain of definitions to a PM sentence or conjunction of PM sentences to the effect that the body is in a certain state (in a similarly broad sense of 'state').

Let us use the function "m has A(O)" to say that in mind m there occurs a mental act of kind A of which the intentional object is O. Thus, A might be *believes*, and C *it is raining*, so that "m has A(O)" says of mind m that it believes that it is raining. Let us give the same subscript to an "m" and a "b" which designate, respectively, a mind and a body which belong together; thus m_1 and b_1. Then we can say that according to the thesis of Logical Reducibility, to each function "m_i has A(O)" there corresponds a *definitionally* equivalent PM function "$\emptyset b_i$".

We are now in a position to distinguish between Philosophical and Scientific (or Psychological) Behaviorism. They have a common substantive thesis, for they both propose the equivalence schema,

$$m \ \ has \ \ A(O) \ \equiv \ \ \emptyset b$$

and consequently agree that for every law involving a mentalistic function there will be an equivalent law in PM terms. But whereas the Philosophical Behaviorist argues that this equivalence is a *logically necessary* equivalence grounded in the logical reducibility of mentalistic to non-mentalistic expressions, the Scientific Behaviorist makes no such claim, and limits himself (*qua* Scientific Behaviorist) to asserting truth functional or "material" equivalences.

We have made it clear in the preceding paragraph that the Scientific Behaviorist is not committed to Philosophical Behaviorism. It is equally important to stress that he is not committed to its rejection. He insists that corresponding to every mentalistic function there is a PM function which is *at least* materially equivalent to it; he does not exclude the possibility that the relation is a stronger one than material equivalence, nor that it may even be logical equivalence. As scientific Behaviorist he does not commit himself one way or the other.

« Very well! the reader may say, "Such self-denial is perhaps a virtue in the scientist, but as philosophers we can scarcely be expected to rest in this agnosticism. For my part", he may continue, "I am not convinced that the Scientific Behaviorist is correct in asserting even a material equivalence between every mentalistic function and a PM function. As a far as I can see, however, it is not my function, as philosopher, to rule on this question. What does concern me is the interpretation to be placed on the thesis of Scientific Behaviorism should it prove worthy of acceptance as sound psychological doctrine. The philosopher could scarcely be content to accept the idea of their being such a material equivalence and let it go at that. Even to *deny* that the relation is anything more than material equivalence is to go beyond the bare thesis of Scientific Behaviorism. As a matter of fact, what would be the alternatives between which the philosopher might choose? You have already mentioned P hilosophical Behaviorism. There is also Epiphenomenalism, according to which the equivalence is not grounded in the logical reducibility of the mental, but is, in effect, a law of nature. Are there any other alternatives? »

The reader's challenge in the preceding paragraph amounts to the question: Can the thesis of Scientific Behaviorism be given a philosophical interpretation which denies the logical reducibility of the mental, and yet avoids epiphenomenalism? Or, if we use the phrase *"causal* reducibility of the mental" to stand for the thesis of Scientific Behaviorism: *Can the joint thesis of the causal reducibility but logical irreducibility of the mental be held in any other form than epiphenomenalism?* I shall argue that it can. But before I turn to this task, let me remind the reader that I am *not* making a case for Scientific Behaviorism. I am dealing with the question "If Scientific Behaviorism, then what?" As a matter of fact, I do find the thesis of Scientific Behaviorism to be reasonable and worthy of acceptance,

60

even though, to use Feigl's expression, it is a promissory note which can not yet be cashed. Yet it is my hope that the following argument will be of interest even to those for whom it falls in the same category as "If Napoleon *had* won the battle of Waterloo,.....".

V

It is clear that the philosophical interpretation of Scientific Behaviorism requires a much closer scrutiny of the latter than we have yet made. We defined it above in terms of the equivalence schema,

$$m \text{ has } A(O) \equiv \varnothing b$$

and it is to an examination of this schema that we must now turn. Perhaps the best procedure is to imagine it under attack. Thus, consider the following dialogue:

Philonous: An interesting equivalence! But tell me more about the right hand side. Just what are these bodily states you have in mind?

Hylonous: Permit me to remind you that the phrase "bodily state" is being used to cover dispositions, and episodes *qua* expressing dispositions, as well as 'states' in the narrower sense of episodes. Thus the above equivalence can be rephrased by saying that every state of affairs in which a mind is enjoying a mental act is a state of affairs in which the appropriate body is behaving intelligently.

Philonous: But surely intelligent behavior is behavior guided by thought, -- the awareness of standards, of means and ends, of circumstances and possibilities. In short, 'intelligent' would seem to be definable only in terms of the "mentalistic" expressions which belong or the left hand side of your equivalence. Perhaps you would be more at home in a specific example. Suppose that there occurs in a certain mind the thought that it is raining. What are we to put on the right hand side in such a case?

Hylonous: We would mention such behavior as reaching for an umbrella (if one were at hand), or putting on a raincoat, and, along with other behavior of this sort and dispositions to behave, tendencies to utter linguistic expressions, particularly of a meteorological variety.

Philonous: I shall not try your patience with attempts to show that the explication of "action phrases" such as 'reaching for an umbrella' and 'putting on a raincoat' leads directly to mentalistic discourse. I shall limit my remarks to your category of tendencies to utter linguistic expressions which, if I am not mistaken, is the very heart of your position. Thus, suppose the mind in question to be a German mind, then the equivalence, highlighting the linguistic component, would look as follows:

$$\left. \begin{matrix} \text{m has thought that} \\ \text{it is raining} \end{matrix} \right\} \equiv \left\{ \begin{matrix} \text{.....and b tends to} \\ \text{utter 'es regnet' ...} \end{matrix} \right.$$

But what is the import of "b tends to utter 'es regnet'"? Obviously the utterance "es regnet" is not being considered here as a mere sequence of noises. It is conceived to be a *meaningful* sequence of noises. But to make this explicit we must surely rewrite the equivalence so that it becomes,

$$\left. \begin{matrix} \text{m has thought that} \\ \text{it is raining} \end{matrix} \right\} \equiv \left\{ \begin{matrix} \text{.....and b tends to utter} \\ \text{'es regnet' where 'es} \\ \text{regnet' means } \textit{it is raining...} \end{matrix} \right.$$

Permit me to point out that 'means' like 'believes' and like the 'has thought that..' of the left hand side of this "equivalence" is at least *prima facie* not a truth-functional connective. It is therefore by no means clear that the right hand side is written (as you claim) in PMese. I doubt, indeed I deny that it is, and I should trace its non-truth functional character to what is to me the patent fact that *meaning* is a *mental* phenomenon, so that "means" cannot possibly belong in a context in which reference is made only to bodies and their states, and therefore cannot possibly belong on the right hand side of your collapsing "equivalences".

Let us turn away before Hylonous begins his reply. Philonous has put his finger on the nerve of the problem, and the point is much too important to leave to eavesdropping. He has argued, in effect, that the causal reduction of mental states to bodily states (in particular, tendencies to utter linguistic expressions) is capable of being realized only on condition that it is possible to reduce sentences of the form " b utters 'es regnet' where 'es regnet' means *it is raining* " to sentences which involve no mentalistic expressions, that is (in terms of the framework we have built up) to PMese about bodily states. At this point, let me remind the reader that I am not seeking to establish the truth of Scientific Behaviorism. It is therefore not my purpose to present arguments in favor of the reducibility of sentences of the form " b utters 'es regnet' where 'es regnet' means *it is raining*" to PMese about bodily states. Rather my aim is to suppose that this reduction can be achieved, and to frame enough of an idea of what it would be like to make it worthwhile to explore its implications for the traditional mind-body problem. Now, to assert this reducibility involves asserting (in principle) a class of equivalences illusrated by

$$\text{b's utterance of 'es regnet' means } \textit{it is raining} \equiv \Psi \text{ b}$$

where "Ψb" says of b that it has certain habits relating its utterances of "es regnet" to other utterances, to other habits, and to sensory stimuli. Once again it should be pointed out that while the Scientific Behaviorist is committed to such equivalences, he is not committed either to asserting or to denying that they are more than truth functional equivalences.

To prepare the way for the next step in our argument, let us rephrase the above equivalence to read

$$\text{"Es regnet" uttered by b means } \textit{it is raining} \equiv \Psi \text{ ("es regnet", b)}$$

where we now use the relational form to convey that b has habits of the above mentioned kinds with respect to utterances of "es regnet". But now consider the case of a Frenchman who utters "Il pleut". We are in any event authorized to write down the equivalence

$$\text{"Il pleut" uttered by b means } \textit{it is raining} \equiv \theta \text{ ("il pleut", b)}$$

But clearly the Scientific Behaviorist is committed to the thesis that if "es regnet" uttered by Germans *has the same meaning* as "il pleut" uttered by Frenchmen, then the habits of the latter with respect to "il pleut" (expressed by ' θ ("il pleut", b)') share a common generic feature with the habits of Germans with respect to "es regnet" (expressed by 'Ψ ("es regnet", b).' Let us represent this common generic feature by the form 'K (".....", b). Then we can write down the two new equivalences

$$\begin{matrix} \text{"Es regnet" uttered by b} \\ \text{means } \textit{it is raining} \end{matrix} \equiv \text{K ("es regnet", b)}$$

and

$$\begin{matrix} \text{"Il pleut" uttered by b} \\ \text{means } \textit{it is raining} \end{matrix} \equiv \text{K (" il pleut", b)}$$

or, generally,

$$\begin{matrix} \text{"...." uttered by b} \\ \text{means } \textit{it is raining} \end{matrix} \equiv \text{K ("....", b)}$$

Now we are all familiar with the fact that when we say "Jones' utterances of 'es regnet' mean *it is raining*" we are *mentioning* "es regnet" and *using* "it is raining" to convey what is meant by "es regnet" as uttered by Jones. According to Scientific Behaviorism, if what we say of Jones' utterances is true, then the utterance "it is raining" which we *use* is the manifestation of habits generically identical with Jones' habits with respect to "es regnet". Thus, when I utter

$$\begin{matrix} \text{"Es regnet" uttered by b} \\ \text{means } \textit{it is raining} \end{matrix} \equiv \text{K ("es regnet", b)}$$

the *"it is raining"* of the left hand side is a *manifestation* of the habits *mentioned* by 'K ("it is raining", Sellars)', and when I utter

$$\begin{matrix} \text{"It is raining" uttered by} \\ \text{Sellars means } \textit{it is raining} \end{matrix} \equiv \text{K ("it is raining", Sellars)}$$

the unquoted "it is raining" of the left hand side is a *manifestation* of the habits *mentioned* by the right hand side. Furthermore, while it would not be in the strict sense a self-contradiction for me to say

$$\text{"It is raining" uttered by Sellars means } \textit{it is raining}$$
$$\text{but} \sim \text{K ("it is raining", Sellars)}$$

I would be *exhibiting* on the left hand side what I was *denying* on

64

the right hand side. That is to say, I would be doing this if the equivalence

$$\text{``....'' uttered by b} \atop \text{means } \textit{it is raining}} \equiv K \ (\text{``....''}, \ b)$$

does indeed obtain; and I would be doing this in addition to making a statement which was logically incompatible with the latter equivalence. This enables us to see that the equivalences of the form

$$\text{``....'' uttered by b} \atop \text{means ****}} \equiv F \ (\text{``....''}, \ b)$$

envisaged by Scientific Behaviorism are subject to the general condition that they can only be true if utterances of them are "pragmatically consistent", in other words if the component utterance of "****" on the left hand side is a manifestation of the kind of habit mentioned on the right hand side.

VI

Let us now return to Hylonous and Philonous who have been patiently waiting to continue their argument.

Hylonous: In replying to your lengthy argument*, dear Philonous, I must begin by expressing agreement with *almost* everything you have said. In particular, I agree that the right hand side of the equivalence schema

$$\text{m has thought that} \atop \text{it is raining}} \equiv {\text{..... and b tends to} \atop \text{utter 'es regnet' ...}}$$

must be so constructed that it does justice to the *meaningfulness* of the utterances in question. I agree that one way of doing this is by rewriting the equivalence schema so that it becomes

---

*) The reference, of course, is not to the above discussion, but to the speech by Philonous (p. 60) which was its occasion. Both Hylonous and Philonous, however, are presumed to be familiar with the considerations advanced since their dialogue was interrupted.

$$\left.\begin{array}{l}\text{m has thought that}\\\text{it is raining}\end{array}\right\}\equiv\left\{\begin{array}{l}....\text{ and b tends to}\\\text{utter 'es regnet' where}\\\text{'es regnet' means }it\ is\\raining...\end{array}\right.$$

I also agree that the right hand side of this reformulated equivalence (1) is not in PMese, and (2) does not, in taking account of the meaningfulness of the utterances of 'es regnet', describe or mention any *bodily* states of b. When, however, you attribute the non-truth functional character of "means" to "the patent fact that *meaning* is a *mental* phenomenon" and argue that "'means' cannot possibly belong in a context in which reference is made only to bodies and their states", I am afraid that we must part company.

To begin with the heart of the matter, the right hand side of the modified equivalence does indeed inform us that the utterances by b of "es regnet" are more than the string of noises which might be voiced by a parrot; and it does indeed do this without mentioning other bodily states and dispositions of b. It is, however, a mistake to infer from this that it gives us this information by mentioning mental states and dispositions of m. The plain and simple truth is that when it is said of Jones' utterance of "es regnet" that it means *it is raining, no* state or disposition of Jones is being mentioned, whether of his body or of his mind. If anything is being mentioned, it is the state of affairs *raining now*, which state of affairs may or may not be the case.

Philonous: But even if I grant that "...means *it is raining*" doesn't *mention* any states or dispositions of Jones, have we not agreed that it *conveys the information* that Jones' habits with respect to "es regnet" are of the same kind as the speaker's habits with respect to "it is raining"? Surely these habits include habits of mind as well as habits of body! I conclude that even if "...means *it is raining*" doesn't *mention* any mental states or dispositions, it conveys (and it is its function to convey) the information that Jones has certain mental habits with respect to "es regnet". In this sense, propositions about meaning cannot be *understood* apart from reference to minds and mental states as opposed to bodies and bodily states, even if they do not mention minds and mental states.

Hylonous: Permit me *now* to agree with you (I could not have done so before without being misunderstood) that "meaning is a mental phenomenon." Indeed, I will go further and say that meaning is *the* mental "phenomenon" in that it is the essential ingredient in every state, process or disposition which is properly called mental. Thus, of every mental state it can be said that it either is or includes a state which "means ****". But if this is the case, then if I admit that "... means *it is raining*" said of Jones' utterance conveys the information that Jones has certain *mental* habits with respect to "es regnet", then I am admitting only that certain of Jones' habits with respect to "es regnet" can *themselves* be characterized as "meaning ****". But have you faced up to the possibility that though these habits are correctly called "mental" (as being correctly said to "mean ****") they might also be correctly called "bodily" (though of course not "merely bodily") habits? Might it not be the case that a mental state is (schematically) a bodily state which means **** (where to say "State S of b means ****" conveys, but does not mention, the information that S plays the same role in the behavioral economy of b as does the utterance of "****" in the economy of the speaker? Might it not be the case that instead of "mental" and "bodily" being mutually exclusive categories, it is bodily states, though of course not all bodily states, which are correctly called "mental"?....

It is clear that Hylonous has taken the bit in his teeth and is racing over precarious ground. Let us leave him to Philonous, and follow, where we can, at a cautious pace. We can locate ourselves by noticing that whereas Hylonous began by limiting himself to the *equivalence* schema,

$$\text{m has A(O)} \equiv \text{øb}$$

where " øb" is PMese about b's bodily behavior in relation to his environment, our last encounter found him moving towards the assertion of the identity of mental states (using, again, the word "state" in a suitably broad sense) with bodily states *qua* meaning thus and so, or *qua* including component bodily states which mean thus and so. If we oversimplify for the moment, we can say that Hylonous is now proposing the *identity* schema,

$$\text{m has A(O)} = \text{b has S, and S means O.}$$

He is proposing, in effect, (and again we oversimplify) the identification of *minds* with bodies *qua* disposed to have states of which it can correctly be said that they "mean ****".

Now, it is essential to note that while this position is "stonger" than scientific Behaviorism as we have defined it, in that, to speak loosely, it holds an "identity" theory of mind and body, it must not be confused with the position we have called "Philosophical Behaviorism". The latter, it will be remembered, interprets the equivalence

$$\text{m has A(O)} \equiv \text{\o b}$$

(where " ∅b" is PMese about b's bodily behavior in relation to his environment) to be an *identity*; whereas Hylonous is not committed to this identity unless he is prepared to assert

$$\text{b has S, and S means O} = \text{\o b}$$

and this, in the light of our discussion of " 'es regnet' uttered by b means *it is raining* ", he is not prepared to do.

VII

What are we to make of this "identity" theory proposed by Hylonous? Is it a reasonable interpretation of the equivalences affirmed by Scientific Behaviorism? Let us begin our discussion with some further remarks on the mentalistic language. We have already called attention to the obvious fact that many mentalistic expressions are definable in terms of other mentalistic expressions. Now, a scrutiny of the psychological (and philosophical) literature devoted to the descriptive phenomenology of the mental suggests that an adequate basis for the definition of all mentalistic terms can be found in "act of thought" (which we shall abbreviate as "thought") and "about" together with expressions of a non-menta listic kind. Thus, "x is a thought about O" would be the form of a basic sentence of the mentalistic language. It is important to note that while the thought of O is (to use Ryle's term) *episodic* as contrasted with, say, the ability to have thoughts about O, it must not be assumed that an act of thought is a "pure" episode without dispositional components. When it is said about x that it is an act of thought about O, no dispositions are being attributed to x. Yet it may well be the case that in order correctly to be characterized as a thought about O, x must be a complex including both episodes and dispositions. As a parallel it may be pointed out that (according to our previous discussion) when a series of grunts and groans is characterized as a sentence which means ****, no dispositions are being asserted of the sounds in question, although it is only if these grunts and groans are the manifestation of certain habits that they are correctly characterized as a sentence meaning ****.

Now it is not my purpose to define a set of mentalistic terms on the above basis. I shall suppose that this can be done, though it may be helpful to point out that mentalistic verbs relating to motivation ("desires", "chooses", "hates", etc.) can presumably be defined in terms of the tendency to have certain thoughts, and the tendency of thoughts about certain lines of conduct to bring about this conduct. I want rather to move in the opposite direction, and suggest that the basis proposed above for the definition of the mentalistic vocabulary is redundant, and, indeed, that it can be reduced to the single term "about". After all, it would be absurd to speak of an act of thought that was not about something, and our knowledge that an act of thought is necessarily about something would seem to be not only a priori but analytic. Can we not, therefore, define an act of thought as an event which is about something? One might be tempted to suppose that the definiens should read "a *mental* event which is about something". But surely "mind" and "mental" are to be defined in terms of thought, and not vice versa, so that if this approach is sound the definition as originally given must stand.

If, however, we take this step, we are clearly just around the corner from Hylonous. For if to be a thought is defined as to be about something, then we cannot rule out *ex vi terminorum* the idea that the items which are correctly said to have aboutness, and therefore to be thoughts, are bodily states (though not *mere* bodily states). Now, Hylonous originally proposed the identity schema

m has A(O) = b has S, and S means O.

This on reflection, is a most implausible identity schema since it apparently requires us to hold that the concept of a mental act is the concept of some kind of bodily state. If this were the case, however, mind-body dualism would not only be false, but absurd, which it does not seem to be. On the other hand, the above line of thought is sound, we may expect Hylonous to reformulate his identity schema to read

     .... y has x, and x is about O = b has S, and S means O

where the omitted segment of the left hand side contains the information that y is a mind, -- a matter, according to this approach, of its ability to have still other states characterized by aboutness.

Hylonous, thus interpreted, is clearly contending that y is identical with the body (b) more accurately, as we have seen, with the body qua able to have states which can correctly be said to "mean***", and x with a bodily state (S). He can scarcely be contending, however, that we are aware that y is identical with the body, or x with a bodily state. To do so would be to run afoul of the objection raised above against the earlier formulation of his identity, namely that if this were the case we should find dualism absurd, which it is not. It is clear, however, that Hylonous can hold that x, which is a thought, is identical with S which is a bodily state, without holding that x is known to be a bodily state. And, consequently, he can hold that a mind's having a thought about O is identical with a body's having a state which means O, without being committed to the obviously false proposition that we know this to be the case. As a not too distant parallel it may be noted that Bacon's writing *Novum Organum* may be identical with the author of *Hamlet*'s writing *Novum Organum* although a person may understand both "Bacon wrote Novum Organum" and "The author of Hamlet wrote *Novum Organum*" without knowing this to be the case ([7]).

But the heart of the identity proposed by Hylonous is its equation of the "about O" of the mentalistic language with the "means O" of the right hand side. It will be remembered that the language of the right hand side is the language of behavior supplemented by statements of the form "S means ***", where S is a bodily state, and where to say of S that it means **** is not to *mention* additional facts about the body, nor even to mention states of another object

---

[7] For a valuable discussion of the 'identity theory' along these (and related) lines, see HERBERT FEIGL's "The Mind-Body Problem in the Development of Logical Empiricism", *Revue Internationale de Philosophie*, 11, 1950 pp. 64-83.

called the "mind", but rather to convey, without mentioning, the information that S plays a role in the economy of Jones of the same kind as that played by utterances of "****" in the economy of the speaker. But here it is important to note that although, if Scientific Behaviorism be true,

$$\text{b has S, and S means **** } \equiv \text{ K(S, b)}$$

where "K(S,b)" says of S that it is the expression of bodily habits of a certain kind (the same kind, though not asserted to be such, as those which are expressed by the speaker's use of "****"), this equivalence also can obtain without being known to obtain. Thus, when someone says

"es regnet" uttered by Jones means *it is raining*

while we are able to infer that if he is not mistaken, then Jones has the "same" habits with respect to "es regnet" as the speaker has with respect to "it is raining", and while we may be able to specify some of these habits, we should certainly be unwilling to say that we knew all the relevant habits to be "bodily". And in our attempt to explain these habits we should find ourselves frequently driven to make statements on our own hook of the form "S means ****". While we can convey how Jones uses "es regnet" by the use of "'es regnet' uttered by Jones means *it is raining*" only to someone who shares our habits with respect to "it is raining", we can convey this information even though neither of us has a "clear and distinct" idea of what these habits are, and even though neither of us is able to characterize these habits without the repeated use of statements of the form "S means ****", and, indeed of the form " in Jones' mind there is a thought about ****".

Now, it is obvious that when Hylonous propounds the thesis of Scientific Behaviorism in terms of the equivalence schema

$$\text{b has S and S means O } \equiv \text{ } \emptyset \text{b}$$

he is presupposing that the right hand sides of the equivalences represented by this schema are formulated in the language of an ideal behavioristic psychology which at present exists only in the dreams of the tough minded. The same is, of course, true of the left hand sides-in so far, that is, as they attribute states S to bodies b. (For it will be remembered that in so far as the left hand sides say of bodily states S that they mean O, they are not in behaviorese. "Means

****'' *mentions* neither behavior nor mental states, but is rather, in recent terminology, a semantical function, and, *even though properly used to convey psychological information*, not a psychological function ([8]).

Thus, when we look at the identity schema

m has A(O) = b has S, and S means O

we realize that we simply do not have the behavioristic resources which would enable us to formulate the specific identities which cons'itute its cash value. What we actually have is a language in which mention of *aboutness* or *meaning* is primarily made in the vocabulary of mental acts and dispositions, to such an extent, indeed, that when, on occasion, we speak of utterances as "meaning ****'' we suppose it necessary to explain this by saying that they are the expressions of mental states ("ideas", "judgments", etc.) which are about ****, and when we do begin sentences with "Jones' behavior means..." it turns out that what we are saying is not that Jones' behavior means, e.g., *it is raining*, but rather that it means *in the different sense of 'is evidence for'* the occurrence in Jones' mind of the thought that it is raining. (On the other hand, it must be granted that, as has been pointed out by many recent writers (e.g. Ryle), in ordinary usage statements about dispositions to behave are entailed by statements about mental states, even though it has not always been appreciated that the careful specification of these dispositions leads to other mentalistic language ([9]).

Hylonous, therefore, must be interpreted as asserting not that our mentalistic vocabulary has the same meaning as available expressions in behaviorese supplemented by semantical clauses of the form "S means ****", but rather that in the language of an ideal behavioristic psychology it would be possible to define semantico--behavioral functions of the form "b has S, and S means ****" which could be used where we now use "m thinks about O" and which would enable us to say everything which we now say by means of our mentalistic vocabulary.

---

[8]) It is interesting to note that if, as seems proper, we define a linguistic event as an event which is correctly said to "mean ****" then the class of linguistic events is obviously much more inclusive than the class of events belonging to conventional languages. It is only if "language" is taken in this broader sense that thought can with any plausibility be identified with the use of language.

[9]) See RODERICK CHISHOLM's challenging paper "Intentionality and the Theory of Signs", *Philosophical Studies*, **3**, 1952.

VIII

But perhaps the most illuminating approach to the "identity" theory is by way of the question, "What is the alternative?" If it be granted that to say of an event in the biography of Jones that it *means* **** or is *about***** is not to mention other biographical information about Jones, and if it be granted that meaning or aboutness is the defining trait of the mental, then the crux of the mind-body problem is to determine what kinds of items belonging to the biography of Jones are correctly characterizable as "meaning ****". From this point of view we should conceive of dualism as the position that it is primarily items of a non-bodily kind which are correctly said to be "about ****". It cannot be the *mental* kind, for ex hypothesi events of the kind in question are mental qua 'having aboutness', and to say of an event that it is "about ****" is not to describe its nature. Thus, on the above assumptions, mental events must, in principle, be describable in non - mentalistic terms. But what terms might these be if not behaviorese?

Now, no one is likely to claim that the kind of event which 'has aboutness' is a kind of event which has not as yet been discovered. And, as a matter of fact a glance at the history of psychology immediately suggests the idea that it is images which are mental as being correctly said to be "about ****". Here it is essential to realize (and the point has frequently been made) that an image as such is not a mental fact (though the *imagining that* something is the case is, of course, a mental activity which, even though it frequently involves the having of images, can by no means be identified with having images). Suppose it to be granted that some images can correctly be said to be "about ****" and as such to be mental events. Why is it so frequently assumed that *only* images 'have aboutness', items other than images, e.g. utterances, 'having aboutness' only as causally related to images? The answer is not difficult to find. It has not always been realized that to say of an image that it is an image is not yet to say that it is mental. Images have been thought to be mental antecedently to their being correctly characterizable as "about ****", and therefore as capable of being characterized as "about ****" *because they are mental*, rather than as being mental qua correctly characterizable as "about ****". One who is guilty of this confusion will argue that only images can have aboutness because only mental events can have aboutness. The primary source of this confusion has of course, been exposed by Moore and Russell as the confusion between being "in the mind" as a state of mind, and being "in the mind" in the sense of *before the mind*. An image *i* may not only be a mental state *qua* being correctly said to be "about ****" but may also be "in the mind" by virtue of there being another mental state which is "about *i*." In this case, *i* is *before the mind*, and might, therefore, by the above confusion, be thought to be a mental state independently of its being about ****. The truth of the matter is that while an image is not as such a mental fact, the consciousness of an image is a mental fact.

At this point, an objection will doubtless occur to the reader which, if sound, would force, at the very least, a radical revision of the argument to date. "The consciousness of an image may be a mental fact." the objection proceeds, "but the consciousness of an image cannot be identified with the occurrence in the mind of an item which is about the image, for there occurs in my mind an item which is about the rock of Gibraltar, yet I am not conscious of the rock of Gibraltar in the sense in which I am conscious of an image. "In general", the objection continues, "we are conscious of the colors we see or imagine in a more *intimate* way than by mere aboutness. I do not mean more *direct*, for our consciousness even of Gibraltar is of Gibraltar itself, and not of some replica of Gibraltar. This more intimate mode of consciousness is *givenness*, or, to suggest the active voice, *awareness*, and it is awareness rather than aboutness which is the basic mental fact."

Now, there are two lines along which we might reply to this objection. Both begin with the admission that consciousness in the sense of awareness is to be distinguished from *mere* aboutness. The first identifies awareness with the aboutness characteristic of what it calls "logically proper names" (which it confuses with ego--centric or token-reflexive expressions such as "this" and "that"), so that "x is the awareness of y" has the force of "x is the name of y", and "m is aware of y" the force of "in m occurs a name of y". One's consciousness of Gibraltar, on the other hand, would involve the aboutness characteristic of descriptions, that is, of discourse represented in the artificial language of the logicians by the use of variables and the existential operator. I have criticized this approach on another occasion ([10]), and shall say nothing more about it here.

---

[10] "Acquaintance and Description again", *Journal of Philosophy*, **46**, 1949, pp. 496-504.

The second line of reply, which I should defend, argues that awareness is to be distinguished from mere aboutness because the notion of awareness is a richer notion than that of aboutness, even the aboutness of logically proper names. Thus, it seems to me that "m is aware of y" can be defined in terms of a tendency of m to have thoughts which (a) are *about* y, (b) are direct responses to y, and (c) are, by virtue of the manner in which the tendency to have these responses is learned, ex remely likely to be true. I recognize, however, that this is an extremely delicate matter on which it is difficult to speak with any degree of confidence, and I should certainly not wish to be pinned down to the above formulation. What I do wish to emphasize is that any account (including the first of the above approaches) must, to be plausible, tie up the notion of awareness with the notion of a direct response of the mind to the object of awareness, the object being distinguishable from the mind's awareness of it, and evoking the thought or thoughts involved in that awareness.

It is more than likely, however, that neither form of the above attempt to equate awareness with (roughly) aboutness evoked by the object of aboutness satisfies the reader who raised the above objection. We may imagine him to continue by pointing out that "we can conceive of an electronic machine which reacts to certain stimuli with a response which we should be willing to say are about these stimuli. Thus, a computing machine may not only have 'thoughts' about an aeroplane in flight but may also be 'aware', as you propose to use this term, of the stimuli which set it to work. But even if a machine can be said to be conscious in both the senses you have been describing, there is obviously a sense in which machines are not conscious but human beings are, and since your account makes no reference to consciousness in this sense, it is clearly inadequate as an account of the human mind".

Fortunately, to answer this objection it is not necessary to explore the question "Can Machines Think?" For the answer consists in admitting that there is a sense in which human beings are conscious and no machines are or, for that matter, ever will be conscious, but denying that consciousness in this sense is a *mental* fact. To put the matter simply, human being have sensations (and imagery) and machines do not. Now, it might be thought that to have a sensation is to be *aware* of, say, a color, so that since sensations can exist (e.g. in new born babes) where there is as yet nothing that can be called a "symbolic process", no process, that is, which can correctly be said to be "about ****", there is a mental activity, namely sensation, which is more basic than, and a necessary condition of, meaning or aboutness. But this would be a mistake. There is no *mental* activity more basic than meaning or aboutness, even though seeing colors, hearing sounds, having images, etc., is more basic than aboutness. Seeing a color, as Prichard emphasized ([11]) is not the same as being aware of a color, even though when we see colors we are, in point of fact, aware of colors. And while no mistake need be involved in stipulating that the word "sensation" be used as a technical term in philosophy to stand for the awareness of colors, sounds, etc., the philosophers who have proposed this usage have as a matter of fact done so because, starting from the fact that awareness is a form of consciousness, and realizing that to see a color is to be conscious, they have inferred that to see a color is to be aware of a color. It must be granted that ordinary usage is not *clear* (and, for the most part does not need to be clear) about the distinction between merely having a visual sensation (seeing a color) and being *in addition* aware of (seeing) the color, but this distinction can be tickled out of it (*vide* Prichard), and the correct drawing of this distinction is essential to the cl rification of puzzles about consciousness. In particular, if we use "having a visual sensation" or "seeing a color" in the sense of *being aware of a color*, we shall find ourselves using some such expressions as "sense-datum genesis" for what we ordinarily call "seeing a color" or "having a visual sensation". And while there can be no objection to "sense datum genesis" as a cautious, aseptic term, by using it where we should ordinarily speak of seeing a color or hearing a sound, we simply cut ourselves off from the fact that we *know* that to see a color is *ipso facto* to be conscious of a color, even though, at the common sense level, we are unable to give an adequate account of what seeing a color is. We might come to many conclusions about sense-datum genesis, --for example we might conclude that it doesn't occur apart from certain neuro-physiological processes. But how could we conclude that if Jones participates in sense datum genesis then Jones is conscious (in one sense of this term) unless we realized both that the process we were aseptically calling "sense datum genesis" was the process ordinarily referred to by such expressions as "seeing a color" and "hearing a sound", *and* that to

---

[11]) H. A. Prichard, "The Sense-datum Fallacy" *Aristotelean Society Proceedings*, 1938 (reprinted in his (posthumous) *Knowledge and Perception*, Oxford, the Clarendon Press, 1950).

see a color or hear a sound is *ex vi terminorum* to be conscious (in one sense of this term).

To sum up the argument of the last few paragraphs, we can say that there is indeed a sense of "consciousness" distinct from both "mere aboutness" and "awareness", and more basic than either. However, consciousness in this sense is not a *cognitive* or *mental* fact, even though if we were not thus conscious, that is, if we did not have sensations, we would not come to have thoughts, and even though "Jones is aware of y" entails "Jones has a sensation". But to agree that consciousness in this sense, namely seeing colors, hearing sounds, and especially having visual and other forms of imagery, is not a *mental* fact, is not yet to espouse the thesis of Hylonous. For he argued not only that the items which are mental *qua* correctly said to be "about ****" must have an intrinsic nature describable (in principle) in other than mentalistic terms, he also argued that in their intrinsic nature these items are bodily states. Thus, we may imagine an anti-Hylonousian to claim that it is items belonging to consciousness in this non-mentalistic sense which are correctly said to have aboutness, and to deny that consciousness in this sense is a bodily state.

Now, the question "Is having a sensation or image a bodily state?" is by no means an easy one to answer. To answer in the affirmative one must argue not only that the colors we see or image are causally dependent on bodily process (which might justify us in saying that they are events in the perceiver's biography, but not that they are events in the biography of the perceiver's body) but also that the genesis of colors, sounds, etc. is itself a bodily process. It is not my purpose to put forward such an argument. I shall limit myself to pointing out that two familiar arguments against the view that sense-datum genesis is a bodily process are based on simple confusions. It is argued that since a bodily process is a process definable in the language of physics, and since the sense qualities are not definable in the language of physics, it follows that sense datum genesis is not a bodily process. But to suppose that 'x is a bodily state of Jones' means 'x is a state of Jones which is definable in the language of physics' is to commit a howler. "Bodily" is a term in ordinary discourse which has meaning primarily as a contrast to "mental". And while we should be doing violence to this common sense term if we took 'x is a bodily state of Jones' to have a *definite* meaning exhausted by 'x is a non-mental state of Jones', we should be doing it less violence than if we interpreted it as in the above argument.

It is also argued that inspection reveals the colors we see to be outside our body; therefore, it is concluded, they cannot belong to a bodily process.   But what inspection reveals (if we agree to talk in this way) is rather the quite different fact that the colors we interpret as belonging to the surfaces of other physical objects stand in certain relation to the colors we interpret as belonging to the surface of our body.   This clearly does not entail that the colors we see are located in physical space outside our bodies, nor, for that matter, that they have *any* location in physical space.   We cannot decide, merely on the basis of "inspection", that colors, standing in certain relations of the spatial type to each other, cannot be elements of a process which it is legitimate to call a bodily process.

In this connection it should be noted that even if one should come to the conclusion that such things as seeing a color and having an image are not bodily states, the resulting dualism would not as such be a *mind*-body dualism, even though in one sense of "consciousness" it would be a *consciousness*- body dualism.   It would be appropriate to call it a mind-body dualism only if it went on to hold that aboutness is directly predicable only of sensations and images, and predicable of bodily states only as symptoms of sensations and images *qua* having aboutness (i.e. qua correctly said to be "about ****").

Now, the conclusion to be drawn from the preceding section is that Scientific Behaviorism is a most implausible thesis unless it recognizes that its category of 'bodily states' includes items (seeing a color, hearing a sound, having an image, etc.) which are, in a familiar and legitimate sense of the phrase, "states of consciousness". Thus, Scientific Behaviorism must be interpreted *not* as the assertion of the equivalence schema

Jones has state of consciousness C $\equiv$ ⌀b

but rather as the assertion of the schema

Jones has mental state M $\equiv$ ⌀b

where the language on the right hand side permits the formulation of such sentences as "b is seeing red" and "b is (in one sense of the term) conscious". It is only "conscious" in those senses which involve *aboutness*, in other words, "conscious" as a *mentalistic* term which is restricted to the left hand side of the equivalences anticipated by

Scientific Behaviorism.   Thus interpreted, Scientific Behaviorism
loses the air of paradox which belongs to it as long as it is construed
as the claim that it is (in principle) possible to explain human behavior
without mentioning consciousness.

Encouraged by the increased plausibility of Scientific Behav-
viorism, let us return to the question of its implication for the mind-
-body problem. It will be remembered that at first sight there were
two alternatives, Epiphenomenalism and Philosophical Behaviorism,
the former denying and the latter affirming the logical reducibility
of the mentalistic language to PMese about bodily states. From there
the line of argument went first to the notion of an ideal Behaviorese
enriched with semantical expressions of the from "—— means****",
and then to the interpretation of the mentalistic frame as definable
in terms of aboutness.   This led to the suggestion that it might be
possible to affirm (in principle) the identity schema

$$\text{m has A(O)} = \text{b has S, and S means O}$$

where the expressions on the right hand side are supposed to be in
ideal Semantico-behaviorese.   In a sense, then, Hylonous accepts
the logical reducibility of mind to bodily behavior, and in this sense
his theory is an identity theory.   On the other hand, while Hylonous
insists on the *causal* reducibility of the mentalistic language to
PMese about bodily behavior (the thesis of Scientific Behaviorism)
he refuses to assert the *logical* reducibility of the mentalistic language
to PMese about behavior.   Thus, he limits himself to proposing
the equivalence

$$\text{b has S, and S means O} \equiv \text{K (S,b)}$$

where, given an ideal Behaviorese, the use of the left hand side would
be a correct way of conveying the information asserted by the right
hand side, even though it would not assert what is asserted by the
right hand side. In other words, while the left hand side does not
assert what is asserted by the right hand side, the equivalence, by
virtue of the pragmatic features of the use of the left hand side discussed at length in section V, is more than a "mere" material equivalence.

The logical irreducibility of the mentalistic language to Behaviorese, insisted on by traditional dualisms, turns out, if our argument is sound, to be exactly the logical irreducibility of semantical
metalanguages to PMese.   And semantical metalanguages are logic-

ally irreducible to PMese because although the use of semantical
statements is a correct way to *convey information* about human behavior, semantical statements do not describe human behavior.
Thus, " 'Es regnet' uttered by Jones mean *it is raining*" does not
mention biographical facts about the role utterances of "es regnet"
in Jones' struggles with his natural and social environment, even
though it is a mode of speech properly designed to convey information
of this kind.   Thus, even though the (ideal) equivalence schema

$$\text{b has S, and S means O} \equiv \emptyset\text{b}$$

has a rationale by virtue of which the equivalences it covers are
more than mere material equivalences, they are neither laws of
nature nor, in any usual sense of the term, logical equivalences. The
equivalence

$$\frac{\text{"es regnet" uttered by Jones}}{\text{means } it\ is\ raining} \equiv \text{K ("es regnet", b)}$$

is validated not by showing that " 'es regnet' uttered by Jones means
it is raining" can be constructed out of the same (PM) primitives
as "K ('es regnet', b)", but only by knowing the circumstances in
which it is correct to use " 'es regnet' uttered by Jones means it is
raining".

As an illuminating parallel it can be pointed out that although
"x is here", said by Smith who is at s, is in a strong sense equivalent
to "x is at s", nevertheless it is not, in any ordinary sense, logically
equivalent to it.

We thus see that semantical discourse is a mode of discourse
which shares with normative discourse the characteristic of being
logically irreducible to PMese. Now it will be rememberd that while
Ought is not logically reducible to Is, we found it to be causally
reducible to Is in the sense that the only way in which moral obligation enters into the causal explanation of human history is via facts
of the form, *Jones thinks (feels) that he ought to pay his debt.* We have
since argued that semantical discourse is causally reducible to non-
-semantical discourse in the sense that (assuming the truth of Scientific Behaviorism) we can assert the equivalence

$$\text{b has S, and S means O} \equiv \emptyset\text{b}$$

I want now to point out that there is a sense in which About enters
into the causal order only via facts of the form, *Jones thinks that*

80

x is about y, and in this respect resembles Ought. Thus, suppose it to be correctly proposed as a causal law that

b has S, and S means O ⊃ b has S'

This must be so, according to our account, because of that which is expressed by the following pair

b has S, and S means O ≡ K (S,b)
K (S,b) ⊃ b has S'

Thus causal laws stated in terms of aboutness (and hence causal laws formulated in mentalistic terms) presuppose causal laws which are not stated in terms of aboutness. It is only because people correctly use semantical statements to convey what is (in principle) mentioned by non-semantical statements that it is correct to make causal statements of the form "b has S, and S means O ⊃ b has S'". But to make correct use of a semantical statement is to think about aboutness. Therefore we can put the above by saying that in spite of the fact that it is correct to make causal statements of the form "b has S, and S means O ⊃ b has S'", it is nevertheless true that there is a sense in which About enters into the causal order only by virtue of the fact that people think about aboutness.

To make one more use of the parallel we have pointed out between "x is here" uttered by Smith, and "'es regnet' uttered by Jones means it is raining" uttered by Smith, we can say that although it is correct to say "x is here", it is nevertheless true that there is a sense in which there are facts of the form *x is here* only by virtue of the fact that people correctly use the word "here", i.e. think about *being here*.

IX

I shall now bring this paper to a close with a few remarks designed to a locate its argument in philosophical space. To begin with let me call attention to the fact that our argument has been formulated in terms of the assumption that scientific discourse can dispense with the modalities. Thus, we have assumed that our ideal Behaviorese is an extensional or PM language. It is clear, however, that the conclusions at which we have arrived in no way depend on that assumption, which was made at a time when we were exploring the influence of *Principia Mathematica* on recent attempts to avoid traditional dualisms, and wanted to pay out as much rope as we could to the "extensionalist" program. And as far as the details of our more recent argument are concerned, we might just as well have taken our ideal Behaviorese to have the logical form of PMese enriched with the logical and causal modalities. For the semantical discourse which we found to be the heart of mentalistic discourse is no more reducible (logically) to a PMese thus modified, than it is to PMese pure and simple.

Now our argument, as we actually formulated it, led us to the conclusion that even if semantical discourse is logically irreducible to PMese, nev rtheless the information which we use it to convey could (in principle) be formulated in a behavioristic PM language. This suggest that even though normative and modal discourse are logically irreducible to PMese (and indeed they are), they also are used to convey information which could (in principle) be formulated in PMese. And this in turn suggests that the "extensionalist" thesis might be reinterpreted as the claim that everything which is *conveyed* by means of mentalistic, normative and modal discourse can (in principle) be formulated in PMese, and consequently that *everything can (in principle) be said in PMese.*

Such a revised "extensionalism" has a certain plausibility if one approaches it from the consideration of semantical discourse, and, in particular, from reflection on the equivalence schema

$$\text{b has S, and S means O} \equiv \varnothing b$$

But from the fact that the left hand side is correctly used to convey that which is (in principle) formulated by the right hand side are we entitled to conclude that the left hand side *says* only what is said (in principle) by the right hand side. Obviously not. Whatever the left hand side may *convey*, it *says* that S means O, and this cannot be said in PMese. Perhaps what the "extensionalist" means to assert, as the fruit of his reflection on the above equivalence, is that *ideally* human beings could dispense with semantical discourse. But clearly human beings could dispense with all discourse, though only at the expense of having nothing to say. What would Scientific Behaviorists who had achieved their goal be able to say if they dispensed with semantical discourse? They would be able to formulate laws of man and nature adequate to predict and control. On the other hand, they would not be able to say that S means O, nor that "It is raining" is true if and only if it is raining. Is there then no point to saying such things? Surely the upshot of all this is that the proper way to interpret the above equivalence is not by propounding an "extensionalist" thesis, but rather by giving a careful and detailed analysis of the relations which would obtain between semantical discourse and an ideal Behaviorese.

The situation is even clearer with respect to normative discourse. Whatever users of normative discourse may be *conveying* about themselves and their community when they use normative discourse, what they are *saying* cannot be said without using normative discourse. The task of the philospher cannot be to show how, in principle, what is said by normative discourse could be said without normative discourse, for the simple reason that this cannot be done. His task is rather to exhibit the complex relationships which exist between normative and other modes of discourse, in particular, mentalistic discourse. It will be noticed that if one combines our assertion of the causal reducibility of Ought to Is, with our account of mentalistic discourse, the ethical naturalist gets everything he can reasonably hope for. Yet the fact remains that what is said by "Jones ought to pay his debt" could not be said in even an ideal PMese.

We have rejected the "extensionalist" thesis with respect to both Ought and About, and we have seen how this can be done without falling into the traditional dualisms. It is my convinction that similar approach would resolve traditional puzzles relating to the logical and causal modalities, and avoid both the Scylla of Hume and the Charybdis of Rationalism. But I have already said enough to indicate the spirit of such an approach, and to work out its details would take another paper([6]).

----

[6]) For attempts along this line see my "Inference and Meaning", *Mind*, forthcoming; and "Is there a Synthetic A priori?" *Philosophy of Science*, April 1953. The argument of both these papers should be supplemented by the above treatment of the mind-body problem.

SECTION I

(313.1,.2; 314.1,.2,.3,.4; 315.1,.2; 316.1,.2; 317.1) Discussions of six possible views concerning "material rules of inference" ending with a summary of these views:

(1) Material rules are as *essential to meaning* (and hence to language and thought) as formal rules, contributing the architectural detail of its structure within the flying butresses of logical form.

(2) While not essential to meaning, material rules of inference have an *original authority* not derived from formal rules, and play an *indispensable* role in our thinking on matters of fact.

(3) Same as (2) save that the acknowledgment of material rules of inference is held to be a *dispensable* feature of thought, at best a matter of convenience.

(4) Material rules of inference have a *purely derivative authority*, though they are genuinely rules of inference.

(5) The sentences which raise these puzzles about material rules of inference are *merely abridged formulations of logically valid inferences*. (Clearly the distinction between an inference and the formulation of an inference would have to be explored.)

(6) Trains of thought which are said to be governed by "material rules of inference" are actually *not inferences at all*, but rather activated associations which mimic inference, concealing their intellectual nudity with stolen "therefores".

SECTION II

(317.2; 318.1,.2; 319.1,.2; 320.1,.2,.3) An account of "formal" and "material" rules of inferences through an exposition of Carnap's distinction between two sorts of "transformation rules", "L-rules" and "P-rules". Carnap commits himself to the dispensability of P-rules in the sense that "everything sayable" in a language with P-rules can be said in a language with only L-rules. Therefore he does not hold view (1) or view (2). Since the discussions of views (5) and (6) made it clear that they deny that there are any such thing as P-rules, Carnap is committed to either view (3) or view (4).

(321.1; 322.1) Does Carnap hold (3) or does he hold (4)? On (3), P-rules would have an "authority" that is not derivative from L-rules; such a situation can arise if P-rules "enable a language to perform a function which

could not be duplicated.....by a language with L-rules alone" even
though that function is "dispensable". On (4), no such nonderivative
authority is possessed by P-rules; they are at best a convenience in
formulating arguments. Carnap does not appeal to any of these matters
in discussing P-rules.

SECTION III

(322.2; 323.1) A suggestion by one "Metaphysicus": Some subjunctive
conditionals "give expression to" L-rules while other subjunctive conditionals "give expression to" P-rules. Thus Metaphysicus concludes that
P-rules *"are essential to any conceptual frame which permits the formulation of such subjunctive conditionals as do not give expression to logical
rules of inference."*

(323.2; 324.1,.2; 325.1) An empiricist rejoinder which includes several
unsuccessful attempts to show that all subjunctive conditionals give
expression to L-rules.

(325.2) Unless some sort of attempt along the empiricist lines sketched in
the preceding paragraphs is successful, we have established that material
rules of inference have an authority "not derivative from formal rules"
and "are essential to the language we speak, for we make constant use
of subjunctive conditionals" of the kind at issue. Yet we cannot conclude
from these points that "material rules of inference are essential to
languages containing descriptive terms" since subjunctive conditionals
might be "dispensable".

(326.1) However, it does not follow from the dispensability of subjunctive
conditionals that P-rules are dispensable. It may be that the *"function
performed in natural languages by material subjunctive conditionals is
indispensable"* and that, in lieu of such conditionals material rules of
inference might perform this indispensable function.

(326.2; 327.1) "Provisionally", (4) is shown to be untenable. Some grounds
for thinking it reasonable to extend the investigation: in particular, to
obtain a better account of rules of inference.

SECTION IV

(327.2; 328.1,.2; 329.1) A review of Carnap's remarks on "transformation
rules" shows that his account does not take seriously the notion of a rule.
A rule must either enjoin or forbid or permit, etc. a "doing." Carnap's
account of transformation rules framed in terms of the "structural
relationships" between expressions, leaves the "normative" element out.

(330.1,.2) Rules of inference permit assertion given other assertions where
"we shall assume" that "to assert a sentence is to bring about the
existence of a token of that sentence". A "proper" syntactical
metalanguage is one that can formulate rules which enjoin or permit
asserting.

SECTION V

(331.1,.2; 332.1,.2) We are now in a position to develop an account of the logical and physical modalities which, though based on Carnap's account in his *Logical Syntax of Language*, is an improvement in that it explicitly takes into account the "*rulishness* of syntactical rules." "The language of modalities in interpreted as a "transposed" language of norms" and not as language having to do merely with the "structural" relationships among "expression designs."

(332.3; 333.1,.2,.3) Two objections to the above account and the replies.

(333.4; 334.1) It is widely agreed that the "conceptual meaning" of a logical, a modal or a normative term is "constituted by its logical grammar," i.e., its use "in accordance with certain syntactical rules," because there is no plausibility to the claim that the meaning of such a term is constituted by the term's "being a learned response to a class of extra-linguistic particulars." But for descriptive predicates like 'red' such a claim is very plausible.

(334.2; (335)) Five points to support the claim that not even descriptive predicates owe their conceptual meaning to being such a "learned response."

SECTION VI

(336.1) Given the argument of paper, particularly that of section V, the upshot is that view (1) turns out to be the correct view of the status of material rules of inference: "According to it, material transformation rules determine the descriptive meaning of the expressions of a language within the framework established by its logical transformation rules."

(337.1; (338)) The view of this paper is not like "dogmatic rationalism" even though, *in a sense*, it recognizes "synthetic a priori truths." This recognition is not that of dogmatic rationalism since, on the view of this paper, "there are an indefinite number of possible conceptual structures (languages) or systems of formal and material rules, each one of which can be regarded as a candidate for adoption by the animal which recognizes rules, and no one of which has an indubitable hallmark of royalty."

INFERENCE AND MEANING

By Wilfrid Sellars

I

TWENTY or so years ago it was received dogma among the great majority of empirically-minded philosophers that the inference which finds its expression in " It is raining, therefore the streets will be wet " is an enthymeme. Explicitly formulated, it was claimed, the argument thus presented would read, " Whenever it rains the streets will be wet, it is raining ; therefore the streets will be wet ". As the validity of this reasoning rests on purely formal principles, it was concluded that the same is true of the briefer argument above, it being in all respects save formulation, identically the same. Thus, when Metaphysicus rehearsed for their benefit the argument " I am releasing a piece of chalk, therefore *of necessity* it will fall ", adding by way of commentary, " Surely that was a reasonable argument. It is not, however, formally valid, so the necessity in question cannot be logical necessity. Must you not, therefore, admit that the inference is based on an appeal to a non-logical or material necessity ? " our empiricists replied with the above analysis, and dismissed the subject with the remark, " It is now obvious that the only necessity involved is the logical necessity with which ' This chalk will fall ' follows from ' All released pieces of chalk fall ' and ' This piece of chalk is being released '."

One need not be persuaded by this retort to feel its force. After all, are there not such things as enthymemes ? and is not the rephrased argument valid on purely logical grounds ? Convincing though the retort may be, however, it scarcely amounts to a disproof of the idea that there are *material* as well as *formal* principles of inference, so that instead of merely being abridged edition of a formally valid argument, " It is raining, therefore the streets will be wet " might well be as it stands a valid argument, though warranted by a *material* principle of inference. On what grounds would our empirically minded philosophers have rejected this idea ? At least a partial answer lies close at hand. A scrutiny of the above clash with Metaphysicus suggests that tacit use is being made of Ockham's razor. The claim seems to be that even if it made sense to speak of non-logical principles of inference, there would be no need for them. For do not logical principles enable us to do all the arguing and inferring which these supposed material principles could warrant, provided we use the generalizations which correspond to these material principles as *premises* in our arguments ? Thus, if we suppose " *x is an acid* may be inferred from *x turns litmus paper red* " to be a material principle of inference, the corresponding generalization would be " (x) x turns litmus paper red $\supset$ x is an acid ". The material rule would certify the argument, " This turns litmus paper red, therefore it is an acid ", while if we use the generalization corresponding to the rule as a premise, we get the logically valid argument, " (x) x turns litmus paper red $\supset$ x is an acid ; this turns litmus paper red ; therefore this is an acid ".

I think it is clear, however, that our empirically-minded friends would have gone much farther than this. They would have attacked the very notion of a material principle of inference. At the very least they would have claimed that if any principles do correspond to this description, they have a thoroughly second-rate and/or derivative status as compared with purely formal principles. We can imagine that something like the following considerations would have governed their thinking on this matter.

' Formal rules of inference are essential to the very possibility of language ; indeed, of thought. Kant was on the right track when he insisted that just as concepts are essentially (and not accidentally) items which can occur in judgments, so judgments (and, therefore, indirectly concepts) are essentially (and not accidentally) items which can occur in reasonings or arguments. Without formal rules of inference there would be no terms, no concepts, no language, no thought. In this sense, our empiricists continue, one could say that logical rules of inference specify, at least partially, the very form of a term or concept. Were it not for these rules, we could not even conceive of the releasing or the falling of a piece of chalk, not to mention the piece of chalk itself. On the other hand, given these rules and given the course of our sense-experience, no other rules of inference (that is, no non-formal or material rules) are necessary conditions of concepts—though rules of inductive inference may be necessary to establish synthetic truths involving them.'

To bolster up this line of thought, they would appeal to the empiricist account of concept formation in one or other of the various forms in which it has been held, since Locke made it the cornerstone of his philosophy, and continue :

' The *form* of our concepts may depend on rules of inference, but their material *content* does not. Even if we were to acknowledge a material rule of inference whereby " This piece of chalk will fall " can legitimately be inferred from " This piece of chalk is being released ", the rule could have nothing to do with our ability to conceive of either *chalk*, the *releasing of chalk*, or the *falling of chalk*. This fact alone would force us to put material principles of inference, should we acknowledge their existence, on a decidedly inferior plane.'

Can one, however, go this far in cutting material rules of inference down to size, without taking the more drastic step of denying that anything is really described by the phrase " material rule of inference " ? Those who take this line claim that " It is raining, therefore the streets will be wet ", when it isn't an enthymematic abridgment of a formally valid argument, is merely the manifestation of a *tendency to expect* to see wet streets when one finds it raining, a tendency which has been hammered into the speaker by past experience. In this latter case it is the manifestation of a process which at best can only *simulate* inference, since it is an habitual transition of the imagination, and as such is not governed by a principle or rule by reference to which it can be characterized as valid or invalid. That Hume dignified the activation of an association with the phrase " causal *inference* " is but a minor flaw, they continue, in an otherwise brilliant analysis. It should, however, be immediately pointed out that before one has a right to say that what Hume calls " causal inference " really isn't inference at all, but a mere habitual transition from one thought to another, one must pay the price of showing just how *logical* inference is something more than a mere habitual transition of the imagination. Empiricists in the Humean tradition have rarely paid this price, a fact which has proved most unfortunate for the following reason. An examination of the history of the subject shows that those who have held that " causal inference " only simulates inference proper have been led to do so as a result of the conviction that *if it were genuine inference, the laws of nature would be discovered to us by pure reason.* But an adequate account of *logical* inference might make it clear that even " causal inference " can be genuine inference, as it seems to be, without this unwelcome consequence.

A somewhat less drastic approach to material rules of inference differs from the above in admitting that there are such rules, and that they are indeed rules of *inference*, but insists that not only do they have second-class status in that, unlike formal rules, they are not necessary conditions of the very existence of terms or concepts, but also that their authority as rules is purely *derivative*. It claims that recognition of a material rule to the effect that " x is B " may be inferred from " x is A " presupposes prior acceptance of what we have called the corresponding generalization, in this case " All A is B ", and owes its authority to the fact that " x is B " is logically derivable from " x is A " together with " All A is B ".   Those who adopt this alternative concede to Metaphysicus that the inference from " It is raining " to " The streets will be wet " is immediately grounded in a material rather than formal rule of inference, but insist that as the authority of material principles is purely derivative, this admission entails none of the rationalistic consequences which he desiderates.   While they might agree with proponents of a more drastic approach that in some cases utterances and in-scriptions of " It is raining, therefore the streets will be wet " are functioning merely as abbreviated expressions of inferences governed by a formal rule of inference, they are more likely to insist (and I believe correctly) that in most cases, at least, these supposed abridgments of formally valid arguments are actually complete arguments as they stand which are validated by material rules of inference.   They would add that it might not be in-appropriate to say that these arguments are " abridgments " or " enthymemes " provided that these terms are taken to imply not that there are no material rules of inference, but rather that their status is purely derivative, and their contribution to thought a matter of convenience.

If neither of these two more drastic lines is taken, it would seem possible (at least at this early stage of our discussion) to take a different tack and combine the ascription of an inferior status to material rules of inference, as not being necessary conditions of the existence of terms or concepts, with the claim that their authority as rules is nevertheless original.   This view in turn, would seem to admit of two variants.   According to the first, material principles of inference, though not essential to meaning, are as indispensable as formal rules to thought about empirical matters.   The second variant denies this, claiming that although the authority of material rules is not inherited from formal rules, but is equally original, they are nevertheless dispensable modes of thought, making no contribution to its penetration or scope which could not be duplicated by a combination of formal rules and factual premises.

Now, all the above possibilities in the way of empirically minded interpretations of material rules of inference have in common the idea that whereas formal rules are necessary con-ditions of the existence of concepts or the possession of meaning by terms, and, in this sense, are generic conditions of meaning—the specific content of a concept, or meaning of a term, is derived from experience, and is prior to any material rules of inference in which this concept or term may come to play a role. But might it not be possible for an empiricist to hold that material rules of inference are as essential to meaning as formal rules ? that the specificic nature of a factual concept is determined by the material rules of inference governing it, as its generic nature is determined by formal rules of inference ? that the meaning of a term lies in the materially and formally valid inferences it makes possible ? In spite of the fact that a position of this kind is incompatible with the so-called " empiricist " theory of concept formation, and is universally relegated to the absolute idealisms and rationalisms of a bygone age, I mention it for the sake of completeness.

In effect, then, we have been led to distinguish the following six conceptions of the status of material rules of inference :

(1) Material rules are as *essential to meaning* (and hence to language and thought) as formal rules, contributing the architectural detail of its structure within the flying buttresses of logical form.

(2) While not essential to meaning, material rules of inference have an *original authority* not derived from formal rules, and play an *indispensable* role in our thinking on matters of fact.

(3) Same as (2) save that the acknowledgment of material rules of inference is held to be a *dispensable* feature of thought, at best a matter of convenience.

(4) Material rules of inference have a *purely derivative authority*, though they are genuinely rules of inference.

(5) The sentences which raise these puzzles about material rules of inference are *merely abridged formulations of logically valid inferences*. (Clearly the distinction between an inference and the formulation of an inference would have to be explored.)

(6) Trains of thought which are said to be governed by " material rules of inference " are actually *not inferences at all*, but rather activated associations which mimic inference, concealing their intellectual nudity with stolen " therefores ".

II

In the above paragraphs we have been led to worry about the dispensability or indispensability of, and the relation to meaning of, material rules of inference. We have not yet, however,

318 WILFRID SELLARS:

given an account of what a material rule of inference is, or pretends to be. We have relied on dangerously vague historical connotations of the terms " formal " and " logical ", as well as on the use of examples. Fortunately, help lies close at hand. Professor Rudolf Carnap, in his *Logical Syntax of Language*, draws a systematic contrast between two types of syntactical rule which if his syntactical conception of logic is sound, are exactly the formal and material rules of inference with which we are concerned. It is to a brief exposition of his views on this matter that I now turn.

In Carnap's terminology, a rule of inference, conceived to be a syntactical rule, is called a " transformation rule ". He emphasizes the central role played by the concept of a transformation rule in the definition of a language. Indeed (p. 168) he contends that once we know the circumstances under which one expression of a language is the direct consequence of another, we have the key to the logical structure of the language. These circumstances are specified by the transformation rules, which are formulated in the syntactical metalanguage of the language to which they apply. Whether stated as rules of inference, or as a definition of " direct consequence in S ",

> . . . all that is necessary is that it be clear to what forms of expression the rules are in general applicable (which gives us the definition of " sentence ") and under what conditions a transformation or inference is permitted (which gives us the definition of " direct consequence ") (p. 170).

Transformation rules must carefully be distinguished from *valid* sentences in the object language. The latter are sentences which require nothing more than an appeal to the transformation rules of the language to justify their assertion. If an object-language sentence is valid, its contradictory is *contra-valid*. If either valid or contra-valid, it is said to be *determinate*, otherwise *indeterminate*. Carnap finds it to be a distinguishing feature of logical symbols and expressions that each sentence constructed solely from them is determinate (p. 177). On page 175 he defines the *content* of a sentence as the class of non-valid sentences which are its consequences (*i.e.* can be inferred from it).

We next note that Carnap draws a distinction between *logical* and *extra-logical* transformation rules. The essential difference, to put the matter in a way which is adequate for our purposes, is that whereas *logically* valid inferences do not, *extra-logically* valid inferences do depend for their validity on the fact that they contain a certain set of descriptive terms. The syllogism so fatal to Socrates remains valid if any three descriptive terms of

appropriate category are systematically substituted for " men ",
" mortal " and " Socrates ". In Quine's useful terminology,
descriptive terms occur *vacuously* in logically valid arguments ;
essentially in extra-logically valid arguments. Now, the most
obvious candidates for the position of extra-logical rule of inference are rules authorizing inferences which, to be *logically*
valid would have to have as an additional premise a sentence
formulating a law of nature. Carnap calls rules of this kind
" P-rules " (Where the " P " is short for " physical " in a suitably
broad sense), as contrasted with L-rules (logical rules). In his
terminology, therefore, he distinguished between L-valid and
P-valid inferences. To illustrate : If we suppose " (x) ϕx
implies ψx " to state a law of nature,

I. (x) ϕx $\supset$ ψx, but ϕa, therefore ψa

would be an L-valid inference.

II. ϕa, therefore ψa

would be a P-valid inference. The P-rule authorizing it, whatever
its most satisfactory formulation might turn out to be, would
be to the effect that " A sentence consisting of ' ψ ' followed
by an individual constant is validly inferred from a sentence
consisting of ' ψ ' followed by that same individual constant ".
(That we cannot rest in this formulation is shown by the fact
that when the phrase " may be inferred from " is correctly used
in ordinary speech, it is preceded and followed not by the names
of sentences, but by the sentences themselves—*e.g.* that it will
rain can be inferred from the darkness of the clouds.)

Corresponding to this distinction between L-valid and P-valid
inferences, we have the distinction between L-valid and P-valid
sentences. Thus,

III.   (x) ϕx $\supset$ ψx . & . ϕa : $\supset$. ψa

would be an L-valid sentence. On the other hand, given the
above P-rule,

IV. ϕa $\supset$ ψa

would be a P-valid sentence, while

V. ϕa & — ψa

would be P-contravalid.

Furthermore, in view of Carnap's definition of the content of a
sentence as the class of the non-valid sentences which are consequences of it, ' ψa ' would be part of the content of ' ϕa ',
though not of its L-content. Given a suitable definition of the
content of expressions other than sentences, a corresponding

distinction would have to be drawn between the content of an expression governed by P-rules, and its content in the narrower sense of L-content.

Let us now raise the question whether, granted that a language must have rules of inference, it must have both L-rules and P-rules. We might expect Carnap to say that whereas a language without descriptive terms need not, and, indeed, cannot have other than logical rules of inference, a language with descriptive (extra-logical) terms must have extra-logical rules. *Carnap, however, makes it clear that in his opinion a language containing descriptive terms need not be governed by extra-logical transformation rules.* Indeed, he commits himself (p. 180) to the view that for every language with P-rules, a language with L-rules only can be constructed in which everything sayable in the former can be said. If we now turn back to our list of six possible accounts of the status of material rules of inference (above, p. 317), we see at once that Carnap's account falls in neither the first nor the second category for according to these, P-rules would be indispensable. Furthermore, since he clearly holds that P-rules are as genuinely rules of inference as are L-rules, it does not belong in the fifth or sixth category. Assuming the adequacy of our classification, we are left with the third and fourth pigeon-holes in which to place his account.

To be sure, Carnap, in the above passage, is not discussing the syntax of natural languages, but rather the construction by logicians of artificial languages. Yet he is clearly conceiving of these artificial languages as candidates for adoption by language users. And presumably, an artificially constructed calculus with an appropriate syntactical structure, becomes a natural language by virtue of (1) the adoption of its syntactical rules by a language speaking community ; (2) the association of certain of its descriptive terms with sensory cues. Thus, in saying that " whether in the construction of a language S, we formulate only L-rules, or include also P-rules . . . is a question of expedience ", Carnap is implying that natural languages need have no P-rules, and that the presence or absence of P-rules in a natural language is a matter of some form of (presumably unconscious) social selection determined by convenience.

Notice that corresponding descriptive terms in two languages, one with and one without P-rules, though they have the same meaning in the sense that they enable the communication of the same information, need not have the same content, in Carnap's syntactical sense of the term. For the content of a term ' ϕ ' is, roughly speaking, the totality of what is entailed *logically or*

INFERENCE AND MEANING 321

physically by the function " ϕx ", and, clearly, a term governed by P-rules will have a greater content than one which is not.

Now, according to the fourth alternative, P-rules are not only dispensable, but have a purely derivative authority. Concretely this amounts to the suggestion that the authority of P-rules derives from the fact that the inferences they certify can be reformulated as logically valid inferences, if the generalizations which have been canonized into P-rules are brought down to earth as additional premises. The contribution made by P-rules would then be one of convenience only, and they would be of little interest to the philosopher. They would permit us to argue " ϕa therefore ψa " provided we accepted the generalization " (x) $\phi x \supset \psi x$ " and could, therefore, argue " $(x) \phi x \supset \psi x \,\&\, \phi a$, therefore ψa ", a saving, perhaps, of some intellectual breath at the level of argument, but one which brings no basic enrichment to the language. Now, Carnap nowhere commits himself—at least in so many words—to this fourth conception of the status of P-rules. Might it not be the case that his views fall into the third category? Perhaps we can find him to hold that although dispensable, and adding nothing to the factual content that can be communicated by the language, P-rules enable a language to perform a function which could not be duplicated (even at the cost of great inconvenience) by a language with L-rules alone. If there were any evidence to this effect, we might attribute to him the view that at least part of the authority of P-rules, even though what it authorizes is dispensable, is not derivative from that of L-rules. However, when one turns to Carnap's book with these questions in mind, one is startled to find no account whatsoever of the grounds on which it might be expedient to adopt a language governed by P-rules as well as L-rules. What we do find is an emphasis on the disadvantage of adopting P-rules. He points out that to the extent that empirical generalizations are erected into P-rules, science is put into a strait-jacket. " If P-rules are stated, we may frequently be placed in the position of having to alter the language " (p. 180). Now, although the phrase " alter the language " is perhaps a bit drastic for the adding or subtracting of P-rules conceived as conveniences with purely derivative authority, there is nothing here which prohibits us from construing Carnap as holding that when the adoption of P-rules is expedient, it is merely because at that time and in those circumstances, the economy in the number of premises required for inferences which is obtained by building scientific generalizations into the very machinery of the language, more than compensates for the resulting tendency of this machinery to impede

322   ·   WILFRID SELLARS :

scientific progress. In any event, the passage from which we have just quoted contains no hint that the expediency of adopting P-rules rests on their ability to authorize something that would not be authorized in a language with L-rules alone.

At this point it is relevant to mention that according to Carnap, P-rules, like L-rules, may take either one of two forms : (1) They may be formulated as rules of inference. This is the form we have supposed them to have in the above discussion. (2) They may be formulated as sentences to the effect that certain sentences in the object language are " primitive sentences ", that is, *privileged* sentences in that their assertion is unconditionally authorized by the rules of the language. Notice, however, that each form may be established on the basis of the other provided that the language contains, as it must, at least one L-rule of the first form, *i.e.* formulated as a rule of inference, in short a rule of detachment or *modus ponens*. It is interesting, however, to note that although P-rules may be introduced in either form, Carnap prefers to state them in the second form as singling out certain object-language sentences (usually generalized material implications) to be primitive sentences. This inevitably suggests he is not thinking of the expediency of the adoption of P-rules as a matter of diminishing of the number of premises needed for inferences. For when P-rules are stated in the second form, the generalizations they characterize as primitive sentences must be used as premises in inferences, even though as being unconditionally assertable on the authority of the P-rules of the language, they are premises of a privileged kind.

III

Now, we may well imagine Metaphysicus to have been following the above exploration of Carnap's views with the most intense interest. He has read with approval Carnap's account of the formal distinction between L-rules and P-rules of inference, but shared our disappointment at Carnap's failure to explain either the status or the specific contribution of the latter. Metaphysicus notes that we have been asking whether Carnap's P-rules authorize any linguistic activity which, dispensable or not, is incapable of being authorized by L-rules alone. Pointing out that we have as yet failed to find any mention of such in the *Logical Syntax of Language*, he now seizes the initiative with the claim that there is indeed such an activity, and that it provides the key to an understanding of the status of material rules of inference.

What Metaphysicus has in mind, of course, are such subjunctive conditionals as " If I *had released* this piece of chalk, it *would have fallen* ", and " If there *were to be* a flash of lightning there *would be* thunder ". But before Metaphysicus attempts an analysis of these statements, bringing out their relevance to our problem, he first turns his attention to those subjunctive conditionals which are clearly true on purely formal grounds. He points out that " If anything were red and square, it would be red " cannot plausibly be claimed to assert the same as " (In point of fact) all red and square things are red ", and suggests that this subjunctive conditional conveys the same information as the logical rule permitting the inference of *x is red* from *x is red and x is square*. This rule is a derivative logical rule, a special case of the logical rule proper, which latter, of course, does not single out the terms *red* and *square*. According to this line of thought, one who asserts " If this *were* red and square, then it *would* be red ", is committing himself to the falsity of " This is red and square ", while in some sense giving expression to a logical rule of inference. On the other hand, a person who says " Since this is both red and square, it is red ", is giving expression to the same rule of inference, while asserting both " This is red and square ", and " This is red ". Metaphysicus now argues that if we accept this analysis, we must interpret the subjunctive conditionals with which we began this paragraph as expressions of *material* rules of inference. " If there were to be a flash of lightning, there would be thunder ", giving expression to some such rule as " *There is thunder at time t-plus-n* may be inferred from *there is lightning at time t* ", and this rule is not in any obvious way a specification of a purely logical rule of inference. He therefore claims to have shown beyond reasonable doubt not only that there are such things as material rules of inference, but, which is far more important, *that they are essential to any conceptual frame which permits the formulation of such subjunctive conditionals as do not give expression to logical principles of inference.* Since we are all conscious of the key role played in the sciences, both formal and empirical, in detective work and in the ordinary course of living by subjunctive conditionals, this claim, if substantiated, would indeed give a distinguished status to material rules of inference.

At this point, our empiricists are tempted to reply by claiming, that even the latter subjunctive conditionals owe their force to purely logical principles and that if this does not appear to be the case it is because the content of these conditionals has not been made fully explicit. This is, of course, essentially the same claim as the one considered at the opening of this paper to the effect that " It is raining, therefore the streets will be wet ", is an enthymeme. It will prove quite rewarding, however, to explore this claim in its present guise.

What, then, would be the explicit formulation of this subjunctive conditional ? Perhaps,

A. *Since every time it rains the streets are wet,* if it were to rain the streets would be wet,

the since clause dropping out to give the usual formulation. The logical principle of inference sanctioning this expanded version would presumably be " From ' (x) ϕx implies ψx ' can be inferred ' ϕa implies ψa ' ", which is a special case of the principle authorizing the inference from " (x) fx " to " fa ". But we see right away that something is wrong. For the subjunctive conditionals which this principles authorizes would be of the form " If (x) fx were the case, then fa would be the case ". Consequently, if " Every time it rains the streets are wet " expresses a material implication, as it must, if we are not to introduce a P-rule in the very attempt to dispense with such, we would get a subjunctive conditional of the form " If it were the case that (x) $\phi x \supset \psi x$, then it would be the case that $\phi a \supset \psi a$ ". But the " since " statement corresponding to this is " Since (x) $\phi x \supset \psi x$, $\phi a \supset \psi a$ ". In other words, the logical principle would justify not A, but rather

A[1]. Since every time it rains the streets in point of fact are wet, it will rain $\supset$ the streets will be wet.

Here the subjunctive mood has disappeared from the consequence clause, and with a merely material implication, we are no longer asserting that a wetting of the streets can be inferred from the occurrence of rain. Nor is it an adequate reply that " it will rain $\supset$ the streets will be wet " is inferable from " all cases of rain are in point of fact cases of wet streets ", and that it is this inferability which makes its presence felt in the original subjunctive conditional. For on this alternative, wherever we accept "all A's are in point of fact B " we should be warranted in asserting " if x were A, x would be B "—whereas whenever we assert a subjunctive conditional of the latter form, we would deny that it was merely in point of fact that all A's are B.

On the other hand, if " Everytime it rains the streets are wet " is interpreted as the expression of an entailment, then the above-mentioned logical principle of inference would warrant a subjunctive conditional of the form " If it were the case that (x) ϕx

entails ψx then it would be the case that *φa entails ψa* ". The corresponding " since " statement would be " Since (x) *φx entails ψx, φa entails ψa* ". Thus we would get,

A". Since *every time it rains the streets are wet* (interpreted now as an entailment), *it will rain entails the streets will be wet*.

Since an entailment statement has the same force as a subjunctive conditional, A" is equivalent to A, and our logical principle of inference has given us what we want. But a moment's reflexion reminds us that to get A" we have had to pay the price of introducing a material rule of inference. *To say that rain entails wet streets is to convey exactly the same information as to say that a sentence asserting the existence of wet streets may be inferred from a sentence asserting the existence of rain.* Thus our ultimate purpose of explaining the original subjunctive conditional without appealing to a material rule of inference would not have been achieved.

Let us try again. Perhaps the explicit formulation would be,

B. If it were the case both that *everytime it rains, the streets are wet* and that *it is raining*, then *the streets would be wet*.

The logical principle which finds expression in this statement is, schematically, " From ' (x) (φx implies ψx) and φa ' can be inferred ' ψa ' ". Notice that on this interpretation the original subjunctive conditional would not be the implicit formulation of a since sentence, as the since clause would include the assertion of " It is raining ", and this would be incompatible with the significance of contrary to fact subjunctive conditionals. Now it is at first sight not too implausible that the original subjunctive conditional is an abbreviated formulation of B. But to see that this won't do it is sufficient to point out that on this interpretation *all such subjunctive conditionals would be true !* Surely some sentences of the form " If a were φ, a would be ψ " are false, in other words some sentences of the form ; " Even though a were φ, it need not be ψ " are true. But on the theory under examination, the former, when explicated turns out to be a logical truth, and the latter a contradiction.

Now, unless some other way can be found of interpreting such subjunctive conditionals in terms of logical principles of inference, we have established not only that they are the expression of material rules of inference, but that the authority of these rules is not derivative from formal rules. In other words, we have shown that material rules of inference are essential to the language we speak, for we make constant use of subjunctive conditionals of

the type we have been examining. It is very tempting to conclude
that material rules of inference are essential to languages containing descriptive terms. Yet to draw this conclusion would
be hasty, for the most we have shown is that if there are descriptive languages which are not governed by material rules, they do
not permit the formulation of material subjunctive conditionals.
We now notice that, as a matter of fact, most of the linguistic
structures Carnap considers, being extensional, do not even
permit the formulation of subjunctive conditionals, and that
though they are not natural languages in actual use, he clearly
thinks that they could be. Carnap, then, is clearly convinced
that subjective conditionals are dispensable.

Does this commit him to holding that P-rules are dispensable ?
Clearly not, no more than it follows from the dispensability of
logically true subjunctive conditionals that a language need have
no L-rules. Thus, even though material subjunctive conditionals
may be dispensable, permitting the object language to be extensional, it may nevertheless be the case that the *function*
performed in natural languages by material subjunctive conditionals is indispensable, so that if it is not performed in the
object language by subjunctive conditionals, it must be performed
by giving direct expression to material rules of inferences in the
meta-language. *In other words, where the object language does not
permit us to say " If a were φ, it would be ψ" we can achieve the
same purpose by saying " ' ψa ' may be inferred from ' φa ' ".*
Since it is the importance of the function served by material
subjunctive conditionals on which we have been insisting, the fact
that Carnap emphasizes the possibility of extensional descriptive
objective languages by no means rules out the idea that material
rules of inference might be indispensable to languages containing
descriptive terms.

To sum up the results of the last few paragraphs : Alternative
(4) has been shown, at least provisionally, to be untenable.
This would leave Carnap with alternative (3)—(material rules
of inference are dispensable but underived). However, in the
process of disproving alternative (4) we have been led to notice
the importance of the function played in natural languages by
material subjunctive conditionals. Since these are object
language expressions of material rules of inference, and since
the same function can be performed by the formulation of a rule
of inference in the metalanguage, it has occurred to us that
alternative (2)—material rules of inference, though not essential
to the meaning of descriptive terms, are indispensable features
of languages containing descriptive terms, and have an authority

underived from formal rules—though rejected by Carnap, is worth reconsidering.

Now, if we were to accept the second alternative, it is clear that we should have to explore the relation of material rules of inference to the meaning of descriptive terms, to see if we could rest in alternative (2) without ultimately embracing alternative (1)—according to which material rules of inference are as essential as formal rules to the meaning of descriptive terms. It is also worth noting, at this stage, that the Humean suggestion that causal inferences are really not inferences at all, but rather habitual expectations masquerading as inferences, loses all plausibility when it is stretched to cover ostensible material subjunctive conditionals, particularly when contrary to fact. Yet if we are now in a position to insist that materially valid inferences are as much inferences as formally valid inferences, we must also recognize that we have as yet given no account of what a rule of inference is (whether formal *or* material). It is to this task that we now turn, in the hope of getting further light on our problem.

IV

We have already had occasion to remark on the central role played in Carnap's conception of a language by the notion of a rule of inference or "transformation rule". Indeed, he writes on occasion (*e.g.*, p. 4) as though a language, formally considered, were identical with its syntactical rules, from which it would follow that the transformation rules of a language would be at least a part, and might—in the light of the passage we have quoted on the power of transformation rules to specify the syntactical structure of a language—be identical with the language. Now, I think we would all grant that there is a sense in which a calculus, or a game (*e.g.* chess) or even a language, is what it is as specified by certain rules. But surely there is a perplexing Hibernian ring to the statement that a calculus is identical with "its" rules. After all, the rules of a calculus belong in the syntactical metalanguage, so that in making this identification, one would be identifying a calculus with expressions in its metalanguage, and thus doing violence to a distinction which is the central theme of Carnap's book. Let me hasten to add that the identification of a calculus, or game or language, with its rules, though strictly a mistake, can be regarded as a paradoxical way of stating an important truth; and I have dwelt on the matter only because Carnap's statement is

328   WILFRID SELLARS :

symptomatic of a carelessness with the term " rule " which
pervades his otherwise admirably incisive and patiently meti-
culous argument.

Another *prima facie* puzzling feature of Carnap's treatment of
transformation rules is his preference for formulating them as
definitions of " direct consequence in S ", where S is the language
whose rules are under consideration.   Thus, in a passage already
quoted, Carnap writes, " In the following discussion we assume
that the transformation rules of any language S, *i.e.* the definition of the term ' direct consequence in S ', are given "
(p. 168).   Now, this term, like any other syntactical predicate, is
for Carnap, a formal predicate.   That is to say it is to be defined
in terms of structural properties of the expressions belonging to
language S.   Thus, by telling us that transformation rules can
be formulated as definitions of " direct consequence in S ",
Carnap gives the impression that the force of a rule to the effect
that expressions of kind A can be " transformed " into expressions
of kind B, relates solely to the existence of a structural relationship between these two kinds of expression.   In ethics the
corresponding thesis would be that moral rules can be formulated
as definitions, in naturalistic terms, of the predicate " morally
right " ; thus, the rule " Happiness ought to be maximized "
as the definition " x is morally right $=_{Df}$ x maximizes human
happiness ".   Here we should all know what to say.   We would
point out that the definiendum is no mere synonym for the
definiens, and that even if it has the same components of descriptive meaning as the latter, it has a surplus meaning over and above
these which can be indicated by the word " ought ".   In other
words, the most that such a definiens can do is specify the type
of circumstances in which a certain kind of action ought to be
done ; it cannot specify *that* it ought to be done.   If one is an
emotivist in one's account of *ought*, one will say that the
" *cognitive* content " of a rule is indeed exhausted by the definiens
in such a definition ; and that provided one does not overlook the
surplus pragmatic meaning of the definiendum, there need be
nothing mistaken about the enterprise of formulating moral
rules as naturalistic definitions of " morally right ".   Intuitionists, on the other hand, would hold, of course, that such
definitions are in principle mistaken.

Now, the basic moral of the above discussion is that if a definition is, with any plausibility, to do the work of a rule, the
definiendum must have the normative flavour characteristic
of " ought ", or " ought not " or " may " or " may not ".   But
when one turns to Carnap's thesis that transformation rules

may be formulated as definitions of " direct consequence in S ",
one finds no such flavour. The term " direct consequence " has
the same sort of feel as " next to " or " between ". This is not
true of the predicate *i.e.* " derivable " in terms of which he
formulates certain transformation rules which are more restricted
in scope than those he associates with the predicate " direct
consequence ". The term " derivable " is one of those " -able "
words which connotes " may be done " in the sense *not* of " can
be done " but rather " is permissible ", an expression which
obviously belongs in the context of rules. Now it is my impression that when Carnap was looking for another word to
share the burden of transformation rules formulated as definitions with " directly derivable ", he failed to bear in mind
that what he needed was another word with this same rulish
force. If he could not find one in current use, it would have
been better to make one up (*e.g.* " directly extractable ") than
to choose a word with such purely cognitive flavour.

The next point I wish to make is the closely related one that a
rule is always a rule for *doing* something. In other words,
any sentence which is to be the formulation of a rule must mention
a doing or action. It is the performance of this action (in
specified circumstances) which is enjoined by the rule, and which
carries the flavour of *ought*. With this in mind, let us examine
Carnap's formulation of certain transformation rules as definitions of " directly derivable in S ". Here the interesting
thing to note is that while the definiendum seems clearly to
mention a kind of action, namely, deriving something directly
from something else, and to indicate that this deriving is permissible, the definiens on the other hand, specifies only a structural
relationship between the *terminus a quo* and the *terminus ad quem*
of the deriving. In short, Carnap's claim that he is giving a
definition of " directly derivable in S " is a snare and a delusion.
It is as though one offered the following " definition " as a formulation of a basic rule governing the activities of policemen :
" X is arrestable $=_{\text{Df}}$ X has broken a law ". It is obvious
that such a definition would be a mistake not only because the
definiendum " arrestable " has, as we saw, a normative force not
shared by the definiens, but also because it designates an act,
the act of arresting, which is not designated by the definiens. I
think we would all be inclined to say that a person who offered
such a " definition " was really attempting, in a confused way,
to do something quite different, namely, specify the circumstances
in which a person is arrestable. " X is arrestable if and only if
X has broken a law " reminds us of " X is a triangle if and only

if **X** is a plane figure bounded by three straight lines ", an analytic statement which is true by definition. In both cases an " if and only if " sentence is affirmed which is not an empirical assertion. Yet it would be a mistake in principle to take " X is arrestable if and only if X has broken a law " to be an analytic proposition which is true by definition. Compare, " I will shoot you if and only if you cross that line ". In short, instead of defining " directly derivable in S " Carnap is at best specifying the circumstances in which it is permissible to derive one expression from another. The same considerations apply *mutatis mutandis* to Carnap's formulation of less restricted transformation rules as definitions of " direct consequence in S ". As the technical difference between the more and less restricted transformation rules considered by Carnap is irrelevant to our problem, and as we have found the term " derivable " to be more satisfactory than " consequence " we shall use the former in a broad sense which covers the ground of Carnap's two terms " derivable " and " consequence ".

What, then does it mean to say of one sentence, B, that it is derivable from another, A ? Roughly, that it is permissible to assert B, given that one has asserted A, whereas it is not permissible to assert not-B, given that one has asserted A. In other words, we have here a rule of conditional assertion (which must not be confused with a rule for the assertion of a conditional). To be contrasted with rules of this type, *e.g. modus ponens*, are rules which specify certain sentences as unconditionally assertable. Rules of this latter type are formulated by Carnap (with all the mistakes criticized above) as definitions of " primitive sentence of S ". Thus, to say that " (x) $\phi x \supset \psi x$ " is a primitive sentence of S, is to say that one is authorized by the rule of S to assert this sentence, *without having to appeal to evidence or grounds, in other words, to other sentences on whose prior assertion the authorization would depend.* It should, of course, be noticed that to say that a sentence is unconditionally assertable entails that its contradictory ought not to be asserted. In this respect an unconditionally assertable sentence differs from a contingently assertable sentence, *e.g.* " It is raining ", whose contradictory is also contingently assertable.

Let us now pause to sum up the substance of the last few paragraphs. We have been pointing out that a syntactical rule, like any other rule, prescribes or permits a certain kind of action in a certain type of circumstance. In the case of syntactical rules, the relevant kind of action would seem to be *asserting,* a concept of which we have offered no analysis, but which is, we shall assume, to be understood in terms of the concept of a token, so that to assert a sentence is to bring about the existence of a token of that sentence. (Though after Ryle's painstaking analysis of mentalistic terms we must be prepared to find that even the "event" of asserting has a dispositional component.) Be this as it may, it follows from our analysis that a syntactical metalanguage cannot permit the formulation of syntactical *rules*, unless (1) it contains a term for the activity of asserting, and (2) it contains an expression having the force of "ought". To the extent that a so-called "syntactical metalanguage" falls short of these requirements, it is an abstraction from a syntactical metalanguage proper. It is undoubtedly convenient to study calculi by means of such truncated metalanguages as mention only the structural inter-relationships of the sign-designs of these calculi, but it is essential for our purposes to stress that these truncated metalanguages become capable of formulating *rules* only when supplemented by the equipment mentioned above.

V

We are now in a position to develop an account of the logical and physical modalities which, though based on Carnap's account in his *Logical Syntax of Language*, is an improvement in that it explicitly takes into account the *rulishness* of syntactical rules. It will be remembered that the central concept of Carnap's treatment is that of a quasi-syntactical sentence. As a simple example we may take the sentence "Red is a quality". This is a quasi-syntactical sentence in that it conveys the same information as the syntactical sentence "'Red' is a one-place predicate". Furthermore, "red is a quality" is a quasi-syntactical sentence in the *material* mode of speech, as opposed to the *autonomous* mode of speech, in that "'red' is a quality" is not a syntactical sentence conveying the same information as "red is a quality". Carnap tells us that

> . . . The material mode of speech is a transposed mode of speech. In using it, in order to say something about a word (or a sentence) we say instead something parallel about the object designated by the word (or the fact described by the sentence. . . .) . . .

Consider, now, the sentence "If a is red and square, then it is *logically necessary* that a be red". According to Carnap's account, this is a quasi-syntactical sentence in the material mode of speech which conveys the same information as the syntactical sentence " ' a is red ' is an L-consequence of ' a is red and a is square '." Now, as I see it, this account is essentially sound, and is vitiated only by the fact that Carnap's account of the consequence relation makes it merely a matter of a structural relationship obtaining between two expression designs. If, in accordance with our earlier proposal, we reformulate the above in terms of the syntactical predicate " derivable ", then the claim becomes that the sentence " If a is red and square, then it is logically necessary that a be red " is a quasi-syntactical sentence conveying the same information as the syntactical sentence, " ' a is red ' is L-derivable from ' a is red and a is square ' ".

To appreciate the significance of this claim, let us remember our previous conclusion that in thinking of one expression as derivable from another, we are thinking of one kind of activity as permissible and of another kind as not permissible, in a certain kind of circumstance, where, for syntactical purposes, the significant feature of both activities and circumstance is that they involve the exemplification of specified types of linguistic structure. Let us now notice that the contrast between the permissible and the non-permissible can be explicated in terms of *ought to be done*, to say of x that it is permissible being to say that it is not the case that it ought not to be done. Let us assume, then, that consciousness of ought to do is the basic consciousness involved in recognizing a set of rules, whether they be moral rules or, as in the present case, rules of syntax ; and that consciousness of *may do* is to be understood in terms of it.

Returning now to the problem of interpreting modal sentences, we notice that Carnap's analysis has become the claim that sentences involving the phrase " logically necessary " convey the same information (the use of the vague expression " convey the same information " is deliberate) as syntactical rules to the effect that we may do thus and so, and ought not do this and that, in the way of manipulating expressions in a language. The language of modalities is interpreted as a " transposed " language of norms.

This theory, as it stands, is open to two related and rather obvious objections. (1) It might be objected that the thought of necessity is radically different from the thought of permission-*cum*-obligation. (2) It might be objected that the sentence " If *a* is red and square, then *a* must, of logical necessity, be red ", mentions neither linguistic expressions nor language users, and consequently cannot mention an obligation of language of language-users to use linguistic expressions in certain ways ;

whereas, as we have seen, the sentence " ' a is red ' is L-derivable from ' a is red and a is square ' " does both.

To answer these objections, it is sufficient to remind ourselves that there are two senses in which an utterance can be said to convey information. There is the sense in which my early morning utterance, " The sky is clear ", conveys meteorological information ; and there is the sense in which it conveys information about my state of mind. Let us use the term " asserts " for the first sense of " conveys ", and " conveys " for the second. Then it is clear that if Carnap's theory is to hold water, it must be reformulated as the claim either (1) that the utterance " ' ψa ' is L-derivable from ' ϕa ' " *asserts* what the utterance " ϕa necessitates ψa " *conveys*, or (2) that the utterance " ' ψa ' is L-derivable from ' ϕa ' " *conveys* what the utterance " ϕa necessitates ψa " *conveys*.

To choose between these alternatives, it suffices to ask What does the utterance " ϕa necessitates ψa " convey ? Clearly it conveys (and does not assert) that the speaker conforms to the rule " ' ψa ' is L-derivable from ' ϕa ' ", and says what he says in some sense because of the rule. In other words, the utterance conveys the existence of a rule-governed mode of behaviour in the speaker. But it is equally clear that the utterance " ' ψa ' is L-derivable from ' ϕa ' ", being a normative utterance, does not *describe* the psychological mechanisms of the speaker. Consequently, " ' ψa ' is L-derivable from ' ϕa ' " does not assert that which is conveyed by " ϕa necessities ψa ", and we are left with the second of the above alternatives.

Moreover, it also follows from considerations like these that although utterances of the term " necessary " have psychological implications which overlap with those of utterances of " ought " in the context of linguistic rules, neither the term " necessary " nor the term " ought " designates a psychological property. In short, modal terms, normative terms and psychological terms are mutually irreducible. Note also that because utterances of " ϕa necessitates ψa " convey but do not assert the existence of a linguistic rule governing the use of ' ϕ ' and ' ψ ', there is no contradiction in the sentence " ϕa would necessitate ψa even though there were no language users ". Opponents of the position we are developing should be wary of saying that according to it " necessities are created by linguistic rules ".

Let us now agree, and in so doing we continue in the spirit of Carnap's philosophy, that everything which can properly be called a conceptual awareness of qualities, relations, particulars or states of affairs, can be identified with the occurrence (in human beings) of symbol-events, events of which it can correctly be said that they " mean such-and-such ". Included in the class of symbol-events are events which belong to languages as social phenomena. I shall, however, for present purposes, assume that the class of symbol-events coincides with the class of linguistic events in the narrower sense. Specifically, I shall assume that concepts are meaningfully used predicates. " Necessary " and " ought ", as occurring in living English usage, then, are concepts. Indeed, they would seem to be as much concepts as " red " or " longer than ". Yet there is an important difference between logical, modal and normative predicates, on the one hand, and such predicates as " red " on the other. In the case of the former, it is obvious that their conceptual meaning is entirely constituted by their " logical grammar ", that is, by the fact that they are used in accordance with certain syntactical rules. In the case of the latter, this is not obvious—though, as we are about to argue, it is equally true.

Why is it obvious (once we escape from the mental eye) that the conceptual meaning of a modal or normative term is constituted by its logical grammar ? Because it is obvious that it cannot be constituted by the term's being a learned response to a class of extra-linguistic particulars. A modal or normative property (if we permit ourselves to speak of them as such) cannot significantly be said to be exemplified by a particular (or pair of particulars). On the other hand, it does make sense to speak of a particular as an instance of *red*, and of a pair of particulars as an instance of *longer than*. It does make sense to speak of " red " as a learned response to red objects. It would therefore seem open to us to hold that the conceptual meaning of " red " is constituted (apart from its purely formal properties) by this relationship.

Now, that at least some of the descriptive predicates of a language must be learned responses to extra-linguistic objects in order for the language to be *applied*, is obvious. But that not even these predicates (" observation predicates ") owe their conceptual meaning to this association should be reasonably clear once the following considerations are taken into account :

(1) By no means all descriptive predicates which are not themselves observation predicates are explicitly definable in terms of observation predicates. The conceptual meaning of those which are not cannot consist in being learned responses to objects of the kind they are said to mean.

(2) To say of a predicate " ϕ " that it is an observation predicate entails that it is a learned response to extra-linguistic

situations of a certain kind K, where K is the kind of which it is
correct to say " 'ϕ' means K ". But, clearly, one can grant
that the successful use of language requires, for certain predicates "ϕ", a coincidence of the kind of object evoking the
verbal response "ϕ" with the kind of object which "ϕ" is
(correctly) said to mean, without identifying " 'ϕ' is evoked
by K " with " 'ϕ' means K ".

(3) " (In Schmidt's language) '*rot*' means red " (S_1) appears
to *assert* an empirical relationship between "*rot*" as used by
Schmidt, and the class of red objects. Once this is taken for
granted, it is natural to infer that this relationship consists in
Schmidt's having learned to respond to red objects with "*rot*".
If one should then notice that " (In Schmidt's language) '*und*'
means and " (S_2) can scarcely be given the same interpretation,
one is likely to say that S_2 concerns a different species of meaning,
and informs us that Schmidt uses " und " in accordance with
rules which are analogous to our rules for " and ". Now the
truth of the matter is that *neither S_1 nor S_2 makes an empirical
assertion*, though both *convey* empirical information about
Schmidt's use of language. The " means " of semantical
statements (idealized as " Designates " in the Pure Semantics
of Carnap and Tarski) is no more a *psychological* word than is the
" ought " of ethical statements or the " must " of modal statements, even though it is correctly used, and gains application
through being used, to *convey* psychological information about
the use of language. And once we cease to be hypnotized by the
form " ' red ' means red " into taking for granted that the psychological fact (conceptual meaning) corresponding to S_1 is a dyadic
relation between Schmidt's " *rot* " and red, and realize that since
the fact in which we are interested is conveyed rather than
asserted by S_1, so that the logical form of the latter is no guide
to the form of the fact for which we are looking, we see that
" *rot* " might well owe its conceptual meaning to Schmidt's
using " *rot* " in accordance with rules analogous to our rules
for " red ".

(4) That it is fruitful to distinguish those aspects of the use of an
observation predicate which relate to its *application* from those
which relate to its conceptual meaning, has been obscured by a
careless use of the term " rule ". There is at first sight some
plausibility in saying that the rules to which the expressions of a
language owe their meaning are of two kinds, (*a*) syntactical
rules, relating symbols to other symbols, and (*b*) semantical
rules, whereby basic descriptive terms acquire extra-linguistic
meaning. It takes but a moment, however, to show that this

widespread manner of speaking is radically mistaken. Obeying
a rule entails recognizing that a circumstance is one to which
the rule applies. If there were such a thing as a " semantical
rule " by the adoption of which a descriptive term acquires
meaning, it would presumably be of the form " red objects are to
be responded to by the noise *red* ". But to recognize the circumstances to which this rule applies, one would already have to
have the concept of red, that is, a symbol of which it can
correctly be said that it " means red ".

(5) A uniformity in behaviour is rule-governed not *qua*
uniformity, for then all habitual responses would be obeyings of
rules—which is clearly not the case—but *qua* occurring, in a sense
by no means easy to define, because of the conception of the
norm enjoined by the rule. Yet the fact that both rule-governed
and merely associative uniformities are *learned* uniformities, and
differ in this respect from, say, the uniformities studied in chemis-
try, has blinded many philosophers to the important respects
in which they differ from one another, and has led to much of the
nonsense peddled under the heading " ostensive definition ".

VI

It will be remembered that at the end of section III we had
arrived at the conclusion that P-rules are indispensable to any
language which permits the formulation of material subjunctive
conditionals, though the use of the latter may be avoided by a
direct statement of the rules themselves. This, in turn, inclined
us to hold that P-rules are essential to any language which
contains non-logical or descriptive terms. This would eliminate
all but the first two interpretations of the status of material
rules of inference listed at the end of section I. If, however,
the argument of section V is sound, it is the first (or " rationalistic " alternative to which we are committed. According to it,
material transformation rules determine the descriptive meaning
of the expressions of a language within the framework established
by its logical transformation rules. In other words, where ' ψa '
is P-derivable from ' ϕa ' (in modal language, ϕa necessitates ψa),
it is as correct to say that ' ϕa $\supset \psi$a ' is true by virtue of the meanings of ' ϕ ' and ' ψ ', as it is to say this where ' ψa ' is L-derivable
from ' ϕa '. In traditional language, the " content " of concepts
as well as their logical " form " is determined by rules of the
Understanding. The familiar notion (Kantian in its origin,
but present in various disguises in many contemporary systems)
that the form of a concept is determined by ' logical rules ',

while the content is 'derived from experience' embodies a radical misinterpretation of the manner in which the 'manifold of sense' contributes to the shaping of the conceptual apparatus 'applied' to the manifold in the process of cognition. The contribution does not consist in providing plums for Jack Horner. There is nothing to a conceptual apparatus that isn't determined by its rules, and there is no such thing as choosing these rules to conform with antecedently apprehended universals and connexions, for the "apprehension of universals and connexions" is already the use of a conceptual frame, and as such presupposes the rules in question. The role of the given is rather to be compared to the role of the environment in the evolution of species; though it would be misleading to say that the apparent teleology whereby men "shape their concepts to conform with reality" is as illusory as the teleology of the giraffe's lengthening neck. After all, it is characteristic of modern science to produce deliberately mutant conceptual structures with which to challenge the world. For primitive thought the analogy is much less misleading.

Our thesis, in short, turns out, as we have developed it, to be quite unlike the dogmatic rationalism of Metaphysicus. For whereas he speaks of *the* conceptual frame, *the* system of formal and material rules of inference, we recognize that there are an indefinite number of possible conceptual structures (languages) or systems of formal and material rules, each one of which can be regarded as a candidate for adoption by the animal which recognizes rules, and no one of which has an intuitable hallmark of royalty. They must compete in the market place of practice for employment by language users, and be content to be adopted haltingly and schematically. In short, we have come out with C. I. Lewis at a "pragmatic conception of the *a priori*". Indeed, my only major complaint concerning his brilliant analysis in *Mind and the World Order*, is that he speaks of the *a priori* as *analytic*, and tends to limit it to propositions involving only the more generic elements of a conceptual structure (his "categories"). As far as I can gather, Lewis uses the term "analytic" as equivalent to "depending only on the meaning of the terms involved". In this sense, of course, our *a priori* also is analytic. But this terminology is most unfortunate, since in a perfectly familiar sense of "synthetic", some *a priori* propositions (including many that Lewis recognizes) are synthetic and hence *not* analytic (in the corresponding sense of "analytic"). That Lewis does not recognize this is in part attributable to his ill-chosen terminology. It is also undoubtedly due to the fact that in

empirically-minded circles it is axiomatic that there is no synthetic
a priori, while the very expression itself has a strong negative
emotive meaning.   Whether or not it is possible to rescue this
expression from its unfortunate associations I do not know.
I am convinced, however, that much of the current nibbling
at the distinction between analytic and synthetic propositions
is motivated by what I can only interpret as a desire to recognize
the existence of synthetic *a priori* propositions while avoiding the
contumely which the language traditionally appropriate to
such a position would provoke.

University of Minnesota

PPE 1. "Pure Pragmatics and Epistemology," *Philosophy of Science* 14 (1974): 181-202.

ENWW 2. "Epistemology and the New Way of Words," *The Journal of Philosophy* 44 (1947): 645-60.

RNWW 3.
RNWWR "Realism and the New Way of Words, "*Philosophy and Phenomenological Research* 8 (1948): 601-34. Reprinted in *Readings in Philosophical Analysis*, edited by Herbert Feigl and Wilfrid Sellars (New York: Appleton-Century-Crofts, 1949).

CIL 4. "Concepts as Involving Laws and Inconceivable without Them," *Philosophy of Science* 15 (1948): 287-315.

APM 5. "Aristotelian Philosophies of Mind," in *Philosophy for the Future*, edited by Roy Wood Sellars, V.J. McGill, and Marvin Farber (New York: The Macmillan Co., 1949): 544-70.

LRB 6. "Language, Rules and Behavior," in *John Dewey: Philosopher of Science and Freedom*, edited by Sidney Hook, (New York: The Dial Press, 1949): 289-315.

LCP 7. "On the Logic of Complex Particulars," *Mind* 58 (1949): 306-38.

AD 8. "Acquaintance and Description Again," *The Journal of Philosophy* 46 (1949): 496-505.

RC 9. "Review of Ernst Cassirer, *Language and Myth*," *Philosophy and Phenomenological Research* 9 (1948-49): 326-29.

ILE 10. "The Identity of Linguistic Expressions and the Paradox of Analysis," *Philosophical Studies* 1 (1950): 24-31.

QMSP 11. "Quotation Marks, Sentences, and Propositions," *Philosophy and Phenomenological Research* 10 (1950): 515-25.

GQ   12. "Gestalt Qualities and the Paradox of Analysis,"
            Philosophical Studies 1 (1950): 92-94.

OM   13. "Obligation and Motivation," *Philosophical Studies* 2
            (1951): 21-25.

RP   14. "Review of Arthur Pap, *Elements of Analytic Philosophy*,"
            Philosophy and Phenomenological Research 11 (1950):
            104-9.

OMR   15. "Obligation and Motivation," in *Readings in Ethical Theory*,
            edited by Wilfrid Sellars and John Hospers (New York:
            Appleton-Century-Crofts, 1952): 511-17. A revised and ex-
            panded version of (13).

RCA   16. "Review of C. West Churchman and Russell L. Ackoff,
            *Methods of Inquiry: An Introduction to Philosophy and
            Scientific Method*," *Philosophy and Phenomenological
            Research* 12 (1951): 149-50.

CHT   17. "Comments on Mr. Hempel's Theses," *Review of Meta-
            physics* 5 (1952): 623-25.

MMB   18. "Mind, Meaning, and Behavior," *Philosophical Studies* 3
            (1952): 83-95.

P   19. "Particulars," *Philosophy and Phenomenological Research*
            13 (1952): 184-99.

ITSA   20. "Is There a Synthetic A Priori?", *Philosophy of Science*
            20 (1953); 121-38. Reprinted in revised form in *American
            Philosophers at Work*, edited by Sidney Hook (New York:
            Criterion Press, 1957); also published in Italy in translation.

SSMB   21. "A Semantical Solution of the Mind-Body Problem," *Methodos*
            5 (1953): 45-82.

IM   22. "Inference and Meaning," *Mind* 62 (1953): 313-38.

PRE   23. "Presupposing," *Philosophical Review* 63 (1954): 197-215.

SRLG   24. "Some Reflections on Language Games," *Philosophy of Science* 21 (1954): 204-228.

NPD   25. "A Note on Popper's Argument for Dualism," *Analysis* 15 (1954): 23-4.

PR   26. "Physical Realism," *Philosophy and Phenomenological Research* 15 (1954): 13-32.

PSB   27. "Putnam on Synonymity and Belief," *Analysis* 15 (1955): 117-20.

VTM   28. "Vlastos and 'The Third Man'," *Philosophical Review* 64 (1955): 405-37.

IIO   29. "Imperatives, Intentions, and the Logic of 'Ought'," *Methodos* 8 (1956): 228-68.

CE   30. "The Concept of Emergence" (with Paul Meehl), in *Minnesota Studies in the Philosophy of Science*, Vol. I, edited by Herbert Feigl and Michael Scriven (Minneapolis: University of Minnesota Press, 1956): 239-52.

EPM   31. "Empiricism and the Philosophy of Mind" (University of London Special Lectures in Philosophy for 1956), *ibid.*, pp. 253-329.

LSPO   32. "Logical Subjects and Physical Objects," *Philosophy and Phenomenological Research* 17 (1957): 458-72. Contribution to a symposium with Peter Strawson held at Duke University, November, 1955.

CDCM   33. "Counterfactuals, Dispositions, and the Causal Modalities," in *Minnesota Studies in the Philosophy of Science*, Vol. II, edited by Herbert Feigl, Michael Scriven, and Grover Maxwell (Minneapolis: University of Minnesota Press, 1957): 225-308.

ITM   34. "Intentionality and the Mental," a symposium by correspondence with Roderick Chisholm, *ibid.*, pp. 507-39.

SFA   35. "Substance and Form in Aristotle," *The Journal of Philosophy* 54 (1957): 688-99. The opening paper in a symposium on

Aristotle's conception of form held at the December, 1957, meeting of the American Philosophical Association.

EAE   36. "Empiricism and Abstract Entities," in *The Philosophy of Rudolf Carnap (The Library of Living Philosophers)* edited by Paul A. Schilpp (La Salle, Illinois: Open Court, 1963): 431-68.

GE   37. "Grammar and Existence: a Preface to Ontology," *Mind* 69 (1960): 499-533. Two lectures delivered at Yale University, March, 1958.

TWO   38. "Time and the World Order," in *Minnesota Studies in the Philosophy of Science*, Vol. III, edited by Herbert Feigl and Grover Maxwell (Minneapolis: University of Minnesota Press, 1962): 527-616. A Metaphysical and Epistemological Analysis of Becoming.

IIOR   39. "Imperatives, Intentions, and the Logic of 'Ought'," in *Morality and the Language of Conduct*, a collection of essays in moral philosophy edited by Hector-Neri Castaneda and George Nakhnikian (Detroit: Wayne State University Press, (1963): 159-214. A radically revised and enlarged version of (29).

BBK   40. "Being and Being Known," *Proceedings of the American Catholic Philosophical Association* (1960): 28-49.

LT   41. "The Language of Theories," in *Current Issues in the Philosophy of Science*, edited by Herbert Feigl and Grover Maxwell (New York: Holt, Rinehart, and Winston, (1961): 57-77.

CM   42. Comments on Maxwell's "Meaning Postulates in Scientific Theories," *ibid.*, pp. 183-92.

PSIM   43. "Philosophy and the Scientific Image of Man," in *Frontiers of Science and Philosophy*, edited by Robert Colodny (Pittsburgh: University of Pittsburgh Press, 1962): 35-78.

RMSS   44. "Raw Materials, Subjects and Substrata," in *The Concept of Matter*, edited by Ernan McMullin (Notre Dame: The University of Notre Dame Press, 1963): 255-68.

CMM   45. Comments on McMullin's "Matter as a Principle," *ibid.*, pp.
          209-13.

NS   46. "Naming and Saying," *Philosophy of Science* 29 (1962):
          7-26.

TC   47. "Truth and Correspondence," *The Journal of Philosophy* 59
          (1962): 29-56.

AE   48. "Abstract Entities," *Review of Metaphysics* 16 (1963):
          627-71.

CAE   49. "Classes as Abstract Entities and the Russell Paradox,"
          Review of Metaphysics 17 (1963): 67-90.

PANF 50. "The Paradox of Analysis: A Neo-Fregean Approach,"
          Analysis Supplementary Vol. 24 (1964): 84-98.

TE   51. "Theoretical Explanation," in *Philosophy of Science: The
          Delaware Seminar*, Vol. II (New York: John Wiley, 1963):
          61-78.

IRH   52. "The Intentional Realism of Everett Hall," in *Commonsense
          Realism: Critical Essays on the Philosophy of Everett W.
          Hall*, edited by E.M. Adams, *The Southern Journal of
          Philosophy* 4 (1966): 103-15.

SPR   53. *Science, Perception and Reality* (London: Routledge and
      .   Kegan Paul, 1963). Includes items (19), (20), (24), (31),
          (37), (40), (41), (43), (46), (47), and a hitherto unpublished
          essay, "Phenomenalism."

IV   54. "Induction as Vindication," *Philosophy of Science* 31
          (1964): 197-231.

NI   55. "Notes on Intentionality," *The Journal of Philosophy* 61
          (1964): 655-65. Presented in a symposium on "Intentionality"
          at the December, 1964, meeting of the American
          Philosophical Association.

IAMB 56. "The Identity Approach to the Mind-Body Problem" *Review
          of Metaphysics* 18 (1965): 430-51. Presented at the Boston

Colloquium for the Philosophy of Science, April, 1963. Reprinted in the same volume as (58).

ML   57. "Meditations Leibnitziennes," *American Philosophical Quarterly* 2 (1965): 105-18. An expended version of the opening paper in a symposium on Rationalism at the May, 1958, meeting of the American Philosophical Association.

SRI   58. "Scientific Realism or Irenic Instrumentalism: A Critique of Nagel and Feyerabend on Theoretical Explanation," *Boston Studies in the Philosophy of Science*, Vol. II, edited by Robert Cohen and Marx Wartofsky (New York: Humanities Press, 1965): 171-204.

TA   59. "Thought and Action," in *Freedom and Determinism,* edited by Keith Lehrer (New York: Random House, 1966): 105-39.

FD   60. "Fatalism and Determinism," *ibid.*, pp. 141-74.

PP   61. *Philosophical Perspectives* (Springfield, Illinois: Charles C. Thomas, Publisher, 1967). Includes items (26), (28), (35), (44), (48), (49), (50), (51), (52), (55), (56), (57), (58), and a rejoinder to Gregory Vlastos on the Third Man Argument, and three previously unpublished essays: "The Soul as Craftsman" (on Plato's Idea of the Good), "Aristotle's Metaphysics: An Interpretation," and "Science and Ethics."

SM   62. *Science and Metaphysics: Variations on Kantian Themes*, The John Locke Lectures for 1965-66 (London: Routledge and Kegan Paul, 1967).

PH   63. "Phenomenalism" in *Intentionality, Minds, and Perception*, edited by Hector-Neri Castaneda (Detroit: Wayne State University Press, 1967): 215-74. An abbreviated version of the essay referred to in (53) above.

RA   64. "Reply to Aune," *ibid.*, pp. 286-300.

FCET   65. *Form and Content in Ethical Theory*, The Lindley Lecture for 1967 (Lawrence, Kansas: Department of Philosophy, University of Kansas, 1967).

KTE   66. "Some Remarks on Kant's Theory of Experience," *The Journal of Philosophy* 64 (1967): 633-47. Presented in a symposium on Kant at the December, 1967, meeting of the

American Philosophical Association.

MP   67. "Metaphysics and the Concept of a Person," in *The Logical
          Way of Doing Things*, edited by Karel Lambert (New Haven:
          Yale University Press, 1969): 219-52.

TT   68. "Some Reflections on Thoughts and Things," *Nous* 1 (1967):
          97-121. Reprinted as Chapter III of (62).

CDI   69. "Reflections on Contrary to Duty Imperatives," *Nous* 1
          (1967): 303-44.

KSU   70. "Kant's Views on Sensibility and Understanding," *Monist*
          51 (1967): 463-91. Reprinted as Chapter I of (62). The
          first of the six John Locke Lectures.

SPB   71. "Some Problems About Belief," in *Philosophical Logic*, edited
          by J.W. Davis, D.T. Hockney, and W.K. Wilson (Dordrecht:
          D. Reidel, 1969): 46-65. Reprinted in *Words and Objections,
          Essays on the Work of W.V. Quine*, edited by D. Davidson and
          J. Hintikka (Dordrecht: D. Reidel, 1969): 186-205.

NDL   72. "Are There Non-deductive Logics?" in *Essays in Honor of
          Carl G. Hempel*, edited by Nicholar Rescher *et al.*, *Synthese
          Library* (Dordrecht: D. Reidel, 1970): 83-103.

LTC   73. "Language as Thought and as Communication," *Philosophy and
          Phenomenological Research* 29 (1969): 506-27.

KBDW 74. "On Knowing the Better and Doing the Worse," *International
          Philosophical Quarterly* 10 (1970): 5-19. The 1969
          Suarez Philosophy Lecture delivered at Fordham University.

SSIS 75. "Science, Sense Impressions, and Sensa: A Reply to Comman,"
          Review of Metaphysics 25 (1971): 391-447.

TTC   76. "Towards a Theory of the Categories," *Experience and Theory*,
          edited by L. Foster and J.W. Swanson (Amherst: University of
          Massachusetts Press, 1970): 55-78.

AAE   77. "Actions and Events," *Nous* 7 (1973): 179-202. Contribution
          to a synposium on the topic at the University of North Carolina,
          November, 1969.

SK   78. "The Structure of Knowledge: (1) Perception; (2) Minds;
          (3) Epistemic Principles," The Matchette Foundation Lectures
          for 1971 at the University of Texas. Published in *Action,
          Knowledge and Reality: Studies in Honor of Wilfrid Sellars*, edited
          by Hector-Neri Castaneda (Indianapolis: Bobbs-Merrill, 1975):
          295-347.

RAL   79. "Reason and the Art of Living in Plato," in *Phenomenology and
          Natural Existence: Essays in Honor of Marvin Farber*, edited by
          Dale Riepe (Albany: The University of New York Press, 1973):
          353-77. (Reprinted as Chapter 1 in *Essays in Philosophy and
          its History*).

I   80. "...this I or he or it (the thing) which thinks" the presidential
          address, American Philosophical Association (Eastern Division),
          for 1970, *Proceedings of the American Philosophical
          Association* 44 (1972): 5-31.

RD   81. "Reply to Donagan," an essay on fatalism and determinism
          (1971). *Philosophical Studies* 27 (1975): 149-84.

OPM   82. "Ontology and the Philosophy of Mind in Russell," in
          Bertrand Russell's Philosophy, edited by George Nakhnikian
          (London: Duckworth; New York: Barnes and Noble, 1974):
          57-100.

RM   83. "Reply to Marras," *Canadian Journal of Philosophy* 2
          (1973): 485-93.

CC   84. "Conceptual Change," in *Conceptual Change*, edited by
          P. Maynard and G. Pearce (Dordrecht, Holland: D. Reidel,
          1973): 77-93.

RQ   85. "Reply to Quine," *Synthese* 26 (1973): 122-45.

AR   86. "Autobiographical Reflections: (February, 1973).
          Published in *Action, Knowledge and Reality*, edited by
          H.N. Castaneda (Indianapolis: Bobbs-Merrill, 1975): 277-93.

DKMB 87. "The Double-Knowledge Approach to the Mind-Body Problem"
          The New Scholasticism 45 (1973): 269-89.

MFC   88. "Meaning as Functional Classification (A Perspective on the
          Relation of Syntax to Semantics)," in *Intentionality, Language
          and Translation*, edited by J.G. Troyer and S.C. Wheeler, III
          (Dordrecht, Holland: D. Reidel, 1974), along with replies to
          Daniel Dennett and Hilary Putnam.

IAE   89. "On the Introduction of Abstract Entities," in *Forms of Representation:* Proceedings of the 1972 Philosophy Colloquium of the University of Western Ontario, edited by B. Freed, A. Marras and P. Maynard (Amsterdam: North Holland, 1975): 47-74.

GEC   90. "Givenness and Explanatory Coherence," (Presented at a symposium on Foundations of Knowledge at the December 1973, meeting of the American Philosophical Association). An abbreviated version was printed in *The Journal of Philosophy* 70 (1973): 612-24.

SSS   91. "Seeing, Seeming, and Sensing," in *The Ontological Turn: Studies in the Philosophy of Gustav Bergmann,* ed. by M.S. Gram and E.D. Klemke (Iowa City: University of Iowa Press (1974): 195-210. The first in a series of three Machette Lectures given at the University of Texas, 1971. See (78).

EPH   92. *Essays in Philosophy and its History* (Dordrecht-Holland: D. Reidel, 1974). Includes items (36), (49), (51), (54), (66), (67), (71), (72), (74), (76), (77), (79), (80), (83), (84), (85), and (89).

BD   93. "Berkeley and Descartes: Reflections on the 'New Way of Ideas' " (Presented in 1974 in the Program in the History of Philosophy of Theories of Perception at Ohio State University). Published in *Studies in Perception: Interrelations in the History of Philosophy and Science,* edited by Peter K. Machamer and Robert G. Turnbull (Columbus: Ohio State University Press, 1977).

ATS   94. "The Adverbial Theory of the Objects of Sensation," in *Metaphilosophy* 6, edited by Terrell Bynum (Oxford: Basil Blackwell, 1975): 144-60.

VR   95. "Volitions Re-affirmed," *Action Theory,* edited by Myles Brand and Douglas Walton (Dordrecht-Holland: D. Reidel, 1976): 47-66. Presented at a conference on action theory at Winnipeg, May, 1975.

KTI   96. "Kant's Transcendental IDealism," (Presented at an international Kant Congress at the University of Ottawa.) Published in Vol. 6 *Collections of Philosophy,* 1976, pp. 165-181.

SRT   97. "Is Scientific Realism Tenable?" (Presented at a symposium at the 1976 Philosophy of Science Association Meeting in Chicago.) Published in Vol. II, *Proceedings of PSA,* 1976.

MMM   98. "Hochberg on Mapping, Meaning, and Metaphysics," in *Midwest Studies in Philosophy*, Vol. II; (eds.) Peter French, Theodore Vehling, Jr., and Howard Wettstein, University of Minnesota Press, 1977, pp. 214-24.

PPHP 99. *Philosophical Perspectives: History of Philosophy*, (Reseda, California: Ridgeview Publishing Company, 1977). A reprint of Part I of *Philosophical Perspectives*. Includes items (28), (35), (44), (57), and a rejoinder to Gregory Vlastos on the Third Man Argument, "The Soul as Craftsman" (on Plato's Ideas of the Good), "Aristotle's Metaphysics: An Interpretation," and "Science and Ethics."

PPME 100. *Philosophical Perspectives: Metaphysics and Epistemology* (Reseda, California: Ridgeview Publishing Company, 1977). A reprint of Part II of *Philosophical Perspectives*. Includes items (26), (48), (49), (50), (51), (52), (55), (56), and (58).

IKTE 101. "The Role of the Imagination in Kant's Theory of Experience," The Dotterer Lecture 1978 in *Categories: A Colloquium* (ed.) Henry W. Johnstone, Jr., Pennsylvania State University, pp. 231-45.

NAO   102. *Naturalism and Ontology* (Reseda, California: Ridgeview Publishing Company, 1980). The John Dewey Lectures for 1973-4.

MGEC 103. "More on Givenness and Explanatory Coherence," in *Justification and Knowledge*, George Pappas (ed.), D. Reidel, 1979, pp. 169-182.

SRPC 104. "Some Reflections on Perceptual Consciousness," in *Selected Studies in Phenomenology and Existential Philosophy*, R. Bruzina and B. Wilshire (eds.), The Hague, 1977, pp. 169-185.

ORAV 105. "On Reasoning About Values," to appear in the *American Philosophical Quarterly*, Nicholas Rescher (ed.), Vol.___, 1980. One of three Tsanoff Lectures presented at Rice University, October 1978.

SSPO   106. "Sensa or Sensings: Reflections on the Ontology of Perception,"
            Keith Lehrer (ed.), *Philosophical Studies Series in Philosophy*,
            Vol.__, Essays in Honor of James Comman. Presented at a
            colloquium at the University of North Carolina, October
            1976.   Research supported by grant from NEH in connection with
            Fellowship at the Center for Advanced Studies in the
            Behavioral Sciences.

BLM   107. "Behaviorism, Language and Meaning," *Pacific Philosophical
            Quarterly*, Vol. 61, Nos. 1 and 2, January-April 1980, pp. 8-29.